OF TRIBES AND
TRIBULATIONS

OF TRIBES AND TRIBULATIONS

*The Early Decades of
the Cleveland Indians*

James E. Odenkirk

McFarland & Company, Inc., Publishers

Jefferson, North Carolina

LIBRARY OF CONGRESS CATALOGUING-IN-PUBLICATION DATA

Odenkirk, James E. (James Ellis), 1928–
Of tribes and tribulations : the early decades of the
Cleveland Indians / James E. Odenkirk.
p.   cm.
Includes bibliographical references and index.

ISBN 978-0-7864-7983-2 (softcover : acid free paper) ∞
ISBN 978-1-4766-1706-0 (ebook)

1. Cleveland Indians (Baseball team)—History.   I. Title.
GV875.C7O34 2015   796.357'640977132—dc23   2015011665

BRITISH LIBRARY CATALOGUING DATA ARE AVAILABLE

Printed in the United States of America

*McFarland & Company, Inc., Publishers
Box 611, Jefferson, North Carolina 28640
www.mcfarlandpub.com*

To Benita—As Bill Veeck once said—
not because I should
but *because I want to,* always and forever

Table of Contents

Acknowledgments

It is imperative that I recognize and thank those who provided assistance in the long haul to the finish line. Among them are the staffs of the Library of Congress, Cleveland Public Library, Western Reserve Historical Society, Arizona State University, Cleveland Baseball Heritage Museum, National Baseball Hall of Fame, and the Society for American Baseball Research Library. I relied heavily on the collections of these institutions, guided at times by their helpful librarians, archivists, employees and volunteers.

Cleveland sportswriters were cooperative in providing behind-the-scenes anecdotes about the Cleveland Indians, particularly Russell Schneider and Hal Lebovitz of the *Cleveland Plain Dealer* and Bob August of the *Cleveland Press*. The following players and club officials were kind enough to grant interviews: Bill Veeck, Bob Feller, Lou Boudreau, Ray Boone, Harmon Killebrew, Tommy Henrich, Hal Trosky, Jr., Herb Score, Jimmy Dudley, Roland Hemond, and Gabe Paul.

Many professional associates, friends, and family members gave encouragement and professional assistance: Lee Lowenfish, Monte Poen, Bob Boynton, Maynard Brichford, John Toland, Morris Eckhouse, Stephanie Liscio, Jim and Linda Kearney, Bob Osterhoudt, Bill Witty, Gerry Soule, Bryce and Lu Gochner, Dale Stadtmueller, Steve Gietschier, Larry Gerlach, my sister Barb and her husband, Al Wadley, and my Wooster, Ohio, connections Harry and Betty Weckesser, Al and Judy VanWie, and Donald Demkee. Last, but not least, my two sons, Tom and Jim, who were baptized Indians fans.

Special thanks are due Fred Schuld, a loyal Indians fan and baseball scholar, and baseball writer Russell Schneider, both of whom provided important materials to help with my research, as did Jacob Pomrenke, web editor/producer for the Society for American Baseball Research. My good friend Gary Krahenbuhl provided invaluable help in preparing and collating photos included in this book. Special thanks go to historians Larry Gerlach and Charles Alexander, author and lawyer Rick Huhn, and sportswriter Russell Schneider of the *Cleveland Plain Dealer* for reading my manuscript and providing important suggestions.

Not enough praise and thanks can be given to my editor, Dr. Kathy Harris, professor emeritus, Arizona State University, who has helped me with many other published papers and one other book.

Finally, to my wife, Benita, untold appreciation for her patience, valid suggestions (among them, Don't write another book!), and skill in typing the manuscript from my long-hand writing. This book is dedicated to her.

Finally, any inaccuracies or errors interpreting the Tribe's history are mine alone and I take full responsibility.

Preface

Jim Bouton noted in closing his best seller, *Ball Four*, "You spend a good bit of your life gripping a baseball and in the end it turns out that it was the other way around all the time." For some, the relationship with the national pastime was a product of childhood; others embraced baseball later in life. For better or worse, they are bonded to the game. True fans become daily purveyors (and proofreaders) of box scores. They are hopefully addicted to green grass and blue skies, and each spring are seduced by the Siren's song, "This is the year that we're gonna win the pennant." The description fits this author.

This book is the product of a lifetime of experiences. First and foremost, it is a matter of loyalty, the kind of behavior which eventually leads to one being defined by Webster as a "fanatic," someone who is "unusually enthusiastic and overly zealous." Growing up during the Great Depression, I was exposed to the rooting interests of members of my immediate family. My mother, sister, uncle, and grandfather were Indians fans, but my father chose to be contrary, supporting the Detroit Tigers and Pittsburgh Pirates. It is recorded in my senior yearbook at Ontario High School that I would become the groundskeeper for the Cleveland Indians.

It was an era when fans could not easily attend games, but rare car trips from our home in Mansfield, Ohio, to League Park and Municipal Stadium solidified my support for the Indians. And each season the radio broadcasts by Jack Graney and Jimmy Dudley over stations WTAM, WHK, WJW, and WERE provided exciting information about games and players which intensified my imagination and interests. A brief tryout with the Tribe in 1950 as a young 22-year-old and with Hall of Famer Tris Speaker standing by, exciting if unsuccessful, personalized my identification with the team.

Then there was the written word that kept fans informed about the happenings in both leagues. Primary sources were *The Sporting News*, the "Bible of Baseball," the red-covered *Baseball Magazine*, and *Who's Who in Baseball*. Cleveland newspapers and the Akron Beacon Journal were the principal sources of game coverage of team activity. The inside scoop was covered by Franklin "Whitey" Lewis and Frank Gibbons of the *Cleveland Press*, Ed McAuley of the *Cleveland News*, and Gordon Cobbledick of the Cleveland *Plain Dealer*, and of course there was the local *Mansfield*

News Journal. It was simpler, more focused time when baseball was not yet influenced by television broadcasts, player unions, and agents, convoluted and expanded schedules, and league expansion and playoff games.

But it was my career as a sport historian that prompted me to undertake this book project. I came to appreciate the need for historical, not just contemporary journalistic accounts of teams, people and episodes that form the world of sport. There have been many fine books written about various Indians players and events by noted historians and journalists, including Charles Alexander, Gordon Cobbledick, David Fleitz, J. Thomas Hetrick, Hal Lebovitz, Terry Pluto, Russell Schneider, John Sickels, and Gary Webster, to name a few. (I am grateful to other Tribe writers whose work appears in the bibliography.) But team histories are lacking. Franklin Lewis's popular *The Cleveland Indians* (1949), part of the Putnam team series, covers the first 50 years without references or endnotes. *Endless Summers: The Rise and Fall of the Cleveland Indians* by Jack Torry, former columnist for the *Columbus Dispatch*, treats the period from 1956 to 1994.

The most important motivation for this book was to research and write a history of the Cleveland Indians for the first half-century, from the founding of the franchise in the 1890s to the glory days of the late 1940s and early 1950s. This required extensive research in national and local newspapers published over the seven decades, perusal of numerous baseball and sports magazines, and innumerable interviews with individuals knowledgeable about the Indians. Hopefully, my literary contribution to Cleveland Indians history proves to be a valuable resource for researchers, authors, and readers interested in the Tribe and baseball in general.

Three colleagues encouraged writing this book. They were the late Bill Kirwin, a Red Sox fan, Larry Gerlach, history professor at the University of Utah and devoted Yankees fan, and Steve Gietschier, a Mets fan and professor of history at Lindenwood University in St. Charles, Missouri. At a NINE Conference, these three gentleman, tired of my fomenting over the magnificent Tribe, bellowed out "Just write the damn book!" Five years later, mission accomplished.

1

Nineteenth Century Baseball in Cleveland

*"Baseball is the very symbol, the outward and visible expression
of the drive and push and rush and struggle of the raging,
tearing, booming Nineteenth Century"*—Mark Twain

Like every other major league baseball team, the history of the Cleveland Indians is unique. It is a story deeply rooted in the distinctive social, economic, and political characteristics of the city. Because the Indians have always been a reflection of the people and the community, it is important to look briefly at the development of the city that first produced and then nurtured the team.

On the eve of the Civil War, Cleveland—now a fully developed city of that era—grew rapidly in population and national influence. Sufficiently isolated from the battlegrounds of the war, yet connected by rail with the rest of the North, Cleveland emerged as a significant production center for war materiel. Railroads revolutionized transportation, eliminating the need for canals and laying the groundwork for transition from commerce to manufacturing. Cleveland was transformed from a small, predominately Yankee commercial burg to a large, multiethnic industrial city. This process had a profound effect on local economic, cultural, political, and intellectual life.

Historian James Whipple characterized this period as one of conflict between the Cleveland mind—deeply rooted in early American values (especially those of Puritan New England)—and the dramatically new social and economic order spurred by the Industrial Revolution.[1] This conflict spilled into the open as the city grappled with rapid ethnic immigration, volatile labor issues, and growing welfare needs and found it difficult to cope with unprecedented demands for social and municipal services.

In *Cleveland: The Making of a City*, William Ganson Rose vividly described the smell and sound of the age: "The smoke of prosperity mingled with the odor of hemp and canvas, oil, and grease.... The air was filled with hoarse blasts from steamship whistles, the clang of ships' bells, and the hoot of tugs and locomotives. Industry was making men rich."[2] In 1860, the *Cleveland Leader* proclaimed, "Cleveland must rise, if at all, by manufacturing."[3] The city accomplished that, but in the decades ahead paid the price in the form of poverty, vice, disease, and other social ills.

3

In the 1860s, six railroads operated in and out of Cleveland, and the Flats teemed with roundhouses, warehouses, oil tanks and factories. A third economic tier appeared—the consumption of raw materials emerged in addition to the manufacture and production of finished goods for export to national and international markets. The first two economic tiers, already in place, were food consumption from surrounding agriculture counties and development as a commercial and service hub for neighboring rural communities.

Strategically positioned for dramatic growth, then, Cleveland—the Forest City[4]—was primed to benefit from industrial and transportation development. A labyrinth of railroad lines connected hamlets throughout the Midwest. These railroads, in addition to Great Lakes shipping and pipelines from Pennsylvania and eastern Ohio oil fields, began to impact Cleveland's incipient manufacturing orders and general economic state. Industrial barons were about to discover what was later touted as the "Best Location in the Nation."[5] By 1870, Cleveland was one of the most beautiful cities in the country, with all the potential associated with urban centers.

The discovery of huge iron ore deposits in the Lake Superior region and on the Mesabi Range in northern Minnesota in the 1850s sparked the growth of the iron and steel industry. The completion of a canal at Sault Ste. Marie made this port arguably the most important one on the Great Lakes in the nineteenth century. This canal opened a water route to the lower lakes which irrevocably changed Cleveland's economy. Vast treasures of iron ore were shipped to this lakefront city. The ore, along with limestone from Michigan and coking coal from the Appalachians, created a broad industrial band which stretched from Wheeling, West Virginia, to Chicago. Positioned in the midst of such a landscape, Cleveland soon was coined the "industrial Ruhr of America."

John D. Rockefeller, one of the so-called robber barons, dramatically influenced Cleveland's economy and growth. Son of a snake-oil salesman, Rockefeller and his family migrated from New York to Cleveland in 1853. In the 1860s and 1870s, oil flowed in from wells in Pennsylvania and eastern Ohio. This daring transplant established a crude oil refinery at the junction of Kingsbury Run (near the Flats) and the Cuyahoga River. He gradually bought out his competitors, and by the 1880s, the Standard Oil Company controlled 90 percent of the nation's refining capacity and Rockefeller was becoming one of the richest men in America. This newcomer to Cleveland inspired local entrepreneurs to invest in various enterprises, namely Mark Hanna (street railways), Alva Bradley (shipping), Charles Brush (electricity), William Mather (iron, mining, and banking), Liberty Holden (Cleveland *Plain Dealer* and *Leader*, banking), Louis H. Severance (finance, oil), and John Hay (diplomat, author).[6] This group was a close-knit aristocracy who dominated the city's business, civic, and cultural life.

In 1865, Cleveland claimed 30 oil refineries (Standard Oil Company). Rockefeller, now a wealthy oil magnate, enticed renowned pioneer chemist Eugene Grasselli to move from Cincinnati to Cleveland in the late 1860s. His talent was a key in the production of massive quantities of sulfuric acid, a component vital to oil refineries.[7] Vast fortunes were amassed by families with familiar names. The total worth of these entrepreneurs would have been 1.2 billion dollars (value in 2013). A string of mansions lined along Euclid Avenue was identified as "Millionaire's Row."[8]

In the fall of 1800, Lorenzo Carter had been the only permanent resident living within

the confines of the Forest City. On October 16, 1879, John Hay, journalist and former secretary to President Abraham Lincoln, invited a few friends to dinner at his home on Euclid
Avenue. The dinner party comprised some of the most powerful political, economic and
intellectual leaders in the nation. Among those from Cleveland and the Western Reserve
were Rutherford B. Hayes, President of the United States, future president James A. Garfield
from nearby Mentor, former congressional leader Richard C. Parsons, nationally prominent
economic leader and bridge builder Amasa Stone, industrialist Samuel L. Mather, and lawyer
and businessman W. J. Boardman. Hay had asked these influential neighbors and friends to
his home to honor another native of the Western Reserve, his old teacher and author William Dean Howells, at the time editor of the *Atlantic Monthly*.[9]

In 1870, 42 percent of Cleveland's 92,000 residents were foreign born. Whereas earlier
immigrants had migrated primarily from Germany and Ireland, those who arrived after 1870
included large numbers of Poles, Russians, Jews, Hungarians, Czechs, Slovenes, Croats,
Serbs, Italians, and Greeks. These new arrivals came largely from agricultural societies and
filled the demand for semi-skilled and unskilled laborers. During the late 1880s, colorfully
named immigrant ghettos evolved: Cabbage Patch, Warszawa, Dutch Hill, the Angle, Kouba,
Birdtown, Little Italy, Chicken Village, and Haymarket.[10]

Into this rapidly growing industrial and ethnically diverse community came a new activity that quickly attracted males, young and old, to participate in games formal and informal,
providing entertainment for numerous spectators and becoming a source of community
identity and pride: Baseball. With the arrival of the National Pastime, Cleveland began its
storied contributions to America's national sporting culture.

French-born scholar Jacques Barzun, distinguished Columbia University historian in
the mid-twentieth century, wrote, "Whoever wants to know the heart and mind of America
had better learn baseball."[11] For baseball aficionados, Barzun's words read much like a parable
from the Bible or a stanza from America's national anthem. Other notable adages paraphrased
the impact of baseball on American's cultural scene:

"Went to the ballgame and didn't care if he ever gets back"—poster caption once displayed
at Yankee Stadium

"There is no game now in vogue which is more simple than that of baseball, and hence its
attraction for the masses ... yet to excel in the game ... requires not only the physical attributes
of endurance, agility and strength ... plenty of courage, luck and nerve, mental powers of
sound judgment, quick perception ... and presence of mind to act promptly in critical emer-
gencies"—Henry Chadwick in 1876

"I see great things in baseball. It's our game—the American game. It will take our people out
of doors, fill them with oxygen, give them a larger stoicism. Tend to relieve us a nervous dys-
peptic set. Repair these losses, be a blessing to us"—Walt Whitman

"A boy's game, with no more possibilities in it than a boy could master, a game bounded by
walls which kept out novelty or danger, change or adventure"—F. Scott Fitzgerald

"Baseball is one of the symbols of those things constant in American Life. Not even the toxic
intrusion of artificial grass and megabuck contracts can spoil the naivety and optimism that
is in baseball. Millions of Americans look to it for a nonviolent escape from the weariness
that exists in the world beyond the center field wall. Baseball is constant and no matter how
bad things get there is always next year. As Emily Dickenson put it, 'A little madness in the
spring is wholesome even for a king'"—*New York Times* editorial, June 5, 1984

"THE GAME IS PERFECT. IT'S THE PEOPLE WHO SCREW IT UP."—sign at Yankee Stadium just before the 1994 players' strike

"The American civilization will be remembered for three things 2,000 years from now: the Constitution, jazz music, and baseball"—Gerald Early, director of the African and Afro-American studies department at Washington University in St. Louis

"The game is played with a round bat and a round ball, and the players run around the bases, and what goes around comes around"—Toronto Blue Jays rookie Frank Wills, when called up in 1989[12]

A ragged spheroid and an unseemly piece of wood were the equipment used in a many-splendored activity that eventually was called baseball. Long before Abner Doubleday supposedly invented baseball at Cooperstown, New York, in 1839, boys and girls played a wide variety of ball games named Rounders, One Old Cat, Two Old Cats, Town Ball, Bittle Battle, and other variations.[13] (Evidence is overwhelming that Doubleday did not invent America's game. As one pundit wrote, "the only thing Doubleday started was the Civil War.")

There is considerable debate about the official origin of organized baseball. American sports historian Charles A. Peverelly credits Alexander Cartwright with having established the first formally organized club—the New York Knickerbockers—in 1845. Likely the Knickerbockers played a form of an earlier game before 1845. It is difficult to ascertain when the first recorded game was played. Historians have generally settled on June 19, 1846, when an organized game was played between the Knickerbockers and the New York Nine at Elysian Field in Hoboken, New Jersey. Cartwright and others were responsible for a set of rules identified as the Knickerbocker Rules of 1845.[14]

In the 1850s, the game spread like wildfire throughout the eastern part of the country. Dozens of "baseball" clubs organized in the greater New York City area. The sport expanded to the South during the Civil War, where Union soldiers demonstrated the game in town after town. News sources and the public soon proclaimed the popular game as the "National Pastime." Soon after the Civil War, Cleveland citizens demonstrated an increasing interest in recreation and sports, some joining the Turner Movement from Germany, others the Muscular Christianity Movement. Sub-cultures were attracted to horse racing and boxing, but it was baseball that met the sporting spirit of the public, particularly at the amateur level. Evidence of baseball in Cleveland dates to 1845, when ball was banned in the Public Square. The ban did not last long.

Parks were established on the east side of Cleveland, often not much more than scraped surfaces earlier dedicated to grazing and gardening. As many as 2,000 curious residents assembled at one of five city parks where a semblance of professional teams competed. One of these parks was Case Commons, an unfenced expanse located on Putnam Avenue (later East 38th Street) between Scovil and Central Avenues.[15]

The beginning of professional baseball in Cleveland is recorded on June 2, 1869. Named the Cleveland Forest Citys, this team played the legendary Cincinnati Red Stockings, the first American team comprised entirely of paid professional players. Noted Cincinnati stars were brothers George and Harry Wright and fabulous John Hatfield, known to have the strongest throwing arm in the game at the time. The local nine were dressed in white pantaloons and bright stockings, while the redoubtable Cincinnati squad, the nation's leading exponents of rounders, set the pace in style by wearing a racy knickerbocker-type pant for the first time.[16] Played at Case Commons, this contest should have been a tipoff to the bleak years ahead for Cleveland. The visiting Cincinnati team won by a score of 25–6.

In July 1868, native Ohioan President Ulysses S. Grant invited the Forest City Baseball Club to the White House:

> "Boys," said the Chief Executive, "I have never seen a game. I haven't had time but I know a great deal about the game. Let me prove it to you. I'll call the positions and then let each man step forward as his position is named. Catcher!" Jim White stood out, "Pitcher!" Pratt answered. "First base!" The President called eight men into line. "Wait a minute," he said, "there are nine men on the team. Hold on, there's the shortstop." Turning to W.R. Rose, five feet six inches tall and acting as cashier for the team, he put his arm around the young man's shoulders and exclaimed, "This must be the short stop!"[17]

Cleveland's Forest Citys, "the most gentlemanly club in the country," beamed as the president went with them to the door, puffing on his black cigar.

In 1870, Cleveland's second year in professional baseball highlighted a sparkling exhibition between the home nine and the Atlantic Club of Brooklyn, New York. The concept of pay-for-play attracted the best players to a limited number of clubs and all but destroyed attendance for the remaining amateur groups in the city. One of these clubs, the Cleveland Nine—composed of local railroaders—was one of the best amateur clubs in Cleveland, having defeated the tough Brooklyn Atlantics in 1867 and 1868. The team's demise was assured, however, when the Forest City team went professional. Amateur teams continued to organize, but for the remainder of the century, attention focused on professional teams.[18]

During a seven-year interregnum from 1872 to 1879, Cleveland had no professional baseball team. During this period, baseball itself was undergoing a critical change. The National League, founded in 1876, signaled the beginning of the modern business phase of the game. The new league was an owners' league composed of individuals or stock companies who ran the teams. The players were now employees, not partners. The imposition of the reserve clause by the league in 1879 sealed the deal. This regulation required players to bind their services to a particular team. No longer could individuals freely move from team to team in search of better pay. Salaries and rosters stabilized, and profits for the owners became more consistent.[19]

Stabilizing teams and cutting costs were just two developments behind the creation of the new league; the third was improving the image of the game. By the 1870s, baseball had begun to acquire a reputation as attracting beer-drinking, boisterous crowds, including gamblers and pickpockets. The league banned beer at games and raised ticket prices to 50 cents (double the standard rate) in order to cultivate a better clientele. To encourage fans further, team owners eventually introduced padded box seats.[20]

In Cleveland, little interest in professional baseball was apparent until the later 1870s. For over 20 years, professional baseball had operated in a topsy-turvy manner as various teams and leagues organized and then disappeared from the scene. It existed in a continuum of haphazard league affiliations, an in-and-out association that prevailed until the end of the century—the formative years of American baseball. Eventually on December 4, 1878, the National League admitted the Cleveland Blues to the league. William Hollinger and J. Ford Evans, who had been involved with the earlier Cleveland team, organized the team.

For the next six years, the Blues played with mixed results. The team compiled three winning seasons, finishing third (47–37) in 1880, fifth (42–40) in 1882, and fourth (55–42) in 1883. However, in 1884, the Blues severed their relationship with the National League. The loss of five star players to an outlaw league had taken the heart out of the team, and major league baseball was absent from Cleveland in 1885 and 1886.

Frank De Haas Robison was determined to return baseball to Cleveland. "I'm going to put Cleveland back in baseball," he promised in the summer of 1886, "if I have to buy a team myself, sell the tickets, and haul it around in my own streetcar."[21] Robison's secretary treasurer was George W. Howe—nephew of Elias Howe, inventor of the sewing machine. Robison, a trolley car magnate, looked for a way to put riders on his transit line and collect from the patrons again at his new ballpark at Kennard (East 46th Street and Cedar). A shrewd businessman, Robison realized that the increasing number of workers in an ever-growing industrial city would patronize Sunday baseball. However, he faced legal charges for violating the Blue Laws. Teams made a special effort to travel to cities where Sunday ball was not strictly challenged, then return to their home fields by the early weekdays.

Meanwhile, the American Association was founded in 1882 with six teams competing against the more highly organized National League. The association expanded to eight teams in 1883 and to 14 teams in 1884, and finished with 13 when Washington dropped out.

After a two-year hiatus, Cleveland competed in the faltering American Association in 1887 and 1888. Due to trades, the depleted team finished in last place in 1887 with a record of 39–92 and two ties. The following year, Cleveland showed improvement with a record of 50–82 and three ties.[22]

When the Cleveland players reported to the city in the spring of 1889, Howe took one look at the aggregation and moaned, "They look awful, all skinny and spindly," he complained, "They're nothing more than spiders."[23] Howe had the players dress in white and dark blue uniforms, a garb that only accentuated their skinny appearance.

In 1889, the Cleveland team moved to the National League and became the Cleveland Spiders. What prompted the move to the older, established league is unknown, other than the fact that a slot opened because Detroit had left the league. Robison thought his interests would be more secure. The choice was a wise one. During the preceding three years, the American Association had reorganized and four teams, including Cleveland, left the association and joined the National League.

However, if the Spiders could not win games, they could and did win most of their fights in 1889 and came to be known as the National League's toughest and roughest team. In fact, when the team hit the skids in August, the pugnacious players were so unruly that league governors considered legislation to restrain team behavior.

At the same time, a second professional team arrived in Cleveland, a member of the upstart Players' League, otherwise known as the Brotherhood of Professional Baseball Players; the teams formed a league to compete against the National League and American Association at the major league level. This Brotherhood had been formed in 1885 to give the players the potential to take control of the game, rather than be exploited by owners.

Defections from organized baseball were numerous. Over 100 players fled the National League to join the Players' League, while another 20 jumped from the American Association, and by 1890, the cream of the baseball world was playing in the Players' League. Several players from the Cleveland Spiders joined the second Cleveland team, including manager "Patsy" Tebeau and rookie outfielder Jim McAleer. The local team was nicknamed the Infants.[24]

The player-led league did well for a few weeks, but by June, all three leagues were drawing low attendances. Despite mounting losses, the Players' League Infants managed to stay afloat through the summer and completed the season finishing seventh in an eight-team league. The league folded after the 1890 season, and several of the Infants returned to the Cleveland Spiders. The Players' League had lost over $125,000 in their venture, when the first peace offerings were made by the National League in October 1890. The Players' League franchises jumped at the chance to return to the National League. Further losses could not be tolerated. However, hindsight revealed that perhaps the Players' League had acted in haste to close shop, for the National League had lost almost $500,000—one more push and it might have gone under.

With the demise of the Players' League, the Brotherhood was broken, and any semblance of player power was lost. The powerful owners were free to have their way with the ballplayers, setting salaries and the like to suit their own needs.

The losses of the Brotherhood had far-reaching implications for Cleveland and the nation. Albert Johnson, also a traction railway magnate in Cleveland and a competitor of Spiders owner Frank Robison, with his brother Tom owned stock in the Brotherhood enterprise. The brothers showed their support in what was essentially a nationwide movement by organized labor, and their intrusion was a blow to Robison and his efforts to stabilize the Spiders.[25]

To add to an already dismal season, the stands on Payne Avenue were hit by lightning and burned to the ground.[26] Better days began on August 5, 1890, a red-letter day in Cleveland baseball history, when the franchise purchased pitcher Denton True Young from the Canton Nadjys semi-pro team. The cost was $250. A huge farm boy—six feet, two inches, 210 pounds—he was considered exceptionally large at the time.

Dressed in a nondescript uniform that was quickly provided for him, his odd appearance failed to detract from his performance. Untutored in pitching skills, Young's main forte, according to sports writers who saw him, was his roaring fast pitch—so fast that writers soon nicknamed him "Cyclone" Young.[27] That name was inevitably shortened to "Cy," and under that tag the right-hander went on to become one of baseball's true immortals. His career lasted until 1912, a total of 22 seasons, of which 12 were with Cleveland; and when statisticians totaled the final figures at the end of the trail, Young had compiled four records that are unlikely to ever be broken: wins, 511; losses, 315; innings pitched, 7356; and 750 complete games of his 815 starts. In 1956 the Cy Young Award was established to honor the major leagues' most outstanding pitcher. (Beginning in 1967, it was awarded to one pitcher in each league.)

From 1891 through 1896, Cleveland had one of the most successful teams in the National League. The club was bolstered not only by Cy Young, but also by other star players. The lineup featured outfielders Jesse Burkett and Jimmy McAleer, versatile Buck Ewing, Cupid Childs, catcher Chief Zimmer, and right-handed pitcher Nig Cuppy. The team also played in a new ball park in 1891. After the fire in 1890, owner Frank Robison constructed a new ball park, National League Park, several blocks eastward to Lexington Avenue and 66th Street. His two trolley lines ran right by the park. The all-wood stands consisted of a single deck behind the plate, a covered pavilion behind first base, and a small bleacher section.

Because owners of a saloon and two residences had refused to sell their properties, League Park likely provided the most unusual dimensions in major league history. The left field foul line was 375 feet from home plate, the right field foul line 290 feet, and the center field wall 420 feet from home plate.[28] The ballpark held approximately 10,000 fans.

For the first time, sales of season reserved seats were available. The cost for an individual ticket was six dollars. The store clerks informed the eager populace, "But if you wish to bring a lady, there is a special deal available ... only ten dollars for yourself, your lady, and your carriage." He added, "The carriage could be pulled up to a specified location behind first or third base and there would be no necessity of stepping down on the turf at any time."[29]

In 1892, the Cleveland franchise experienced the first of several "glory years." The American Association had folded, and the National League had expanded to 12 teams. In order to ease the awkwardness of a packed schedule, the season was divided into spring and fall series. An outstanding Boston Red Sox team led by Hall of Famer manager Frank Selee won the first half championship in the spring campaigns. Cleveland finished in fifth place in the first half, winning 40 while losing 33 games. Robison was not pleased, and he elevated Pat Tebeau from captain to team manager, replacing manager Bob Leadley. From 1893 to 1895, Tebeau would bat over .300. As manager, he was inspirational but also combative, often harassing opposing teams and umpires. The new manager would lead the Spiders to successful performances for the next five years (1892–1896).

The managerial change by Robison had turned out to be a Godsend for the team and Cleveland fans. In the "fall" of 1892, the team won 53 games and lost only 23 to win the second-half championship. "The Spiders are the best team that ever represented the Forest City in baseball," acclaimed the Cleveland *Leader*. "Mr. Robison is to be highly commended for installing Tebeau as manager. He will gain national recognition for not only the Spiders but for Cleveland."[30]

Cy Young, the Spiders' star pitcher, was in a jovial mood all summer. And well he might have been. The 25-year-old won 36 games and lost only 12 with an ERA of 1.93. On October 17, Young tangled with Happy Jack Stivetts, ace of the Boston staff, before six thousand cranks (a term to describe baseball fans in the late 1800s) at League Park in an exhibition game. The two pitchers battled for 11 innings, with the Beaneaters garnering six hits off Young and Cleveland tagging Stivetts for four hits. Not one error marred the game, and the fielding was as spectacular as it was clean. But the "sportsmanship" of Mike "King" Kelly, Boston's pugnacious catcher-outfielder, was neither. Kelly was the most hated player of the era, a man with such an intense desire to win—and to win bets he had placed on his own team—that he would resort to any chicanery.

In this classic scoreless game, the tension mounting into the ninth inning, the Beaneaters received a break when Stivetts popped up one of Young's fast pitches high into foul territory.

The Spiders called for catcher Charles "Chief" Zimmer to take the ball, and Kelly yelled for first baseman Jake Virtue to make the catch. Virtue crashed into Zimmer, who

Denton True "Cy" Young, winner of a record 511 victories, 260 with Cleveland. He was elected to the Hall of Fame in 1937, along with Nap Lajoie and Tris Speaker (Library of Congress).

consequently dropped the ball. The Spiders swarmed onto the field and charged the umpire, demanding that Kelly be thrown out of the game. "It did not benefit the Boston team, as they scored a blank, despite Kelly's dirty work," reported the *Spalding Baseball Guide* for 1893. "He was fined 10 dollars for the call."[31] The game ended in a tie and the rest of the series was downhill for Cleveland as the Beaneaters swept the Spiders in five games (plus one tie). (As an aside, Mike "King" Kelly was elected to the Hall of Fame in 1945.)

The 1893 and 1894 Spiders were formidable, finishing third and sixth in the now 12-team National League. Cy Young continued with his torrid pitching exploits, compiling a 34–16 record in 1893 and 26–21 in 1894. Nevertheless, the Clevelanders seemed to lack the necessary spark. League members were now competing for the Temple Cup. Pittsburgh businessman Charles C. Temple, a fan of his hometown Pittsburgh Pirates, spent $800 for a trophy that he decreed would be contested by the first- and second-place teams in 1894. He further ruled that the winners would receive 65 percent of the gate receipts while the losers divided the rest. The trophy was called the Temple Cup.[32] The Baltimore Orioles, a powerhouse and league champions, faced the second-place New York Giants and met their Waterloo in four consecutive games.

The Spiders vied for the Temple Cup in 1895. Undaunted by Baltimore's reputation, they discarded the defending champions in five games. The locals were led by Cy Young, who won three games, catcher "Chief" Zimmer and Jesse Burkett—all respected in the game.

Burkett batted .500 in the series and grumbled at the Orioles in every game. The Baltimore team was made up of hoodlums and troublemakers considered by many to be a disgrace to the game.

Whatever the social and political ramifications involved in their establishment, the Spiders finally gave Cleveland a winner. The rowdiness of fans in this series was a preface to future episodes of fan rowdiness—notably the 1934 World Series between the Detroit Tigers and the St. Louis Cardinals.

Playing at home, the Clevelanders won the first three games before crowds of between 10,000 and 12,000 people, with Cy Young winning two of those games. During the home games, local fans bombarded the Orioles with potatoes and other missiles. As expected, fan retaliation in Baltimore was such that it threatened the Spiders' safety. Upon leaving the Baltimore park, even after losing the fourth game 5–0, the Spiders were assaulted in their high-sided omnibus: "The Cleveland players had to sprawl on the floor of the bus to escape serious injury," reported a Cleveland *Plain Dealer* correspondent, "Many players later showed their souvenirs of stones and pieces of steel they had picked up from the floor of the bus."[33] Perhaps the fan reaction was a response to Cleveland's unruly style of play. Manager Tebeau advocated "rowdy baseball." He once claimed that "A milk and water, goody, goody player can't ever wear a Cleveland uniform."[34]

The Spiders were bruised but not scared, and Young turned back the Orioles the next afternoon, 5–2, to win the Temple Cup, four games to one. Cleveland sports writers gloated in their home newspapers. The *Plain Dealer* chortled, "the Orioles kept up the clip for a while, but then the streaks of 'yellow' showed and it was all over."[35] Young manager Connie Mack of the Pittsburgh Pirates acknowledged the Spiders' victory, commenting, "I am happy that gentlemen have won the Temple Cup."[36] The Spiders each received $528 for winning the series, and each Oriole received $316.

The two teams finished one-two again in the 1896 race for the Temple Cup. Unlike the 1895 Series, the 1896 rematch for the Temple Cup was marked by considerable apathy. Attendance was down. Cy Young had gone through a strenuous summer, winning 28 games, and was pretty much burned out. Before 4,400 fans, the largest crowd of the series in Baltimore, the Orioles defeated Young and the Spiders, 7–1, and went on to sweep Cleveland in four games.

Mr. Temple's motive for sponsoring the championship series was to see his beloved Pirates win it all. Such was not the case, however, as the Temple Cup Series ceased after the 1897 season. The loss of the Cup in 1896 had signaled the eventual demise of the Cleveland Spiders. The locals finished in fifth place in 1897 and 1898. The baseball scene in Cleveland for the remainder of the century would feature two names: Louis Sockalexis and "The Misfits."

Louis Sockalexis, a Penobscot Indian from Maine, came to the sporting scene with superb athletic ability. Contrary to popular belief, Sockalexis was not a full-blooded Indian nor was he the first Indian to play in the major leagues. That honor went to James Madison Toy, a Pennsylvanian whose father was a Native American, who played for Cleveland's American Association team in 1887 and Brooklyn's AA team in 1890. More than two decades later, Moses "Chief" Yellow Horse, a Pawnee from Oklahoma, became the first full-blooded

Native American to play in the major leagues. He pitched with the Pittsburgh Pirates in 1921 and 1922, winning eight games and losing four.

Sockalexis, strong as an ox and fast as a deer, had caught the attention of college scouts and had played baseball at Holy Cross (1895–1896) and Notre Dame (1897). Unfortunately, he experienced his first taste of alcohol at Notre Dame, which would eventually lead to his downfall. Cleveland slugger Jesse Burkett—"the Crab"—discovered Sockalexis while coaching at Holy Cross and urged manager Patsy Tebeau to sign the swift outfielder.

Enormous expectations accompanied Sockalexis's major league debut. A March 1897, *Sporting Life* article described him as a "massive man with gigantic bones and bulging muscles [who] looks like a ball player from the ground to the top of his five foot, eleven inches of solid framework."[37] Future Hall of Famer Hughie Jennings remembered that Sockalexis had the most ability of any man who had ever played the game. Now expelled from Notre Dame for leaving the campus before the end of the semester, Sockalexis came to Cleveland amidst considerable hoopla, but also in the face of prejudice. The Battle of Little Big Horn (1876) was still fresh in the minds of many Americans.

Sockalexis's exploits, on and off the field, resulted in many falsehoods. The truths during his short major league career are more easily validated. He was an excellent hitter, although not an especially adept outfielder. "Chief," as he was called, was liked by his teammates. In 1897, his most productive season, he played in 66 games, batting 278 times, with 43 runs, 94 hits, 42 RBI, and a batting average of .338 including three home runs. During the deadball era, home runs were a rarity, with top hitters stroking no more than ten to 15 home runs in a season.[38] The deadball era was most prominent between 1900 and 1920 when the game was played with a much less lively ball. Due to certain properties within the component material of the ball, it rebounded less sharply upon impact with the bat.

Alcohol soon overtook the 25-year-old. He played in only 21 games in 1898, batting a meager .224 and driving in ten runs, and was released after seven games in 1899. He played a total of 94 games in two and one-half seasons, batting .313. Sockalexis was sent to the minor leagues for three seasons and then retired from the game. The pioneer Native-American major leaguer, often called the "father of the Cleveland Indians," died in 1913 at the age of 42.[39]

By 1899, The Gay Nineties were not so gay, nor were the Cleveland Spiders, a team in name only. Cleveland was growing rapidly, thanks to oil, coal, and iron ore interests. Interest in professional baseball had declined. Hurt by numerous league manipulations, the season was a flop and so were the Spiders. Owner Frank Robison decided to make several dramatic changes following the 1898 season. One major reason for seeking a change was the continual refusal of city fathers to allow Sunday baseball games, causing severe financial loss. Robison and his brother Stanley bought the lowly St. Louis Perfectos from bankrupt German mogul Chris Von der Ahe. After much legal bickering and secret negotiations, the deal was consummated at a sheriff's sale in early 1899. Robison transferred most of the Spiders stars— Cy Young, Jesse Burkett, manager Patsy Tebeau, Cupid Childs, and John Heidrick—to the St. Louis Perfectos. The remaining Spiders who did not make the St. Louis team were sent back to Cleveland.

The Cleveland Spiders, with a residue of ragamuffin players, remained in the National

League, where Robison now owned two teams. A hapless figure named Lave Cross, who eventually had a 21-year career in the major leagues, was assigned to manage the leftovers. Cross believed that if Robison were to give him five good players, he and this depleted team could win a few games. Robison fixed Cross with a stare: "I'm not interested in winning games [in Cleveland]," he retorted. "Play out the schedule. That's your job."[40] In an uproar over Robison's scurrilous behavior, fans stayed away from League Park. This ineffective collection of players, known by a variety of derogatory names, were charitably called the "Misfits" but continued to be referred to as Spiders in official record books.[41] After 27 games, fans stayed away from League Park, and it did not pay to open the gates. Receipts reached a low of $25 for a game, and opposing clubs protested that it was not worth their time to go to Cleveland.

After the first 27 games, the Misfits played 50 games in a 52-day span away from home, from July 3 to August 23. The team never won more than two games in a row. Morale was low, as defeats mounted. To add to their misery, owner Robison pulled manager Lave Cross up to the St. Louis team in early June, and second baseman Joe Quinn took over as manager of the Spiders.

The newspapers directed humor of various sorts toward the Misfits. The *Brooklyn Daily Eagle* commented: "Will somebody please tell the Clevelands that fly balls are intended, according to the rules of the game, to be caught."[42] The *Plain Dealer* commented that the 100 fans who showed up for a Pirates-Misfits game were treated to the "eighth wonder of the world."[43] After a terribly long losing skein, the locals won, 6–2.

On June 24, the *Plain Dealer* summed up the day-by-day tribulation of the Spiders in a game against the New York Giants:

> Cleveland had a narrow escape yesterday. For some time it looked as if another day would go by without ... meeting their customary defeat, and there was great anxiety felt by friends of the players. There is no telling what effect such an accident would have on them.... It looked so much like rain ... that there seemed little hope of getting in a daily beating.... The game was played and as it resulted as usual, the nervous system of the players and audience sustained no shock.[44]

The New Yorkers defeated the Misfits, 7–2. The beat went on for three more months. The season ended on Sunday, October 15. As if retelling the last moments of life before a condemned man's execution, the *Plain Dealer* remarked, "The end is at hand, and that there would be only one more tale of woe."[45] On the last day, the Misfits lost a doubleheader to Cincinnati, 16–1 and 19–3.

The 1899 Misfits lost 40 of their last 41 games and 134 out of a scheduled 154 games, the worst record in major league history. In an understatement, the *Plain Dealer* uttered philosophically, "It has been a bad season for Cleveland fans." One of the Cleveland faithful added, "I have never seen an audience so loyal to its home team. During [home] games, there was never a hiss or a call down for a Cleveland player."[46] Only 6,000 fans had seen the team play in Cleveland for the entire season.

No doubt those loyal fans soon let loose with a cry so familiar to baseball fandom, "Wait 'Til Next Year." The next year would be 1900, a time of renaissance for modern-day baseball. Unfortunately, Cleveland would not field a professional team in 1900, but better days were ahead.

2

The Clevelanders and the American League

"The town is baseball mad, the addition of Lajoie and Barnard has set the town afire, and now nothing is talked about except baseball."—*Sporting Life*, 1902

As the United States moved into the twentieth century, and despite organizational disruptions, baseball captured the citizenry as America's national pastime, and midwestern and eastern cities vied for major league teams. Starting in 1900, the modern National League—the senior circuit—was comprised of the same eight teams until 1953, when the Boston Braves moved to Milwaukee. A similar stability prevailed in the American League—the junior circuit founded in 1901—with only the transfer of the Milwaukee franchise to St. Louis and the replacement of the Baltimore Orioles by the New York Highlanders in 1903. After a flurry of back room maneuvering, the two leagues coalesced into stable enterprises which survived for over a half century. All of the original 16 teams—eight in each league—were located east of the Mississippi, with the exception of two St. Louis teams situated on the west bank of the country's largest river.

How did Cleveland, after the disastrous season of the Misfits in 1899, end up as one of the four original teams in the American League? It was no surprise that in 1900, the National League had decided to drop four teams, leaving as a core the teams from Boston, Philadelphia, Pittsburgh, Chicago, New York, Brooklyn, Cincinnati and St. Louis.[1]

When the National League was reduced from 12 clubs to eight in the winter of 1899-1900, dropping Cleveland and Louisville in the west, and Washington and Baltimore in the east, the stage was set for expansion of the American League into the junior circuit. This action was sponsored by Andrew "Sly" Freedman, hated owner of the New York Giants, who wanted to lop off so-called "dead wood" of the National League,[2] which left Cleveland without a team.

The National League paid out approximately $150,000 to buy out the four eliminated franchises. Frank Robison, who also owned the St. Louis Cardinals, was given $25,000 for his now deposed Spiders team.[3] Charles Somers, an obtrusive baseball enthusiast, quickly acquired the Grand Rapids (Michigan) club of the Western League and moved it into the vacated National League territory in Cleveland. In the same year, 1900, Ban Johnson and Charley Comiskey moved their St. Paul club into Chicago and changed their circuit from

15

the Western to the American League.[4] Prospects for a major league team in Cleveland were dim until February 21, 1900, a cold blustery day in the Forest city.

David Hawley, president of Cuyahoga Savings and Loan Association, received three visitors that day, one being native Ohioan Bancroft "Ban" Johnson, president of the Western Baseball League. When one of the others—M. E. Gaul of the New York Central Railroad—introduced the stocky president of the Western League, Johnson retorted, "You made a mistake, Mr. Gaul; it used to be the Western League. It is now called the American League."[5] Hence, the birth of a second major league. Johnson was determined to establish a new league, and if necessary, to raid the National League for players.

Johnson wanted to know if Hawley could recommend an owner(s) to take over this new franchise in Cleveland. Hawley replied, "I have two young men in mind. One is Charley Somers, the other is Jack Kilfoyl."[6] Somers was in the lumber and Great Lakes shipping business with his father. The family's fortune had increased over the years, so he possessed ready cash. Kilfoyl owned a men's clothing store on Public Square in Cleveland. With less money than Somers, but more business acumen and an equal amount of enthusiasm, he was a good fit with Somers. Kilfoyl became president and treasurer of the new franchise, and Somers was content with the title of vice-president.

To be expected, there were hurdles to overcome before a team could be ready to compete. A baseball park was the first issue. The Robisons owned League Park and after some haggling, they agreed to rent the park to this new team for $12,000 annually.[7] To resolve impending problems, the National League met in Cleveland on March 3, 1900, and agreed to give the Cleveland owners territorial rights for their team. A similar arrangement allowed Charles Comiskey to field a team on the south side of Chicago.

In 1900, in exchange for these concessions, Johnson and his new colleagues consented to remain a minor league. Although the name change from Western League to American League would remain in effect, the minor league would be subject to a player draft by the National League. Peace would not last long.

In 1901, the Cleveland ownership fielded a team under the management of Jim McAleer, a graceful outfielder who had played with the pre–1900 National League Spiders. He was a local favorite but had little talent to work with in 1901. His star player was a Cleveland native, third baseman Bill Bradley. The team was called the Blues, after the team's blue uniforms. The Blues played their first game at League Park to an announced capacity of 9,000. The park was as large as those of Cleveland's American League counterparts—Boston (Huntington Avenue Baseball Grounds), Detroit (Bennett Park), and Philadelphia (Columbia Park)—but smaller than South Side Park in Chicago (forerunner of Comiskey Park), which held 15,000. Recruiting enough quality players was difficult, and the locals finished in seventh place with a record of 55–82. The home attendance of 131,380 was the worst in the league, but an improvement over the Misfits' season.

One highlight of the season occurred on May 23, 1901, when Cleveland set a major league record by proving the game isn't over until the final out. The Washington Senators led the Blues, 13–5, with two outs in the last of the ninth and nary a runner on base. Most of the 1,250 fans in attendance had already left League Park in disgust. Cleveland erupted for *nine runs* to rescue a potential loss, winning 14–13.[8]

League Park, a cozy ball park built in 1891, wedged into an existing neighborhood block. A short right field necessitated the construction of a 45-foot wall (fence) within, making for a lively game (courtesy of the artist, Jeff Suntala).

The year 1902 was a landmark year, not only for the Cleveland franchise but also for hard-driving Ban Johnson and Charley Somers. Johnson was determined to make the American League a worthy counterpart to the National League, and moved forward with the help of Somers's bankroll. First, he transferred the Milwaukee team to St. Louis, where Sportsman's Park had been improved with the help of Somers's dollars. Cleveland manager Jimmy McAleer was transferred to that team to provide his experience and positive personality.

Somers poured money into the new Boston Red Sox club and put up more than one-half of the money needed to establish a second franchise in Philadelphia under the leadership of Ben Shibe and Connie Mack. This move would soon have important ramifications for the Cleveland club. By now, Somers had invested over $800,000 in the American League in support of Johnson's efforts to establish a second major league.[9]

But as it happened, Somers's interest in the Philadelphia Athletics was brief. Shibe, a sporting goods manufacturer, bought half of Somers's share, and a few months later, Shibe and Connie Mack purchased the remainder. Somers was unable to surrender his interests in Boston until 1903, when he sold out to Henry and Matthew Killilea of Milwaukee.

The newly named Cleveland Bronchos—the players believed the nickname Blues was too sissified—hired William Armour to manage the Bronchos in 1902. Although Armour did not distinguish himself as manager of the Bronchos, he was noted for two innovations. First, after leaving Cleveland in 1905 to manage the Detroit Tigers, he reportedly asked his wife for her daily starting pitcher selection. His Detroit team finished third in 1905 and sixth in 1906.

Armour's second innovation was of a more serious nature. Sabermetrician Bill James claims Armour initiated the platoon system at Detroit in 1906 when he platooned catchers Boss Schmidt and John Warner. Later in the 1920s, Cleveland manager Tris Speaker was the first manager to platoon extensively, doing so at three or four positions.[10] Armour's Bronchos floundered until June 4, 1902, when Cleveland's fortunes took a major turn for the better. Under Ban Johnson's urging, over 100 players fled from the National League for the fledgling American League.

Armour's young team did not have much to look forward to early in 1902. The arrival of several noted players changed the landscape much for the better. What made 1902 such a remarkable year in the history of the Cleveland franchise was the arrival of second baseman Napoléon "Nap" Lajoie, and the equally valuable addition to the roster of pitcher Adrian "Addie" Joss, whose name will be in the annals of Cleveland baseball history forever. Joss was born on April 12, 1880, in Woodland, Wisconsin, the only child of immigrant parents. When Joss was ten years old, his father died from the effects of alcoholism. To support the family, his mother worked as a milliner.[11] Joss graduated from high school, pitching successfully for Wayland Academy in Beaver Dam, Wisconsin, and playing amateur ball in Oshkosh and Manitowoc, Wisconsin. He signed a contract with manager Charles J. Strobel's club in Toledo, Ohio, then in the Inter-State League, for the 1900 season. Joss found his experience in Toledo formative for his professional development. In the two seasons he pitched for the Mud Hens—playing in the Western Association in 1901—he won 46 games, and learned the pro game from team captain and former Cleveland Spider Bobby Gilks.[12]

After Joss's minor league sojourn, Somers signed him; during the next nine years, the right-hander anchored the Cleveland team's pitching staff. He pitched a one-hitter in his major league debut against the St. Louis Browns on April 26, 1902. In his third start on May 4, he allowed the Detroit Tigers no hits until the ninth inning.

Shortly thereafter, two important players jumped from the National League to bolster the Cleveland roster. Elmer Flick, a native of Bedford, Ohio, played briefly with the Athletics before going to Cleveland. An outfielder, he became a fan favorite for the next nine years. Flick was inducted into the Hall of Fame in 1963.[13] Right-hander Bill Bernhard, who had short stays with the Phillies and Athletics, also bolted to the American League and joined the Cleveland Indians.

The patient and soft-spoken Connie Mack—his given name was Cornelius McGillicuddy—was asked by Ban Johnson to build a new team to compete against the well-established Philadelphia Phillies and their headstrong owner, Colonel John I. Rogers. Shibe was a good friend of Al Reach, manufacturer of baseball equipment, and part owner of the Phillies. Shibe's relationship with Colonel Rogers had become more distant, and eventually he was an important cog with the Philadelphia Athletics and later became their owner.[14]

Connie Mack had great respect for Napoléon Lajoie, who was one of the premier players in the major leagues. Lajoie was born in Woonsocket, Rhode Island, September 5, 1875, of pure French stock, à la Lou Boudreau, who also was of French descent. As he grew to 6'1" and 195 pounds, Lajoie demonstrated matchless grace and smooth physical power that enabled him to field and throw with a minimum of effort.[15]

In 1896, a local scout signed Lajoie to play for the Fall River, Massachusetts, team in the New England League. The newcomer tore up the league. A Philadelphia Phillies scout quickly signed him and rushed him off to the City of Brotherly Love. He batted .361, .324, .378, and .337 the next four years for the Phillies.

Lajoie needed little prodding to throw his lot with Johnson's and Mack's American League. Like most Phillies players, Lajoie was unhappy with Colonel Rogers' one sided contracts and the National League's mandated salary limit of $2,400. Mack persuaded Lajoie to play for him in 1901 at a higher salary. Both Lajoie and star pitcher Bernhard jumped to the American League with the Athletics, and Lajoie led the American League with a remarkable .426 batting average.[16]

John I. Rogers, president of the Phillies and a lawyer, had permitted Lajoie to play one year with the Athletics, but now was made livid by Lajoie's departure. He petitioned a Pennsylvania Superior Court and obtained an injunction to restrain Lajoie, Bernhard, and any other "jumping" players from appearing with any team but the Phillies.[17] The injunction was due back on April 21, 1902. The plot thickened and many of the legal entities involved are beyond the scope of this discussion. In reality, it became a battle between the National League and the American League. The Superior Court released its long-awaited decision on April 22, ruling that Lajoie was the property of the Phillies and bound to the franchise for the 1902 and 1903 seasons. This decision was tilted toward the Phillies, particularly because Lajoie had had such a great season for the Athletics in 1901, making him "the king of ballplayers" and irreplaceable.[18]

Lajoie was disappointed with the decision, but remained defiant. Shortly after the court decision was released and the ten-day notice that he had to return to the Phillies was served, he retaliated, "If Mr. Mack wants me to play for his club, either in [Philadelphia] or outside it I will do so. I am under contract to him, and will faithfully live up to the terms of it."[19]

Stunned by the ruling, the Athletics traveled to Baltimore on April 23 to open their season. Lajoie started the game at second base. In the bottom of the eighth inning, Mack received a telegram informing him that the court had granted a five-day temporary injunction requested by Colonel Rogers. Lajoie was, for the time being, barred from playing for any team but the Phillies within the state of Pennsylvania. After weighing the situation, and not wanting to anger the judges by appearing to defy their order, Mack pulled Lajoie from the game. Pitcher Bill Bernhard, who was not yet enjoined from playing, remained on the mound, finishing the last game he would pitch for the Athletics. Lajoie watched the next few games in an Athletics uniform and pondered his next move.

According to biographer David L. Fleitz, Lajoie's situation in May 1902 was unique in baseball history. "No other star of Lajoie's magnitude had ever found himself cast adrift during a season while owners of other teams competed for his services in a flurry of high stakes bidding and record-setting salary offers." In reality, Lajoie was a free agent.[20] The second baseman had the option of signing with the Phillies, distasteful though it may have been, to return to the employ of Rogers. The major advantage of doing so would be an end to his legal problems.

Likely, Lajoie would have returned to the Phillies, but the arrogant Rogers overplayed his hand. His salary offer was lower than those of other teams. In a bewildering burst of bad judgment, the owner demanded that Lajoie pay a penalty for the time he had missed with the Phillies. This was an insult to the proud star who still believed that the owner had cheated him out of $400 in his 1900 contract. Lajoie would not accept this offer, but Rogers stood firm. The Colonel's stubbornness opened the door for the Cleveland Bronchos to swoop in and carry off the prize. Negotiations with the Phillies had stalled. The Bronchos had already signed Elmer Flick, and had hoped to capture Bill Bernhard as well as Lajoie.

Lajoie and Bernhard arrived in Cleveland on May 25, 1902, and met with owners Charley Somers and John Kilfoyl. The young and weak Cleveland franchise needed the help these two players could provide. Lajoie was impressed with an offer of a guaranteed salary of $7,000 per year for four years, the largest sum ever offered to that date. Two days later president John Kilfoyl held a press conference to confirm that Napoleon Lajoie, "the best player in the game," had signed a contract with the Bronchos.[21] His first game would be against the Boston Red Sox on June 4. Bernhard also joined the Bronchos.

The legal status of Lajoie and Bernhard continued its status quo throughout the summer months. In June, Rogers succeeded in having a Pennsylvania Common Pleas Court issue a charge of contempt against the two players. He then filed suit in an Ohio court to force both men out of uniform. On June 8, District Judge Francis J. Wing in Cleveland dismissed Rogers's suit, ruling his court had no jurisdiction in the case. Rogers was angered by this decision, complaining, "The cases were not really tried. Judge Wing objected to sitting in court during such hot weather, and so he just threw us out to bring the session to an end."[22] For all practical purposes, the battle was over.

The players were still subject to arrest in Pennsylvania, so the ex–Phillies traveled on the New York Central Train through Buffalo to New York and Boston. Their southern route to Washington and Baltimore went through Ohio, West Virginia, and Virginia. The Pennsylvania authorities tried to catch them but they were hiding in the baggage compartment when in train stations such as Erie, Pennsylvania, and then they exited the train and caught a bus to Cleveland. In one case, manager Bill Armour told an officer that Lajoie took "French leave. That's Frenchie's worst habit."[23]

On June 4, 1902, an overflow crowd of 10,000 fans filled League Park to watch their new hero. Lajoie did not disappoint his Cleveland fans. He hit .379 for the season and led the team to a 58–43 record, giving the future Naps an overall 69–67 record, good for fifth place. He was assisted by Bernhard who fashioned a 17–5 record with a 2.20 ERA.[24] Rookie Addie Joss gave strong evidence of his future contributions to the Clevelanders. He posted a 17–13 record, along with a 2.77 ERA, the worst ERA he would compile in his nine-year career with the Naps. His five shutouts led the league. The much-improved Cleveland team finished 14 games better than the previous year.

That Lajoie was the dominant force in the local team's potential success was demonstrated prior to the 1903 season. The *Cleveland Press* conducted a contest to select a new name. The choice was a forgone conclusion and the Bronchos became the Cleveland Naps in honor of Napoleon Lajoie. His popularity swept throughout the city as the new team captain led the Naps to New Orleans for spring training and their second season under manager Bill Armour.[25]

Though the Naps had basically the same team that finished fifth in 1902, many baseball writers picked them to win the pennant. One of the teams that would be a nemesis was the New York Highlanders. The Highlanders, formerly the Baltimore Orioles, were the last piece to complete the major league team alignment for the next 50 years. They became the most dominant team in the major leagues under a different name in 1913—the New York Yankees.

In 1903, owners in the American and National Leagues agreed to an all-embracing national agreement. Despite occasional glitches, the two leagues coexisted as the years went by. The first World Series between the two leagues took place in the fall of 1903, when the Boston Red Sox defeated the Pittsburgh Pirates in what was then a nine-game series, five games to three.

In 1903, the Naps did not do as well as the press had predicted, but Cleveland fans stuck with the club. After losing their first three games on the road to Detroit, the Naps returned for their home inaugural game before a record gathering of 19,867 and to overflowing stands and bleachers. At one stage of the game, reserve players had to grab hands and form a ring around the outer edge of the outfield to push fans back so that the game could continue.[26]

The Cleveland team started off poorly, but reached .500 in mid–May. Three of their best pitchers suffered injuries later in the season. Bill Bernhard suffered a broken finger on July 24; Addie Joss was injured in a train wreck and by August 31 was finished for the season; and Earl Moore missed the final month with a sore arm.[27] Moore compiled a fine 20–8 record and a league-leading ERA of 1.74. The team rallied at the end of the season, however, finishing in third place with a respectable record of 77–63, 15 games behind the Red Sox. Lajoie led the American League with a .344 batting average, and center fielder Harry Bay was the front-runner in stolen bases with 45.

For the next ten years Cleveland attendance was relatively consistent, fluctuating between 300,000 and 400,000. One major change in Naps management during the 1903–1904 off-season had an important impact on the franchise for years to come. During one of several trips to Columbus, Ohio, owner Charley Somers, after several visits with Ernest S. Barnard, sports writer for the Columbus *Dispatch*, had come away impressed with the studious and pleasant writer. Barnard had been a football and baseball coach at Otterbein College in nearby Westerville. He sold Somers on the idea of a full-time, salaried secretary for the Naps.[28]

In 1904, the Cleveland team was picked by many to be the top team in the American League. A strong pitching staff and otherwise solid team supported this judgment but again, the results did not turn out as predicted. Five teams fought for the pennant—Cleveland in the thick of the race—until August. Then, New York and Boston pulled away, with Boston winning its second straight pennant.

Once again the Naps were beset with a series of injuries to key players. Even worse, the team suffered from dissension, team disorganization, and internal problems. For example, the press tended to ignore manager Bill Armour and devoted journalistic efforts toward promoting Lajoie, the fair-haired young man loved by players and fans alike. On May 29, Lajoie was thrown out of a game for flinging his well-molded wad of tobacco at an umpire. A few days later, the Naps made ten errors in a game, and on July 14 folded before the New York Highlanders 21–3.

The Naps continued to play winning ball until early September, when Armour finally called Somers: "I'm resigning, Charley. This team doesn't want to be managed. Lajoie isn't aggressive, although he's a great ball player. I'm through."[29] Somers accepted the resignation with some reluctance, as he believed that Armour was a good manager. His judgment was somewhat validated later, when the Detroit Tigers hired Armour to manage for two years.

Team captain Nap Lajoie took over temporary managerial duties until the season's end, and soon thereafter he was appointed Cleveland's manager. As interim manager, Lajoie brought the team to a fourth-place finish. The Naps led the league in batting with an average of .260 and in runs scored, and Lajoie again won the batting title with a .376 average, but the pitching staff, with the exception of Bill Bernhard, was dismal.

As always, the cry was "Wait 'Til Next Year," and in 1905 Lajoie was prepared to guide the ship. Somers took the team back to New Orleans for spring training. He was interested in buying the New Orleans minor league team, and there was more possibility of obtaining some ready cash in the Crescent City if need be. Somers was not broke, but he remembered an embarrassing situation in San Antonio the spring before.

The training period in Texas had been expensive, and Somers had hoped to recoup enough funds from the last two exhibition games to pay bills accrued in San Antonio. Unfortunately, a two-day cloudburst had washed out both games, and Somers did not know where to turn for cash. His plight became known to the players. Pitcher Robert "Dusty" Rhoads came to the rescue. A handsome, strapping young man who dressed in the height of current fashion, Rhoads was a man about town in many cities, including San Antonio. Rhoads asked the Naps' owner how much money he needed. Somers told him that he required approximately $1,600 to pay bills and purchase railroad tickets. Rhoads smiled and told Somers, "not to worry." Rhoads headed for the craps table at the notorious gambling hall in San Antonio known as the Crystal Palace. As luck would have it, the young pitcher hit it big, winning $1,800. He lent the money to Somers, allowing the team to settle its bills and leave town.[30]

Rhoads' on-field performance as a consistent winner for Cleveland was equally adept. The right-hander won 22 games in 1906 and pitched a no-hitter against Boston in 1908 using a pitch he called his "Merry Widow" curve. He won 88 games over six-plus seasons for the Naps before returning to Barstow, California, where he became known to be a frequent hunting companion of Ty Cobb.

An accident to Lajoie in his first full year as manager ruined the Naps prospects for 1905. The team led the league through July, and Cleveland fans anticipated the first clear-cut championship in the city's professional baseball history. However, they were destined to wait. In a routine play at second base, Lajoie was spiked, and after a cursory check of the wound, he continued to play. The next day he could barely walk. Dye from his stockings had infected the wound, and blood poisoning developed. This injury devastated the Naps' chances for a pennant. Lajoie did not return to the lineup until late August, but after five games, a foul tip hit his ankle, and this injury benched the manager for the rest of the season.[31]

In late September, the Naps set a record no team would want to duplicate. Playing the Chicago White Sox, they made seven errors in the eighth inning, allowing the White Sox to score eight runs and a 9–6 victory—a gift to say the least. Twelve men batted for Chicago, and seven times the Naps failed to field properly.[32] The Naps achieved a more enviable feat in 1908. In a run-of-the-mill game against Boston, the Red Sox took a 2–1 lead as the Naps came to bat in the bottom of the fifth inning. In that inning each player in the Naps lineup, including pitcher Heinie Berger, delivered a hit *and* scored a run. Cleveland scored ten runs and went on to win the game, 15–6.[33]

The team situation in 1905 deteriorated with further injuries to third baseman Bill Bradley and outfielders Harry Bay and Elmer Flick. The Naps finished in fifth place, not what had been expected at the beginning of the season. It was the deadball era, and Lajoie and Flick were two of only four American League players to hit over .300. Addie Joss recorded the first of four consecutive 20-game-winning seasons with a 20–12 record.

By 1905, physical conditions of major league facilities began to change, particularly in the young American League. Wooden stands had prevailed for 40 years. Now owners contemplated building parks with a foundation of steel and concrete. In early ball parks, players had drunk out of a water-filled wooden barrel with a long-handled, tin dipper hanging on the side. In 1904, opening game at Comiskey Park was played in a 30-degree temperature, and between innings players had to break ice in the barrel for a drink. In the mid–1900s, a water fountain was installed in each dugout. Visiting teams dressed at their hotel and rode in open horse-drawn busses to the home park. These accommodations were unavailable for umpires.

The 1906 and 1907 seasons were reminiscent of so many in Cleveland baseball history. In 1906 the team had three pitchers who won at least 20 games; led the league in batting average, runs, total bases, and fielding; had five batters who hit .300 or better; owned the league leader in runs and stolen bases; yet could not capture the pennant.[34]

The Naps were considered one of the American League's premier teams that year and rated a favorite to win the franchise's first pennant. But after the team made a fast start, the season turned into a virtual repeat of 1905. The Naps remained in or near first place until late July, but they were hit hard with injuries, this time to third baseman Bradley and center fielder Harry Bay, both key players. Addie Joss, the team's top pitcher, showed his mettle with his second straight season of 20-plus wins.

In the first week of August, the three-team race for the pennant intensified when the fourth-place Chicago White Sox launched their famous 19-game winning streak. The White Sox, managed by Fielder Jones from Shinglehouse, Pennsylvania, were rescued by outstanding pitching. The staff included five strong starters—Nick Altrock, 20 wins; Frank Owen, 22 wins; Ed Walsh, 17 wins; Doc White, 18 wins; and Roy Patterson, 10 wins. The Naps, with Joss, Otto Hess (20 wins), and Dusty Rhoads (22 wins), could not overcome the White Sox's pitching performance.[35]

The White Sox, appropriately called the "Hitless Wonders" with a team batting average of .228—the worst in the league—raced to the pennant over the Highlanders and Naps in spite of Cleveland's league-leading team batting average of .279. It was another realization of the age-old axiom that excellent pitching outperforms batting prowess. The Chicago White Sox went on to win the World Series over the heavily favored Chicago Cubs, their cross-town rivals, four games to two. The White Sox batted only .198 in the Series, but the Cubs did even worse, batting .196. Cleveland finished a disappointing third, five games from the top.

The 1907 and 1908 seasons became watershed years for amateur and professional baseball in the United States. At the same time, the country suffered through its fourth financial panic. From 1900 to 1910, more than eight million people crossed the ocean to the U.S. The term "melting pot" came into use, derived from a play by that name which debuted in 1908. The immigrants, many of them tossed by the tempests of rural Italian poverty and the pogroms of eastern Europe, were not entirely welcomed, hence the eventual restrictive immigration laws of 1924. The census of 1910 indicated that about half of the U.S. population lived in cities. Cities were still regarded as sinful Babylons, but they were coming into their own as places of culture, opportunity, glamour, and, finally, graciousness.

Baseball accompanied America's emergence as a world power. The U.S. cherished its heritage, calling the game our "National Pastime" as early as 1856. Organized baseball relished this designation, for it reflected the national temperament and was linked to well-established virtues such as patriotism, team loyalty and civic pride. Ladies' Days flourished and women became established followers of the national pastime. And there was always the ongoing push to capture the younger generation, who would become life-long fans.

Often, what is unsaid by baseball aficionados is that this affinity of baseball and the nation's love for the game was not strictly a positive one. There was the "Abner Doubleday myth," which intimated that the purity of the origin of baseball rests solidly in America. This myth has been dispelled by reliable research. Baseball began building attractive ballparks while cities were trying to become beautiful; at the same time, the United States was tightening the color line against black Americans in the late nineteenth century, and so was baseball. As American corporations grew into monopolies, so, too, did baseball. When organized labor began to stir in the early 1900s, baseball players tried to follow suit—with little success.

At the turn of the twentieth century, baseball was still coming out of its infancy. The game was rapidly spreading throughout small towns and large cities. Non-professionals played an entertaining and high-caliber brand of baseball. Rules of the game changed, new or improved ballparks were built, and the quality of equipment, particularly of gloves and bats, improved. A. G. Spalding, Rawlings, Hillerich and Bradsby, Adirondack, and A. J. Reach became trade names for the early manufacture of bats, balls, and gloves.

In 1907, a major step took place in the United States to organize sandlot baseball. This move first occurred in Cleveland. Before 1908, sandlot baseball in Cleveland had been chaotic. The Cleveland *Plain Dealer* was the medium by which hundreds of teams scheduled their games. Each morning the *Plain Dealer* listed hundreds of challenges and acceptances. Fights on the fields were common. In short, sandlot baseball was disorderly.

Clayton Townes, a law student working at A. G. Spalding and later mayor of Cleveland, was a believer in organization. Through his efforts, and with the help of local sports writers Henry P. Edwards and Ed Bang and city officials, he formed what eventually grew to be the Cleveland Amateur Baseball Association. Overcoming roadblocks, this group reorganized in 1910, with the assistance of Ban Johnson, into the National Baseball Federation.[36] At the same time, many local fans were more interested in these amateur teams than in the Naps, and later the Indians. Amateur baseball grew dramatically. Many first generation immigrants, migrating from European ethnic groups that had settled in the rapidly growing city, played the game.

By 1910, so many teams were playing sandlot ball that the Cleveland Amateur Baseball Association organized these teams into leagues and oversaw the rules. By the 1920s, teams were categorized in a series of classes, ranging from E to AAA—classes A to AAA were semi-professional and formed the basis for many young players being picked for minor league baseball throughout the country. These categories spanned dozens of leagues throughout metropolitan Cleveland. Noted diamonds were located at Edgewater, Gordon, Brookside and Washington parks.[37]

In 1914, an estimated crowd of more than 80,000 people congregated in a natural amphitheater at Brookside Park to watch the Telling Strollers beat the Hanna Street Cleaners in a decisive city championship game. The following year, a legendary 100,000+ fans overflowed Brookside Park to cheer the Cleveland White Autos to victory over the Omaha Luxus for the world amateur baseball championship. A panoramic photograph of this huge crowd—the largest crowd ever for a baseball game in Cleveland—hung in Brookside area sporting bars. For years, Cleveland was recognized as the "amateur baseball capitol of the world."[38] It is estimated that more than 100 players from this program reached the major leagues. During World War II, the city claimed that 25,000 sandlot "veterans" served in the United States armed services.

The 1907 season was another good year for the Naps, if not for their manager. For the third year in a row, the team stayed in contention though they failed again in the late stages of the campaign. The Naps were knocked out of contention in the final ten days of the season. They finished in fourth place with an 85–67 record, eight games behind Hughie Jennings's Detroit Tigers. Everything considered, it is surprising they did even that well. Lajoie suffered a recurrence of the blood poisoning that had sidelined him in the 1905 season, causing him to miss 15 games. His batting average dropped to .301. The overall offense suffered with the exception of Lajoie and Elmer Flick, who batted .302, and the team average fell to .241. The pitching was not much better with the exception of Addie Joss. The right-hander posted an excellent league-leading 27 wins (tied with Chicago's "Doc" White) and an ERA of 1.83.

In the annals of baseball history, fans debate, "What was the best season in baseball history?" Cait Murphy makes a strong case for the 1908 season, reflecting that:

> Besides two agonizing pennant races ... and history's finest pitching duel ... the year is full of iconic performances by baseball's first generation of iconic heroes ... i.e., Tinker, Evers, Chance, Honus Wagner, Ty Cobb, Christy Mathewson, Napoleon Lajoie, Cy Young, Walter Johnson. In the dugouts [were] Connie Mack and John McGraw ... opposites in temperament [and] united in their passion for the game.... The whole season [was] rife with drama—comic, tragic, odd, and merely incredible.[39]

The following anecdotes captured the personality of the Cleveland manager, the great Napoleon Lajoie, as the 1908 season unfolded. In a game at League Park in 1904, an opposing batsman hit a "shot" sharply past first base, where Charley Hickman made a grab for it and missed. Then he stood in amazement as Lajoie, with his famous grace, glided over the grass and made a one-handed pickup. The batter was still two feet from the bag, but so was Hickman. When Lajoie saw he had no one to whom to throw the ball, he yelled to Hickman: "Spectators are supposed to pay to get in the park. If you are just going to watch me, sit in the grandstand."[40]

Henry P. Edwards, baseball writer for the Cleveland *Plain Dealer*, later commented on the following scene: "Napoleon Lajoie bowed his head as the tears streamed down his cheeks the night of October 5, 1908. Why did he cry? Because the Cleveland [Naps], of which he was manager, had lost the pennant by half a game."[41] For Edwards, the 1908 American League race had truly been one of the greatest in American League history.

Many circumstances affected the outcome in 1908. The first had taken place before the season began. During spring training in Macon, Georgia, owner Charley Somers made a decision that would have a profound effect on the Cleveland franchise, not only for that year, but long into the future. While meeting with a group of sportswriters before practice one day in March, Somers received a call from Hughie Jennings, manager of the Detroit Tigers, who proposed a trade—Ty Cobb for Elmer Flick. Cobb had led the American League in 1907 with a .350 batting average, 116 RBI, and 53 stolen bases. Flick had hit .302 with 41 stolen bases that same season, and had won the batting championship in 1905. Cobb was 22 years old whereas Flick 32, played only three more seasons.

Somers pondered the offer and asked why Jennings wanted to trade Cobb. Jennings assured Somers that there was nothing physically wrong with Cobb but repeatedly said, "[Cobb] can't get along with our players, and we want to get him away. He's had two fights already this spring. We want harmony on this team, not scrapping." Somers made his decision immediately. "We'll keep Flick," he said, "Maybe he isn't as good as Cobb, but he's much nicer to have on the team."[42] Cobb went on to hit .324 that season, winning the second of his 12 batting titles, and compiled a lifetime batting average of .366, the best in the history of baseball. Meanwhile, Flick encountered injuries and played in only 99 more games before retiring in 1910. With Cobb in Cleveland instead of Detroit, which went on to win the pennant, the Naps probably would have won in 1908.

Like most baseball seasons, the 1908 season dragged along with typical ups and downs for the Naps. The Cleveland team attempted to avoid the pattern familiar under Lajoie, that of a good Fourth of July team that lost it for the rest of the season. This team was different. It started out strong, recovered from their traditional July swoon, and fought to the bitter end.

Early setbacks included injuries to Elmer Flick, who played in only nine games that season. Lajoie had a decent season for the average player but not for him. Then there was starting catcher Jay Clarke, better known as "Nig" for his swarthy skin. Lajoie and Clarke disliked each other. As an anxious husband, Clarke asked Lajoie for a couple of days off to see his new wife. When Lajoie said no, Clarke took matters into his own hands and deliberately stuck his index finger in the path of a pitch, hoping to suffer a bruise so he could take those days off. Instead, he suffered a bloody break and missed five weeks of action.

Lajoie, in spite of his marvelous fielding and tremendous batting, was not exactly the darling of the grandstand managers or even the press. When the team lost a pair of ten-inning games at the beginning of the season, the Cleveland papers were less than cordial: "How long should a pitcher stay in a game before everybody knows he's no good?" asked the *Cleveland Press*.[43] All the city's newspapers printed daily suggestions concerning selection of pitchers, which fielders should play, and which batters should bat in the more advantageous positions in the lineup. So the beat went on day after day during the season.

During the 1908 season, 2,000–3,000 fans attended the average Cleveland game. There were exceptions only when a special game came along. By June 15, the Naps were in fourth place, but only one and one-half games out of first place. The next day the locals won a doubleheader from the St. Louis Browns and were briefly in first place. During July, the Naps went into their routine slump, and by late July were nine games behind the league-leading Tigers. In August, the team regrouped for an exciting finish to a great season.

The Naps stunned the league by winning 12 of 14 decisions during one stretch in August. In early September, fans warily began to stir. The race to the finish for the American League pennant now included four teams: the Naps, Tigers, White Sox, and Browns. The Browns soon fell by the wayside and became the league spoilers in the final days. Cleveland fans had had their hearts broken before. To add to the team's misery, the Naps suffered, not one, but two train wrecks rushing to get home for a Labor Day doubleheader. The players made it to League Park a few minutes after the game was supposed to begin.

Fans continued to stay home in droves. Cleveland might well be "the poorest rooting town in the league," the *Plain Dealer* bemoaned.[44] On September 9, 1908, the Naps drew just 2,429 fans; on the same day the seventh-place Nationals, at home to the sixth-place Red Sox, drew 3,200. In mid–September, the Naps returned home after taking four of five games from Chicago. The local cranks began to wake up and rally behind their team.

On September 17, thousands of rooters practiced cheers in Public Square and then proceeded to League Park. Almost 11,000 fans saw Addie Joss outduel Boston legend Cy Young, 1–0. On September 18, Bob "Dusty" Rhoads did Joss one better, tossing a no-hitter—eleven years to the day since the last no-hitter had been recorded by a Cleveland pitcher in 1897. Cy Young had turned the trick for the Spiders, before that team became a joke.

The next day, for the first time during the season, club officials roped off the outfield in order to control a crowd of 16,000 fans. Despite a number of mental errors, the Clevelanders scored an unearned run in the ninth inning to defeat the Red Sox. That win, combined with a Detroit loss, put the Naps just three percentage points behind the slumping Tigers. Fans were jubilant, thousands running on the field to lift the game's hero, Bill Bradley, onto their shoulders and parade him around the diamond.

On September 21, the Naps entered uncharted territory so late in the season: first place! The front-page banner on the Cleveland *Plain Dealer* read, "Hooray!" Rural Ohio joined in on the excitement. Visitors to farm country reported that after a long day in the fields, farmers were driving miles to the nearest telegraph office to stand around and talk baseball until the operator gave scores.[45]

The Naps won two more—making it 16 victories in their last 18 games. Then the Naps lost two tough games to the lowly Washington Nationals. The *Plain Dealer* described the agony of the second loss: "A brutal defeat ... comes as a result of a hit, a bunt that almost, but never goes foul, an error, and some dubious calls from Jack Egan, [the Naps'] least favorite umpire."[46] At the same time, word was received that former Cleveland owner Frank Robison, listening to a friend give the play-by-play over a telephone, had become so excited, then distressed, that he suffered a cerebral hemorrhage and died at the age of 56.

On October 2, the Chicago White Sox traveled to League Park for a pivotal game. With six games to play, Cleveland trailed Detroit by one-half game. Chicago was also in the

hunt. An overflow crowd of 10,598 fans crammed into League Park on this crisp fall afternoon. This ballpark still held only 9,000 fans. Why was this contest acclaimed as one of the
greatest pitching duels ever? Let us consider the two rival pitchers.

Right-hander Ed Walsh, the White Sox pitcher and a future Hall of Famer, compiled
a 1908 record of 40–15 with an incredible 1.42 ERA. He pitched 464⅔ innings—a modern
record that in all likelihood will never be broken. A strapping man, Walsh never saw the
inside of a college classroom, matriculating instead in the coal mines of Pennsylvania starting
at age 11. When he graduated from high school at the age of 20, he was driving a mule for
$1.25 a day. It was well known that Walsh threw a spitball—legal at this time. Walsh mois-
tened the ball with delicacy, as befit a sophisticated ballroom dancer. Addie Joss also enjoyed
another outstanding season with a 24–11 record and a major league-best ERA of 1.16. He
was pitching for a team with an anemic .239 batting average in contrast to the Detroit team's
leading .264 average. Contrary to Walsh, Joss was one of the few major leaguers who had
attended college.[47]

During the first two innings, each pitcher was masterful. But in the third inning, Cleveland's Joe Birmingham led off by smacking a single to center field. Birmingham, master of
the delayed steal, employed his trick on Walsh. When the big hurler tried to pick him off,
Birmingham was already racing to second. First baseman Frank Isbell's throw struck Birmingham in the shoulder and caromed into the outfield, and the runner continued to third
base. Walsh bore down. With no outs and Birmingham dancing off third, he enticed shortstop George Perring to tap out to a drawn-in infield. Walsh then struck out Joss for the
second out, which brought up right fielder Wilbur "Lefty" Good.

Walsh fired two strikes past Good—hitting .258—and it appeared that "Big Ed" would
escape the jam without surrendering a run. However, according to author Jack DeVries: "The
legacy of the most miserable team in Cleveland's history was about to rear its ugly head."[48]

Behind the plate for the White Sox was Ossee Schreckengost, a former member of the
1899 Cleveland Spiders [Misfits]. Known for his eating, drinking and ability to drive managers crazy, "Shreck" was one of the league's wackiest characters. Among the last catchers
to adopt shin guards, he was one of the first to catch one-handed. As Good waited, Schreckengost called for a pitch, but the delivered pitch was not the one he expected. As he stuck
out his bare hand to stop the pitch, the ball tore through his fingers, rupturing a tendon and
leaving him bleeding as it rolled back to the grandstand.[49] The pitcher was charged with a
wild pitch but disagreed with the ruling. For more than twenty years, Walsh argued with
scorekeeper Henry Edwards that the pitch should have been scored a passed ball. The errant
run turned out to be a monumental mistake as Walsh fanned Good for the second of four
times that the lead-off hitter struck out that day. Walsh regained his form, limiting the Naps
to four hits, a walk, no runs and 15 strikeouts.

Through six innings, Joss had not allowed a runner, a fact that spread through the
crowd by baseball osmosis. League Park became quiet; even the amateur bands put socks in
their pipes. The cowbells were stilled; noise makers were silenced; cigars went unlighted. In
the seventh inning, Joss had a dangerous moment. With one out, White Sox player-manager
Fielder Jones stepped to the plate, determined to break the spell. He crowded the plate and
worked the count to 3–1. Joss fired a fastball over the plate for strike two, and on the next

pitch Joss shot a sidearm curve under Jones's wrists. Umpire Thomas Connolly, who in 1953 joined Bill Klem as the first umpires inducted into baseball's Hall of Fame, never hesitated, raising his right arm to signal strike three. Jones argued vehemently before stalking back to the bench muttering to himself. A ground ball to Lajoie ended the seventh inning.

Joss retired three batters in the eighth inning, one on a fine play by Lajoie. The second baseman was having an unusual, sub-par year, playing this game with a cold. He handled ten chances, including a bad hop in the eighth inning. Joss waited out the home eighth inning in the dugout—a fancy name for a roof and a bench. He isolated himself from his teammates, who were not speaking to him. "No one on the bench dared breathe a word about what was apparent to all," Joss recalled. "Had [someone] done so, he would have been chased to the clubhouse."[50] During this period major league baseball games, with rare exception, began at 3:00 p.m. It hardly seemed like 4:00 p.m. when Joss took the mound for the ninth inning.

Addie Joss, "King of the Pitchers," a brilliant hurler with an overwhelming fastball, recorded two no-hitters, one perfect game, and a career all-time ERA of 1.89, second only to Ed Walsh. He died prematurely at 31 of tubercular meningitis, and was elected to the Hall of Fame in 1978 (courtesy Scott H. Longert).

White Sox manager Fielder Jones refused to go quietly, sending pinch-hitters to the plate. The first two outs were routine, a ground out to Lajoie and a strikeout, one of only three by Joss in the contest. The next pinch hitter was "Honest John" Anderson, of Norwegian descent. A 14-year veteran with a lifetime batting average of .290, he posed a serious threat. The crowd went from quiet to silent to something deeper than silence so palpable that it became thickly tangible. On an 0–2 pitch in what would be his last at-bat in the majors; Anderson hit a ground ball sharply down the third base line. Bill Bradley had no trouble reaching the ball, fielded it cleanly, and threw to first base—not all that quickly and not all that well. First baseman George Stovall made a pick-up of the ball, and then dropped it. The 34-year-old Anderson lumbered like an ice wagon toward first base, but Stovall picked up the ball in time for the third out, and the 27th out of the game.

After 74 pitches and 90 minutes, Addie Joss had pitched his ninth shutout of the season, a perfect game—the first in Cleveland franchise history, and only the second one in league history.[51] The fans rushed onto the field and Joss used what energy he had left to sprint to the clubhouse behind center field, beating his admirers by an eyelash.

After the game, Walsh, a good friend of Joss, commented: "I'm glad that Addie took down a record that goes to so few. I guess way down in my heart, I was sort of glad when [umpire] 'Silk' [O'Loughlin] called Anderson out.... It would have made no difference anyway."[52] This classic game, described for years to come as one of the great pitching matches of all time, was the season's high point for the Naps. Yet, there was still a pennant to win.

They were one-half game behind Detroit with four games to play. The next day was the last home game, and nearly 21,000 fans showed up to give support to their team. Young Cleveland capitalists did a thriving business selling boxes providing a better view of the game for those folks stuck behind the outfield ropes.

Glenn Liebhardt started for the Naps. He had experienced a hard-luck season but ended with a creditable 15–16 record and ERA of 2.20. The Naps fell behind, 3–1, and with two outs in the seventh inning, the locals loaded the bases with Lajoie at bat. Manager Jones of the White Sox called on ironman Ed Walsh to face Cleveland's premier hitter. This strategy worked to perfection as Lajoie was caught looking at a two-strike fastball to end the threat. Cleveland scored a run in the eighth inning but fell to the White Sox, 3–2, in a crushing defeat. The game capped a miserable season for Lajoie. Earlier in the game, he had committed an error that had led to two runs for the opponents. His season-ending batting average of .289 was the first time in 13 years he had failed to bat .300 or better.[53]

Still, the demoralized Naps were not yet out of the race. The team traveled to St. Louis for their next game on October 4. The Naps trailed the Tigers by one and one-half games with three games to play. This game was noted for right fielder Bill Hinchman's "boner," and for another controversial call against the Clevelanders by the Naps' least favorite umpire, Jack Egan.

In the ninth inning, Hinchman appeared to be safe on a ground ball to Browns shortstop Bobby Wallace, driving home Joss to give the Naps a 4–3 lead. However, Hinchman was called out by the hated umpire. Teammates rushed to Egan to protest but he would not change his mind. Egan and some observers claimed that Hinchman had not run full-speed to first base and otherwise would have beaten the throw. Others blamed Egan and had questioned his work in Cleveland games during the season. Either way, the game remained tied after 11 innings and had to be replayed the next day. Ultimately, the coup de grâce came when the Browns ended Cleveland's pennant hopes with a 3–1 victory.

Another glitch affected the final standings. Cleveland had finished four percentage points and one-half game behind Detroit. At that time, baseball rules did not require that rainouts or games called because of darkness be made up, despite the potential effect on the final standings. Cleveland finished with a 90–64 record, Detroit with a 90–63 record. With the exhausting pennant race over, Lajoie was not the only disconsolate Nap. Addie Joss alone seemed to feel that all had not been lost. The gentlemanly pitcher remarked, "We'll win next year. We had some bad breaks this year, but watch us in 1909."[54] Unfortunately, his prophecy fell far short of the mark.

The 1908 season was the plateau of the Lajoie era of baseball in Cleveland. The season had been too strenuous for President Kilfoyl, and he gradually stepped out of administrative responsibilities for the Naps. Charles Somers, who had been virtual ruler of the franchise for eight years, assumed the presidency and appointed former sportswriter Ernest S. Barnard as vice-president and eventually general manager. This appointment was a classic example of being in the right place at the right time because Barnard was not finished in his move up the administrative ladder in major league baseball. Together Barnard and Somers envisioned a general expansion of the Cleveland farm system, which was nil. With Somers's money, the two soon gained control of franchises in Ironton, Ohio, Waterbury, Connecticut, and Toledo of the American Association League, Portland of the Pacific Coast League, and New Orleans of the Southern Association.

Somers attempted to give the Naps a "shot in the arm" by bringing 42-year-old Cy Young back into the fold. John J. Taylor, the dashing young president of the Boston Red Sox, believed Young was about finished, even though he had won 21 games for the Red Sox in 1908. So he offered Young and his catcher Lou Criger for three Cleveland players who were not in the future plans of the Naps. As it happened, all three were released by the Boston club by the end of the next season.

Catcher Lou Criger was sick and never played a game for Cleveland, and Young performed well, winning his 500th game—plus a few more—in 1909 with a 19–15 record. He retired in 1911 with 511 victories, a record likely never to be broken. Lajoie regained his batting form with a .324 average, but Addie Joss began to fail physically, winning only 14 games.[55]

The team struggled from the onset of the season. This was, in fact, a troubled team. Lajoie discovered one of the facts of baseball life: In Cleveland, as in most cities, fans have little patience with a manager who does not deliver victories, and the press can be vicious. As the team sank into the second division, Cleveland newspapers reacted: "Naps?... They ought to be known as the Napkins, the way they fold up."[56]

Lajoie was under fire for his handling of pitchers. Fans suggested that if Cy Young could be so good at 42, perhaps Somers should get rid of all his players and sign up a new team 40 and older. All of this criticism did not sit well with Lajoie, and although he continued to field and hit well, he no longer had patience with players. His temper flared often, and he complained time and again that his job was to win games, not run schools on teaching players how to play. Twice, Lajoie went to Somers and asked to be relieved as manager, but both times the answer was no.

Finally, he told Charley Somers: "Maybe [the players] would do better with someone else running the club," and added, "I'd like to keep playing for you, but I'd suggest a new manager."[57] After a few days of cooling down, Lajoie was determined to quit managing and would take a salary adjustment if need be. Lajoie's salary was $10,000 a year, making him the highest paid player in the American League. He was able to retain his salary for the remainder of the season.

Somers picked Jim "Deacon" McGuire, one of Lajoie's coaches, to take over the helm in August. Lajoie finished the season and spent the next five years in a Cleveland uniform playing for three managers, one of them his former player. The aging team began to unravel in 1909 with shortstop Terry Turner disabled for 100 games. Elmer Flick was unable to play regularly and missed 87 games; Bill Bradley was sidelined for 58 games; and even the great Lajoie sat out 25 games due to injuries. And an ailing Addie Joss suffered through a subpar year with a 14–13 record. The team finished in sixth place with a 71–82 record.

One of the Naps' few highlights of this dismal season occurred on July 19. Shortstop Neal Ball, who had been purchased from the New York Highlanders to replace the injured Turner, pulled off the first unassisted triple play in major league history. The play took place against the Boston Red Sox in League Park in the first game of a doubleheader. With Heinie Wagner on second and Jake Stahl on first, both runners were running on Cy Young's 3–2 pitch to Ambrose McConnell, who sent a scorching line drive past Cy Young's ear. Ball raced to his left, speared the ball, took a few strides to step on second base, and then easily tagged Stahl coming from first base. The crowd sat stunned momentarily and then broke into a roar. To add to his glory, Ball came to bat in the bottom half of the second inning and stroked an inside-the-park home run.[58]

The 1910 season started with promise but again soon disappointed. A highlight of the season was the renovation of League Park. Work had begun soon after the end of the 1909 season. The project was a six-month rush job to put steel, brick, and concrete into a baseball palace. Construction was handled by the Hunkin Brothers Company and Forest City Steel and Iron Company. It was a rough winter, and blizzards whipped the steel frames as they rose impressively above the frame houses in the neighborhood. The project needed additional labor; the proud plant's final cost was approximately $325,000. The Osborn Company reported the estimated cost had come close to $16.25 per seat. One mistake had been made in the construction of the new park. Non-union labor had been used on some subcontracts. Pickets stood around the park on Opening Day, and the union boycott continued late into the season. The boycott and a losing season contributed to an unprofitable 1910 season. The final attendance tally was 293,456—a six-year low.[59]

League Park was one of a growing number of new major league stadiums. Forbes Field in Pittsburgh, Sportsman's Park in St. Louis, and Shibe Park in Philadelphia had opened in 1909; Comiskey Park in Chicago opened in 1910, Griffith Stadium was finished in 1911, Navin Field in Detroit opened in 1912, as did Boston's Fenway Park. Others were to come later, with the addition of Yankee Stadium in 1923 and Cleveland's Municipal Stadium in 1932. All were engineered by Cleveland's Osborn Company.

The biggest and most startling feature of new League Park was a 40-foot-high wall in right field. It started at the juncture of the right field pavilion and the foul line, 290 feet from home plate, and extended east on Lexington Avenue for more than 400 feet. It was not a barrier of solid concrete. Only the lower 20 feet were permanent; the upper 20 feet were covered by wire screening. It replaced wooden bleachers, which were moved to center field with a scoreboard between the wall and bleachers.[60] This wall was to play an important part in the fortunes of future teams.

Jack Graney, a familiar name with future Indians fans, was a rookie on the 1910 team. He marveled most over the clubhouse: "Why, they had gas driers for our uniforms."[61] Frank Van Dellen, the team's groundskeeper for many years, manicured the playing field in billiard-table shape for the season's opener. It had been a grim winter, but spring was soft enough to make the grass greener. League Park served the Cleveland franchise for the next 36 years. Seating capacity was 19,200. Of these, only 600 were box seats. The team, which trained in Alexandria, Louisiana, for the 1910 opener, was thought to have the potential for a winning season.

Two aging veterans, Bill Bradley and outfielder, Elmer Flick, had reached the end of their careers. Cy Young, now 43, was no longer a dominating pitcher, and Addie Joss had been sidelined with a sore arm, finishing the season with a depressing record of 5–5. Forty-four players spent time on the Naps' roster in 1910, which began with the rededication of League Park. On April 20, Addie Joss pitched his second no-hitter, beating the White Sox in Chicago, 1–0. It was the last victory of significance in his illustrious career. The following day Cy Young, nearly ready to retreat from the limelight, lost to Detroit, 5–0, in the first game at the new League Park. A crowd of 18,835—3,978 more than ever had attended a Cleveland opener before—initiated "the world's best ball plant," as reported by the Cleveland *Plain Dealer*.[62]

The Naps started with great promise, but soon disintegrated into failure. The team fell out of contention in late May and soon was ridiculed by the press as "Molly McGuires." By mid–July, a rebuilding program was launched by Charles Somers and Ernest S. Barnard. Four players were added to the team from the Portland affiliate.

There were a few diversions for Naps fans in spite of a disappointing season. Cleveland reached a population of 560,000 and became the sixth largest city in the country. Glenn Curtiss, a noted racing pilot, thrilled the natives with a "daring" airplane flight from Euclid Beach to Cedar Point. Other notable events focused on baseball and the Naps. Rube Marquard, one of Cleveland's most famous sandlotters at the turn of the twentieth century, caught the attention of Henry Edwards of the *Plain Dealer*. Edwards obtained a professional contract for the left-handed pitcher playing with a team in Lancaster, Ohio. He caught a cold in his pitching arm and was released. He received a second chance with Indianapolis and then was farmed out to Canton.

Edwards begged Somers and Lajoie to go to Canton to watch Marquard pitch. Two scouts joined the entourage. Although Marquard registered a shutout, the four "experts" turned him down. Their wrongheaded opinion was that he "cannot field his position and has a poor move in throwing to first." As it happened, Marquard was signed by the New York Giants in 1908, where he won 19 straight games in 1912. Marquard, in an 18-year career, won 201 games and was elected to the Hall of Fame in 1971.[63]

However, Somers did not make a player mistake with his acquisition on July 25, 1910. After receiving word of the batting exploits of "Shoeless" Joe Jackson with the New Orleans team, he called Connie Mack, who held Jackson's contract. Somers offered Bristol Lord, a rising young outfielder. Mack agreed, and Jackson reported to League Park on September 16. He would eventually supplant Lajoie as the Naps' premier hitter. Jackson came to Cleveland from his home in Brandon Mills, South Carolina. Despite his lack of education, the quiet, dark-haired youngster was intelligent, particularly on the ball field. Frank Gibbons of the *Cleveland Press* wrote: "He could run like a deer, throw like an arrow, and hit like a demon." He batted .387 in the final 20 games of the season. At an Old Timers game in Yankee Stadium decades later, a writer asked Ty Cobb, "Who's the greatest hitter in history?" Cobb paused and replied, "That's easy. Joe Jackson, of course. A natural. Nobody could touch him, including me."[64]

A season-ending controversy involved Lajoie and Cobb. Acting upon an idea conceived by Hugh Chalmers, an auto magnate looking for publicity, the Chalmers Automobile Company decided to give the batting champion of the major leagues for 1910 one of its best cars. Few citizens had a car at that time. The vehicle was valued at $1,500. These two players performed extremely well at the plate throughout the year. During the last week of the season, the race for the batting crown became convoluted and full of chicanery, and the question as to who really won the batting championship remains unsettled. Entering the final day of play, the St. Louis *Post Dispatch* put Cobb's average at .382 and Lajoie's at .377.

Napoleon Lajoie with a silver dollar horseshoe worth $1,009, presented to him in recognition of his tenth anniversary with the Cleveland Naps. In 1937, Lajoie—with a .338 lifetime batting average—was the first second baseman to be elected to the Hall of Fame (National Baseball Hall of Fame, Cooperstown, New York).

Thinking that he had won the batting title, Cobb did not play in his last two games of the season Instead, he went to Philadelphia, where a team of American League stars played a couple of games against the Philadelphia Athletics to prepare them for the World Series.

Meanwhile, the largest crowd of the season—nearly 10,000—gathered at Sportsman's Park for the season-ending doubleheader between St. Louis and Cleveland. The chicanery intensified. According to published accounts of this batting duel, since the Browns detested Cobb, they tried their best to help Lajoie win. Lajoie hit a legitimate triple in his first at-bat. After that, third basemen John Corriden, a rookie, played far back on the grass. Lajoie bunted seven times for hits and once for a sacrifice not charged as a time at bat. Mixed reports of the embarrassing crisis came In to American League President Ban Johnson, a member of the three-man National Commission, who investigated the incident and announced an unceremonious end to bonuses or awards such as a new car. The question remained whether the St. Louis team had played the game fairly.

Finally, Johnson declared the final averages to be .384095 for Lajoie and .385069 for Cobb. Cobb was clearly the winner—or was he? Baseball researchers reject any notion of "statute of limitations." The hunt for statistical accuracy persists. Some 70 years later, baseball researchers discovered that Cobb was erroneously credited with two hits. In 2010, historian Steve Gietschier wrote, "The solution is deft, recognizing Cobb as the acknowledged batting champion (.383), but listing Lajoie as the statistical leader (.384). More than a century ago, Chalmers Automobile Company was equally magnanimous, giving a car to both players."[65] Baseball made important advances during its first decade of the twentieth century. The same held true for the Cleveland Naps. The second decade for the soon-to-be-named Cleveland "Indians" provided more tragedy, an interruption due to World War I, and finally a happy ending. In 1920 the Tribe captured their first World Series Championship.

3

A "Dunn" Deal,
Then Tragedy and Triumph

*"Ohio has two contenders for the presidency ... [in 1920] and
one for the baseball championship.... Ask anyone ... who
is going to win, and they'll answer CLEVELAND."*

During the second decade of the twentieth century, franchises stabilized with new ownerships and benefitted from little or no effort to move teams to new locations. However, there were challenges, which included contract jumping, labor issues, restrictions related to the reserve clause, a brief challenge to the major leagues by the Federal League (1914–1915), and impending war clouds culminating in America's entrance into World War I on April 2, 1917.

Until the mid–1920s, baseball was publicized mainly through journalism. The main source of baseball news before 1886 had been a robust publication called *Sporting Life*, which covered all aspects of the sporting world. From 1886 onward, the dominant baseball periodical of the first half of the twentieth century was *The Sporting News*, founded in 1886 by Alfred H. Spink, a St. Louis promoter of sports and theatrical events. Initially, this weekly newspaper covered racing, boxing, baseball, and theater. By the close of the nineteenth century, its coverage under the direction of Charles C. Spink, Al's younger brother, was devoted exclusively to baseball.[1]

From 1903 forward, *The Sporting News* became what amounted to a house organ for organized baseball, and the paper was often referred to as "The Bible of Baseball." In the 1940s, this weekly employed over 300 correspondents and 50 freelance writers. In 1942, *The Saturday Evening Post* called J. G. Taylor Spink, a son of Charles C., "Mr. Baseball: the game's unofficial conscience, historian, watchdog and worshiper."[2] Baseball guides became popular. Most notable were *The Spalding Guide*, first published in the mid–1870s, *The Reach Guide* in 1876, and later *Spalding's Official Base Ball Record*, first published in 1908—an annual publication of the National League until 1941. In addition, the American League published the *Red Book* and the National League the *Green Book*, both of which contained annual statistical summaries.[3]

Beginning in 1908, *Baseball Magazine*, with a red cover, was devoured by baseball aficionados each month. It continued publication into the late 1940s, its cover claiming it to be "For Red-Blooded Americans." Considered one of the best baseball magazines of the twentieth century, this monthly publication was edited from its inception through the next 27 years by F. C. Lane, who lived to be 99.[4] Beginning in 1915, *Who's Who in Baseball* reached the newsstands in January or February each year, offering compilations of statistics for major leaguers who had competed during the previous season. The *Saturday Evening Post* and *Collier's* often published excellent baseball articles.

As early as 1887, baseball writers covering major league games complained of their treatment by club owners. A short-lived Baseball Reporters Association (1887–1890)

> Assure[d] the writers of a proper seat from which they could do their daily stint, without interference. It's pretty difficult to run out deathless prose with a typewriter precariously on your knees, and your posterior balanced on an upturned beer case from a sympathetic concessionaire, it's doubly difficult when you face the added obstacle of free-loading spectators, yelling in your ear, stomping on your feet, and waving madly to friends while you try to write.[5]

Club owners ignored the problem for several years. There had been talk during the 1906 and 1907 seasons that a baseball writers association should be organized. The writers continued to be disgruntled over the way baseball owners treated them, such as lack of space, poor working conditions, and lack of respect for their coverage of these games.

This issue came to a head in the 1908 World Series between the Chicago Cubs and Detroit Tigers. Team officials in Detroit had done little to discourage fans from sitting in the press box, forcing scribes to seek seats elsewhere. Ford Frick wrote that the Baseball Writers' Association of America was created after actor Louis Mann took sportswriter Hugh Fullerton, Sr.'s, seat in the press box and refused to move, so Fullerton sat on his lap the entire game. Other reporters were compelled to climb a ladder to the roof of the first base grandstand and on occasion were forced to write in the rain and snow.[6]

At the conclusion of the Series, a cadre of writers formed a temporary working organization known as the Baseball Writers' Association of America. Henry Pierrepont Edwards, from Cleveland, Ed Grille of Washington, and Sid Mercer of New York were elected to a committee to design a simplification and unification of scoring and rule interpretation.[7] The first formal meeting was held in New York City in December 1908. Subsequently Edwards, Hugh Fullerton, Sr., from Chicago, and William G. Weart from Philadelphia were appointed to draft a constitution. Working conditions and facilities improved dramatically over the years, particularly because of the construction of new ballparks and improvements at existing facilities. The Association, growing in strength and numbers, celebrated its 100th anniversary in 2008.

Henry P. Edwards, an important figure in the early history of the Cleveland franchise, was representative of the early founders in the promotion of major league baseball through journalism. Edwards was born in Dunkirk, New York, December 11, 1871, and became a reporter for the Dunkirk *Evening Observer* in the late 1880s. The story goes that he was the only man in town who could make out a scorecard. He covered games for Dunkirk, whose team was a member of the New York–Pennsylvania League. Among the players who came under his scrutiny were John McGraw, a 116-pound third baseman playing for Olean, New York, and Jack Doyle, later with the Cubs.[8]

In 1898, Edwards became sports editor for the Cleveland *Recorder*. Edwards was the loneliest man in Cleveland during the summer of 1899. His job: official scorekeeper for the Cleveland Spiders, otherwise known as the Misfits. Spiders president Frank Robison hired Edwards because the Cleveland reporters were flaying at team management. The Spiders won 20 games and lost 134, the worst record in major league history. Later in 1901, the young journalist was offered a position as sports editor of the Cleveland *Plain Dealer*, which he readily accepted.[9] Edwards had gone to Cleveland because he sensed a semblance of big-league baseball and he wanted to write about the National Pastime. His wish came true in 1900 when the Cleveland Blues became a member of the fledgling American League. Edwards served as sports editor of the *Plain Dealer* until 1913, when he asked to cover baseball full-time, which he did until 1928.

Sunday was Edwards' day off, and the baseball zealot devoted his time to watching amateur and semi-pro games in the highly acclaimed Cleveland Baseball Federation program. The sharp-eyed sleuth was instrumental in sending 14 Cleveland youngsters to the minor leagues, of which 11 made the "big time." The most prominent aspirants included Roger Peckinpaugh, and Hall of Fame pitcher Rube Marquard. Edwards was close to Cleveland management and tried to encourage the ownership to consider signing Marquard, but to no avail.[10]

In 1902, Edwards was directly involved in a situation affecting the Cleveland Bronchos. Bill Armour, manager of the Bronchos, was in desperate need of pitchers and asked Edwards to run a boldface type announcement in the *Plain Dealer* requesting that any semi-pro or amateur pitchers who thought they were good enough to pitch for the Cleveland team report to League Park the next morning for a tryout. Seven or eight hopefuls showed up at the park.

Later Edwards asked the manager if there had been a kernel of pitching wheat in the group. Armour pointed to a lanky, blond, handsome left-hander and replied, "I'm going to pitch him against Washington today." His name was Otto Hess.[11] Tom Loftus, the Nationals manager, a crafty individual, told his players to "bunt the kid to death." The Senators bunted 15 times against Hess. Five were base hits, seven were sacrifice hits, and Hess was charged with three errors. But he had moxie, and the Bronchos won in ten innings. The crafty southpaw, originally from Berne, Switzerland, went on to win 20 games for the Naps in 1906. He completed his ten-year pitching career with Cleveland and the Boston Braves, winning 70 games and losing 90 and registering a 2.98 ERA.

Edwards became the third secretary of the Baseball Writers' Association of America in 1924. He held this position for 14 years, representing noted baseball journalists including Ed Bang, Grantland Rice, Paul Gallico, Abe Kemp, Dan Daniel, Fred Lieb, Ring Lardner, Damon Runyon, and Arch Ward.

The five-year period from 1911 to 1915 was a low point in Cleveland franchise history. This period signaled the beginning of a term often ascribed to the Cleveland franchise, that is, "graveyard of managers." The turnover of managers was brutal, leading to franchise instability, poor attendance, lack of interest in the club's fortunes, and migration of fans to nearby community parks to witness top-flight amateur baseball.

The 1911 season started on a sad note. When the team departed for spring training to New Orleans, there was concern about Addie Joss's health. As the mainstay of the pitching staff, everyone was pulling for him after his subpar 5–5 record the previous year. He did not look good, but everyone said, "Wait til it gets warmer. Old Addie will buggy whip them with that loose arm of his."[12]

On April 3, the Naps played an exhibition game in Chattanooga against the Lookouts, a local Southern Association team. Joss, Jack Graney and Ted Easterly were late suiting up at the hotel and dashed for a taxi to the ball park. They crossed the field together. "We were near the dugout," Graney remembered, "when suddenly, there was Addie collapsed at my feet."[13] Joss was rushed to the hospital, where he recovered sufficiently to return to the hotel that evening. The players gathered around the man they loved for his ability, unpretentious philosophy, and steady temperament. Joss went home to his wife Lillian and their two children in Toledo. Dr. M. H. Castle, Cleveland's team physician, diagnosed Joss's illness as tuberculous meningitis, for which there was no cure. Only 31, Addie Joss died a few days later on April 14. "The game will never have another man who was a bigger tribute to it," said his teammate Dode Birmingham.[14]

Jess's funeral was scheduled on Opening Day at the same time that Cleveland was to play at Navin Field in Detroit. Neither Detroit nor Cleveland was especially anxious to call off a traditional game expected to bring a large crowd. On the evening of Joss's passing, several older players met with manager McGuire, asking that the game be cancelled so the entire team could attend the funeral. McGuire carried the players' wish to owner Charles Somers, who readily agreed and, in turn, telephoned Detroit president Frank Navin asking for postponement of the game. At first, Navin agreed—and then wavered. Navin referred the matter to league president Ban Johnson, who emphatically stated that the game must go on. Author Cait Murphy commented cynically, "[He] naturally registered a show of humanity."[15]

When informed of Johnson's decision, the emotionally drained Cleveland players assembled in captain George Stovall's room to decide upon their response. Stovall, Lajoie, and Birmingham drew up a petition stating, in effect, that the team would not play on Opening Day. The veterans pressured every player to sign, and Stovall handed the petition to unsuspecting manager McGuire. The manager wanted to avoid problems with the league president and chastised Stovall for having failed in his duties as team captain. Supposedly, Stovall retorted, "I may be captain, but I'm still a ballplayer."[16]

McGuire huddled with Cleveland vice-president Ernest Barnard, and the two carefully considered the petition. When Somers learned of the players' revolt on Sunday, he implored Johnson to reconsider his decision. Rumors had circulated that Detroit players backed this petition and would join Joss's teammates in refusing to suit up for the game. Convinced that the players, indeed, meant to strike, iron-fisted Johnson—who had never before backed down—averted a public relations disaster by magnanimously calling off the season opener, and the game was rescheduled for later in the season.

The entire Naps aggregation boarded a special train from St. Louis to Toledo. Vehicles waited at the Toledo station to transport the players to the nearby Masonic temple. Billy Sunday, a nineteenth century major leaguer who had become a renowned evangelical preacher, declared, "No longer will the umpire walk in front of the grandstand and cry out, 'The pitcher for today will be Addie Joss.'"[17]

Monies poured in from the baseball world to help the Joss family, as players, owners, managers, and ordinary folks contributed small and large gifts. On July 24, a benefit game played at League Park featured top American League All-Stars playing against the Naps. Over 15,000 fans attended the game, and proceeds for the Joss family exceeded $13,000— a considerable sum in 1911.[18] Some observers believed that Joss would have lived a normal life span had he been handled more carefully as a youth. He was six feet, three inches tall and weighed only 150 pounds as a rookie. It was surmised that Joss's heavy training and pitching regimen may have been too much for his slim frame.

Joss completed nine years in the major leagues, compiling an outstanding record. In addition to four consecutive 20-win seasons, he recorded a win-loss record of 160–97, a life-time ERA of 1.88, second only to Ed Walsh (1.82), two no-hitters, seven one-hitters,[19] and 45 shutouts. Unfortunately, when the Hall of Fame opened in Cooperstown, New York, in 1939, an ironclad rule stated that a player must have played in a minimum of ten seasons in order to be eligible for induction into the Hall of Fame.

Dr. Bill Swartz, a cousin of Addie Joss, began writing letters in support of Joss to the Hall of Fame.[20] Joe Reichler, former sports writer and special assistant to baseball commissioner Bowie Kuhn, believed the ten-year rule should be relaxed, so the veterans committee changed the rule in 1977 in order to allow exceptions to great careers shortened by death or illness. "Your letter urging the election of Addie Joss struck a chord here. I have been advocating the same thing for some time."[21] On January 30, 1978, the committee elected Joss to the Hall of Fame.

During the first decade of the 1900s, the Cleveland professional baseball team was disallowed by state law to play on the Sabbath. The Tribe's first Sunday game could not arrest the growing dissension within the franchise. After a state law passed by the Ohio Legislature permitting Sunday baseball, the first Sunday Naps game took place on May 14, 1911. Cleveland churchmen bitterly opposed the advent of Sunday ball, but the game's popularity was strong enough to withstand such criticism.[22] This game in League Park resulted in a victory over the New York Highlanders but did little to boost the spirits of disheartened Naps, for key elements that had kept the club together were disintegrating. Players were disenchanted with manager McGuire; many thought fiery first baseman George Stovall would make an ideal leader. Others in the clubhouse began to lose faith in owner Charley Somers, who encountered a dire financial situation because of losses in his various enterprises.

By mid–May, the Naps were 13 games out of first place. McGuire attempted to rebuild the aging team. Lajoie ruptured a leg muscle but still batted .365, though playing only 90 games. Brittle third baseman Terry Turner was hurt again and missed 40 games. Peerless Bill Bradley had ended his ten-year tenure with the Naps, and ageless Cy Young, now 44, could no longer whip his blazing fast ball across the plate, and was released after pitching seven games.

However, three new faces provided relief for the departed players: catcher Steve O'Neill, pitcher Vean Gregg, and "Shoeless" Joe Jackson, who had played only ten games over a two-year period with the Philadelphia Athletics. Unfortunately, Somers was just completing another acquisition which would grease his slide out of baseball. Harry Davis, a first baseman for the Athletics now in the twilight of his playing career, was Connie Mack's first lieutenant, and when the Athletics visited Cleveland, the injured Davis sat with Somers. The next day, the *Cleveland Press* carried a story that Davis would manage the Naps the following year. Somers believed that Davis had the same managerial qualities that had made Connie Mack a winner.

On May 1, after the Naps posted a 6–11 record, McGuire quit under fire from the front office, which had become more peevish as Somers sank further into debt. Popular first baseman George Stovall, who had already been mentoring young Jackson—the two roomed together, socialized, and discussed the game constantly—replaced McGuire.

During the 1911 season, a more lively baseball was introduced. The new ball had a cork center inside a rubber core. This baseball was not the modern lively ball introduced in 1920, but a step in that direction. For example, two critical offensive statistics increased. In 1911 and 1912, the aggregate batting average jumped from .249 in 1910 to .266 and .269 respectively, and total runs scored per game increased from 7.7 in 1910 to 9.0 in 1911.

Joe Jackson was one player who did respond positively to the new manager. The outfielder batted a career-high .408 in 1911, only to be outdone by Ty Cobb's .420 average. Vean Gregg recorded the first of three consecutive 20-win seasons. The *Plain Dealer*, reacting to Stovall's managership, wrote, "[He's] got them all up on their toes, and ... they jabber away like a lot of poll parrots. They are full of fight, back each other up like champions, and you can look for them to be very much in next year's pennant."[23] With Stovall's energy and leadership powering the club, the Naps started winning and finished with an 80–73 record, good for a third-place finish. Stovall was so popular that it might have been assumed that he would be reappointed for the 1912 season; unfortunately, Somers shipped him to the St. Louis Browns.

Instead, he hired Harry Davis from the Athletics. Davis had been skeptical of finding favorable conditions in Cleveland, and his assessment proved accurate. Disgruntled players, who had not wanted Stovall to leave, were ready to undermine his successor. Davis tried to rebuild the Naps but did not endear himself to team members. During 1912 spring training, he implemented a series of strict rules, among them the banning of handshakes and conversations with opposing players before and during games.

The team's misery began on their way north from New Orleans after spring training, when the Naps encountered spring flood waters from the Mississippi, Ohio, and lesser rivers. Henry Edwards of the *Plain Dealer* recalled a stopover in a small town in Kentucky. The conductor had called ahead to an elderly proprietor of a lunch room attached to the station. Thirty-five players wanted breakfast served in 20 minutes.

When the players arrived, they soon saw how bewildered the proprietor appeared and took over. "Dad," said Nap Lajoie, "Let me have your apron and sit down and take the money when we are through. But first bring out the ham." Vean Gregg asked, "Where are the eggs?" Steve O'Neill made the coffee. "I'll cut the bread," said Jack Graney. Ray Chapman replied, "Let a right-hander do that. You go sit down and let us real cooks do the work."[24] Steve O'Neill's coffee was pretty good, and 35 men enjoyed their breakfast of ham and eggs, coffee, bread, butter, jelly, and canned fruit. Team secretary Bill Blackwood asked, "Dad, how much?" The proprietor replied, "Twenty-five cents a person, but perhaps I ought to throw off 5 or 10 cents as the boys cooked their own meals." The bill was $8.25 for 35 breakfasts.[25]

The 1912 season started well when the Naps won their first series over Detroit in League Park. Davis continuously urged his team to hustle, and the fans did their part, yelling "swell-head" and much worse at the hated Ty Cobb, who went hitless for the series and later in the season was suspended for beating up a bleacherite.[26] But the Naps' early success would not continue, and the team tumbled into the second division. Injuries to Lajoie and Graney exacerbated the club's problems. Before Lajoie's injury, the future Hall of Famer had pronounced, "It is a fellow's own fault if he grows old. A player should be in bed by 10:30 p.m. and eat one good meal a day. Do little reading. A briar pipe at night, not before." He added, "There are many future stars in Cleveland's sandlots.... They won't arrive [in the major leagues] unless they go home early to their mothers and lead clean lives."[27] Cleveland fans showed their appreciation to Larry Lajoie in August, his tenth anniversary with the Naps, by presenting him a floral horseshoe studded with more than 1,000 silver dollars.

At the end of August, Davis abruptly walked into Somers's office and resigned. Connie Mack accused the Naps of "knifing" him.[28] Reminiscing, Somers reflected: "Ever since I have been in baseball, I have been looking for a man of the caliber of Connie Mack. You can count such men on one hand. George Stovall came the closest to the mark, and I made an error when I failed to keep him."[29]

From 1900 through 1912, six managers came and departed from the helm. Somers now appointed a manager from within the organization, namely, outfielder Joe Birmingham, a 28-year-old who had been with the Naps for seven years. After making the mistake of releasing Stovall prematurely, Somers was determined to keep Birmingham indefinitely. The Naps bounced back under Birmingham's leadership, winning 21 of their last 28 games. The contributions of rookie Ray Chapman, Steve O'Neill, and Doc Johnston were important in the team's late surge. Chapman, a bundle of nerves and fighting energy, replaced Wooster native Roger Peckinpaugh, who had struggled at the plate and yet was coveted by the New York Highlanders. "Shoeless" Joe Jackson hit an amazing .395 playing in every game, along with Lajoie batting .368. Both men recorded 90 RBI. The team moved up one notch, finishing fifth.

In 1913, it appeared for a time that Somers had finally reached an era of good fortune. His team, under "Boy Wonder" Joe Birmingham, made a fight for the pennant race throughout the long season. But inevitably there would be serious distractions. The first was the threat of competition from the forthcoming outlaw Federal League. In 1913, this league began playing with six teams, with one located in Cleveland and managed by Cy Young. The club played in Luna Park and finished in second place with a respectable 63–54 record. Amateur baseball also started to boom, and more people watched the sandlotters at Woodland Hills and Brookside than watched the Naps.

The Naps responded with a competitive team of their own. Attendance began to increase as the team played well and clung to second place until late in the season. But the team suffered from additional distractions. For example, Larry Lajoie clashed with Birmingham, and Lajoie began to feel his years. The ambitious, hustling Birmingham benched him in the throes of a batting slump. Lajoie responded by cursing the manager to his face and in the newspapers.

On July 3, 1913, a crowd gathered at Cleveland Public Square to support the much maligned manager. Injuries to Birmingham, who broke his leg, catcher Grover Land, and pitcher Bill Steen slowed the team's pennant drive. On the bright side, Fred "Cy" Falkenberg came on the scene, discovering that rubbing a baseball with emery paper made the ball move in weird ways. The left-hander won his first ten games and ended with a 23–10 record.

To add insult to injury, in August, Falkenberg and the Naps' other stellar pitcher, Vean Gregg, engaged in a friendly wrestling match on an east-bound train from New York to Washington. Both developed sore arms and were of little use for the remainder of the season.[30] Jackson had another outstanding season with a .373 batting average, and Lajoie contributed with a .335 average. Unfortunately, the Naps stumbled near the end of the season. The Washington Nationals overtook them, and the Naps finished in a respectable third place. Attendance was strong throughout the season, and the Naps drew 541,000 fans, the largest attendance since the inception of the franchise in 1901.

However, the 1914 season was one of the worst in the history of the franchise. First, the departure of Falkenberg—who joined the Indianapolis Hoosiers and led them to the Federal League championship in 1914—and the departure of Vean Gregg—traded to the Boston Red Sox in mid-season—left the pitching staff depleted. Second, Somers used his business acumen to thwart the Federal League threat in the Forest City by shifting his Toledo Spiders farm team from the American Association to play in Cleveland when the Naps were out of town. With no Federal League team located in Cleveland before the 1914 season, Somers called all of his players into Cleveland to sign their contracts so that the only person lost was Falkenberg.

Readers of the four dailies wrote letters blasting Somers. One gentleman wrote, "Napoleon Lajoie must make room for a younger man."[31] As the season wore on, it became evident that Lajoie, Cleveland's first "franchise player" (a term that wasn't coined until decades later) was near the end of his career. The great second baseman garnered his 3,000th hit in August but ended the season with an embarrassing .258 mark, the second worst in his 21-year career. Lajoie was sold that winter to the Athletics of Connie Mack. Mack, in need of money, made the horrible mistake of selling Eddie Collins, another future Hall of Fame second baseman, to the Chicago White Sox.

The 1914 season ended dismally; Cleveland finished in last place with a 51–102 record and the lowest winning percentage ever at .333. It was one of only two times in the first 66 years of the franchise that the Tribe finished in last place—the second time was in 1967. (The Indians finished last four times during the "Dark Ages" of 1970–1994, in 1983, 1986, 1987 and 1991.) Poor attendance matched the losing season with a final low count of 185,000. The following year proved even worse, when only 159,000 fans showed up. The earlier mentioned letter-writing critic wrote after the 1914 season, "Charley Somers will not hear the merry metallic ring of silver and gold and crackle of greenbacks."[32]

On January 6, 1915, the *Plain Dealer* reported that Somers proposed a conference of Cleveland baseball writers to choose a new nickname for his club that would be "short, expressive, and appropriate." Numerous suggestions were sent in to Cleveland papers. The *Leader* reported that "Grays" was the favorite choice of Vice President Ernest Barnard. A meeting of club officials and local baseball writers settled on "Indians." On Monday, January 18, 1915, the following appeared in the *Plain Dealer* entitled "Looking Backward":

Many years ago there was an Indian named Sockalexis who was a star player of the Cleveland baseball club. As a batter, fielder, and base runner he was a marvel.... The fans throughout the country began to call the Clevelander the "Indians." It was an honorable name, and while it stuck, the team made an excellent record.[33]

Author David Fleitz recalled the most exciting period of Cleveland baseball—the first few months of 1897, "when League Park shook with war hoops and Indian yells, when a (Penobscot Indian) from Old Town, Maine, [Louis Sockalexis] lined out hits and made incredible throws."[34] Selecting the name "Indians" for a major league team may have seemed innocuous to Cleveland fans. However, Oklahoma in 1907 and New Mexico and Arizona in 1912 had only recently become states, and much animosity existed between white settlers and Native Americans, particularly in the west. Likely, Louis Sockalexis would not have particularly welcomed the "Indians" name: "No matter where we play, I go through the same ordeal, and ... I am so used to that at times, I forget to smile at my tormentors, believing it to be part of the game."[35]

This Chief logo was used during the 1947 season to the 1951 season. He is the grandfather of the current Chief Wahoo. The Indians won the 1948 World Series wearing this logo. This design was created by Walter A. Goldbach (courtesy of the artist, Walter A. Goldbach).

The American Indian Center of Cleveland filed a lawsuit, charging that displays of Native American images as part of public relations by the Cleveland baseball franchise projected a disrespectful attitude toward the contemporary Native American community. The lawsuit was dismissed. More recently, similar complaints have been directed toward the Atlanta Braves. Activists insist, "We are not going away until we get rid of the Big Four: The Kansas City Chiefs, the Washington Redskins, the Indians, and the Braves."[36] However, a significant element of the Native American population take pride in the use of these nicknames by professional teams, and after nearly 100 years, a name change for the Cleveland club is unlikely. The Tribe media guide (2010) continues to honor Louis Sockalexis with a vignette about his brief career with the Cleveland Spiders.

However, a name change did not help the Indians in 1915. The season started, and the locals played the same as usual. Mired in sixth place, Somers relieved Joe Birmingham of his duties after 28 games and a record of 12–16: "I felt the Cleveland fans demanded a change," he said. Birmingham charged Somers with interference. "Maybe I did tell him to play Jackson on first and Elmer Smith in right field," Somers admitted. "But I backed [Birmingham] up in a thousand other ways."[37]

Lee Fohl, an ex-catcher who had played only five games in the major leagues and later coached for Cleveland in 1914, took over as manager. The Indians now had a promising group of young players who had the potential to produce winning teams, namely Elmer Smith, Guy Morton, Jack Graney, Ray Chapman, Steve O'Neill, and Bill Wambsganss. The team moved up one notch in the standings, winning six more games than had the 1914 cellar dwellers.

However, serious problems continued. Somers was in deeper financial difficulty, and lack of fan support had helped put him near bankruptcy with a debt of nearly $2,000,000, a large sum at that time. In addition, Somers's coal business had fallen off, and he had lost money in several real estate ventures. On August 21, 1915, in order to allay his financial dilemma, the owner traded Joe Jackson, his only star, for outfielders Bobby "Braggo" Roth and Larry Chappell, pitcher Ed Klepfer, and most importantly a much needed $31,500. Klepfer posted one winning season, 14–4 in 1916, and Roth, three decent years as an outfielder—he led the American League in 1915 with seven home runs. But this trade only delayed an inevitable decision concerning team ownership.

Local bankers had been carrying Somers for a year, and the American League was willing to stand by and carry him indefinitely, for he had been a major catalyst in financing the early development of the league. The bankers told Somers that he needed to get out of baseball and real estate properties, and give up his minor league franchises as well. "Charley, we like you and believe you could weather this if conditions were better. But you owe $1,750,000; we've got to put you through the wringer."[38] They issued notes on his vast coal and hotel holdings and liquidated several real estate properties and minor league holdings. Sorrowfully, Somers moved out of League Park, where he had ruled since 1901. Lest one shed tears for Charley Somers, the gray-haired, still handsome coal baron recouped his fortune. He died at Put-in-Bay, Ohio, June 29, 1934, at the age of 65, and left approximately $3 million and the New Orleans Pelicans minor league team, a notable comeback for a man who had been $1,750,000 in debt.[39]

American League president Ban Johnson was stuck with finding a new owner. Johnson met with some of his cronies, including Charles Comiskey and Jim Dunn, a railroad contractor—specializing in laying railroad rails and ties—whose office was across the street from American League headquarters in Chicago. Johnson turned to Dunn and said, "You're going to own the Cleveland ball club." Dunn gulped, "Me?" "Yes, you," repeated Johnson. "How much money can you get together in a hurry?" Dunn looked up at the ceiling and responded: "Well, I could lay my hands on fifteen thousand right this minute, but I might get more if I had some time."[40]

Pat McCarthy, Dunn's business partner, volunteered to put up $10,000. Another voice, that of Tom Walsh, a former catcher for the Chicago Cubs who had only caught two games in the major leagues, chimed in, "I'll take a good block of that stock off of your hands."[41]

Johnson pledged $100,000 on behalf of the American League, and Comiskey agreed to a $100,000 loan. Jim Dunn raised the remaining money from several friends by selling small blocks of stock. The total purchase price was $500,000.

Jim Dunn, nicknamed "Sunny Jim" for his smiling disposition, energized Cleveland fans with his "go for it" outlook. He commented, "I'm going to give this city a pennant," as he smiled under his ever-present derby hat, adding, "I will not stand for a tail-ender. If I thought the Cleveland club was destined to be a second division team, I would not buy it. Cleveland is a corking good town, and I think it will [make] a comeback."[42] *The Sporting News* commented,

> He's of the sort that the game needs—eager to win, if he can fairly, but the same old smile if his team loses; the even temperament that gave him the nickname of "Sunny Jim." In fact, he feels insulted if anyone calls him Mr. Dunn. He is "Jim" to everybody, which indicates pretty well the stuff he's made of.[43]

Dunn had a healthy ego and liked to see his name in the papers. When he decided to purchase the Cleveland franchise, he told Ban Johnson, "Look, Ban, I know nothing about the business of baseball. I've got to have some help." Johnson told him not to worry: "I've got just the man for you. [Bob McRoy] used to be my secretary until he went to the Boston Red Sox. He'll buy five thousand dollars' worth of stock and be your general manager. He knows baseball and how to run it."[44]

"Sunny" Jim Dunn, the colorful and successful owner of the Cleveland franchise (1916–1922). He purchased Tris Speaker from the Red Sox in 1916. Speaker led Cleveland to its first World Championship in 1920 (courtesy Scott H. Longert).

In February 1916, the final transfer of the team to Dunn took place at the luxurious Hotel Statler in downtown Cleveland. The press from four Cleveland dailies was present and interested to know his plans. The new owner was a novice in dealing with writers, so he usually maintained a standoff with them until the potential adversaries became better acquainted with each other. Reporters clustered around and asked Dunn if there would be any changes. "Hardly any," he promised, "Lee Fohl stays as manager.... McRoy will be general manager ... and I'll be president. Bill Blackwood will remain road secretary." Sensing more to come, reporters asked about Somers's vice-president and general manager, the friendly and beloved Ernest S. Barnard. "He goes," Dunn replied bluntly.[45]

Old-timers insist that the Hotel Statler has not been rocked with such an oral explosion since. Ed Bang of the *News*, highly respected and powerful, got to his feet, and baseball writer Henry Edwards went white. The two men reproached Dunn severely. Friends of Barnard, both insisted that he was the most knowledgeable

individual in the entire baseball world. He had been instrumental in building the Indians' farm system; moreover, he
was familiar with the details of running a ball club.[46] After
the writers told him he was making a mistake, Dunn backed
off and kept Barnard, though he demoted him to director of
park operations. Barnard withheld his anger and forged ahead
like a good team member. His cooperative manner was most
evident during the World Series of 1920, one of the most
exciting, which he did not get to see, for he was kept busy in
the front office handling tickets.

At a much later date, Ed Bang and Henry Edwards
learned of Dunn's reason for ousting Barnard: Ban Johnson
had influenced him to do so. Johnson knew the American
League owners thought highly of Barnard, and if ever the
club owners sought to replace him as president, Barnard
would have been a likely choice. What Johnson feared eventually happened: His power eroded, and he had become a fig-
urehead by 1925. In July 1927, he resigned, and Barnard was
appointed president of the American League, serving in that
capacity for over three years until his death in 1931.[47]

Ernest S. Barnard left the *Columbus Dispatch* to join the
Naps in 1904 as a traveling secretary, the first in baseball history.
He was promoted to president
of the Indians in 1922, when
Jim Dunn died, and was later
elected president of the American League, serving from 1927
until his death in 1931.

General Manager McRoy was desperately ill and died
on December 2, 1917. Now there was no one to run the Cleveland team. Dunn apologized to Barnard, saying he had made
a serious mistake, "Barney, they have been making a fool of
me long enough. You are the general manager of this club.
Here is your contract. Write your own salary on this contract
and then sign it."[48] Barnard penned a modest figure. Dunn objected, "You're worth much
more." Barnard said it was enough for him and they could discuss the issue later. After Dunn
died in 1922, Barnard was appointed president of the Cleveland club, as Dunn had directed
his wife, Emily, to retain Barnard as president for as long as she controlled the team.[49]

The new ownership was only one part of the revival of professional baseball in Cleveland. Dunn loved the celebrity his new team brought him. He changed the name of League
Park to Dunn Field, a vanity which was not uncommon in entrepreneurship during this era.
But making the team into a plausible contender was easier said than done. He needed a star
such as Lajoie had been for Somers starting in 1902. In a most convoluted manner and with
the help of sportswriter Ed Bang, Dunn got his man, the "Gray Eagle," Tris "Spoke" Speaker.
The great outfielder seemed an ideal choice to lead the Indians out of the second division
into the Promised Land. The trouble was that Speaker wanted no part of Cleveland.

During the Federal League years of 1914–1915, owners had increased salaries, especially
for their star players, in order to prevent them from jumping to the new league. The Boston
Red Sox had increased Speaker's salary to a reported $18,000, but with the Federal League
no longer a threat in 1916, salaries dropped, and Speaker received a contract for $9,000 for
the coming 1916 season even though he had asked for $15,000. Speaker sent the contract

back to Red Sox owner Joseph Lannin, while he sat at home in Hubbard, Texas, enjoying his mother's cooking.

At spring training in Hot Springs, Arkansas, Boston manager Bill Carrigan was suffering without Speaker's help. He finally called Speaker: "You're getting a bad deal, 'Spoke,' but come up here and we'll straighten it out."[50] With Carrigan's help, Speaker worked out a deal whereby he would be paid for exhibition games regardless of the final results of his contract issue. Speaker traveled with the Boston team back to Brooklyn for an exhibition game, in which he hit a home run. Speaker expected to solve his contract issue when Lannin, who approached Speaker after the game, told him, "Your terms are okay. We'll sign in Boston tomorrow."[51] The plot had thickened the day before, when sports editor Ed Bang of the *Cleveland News* noticed a press release stating that Lannin was disgusted with Speaker's hold-out campaign and wanted to trade him. Bang immediately called general manager Bob McRoy and said, "Bob, I think we can get Tris Speaker, and I think we ought to grab him." He added, "I know Lannin and he'll sell any player for enough money."[52]

For the next 24 hours, Speaker was unaware that his future was being decided by a series of phone calls between McRoy and Lannin. On Sunday evening, after the Brooklyn-Boston exhibition game, Speaker remembered a call from McRoy asking him to come to his hotel room to visit. After salutations, McRoy asked Speaker how he would like to become an Indian. "I think you've got a bad ball club," Speaker shot back. "Cleveland has become a bad baseball town. Boston should win again. No, I wouldn't like it. Why should I go to Cleveland?"[53] McRoy's face showed disappointment. "I'm sorry Tris," he finally said. "We've bought you for $57,500 [including] pitcher Sam Jones and infielder Freddie Thomas."[54] The dazed Speaker told McRoy to call the trade off and threatened to quit baseball and return to his native Texas. Then Speaker realized the amount of cash involved and his animosity against Lannin, and devised a plan. He would report to Cleveland as long as he was paid $10,000 of his purchase price, and the money had to come from Lannin, not Dunn. Predictably, Lannin balked at this idea. Ban Johnson knew how important this deal was for Cleveland. Instead of dealing with the stubborn Speaker, he leaned on Lannin, who finally agreed to give Speaker his money and complete the deal.[55]

Historian Charles C. Alexander succinctly analyzed the impact of this trade for Cleveland:

> As reluctant as he had been to come to Cleveland, Speaker discovered that the city's fandom had quickly taken him to heart. Speaker was welcomed as something of a baseball messiah. Some of his greatest seasons were still ahead of him, and as the key figure in the regeneration of Cleveland's fortunes, he proved a far more valuable asset to James C. Dunn than Joseph J. Lannin could have imagined.[56]

The 1916 season, the first for "Sunny" Jim's syndicate, did not result in a major change in the final standings. There were, however, significant signs that happy days were on the horizon.

In fact, the acquisition of Tris Speaker soon showed itself to be the main asset in the Tribe's forthcoming success. Speaker, a former semi-pro pitcher, had been the key player in the biggest deal in major league history to date. Admittedly, he had not wanted to leave Boston, where he had been a member of the 1915 world champions and a teammate of Babe

Ruth. However, Speaker soon changed his mind about Cleveland being a bad baseball town. The graceful outfielder admitted he was dead wrong and soon found it to be the friendliest of parks in spite of a few boos. He immediately showed fans his batting prowess, finishing with a .386 batting average in 1916 and finally dislodging Ty Cobb from the batting title which he had held for nine consecutive seasons.

Before the 1916 season, several teams had promised to help the newly purchased Cleveland franchise. Washington sent first baseman Chick Gandil, an eventual member of the Black Sox Eight, and the Chicago White Sox unloaded catcher Tom Daley and infielder Ivon Howard. The three contributed little, but two young pitchers, Jim Bagby, Sr., and Stan Coveleski, soon became household names for Cleveland fans. These two right-handers were the hardest working pitchers on the staff in 1916. Each was noted for a particular pitch. For Coveleski, the pitch was a spitball, still legal until 1920. While pitching for Portland in the Pacific Coast League, he learned this new pitch. "I had as good control over the spitball as I had on my fastball. There was an art to throwing a good spitter." He revealed his technique: "One thing you needed was a jaw full of slippery elm. Went to my mouth every pitch." He added, "I'd go maybe two or three innings without throwing a spitter, but I'd always have [the batter] looking for it."[57] Bagby was equally effective with his "fadeaway" pitch.

Although the Clevelanders led the American League through May and June primarily due to Speaker's hitting, they soon faltered and ended in sixth place, one step above their

Tris Speaker, the "Gray Eagle," one of Cleveland's greatest player-managers. Speaker led the Tribe to its first World Championship in 1920, finishing his career with a .344 batting average (seventh all-time) and was an outstanding center fielder. He was elected to the Hall of Fame in 1937 (Library of Congress).

1915 record. Amazingly, the team finished with a .500 record, 77–77, an unusually good record for a sixth-place team. On the positive side, the Indians won 20 more games than in the preceding year. Speaker helped push attendance to 492,000, a major increase of 333,000 or approximately 300 percent over the 1915 attendance. Boston won the pennant for the second straight year as well as the World Series. Speaker's thoughts on this issue as a deposed Boston player are unknown.

The Cleveland team did much better in 1917, in spite of several on-the-field pyrotechnics. The club finished in third place, retaining that position during much of the season. An improved record of 88–66 left the team behind the pennant-winning White Sox and second-place Boston. Pitching was the highlight of the year, with Bagby winning 25 games, Coveleski 19, and Ed Klepfer 13. Famous names in Cleveland baseball history began to blossom into seasoned players, including outfielders Elmer Smith, who returned to Cleveland after a year with Washington, Jack Graney, and Bobby "Braggo" Roth, second baseman Bill Wambsganss, shortstop Ray Chapman, and catcher Steve O'Neill. Speaker, now captain of the team and often referred to as "assistant manager," continued to lead the team in batting with a .352 average.

The routine of the team was interrupted by two unrelated events. First, Larry, the world famous dog owned by Jack Graney, died on July 25, 1917. The popular Larry had accompanied the team on road trips and performed tricks at all of the ballparks.* Second, the United States entered World War I on April 2, 1917, and players were subject to the draft. Later in the season, military drilling was instituted for the players. The army assigned drill experts to each team. With bats serving as rifles, the pantalooned athletes went through formations daily. Near the end of the season, contests were held to determine the championship drill team. The Indians finished third behind the second-place Senators and the Browns, winner of a $500 prize.[58]

Led by Speaker, the Clevelanders at times showed their grit. The season began with the largest Opening Day crowd in the city's history, as 21,000 packed League Park. Late in April, Ross Tenney, sports editor for the *Cleveland Press*, publicly expressed his astonishment at catcher Steve O'Neill, who had lost his temper in a game against St. Louis: "Never since 1912, had we seen O'Neill let his temper get the best of him." The writer added, "Steve got so mad at a decision ... at the plate that he threw the ball into left field and the Brownies beat our side, 6–5."[59]

In early May, Speaker suffered his first banishment from a Cleveland game. As team captain, he raced in from center field to protest a decision by umpire Tom Connolly at second base. "Keep goin'," Connolly yelled at the onrushing Speaker. "Don't stop until you get in the shower."[60] Speaker slowed his pace some, dropped his hands to his side, and kept going.

But as he passed Connolly, he nudged the umpire with his shoulder. Connolly staggered a couple of feet, enough to cause the umpire to write a report to Ban Johnson, American League president, who suspended Speaker for three days.

A "first" in Cleveland American League history occurred on September 9 in Comiskey Park where, for nearly three hours, the Tribe and White Sox had battled and wrangled. In the top of the tenth inning, the Indians had the bases loaded, Graney on third base, and two outs. The fast, smart outfielder took a long lead off third. Dave Danforth, pitching for

Jack Graney, senior member of the Indians in the early 1900s, played 14 years for Cleveland. In 1931, he became the first ex-player to broadcast major league games, becoming a popular announcer for over 20 years (courtesy Scott H. Longert).

Chicago, fired the ball to catcher Ray Schalk, who threw to third baseman Fred McMullin. Graney turned to slide back into the bag, and in doing so toppled McMullin. Schalk's throw rolled several feet from the bag. Graney struggled to his feet, only to discover that McMullin held him by the belt. Graney wrenched free and raced across home plate, followed by Ray Chapman.

At the plate, umpire Clarence "Brick" Owens threw up his hands and indicated that Graney was out and that no run had been scored to break the 3–3 deadlock. Owens claimed that Graney had interfered with McMullin on the throw to third. Graney and infielder Terry Turner charged Owens and had to be pulled off by manager Lee Fohl. Umpire Billy Evans went to Owens's rescue. Owens "pulled his watch" and ordered the Indians to take their positions. A long delay ensued before he was obeyed.

After the argument, Ivan Howard, a utility infielder, replaced Turner, who had been thrown out of the game. In the last of the tenth inning, after one out, O'Neill and Owens began to argue. O'Neill became angrier and angrier and finally intentionally threw the ball far over Howard's head and into left field. Owens promptly forfeited the game to the White Sox, one of the rare forfeitures in modern day baseball.[61] The record books list 38 forfeits since 1901.

Finally, the team was disrupted not only by the daily military drills but also by the loss of nine players to the military draft during the 1917 season. Cleveland, Philadelphia, and Boston were hardest hit. For the first time in professional baseball history, a season began with the country at war. According to Cleveland journalist Russ Schneider, most baseball historians believe the Indians would have won their first pennant in 1918 had it not been for World War I. On July 19, 1918, Secretary of War Newton D. Baker[62] had ruled that baseball was not an essential occupation and that all players of draft age were subject to the "work-or-fight" rule, so many players left their teams for jobs in the shipyards and other defense industries. Players were exempt from this edict until September 1, and baseball decided to end the season the following day—Labor Day. Cleveland lost seven players to military service or defense industries for all or part of the season.

In spite of this unavoidable edict from Secretary Baker and a patched-up lineup, the Tribe began well. An incident on the diamond on May 20, 1918, would have considerable significance in two years. Captain Speaker was hit in the head by Boston's Carl Mays, a submarine-style pitcher who had been earlier accused of intentionally beaning batters. Though Speaker was not injured, he was furious with Mays and reportedly shouted to the pitcher, "I was on the same team with you long enough to know what you do. If you throw at anyone else on [this] ball club, you might not even walk out of this park."[63]

The Clevelanders were in first place in early July when they were caught and surpassed by Boston. But they kept charging and trailed the Red Sox by only four games going into the final week. That last week became disorderly. In the third game of a series with the hapless Athletics, Speaker tried to score on a ball that rolled away from first baseman George Burns. He was called out by umpire Tom Connolly—not Speaker's favorite umpire. Speaker stormed the umpire and bumped him. According to biographer Charles Alexander, after both teams tried to restrain Speaker, he broke loose and clipped Connolly on the chin, whereupon he was ejected. That night, Ban Johnson levied an indefinite suspension on Speaker. Amazingly, Johnson lifted the suspension after the next game and a day of travel.

On Sunday, September 1, the Indians clinched second place with an 8–5 victory over Chicago, their highest finish since 1908. Cleveland was scheduled to play a doubleheader against the Browns in St. Louis on Labor Day. Since the games did not mean anything in the standings, manager Fohl, with the approval of owner Jim Dunn, forfeited those games, in accordance with Secretary of War Baker's ruling that the season end on September 1. Teams in the two leagues ended up playing between 122 and 129 games. Speaker slumped to a .318 batting average, but Stan Coveleski completed his second straight outstanding season with 22 victories and an ERA of 1.82.

The 1918 season was no sooner over than ten more Indians, including Speaker, enlisted. Most of the players remained stateside and returned to their teams after the armistice was signed on November 11, 1918. Pitcher Ed Klepfer survived several weeks of combat but lost his capacity to pitch. First baseman Lou Guisto was gassed and retired from the game for two seasons before returning to Cleveland in 1921.

During the 1918-1919 winter, Speaker and teammates escaped the influenza pandemic that eventually killed nearly 700,000 Americans. Because of the financial losses from the previous season, club owners voted for a 140-game schedule in 1919, rosters limited to 21 players, and salaries reduced by two weeks due to the shortened season which would begin on April 25.

Cleveland management, with Speaker's advice, sent temperamental Braggo Roth to the cellar-dwelling Athletics for third baseman Larry Gardner, pitcher Elmer Myers, and outfielder Charlie Jamieson, who had done little to distinguish himself with either Washington or Philadelphia. Jamieson later described Speaker as "my best friend. He was the one who helped get me traded to Cleveland."[64] Jamieson proved to be one of Cleveland's great outfielders during his 14-year career, compiling a career .303 batting average. Speaker also reunited with Smoky Joe Wood, pitcher and former Boston teammate. Wood is best remembered for his phenomenal pitching record in 1912, with a 34–5 record, ERA of 1.91—bested by Walter Johnson's 1.39—and three World Series victories for the champion Red Sox. His pitching arm was now gone, but for five years he made valuable contributions in the Indians outfield.

The 1919 season began with Speaker serving as both captain and manager Fohl's trusted confidant. As it played out, the season ended with Fohl out of a job and Speaker as manager. Fohl had been sound, if not spectacular, in his role and finished with a creditable .547 winning percentage, one second-place finish, and a third-place finish in his four-year tenure.

Without Speaker's usual offensive weapons, the Cleveland team continued to stay within reach of the favored Chicago White Sox. After 17 games, Speaker was batting an unbelievably low .234, which by his standards led to a season-long slump. The center fielder finished with a .296 average, the only time in his 11 years with Cleveland that he finished below .300. His subpar year may have affected his sometimes bellicose behavior. On Friday, May 31, Chicago and its star pitcher Eddie Cicotte defeated the Tribe, holding Speaker hitless. In the eighth inning, Chick Gandil fielded Speaker's sharp grounder and tagged the base for the out, evidently thinking Speaker might spike him. Historian Charles Alexander tells what happened next:

> The two jawed at each other as Speaker went back to the nearby visitor's dugout. Before Elmer Smith flied out to end the inning, Gandil, according to a naval officer sitting in back of the [White Sox] dugout, made a megaphone of his hands and let loose with a torrent of vile abuse at Speaker. As the sides changed, Gandil lingered off the base line, [and] ... struck [Speaker] in the face.... Enraged, Speaker leaped at Gandil and knocked him down, shoved

umpire Tom Connolly aside [him again!] as though he were a child ... decked Gandil again and began pounding him on the ground. Plate umpire Dick Nallin finally got between the combatants and ordered both from the game.[65]

Speaker left the field escorted by a policeman, several Cleveland players, and Chicago manager William "Kid" Gleason. When play resumed, spectators in the left field bleachers threw bottles at Jack Graney, who had repeatedly complained to umpire Nallin about Cicotte's doctoring of the ball.

The Speaker-Gandil encounter was a genuine one-on-one brawl between men who had disliked each other for years. Hence, players from both teams gathered around and did nothing to interfere. Speaker ended up with a bleeding mouth, bruised cheek, and scratched ankle and arm. Gandil had cuts on his lips and forehead, lumps on his face, and one eye nearly closed. They both received a five-day suspension from league president Ban Johnson.

The last momentous game for the Tribe in 1919 took place on July 18 in Dunn Field. In spite of injuries to Ray Chapman, Jack Graney, and others, the Cleveland team was staging a comeback. The opponent was the seventh-place Boston Red Sox, a dangerous team with Babe Ruth pitching one day and playing left field other days. The Tribe was just 4½ games behind the White Sox. Downtown Cleveland was in the midst of a trolley car strike, so thousands either had to walk or hitchhike to Dunn Field to see the game.

In the fourth inning, Babe Ruth stroked his 12th home run over the short right field wall. The score was 3–3 when Cleveland plated four runs in the eighth inning to take a 7–3 lead. In the ninth inning, the Tribe's Elmer Myers relieved starter Hi Jasper. The reliever gave up one run on a double, then walked two men to load the bases. Babe Ruth came to the plate. In the right field bull pen, a slight southpaw named Fritz Coumbe was warming up as well as right-hander Tom Phillips.

According to Frank Gibbons, there was talk that Coumbe was a pop-off and a braggart. Mike McNally, then with the Red Sox, added, "Coumbe told us he didn't have any trouble with Ruth," and bragged that "he knew how to pitch him slow spot curves."[66] The left-hander had won 13 games the year before but only one so far in 1919.

Replacing Myers, Coumbe first pitched a curve ball right over the middle of the plate; Ruth took a savage swing and missed. The crowd shuddered, and then roared. Catcher Steve O'Neill marched out to the mound shaking his head. "Want to get killed?" he asked the southpaw. "You got away with that, but don't do it again. Keep the ball low and away."[67] Coumbe shrugged. The next pitch was a slow curve, slightly inside, and the ball looked like a white basketball as Babe stepped back a trifle and took a mighty swing. The ball looked like a white pea as it soared beyond the high fence and over Lexington Avenue into a back-yard. Gordon Cobbledick wrote, "The ball skulled a taxpayer puttering in his back yard." Right fielder Elmer Smith did not even look up and bowed his head as four runs scored, the last one by Babe Ruth as the winning run. Fohl later maintained that "[Coumbe] was the logical choice and I'd pick him again.... I told him to keep the ball low and away from Ruth and walk him rather than give him a good ball to hit."[68]

Fohl walked the last mile upstairs to see owner Jim Dunn. He offered to resign and Dunn accepted, making him a scout for the Indians. Dunn called 31-year-old Speaker in to his office to offer him the managership. Speaker refused to take it unless his friend Fohl agreed. Dunn and business manager Ernest Barnard called Fohl, and Speaker heard what he wanted from Fohl. For obvious reasons, Fritz Coumbe never pitched another inning for Cleveland. Ironically, on the day Dunn appointed Speaker, he gave up his efforts to make a trade for a pitcher named Carl Mays, who had just quit the Red Sox.[69] The next day 10,000 fans came to Dunn Field for Speaker's debut as manager. He obliged the supporters by rapping two singles and a triple as Cleveland defeated Boston for a ninth time in ten meetings.

During the remainder of the season, Cleveland gained some pitching strength. One of these pitchers was George Uhle, a home-grown product. After going through spring training in 1919, he won his first of 147 games with the Indians in the opening series against the St. Louis Browns. When Tris Speaker became manager, he looked for pitching strength. He put Uhle into a tight game with Washington on August 14, and the husky right-hander granted only one hit in two innings, winning the game 4–3. Six days later Uhle started his first game in the majors and turned back the Boston Red Sox 5–2. A headline in a Cleveland newspaper read "Uhle, the Sandlotter, Arrives." The second acquisition was Ray Caldwell, who sports writer Grantland Rice said "could be as great as Matty or Walter Johnson, but instead of choosing their careers, he is evidently going to be another Rube Waddell."[70] This statement may have been true until August 1919, for Caldwell's pitching career was about to be revived.

Speaker had a propensity for picking up released players who might make a contribution. "Slim" Caldwell, with a serious drinking problem, was a most amazing example. His checkered career included a jaunt with the Yankees, when manager Miller Huggins assigned two private detectives to track his nighttime activities—to no avail. Subsequently, he experienced a short stay with taciturn manager Ed Barrow of the Red Sox. His road roommate was Babe Ruth, another lover of wild nightlife. On August 19, Speaker signed the 31-year-old, believing he could still contribute. There were stipulations for Caldwell in his contract. Speaker demanded that after each game he pitched, Caldwell must get drunk and was not to report to the clubhouse the next day. The second day, he was to report to Speaker and run around the ball park as many times as the manager stipulated. The third day he was to pitch batting practice, and the fourth day he was to be ready to take his turn on the mound. After reading the contract, "Slim" looked at Speaker. "You left out one word, Tris," he said, "the word *not* has been left out. It should read that I'm *not* to get drunk." Speaker smiled, "No, it says you *are* to get drunk."[71] Slim shrugged his shoulders and signed the contract.

Caldwell had his share of thrills during the final six weeks of the season. On August 24, pitching against Philadelphia in League Park, Caldwell and the Indians led 2–1 with two outs in the ninth inning. Then an electrical storm enveloped the park, and a bolt of lightning smashed into the ground next to the pitcher's mound. Caldwell was flattened and knocked unconscious for five minutes. After first aid was rendered and he was resuscitated, he stood up a bit wobbly but threw two strikes to the batter to end the game.[72]

Two weeks later, Caldwell pitched the best game of his career—a 3–0 no-hitter against the New York Yankees and Carl Mays. The shortened season ended with Cleveland finishing in the runner-up spot for the second straight season, this time behind the Chicago White Sox. The Tribe played well under Speaker, compiling a 40–21 record. The White Sox soon turned into the "Black Sox" after throwing the 1919 World Series to the Cincinnati Reds. It was one of the darkest moments in major league history.

When the season ended, Cleveland players scattered to their respective homes. Several returned later in the fall for a major social event—Ray Chapman's marriage. Ray Chapman married local socialite Kathleen Daley, daughter of the president of the East Ohio Gas Company. Kathleen's family lived on prestigious "Millionaire's Row" (Euclid Avenue). Other residents included notables John D. Rockefeller, Leonard C. Hanna, Samuel Mather, and Frances Bolton. It was uncommon for a Protestant to marry a Catholic. Although Chapman was Protestant, he was obliged to be married in a Catholic ceremony. At Chapman's request, Speaker agreed to serve as best man, even though he had at times expressed his critical attitude toward communicants of the church papacy.

During the winter months of 1919-1920, journalist Hugh Fullerton, Sr., wrote a series of newspaper articles raising questions about strange happenings in the 1919 World Series. He led readers to believe that unusual behavior by White Sox players may have altered results of the Chicago-Cincinnati encounter. Publications like *Baseball Magazine* and *The Sporting News* dismissed such assertions. This issue continued to fester for months until September 1920.

Two playing circumstances influenced baseball as the 1920 season unfolded. First, baseballs became livelier, with a tighter wind of a higher grade of Australian wool around the cork-rubber center. Umpires were instructed to keep clean, white balls in play, so the ball could more easily be seen by the batter. This inaugurated the period known as the "lively ball era," in contrast to the past 20 years when the ball had been lifeless, often soiled and dark, and more susceptible to "treatment" by pitchers. Second, the baseball rules committee banished the spitball and other trick deliveries. An exception was given to 17 veteran spitballers—no more than two per team—which meant Cleveland's Ray Caldwell and Stan Coveleski were exempt from the ban. Babe Ruth, now a member of the New York Yankees, gave evidence that the ball was livelier, astonishing the baseball world by smashing 54 home runs, an increase of 25 from his record-breaking 1919 season.

There have been few if any more exciting, upsetting, yet satisfying baseball seasons than 1920—for Cleveland fans, 1948 would likely be the exception. Journalist George Condon wrote, "It was a time filled with interesting characters, high drama on and off the field, unbelievable heroics, and finally, full triumph. But there also was tragedy."[73]

In Ohio, the key word was euphoria. A Dallas newspaper covering the 1920 presidential election reported, "Ohio has two contenders for the presidency of the United States and one for the baseball championship of the world. Ask anyone in the state who is going to win and they'll answer 'Cleveland.' It ... never occurred to anyone to think the questioner might be referring to Ohioans James Cox or Warren G. Harding and the trifling matter of the country's presidency."[74]

World Champions in 1920! Who could imagine that after 20 years as one of the original teams in the American League, the Cleveland franchise would reach the pinnacle of success? Pundits questioned the legitimacy of the conquest in view of headline-grabbing news of the Black Sox Scandal of 1919. But dark shadows did not diminish the joy along Euclid Avenue and at friendly Dunn Field. Manager Tris Speaker and owner Jim Dunn finally put together a ball club that had power, pitching, and good defense. The pitching staff was led by Stan Coveleski, a wry-faced Pole from Shamokin, Pennsylvania, a drawling Georgian named Jim Bagby, Sr., and Raymond Caldwell, who found alcohol in spite of America's first and only try at prohibition. This trio, led by Jim Bagby's 31 victories, posted 75 of the 98 Indians victories. The only other trio of Cleveland pitchers to match this feat was Mike Garcia, Early Wynn, and Bob Lemon in 1953 with sixty-seven victories.

Walter "Duster" Mails, an addition from Cleveland's Portland farm team, joined the team in late August and won seven games in September without a defeat, posted a 1.85 ERA, and proved to be a lifesaver for the Indians' pennant hopes.

Offensively, the team was the most powerful assembled in Cleveland flannels. The team hit .303, led by manager-player Speaker with a .388 average. The club could not match the Yankees' home run power but did produce a barrage of triples, doubles, and singles. The infield had become a steady and often brilliant machine, with veteran Larry Gardner at third, Chapman at shortstop, Bill Wambsganss at second, and Doc Johnston at first. Future star first baseman George Burns was purchased from the Athletics and played against left-handed batters.

In left field, Joe "Doc" Evans alternated with Charlie Jamieson. When Evans contracted malaria, injured Jack Graney took over in fine style down the stretch. Speaker was in center field, and another Speaker acquisition, Smoky Joe Wood, was a valuable complement to Elmer Smith in right field. Graney recalled, "We played the foul lines and let Speaker take care of the rest."[75] Veteran catcher Steve O'Neill, who caught all but five games, had an outstanding season, batting .321.

Cleveland shot out of the gate with a vengeance, leading the league most of the season and defeating the defending league champion White Sox in nine of their first 12 games. Dunn Field was the focal point for the city's emotions. Sunday baseball was a jam session at the ball yard with crowds spilling out upon the field behind ropes. The Indians drew a record-setting 913,000 fans. Cleveland would not draw 1,000,000 or more fans until 1946, when Bill Veeck arrived on the scene.[76]

A happy, confident Indians ball club left for the east in mid–August. Twenty-nine-year-old Ray Chapman was building a home for his pregnant wife and had every reason for living. On Monday, August 16, the weather was threatening as the Indians went to the Polo Grounds to play the Yankees. The day was overcast and muggy, and a drizzle fell in the early innings. The game attracted an excellent weekday crowd of 23,000. In the crowd were fans and friends of Indians left fielder Charlie Jamieson from his Paterson, New Jersey home. His mother, who was attending her first major league game, and sister were in attendance. Jamieson's mother never attended another game.

In the fifth inning the Tribe led, 3–0. Cleveland shortstop Ray Chapman, in his ninth season with the Tribe, stepped to the plate in his familiar right-handed crouch, hugging the plate. On the mound was dour, barrel-chested Carl Mays, a 5'11", 195 pound submarine-pitching right-hander, whose hand seemed to scrape the mound as he delivered his pitches. On deck, Chapman's friend, Tris Speaker, waited to bat. Mays wound up and his pitch sailed toward the inside of the plate, directly at Chapman. The shortstop waited, his body seemingly frozen by the path of the ball. An instant later, the ball crashed into his left temple, and a horrible sound was heard by every spectator as it echoed throughout the Polo Grounds. He fell immediately to the ground, unconscious, with blood pouring from his left ear. Umpire

Tom Connelly took one look, turned to the stands, and called for a physician. Players from both teams gathered around the fallen batter.

The ball had bounced back to Mays, who thought it had hit the bat. He fielded it and threw over to Wally Pipp at first base. It was only after he saw Pipp's face that he realized what had happened. Chapman regained consciousness after a few minutes, following the ministrations of two doctors, and tried to talk, but no words became audible because the blow had caused a paralysis of the vocal chords. His teammates helped him to his feet finally and with assistance of two of them, he began to walk toward the clubhouse. When he was part way across the infield, his legs collapsed and he had to be carried the remainder of the way to a waiting ambulance.

On the Yankees bench, manager Miller Huggins speculated that the cleats on Chapman's left foot might have caught in the moist dirt, keeping him anchored in the batter's box, and Mays was quoted as saying he had complained to Connolly that the ball had a dark spot on it and should be discarded. Speaker tried to lift spirits, comparing the blow Chapman took to one that pitcher Dave Danforth had dealt him in 1917. Meanwhile, the game resumed, and Cleveland scored a fourth run in the fifth inning. The New Yorkers rallied for three runs off Coveleski in the ninth inning before Frank "Lefty" O'Doul hit into a force-out to end the game, 4–3. With six weeks remaining in the season, the records of the three contenders read Cleveland, 71–40, Chicago, 72–42, and New York, 72–44.

That evening, the Cleveland players waited anxiously at the Ansonia Hotel for word on Chapman's condition. At the hospital, doctors discovered that Chapman had suffered a multiple skull fracture. As his pulse grew weaker, surgeons decided on an emergency operation, which took 90 minutes. Chapman's condition seemed to improve immediately after surgery, but before long, he relapsed and died at 4:40 the next morning.

The news shocked the baseball world. Over the past 50 years, a handful of minor leaguers had died from errant pitches, but Chapman's death remains unique in major league history. The team was distraught and disconsolate. In a statement to reporters, Speaker said, "Ray Chapman was the best friend I ever had," and added, "I would give up any hopes for a championship and retire from the game, if in doing so I could bring my friend back to life."[77] Jacob Ruppert, owner of the New York team, willingly agreed to cancel the next day's game. Speaker and Joe Wood accompanied Kathleen Chapman and members of her family back to Cleveland with Chapman's body.

On the day of the funeral, Steve O'Neill and Jack Graney broke down at the Daly home. The team was scheduled to play in Boston that day, but the game was postponed, to be played as part of a doubleheader the following day. Graney was so overwrought that Napoleon Lajoie, who had come to pay his respects, put the outfielder in his automobile and drove him around the city during the services. Speaker, in seclusion at the Hotel Winton, became ill with a stomach or intestinal disorder and was ordered to bed by his physician. The Chapman funeral was originally scheduled at St. Philomena's Catholic Church. However, to accommodate the great number of people who wanted to attend, it was moved to historic St. John's Cathedral in the heart of Cleveland on Ninth Street—only a few blocks from present-day Progressive Field. With 36 priests participating, the requiem mass lasted two hours. Baseball dignitaries were in attendance, and the overflow crowd gathered on steps outside the cathedral.

Cleveland players did not accompany the funeral cortege to the burial site in nearby Lake View Cemetery because they had to hustle to catch a train to Boston. Speaker stayed behind, remained in bed, and ultimately lost 14 pounds over a five-day period. After an all-night train ride, Speaker's players arrived in Boston early in the afternoon of August 21 and went directly to Fenway Park. The mood of the team was as black as the mourning bands they wore on their uniform sleeves. Tired and downcast, the Indians were shut out, 12–0 and 4–0, by Waite Hoyt and Herb Pennock, two future Hall of Fame pitchers. To syndicated Boston writer Burt Whitman, "The Indians seemed stunned."[78] The Cleveland team was no longer in first place.

Ray Chapman remains the only major league player to be killed by a pitched ball. An outstanding shortstop, he was having another strong season when struck by a fatal pitch from Yankee pitcher Carl Mays on August 17, 1920 (National Baseball Hall of Fame, Cooperstown, New York).

The first thing Speaker did when he rejoined the team two days later was allay the anger that had spewed out against Carl Mays, particularly by certain members of the Boston and Detroit teams. Speaker spoke out firmly, "I do not hold Mays responsible in any way," and added, "I can realize that Mays took this thing as deeply as any man could, and I do not want to add anything to his burden."[79] Speaker's surmise about Mays's reaction was accurate. The New York pitcher had paced the floor of his locked hotel room during the night after the beaning, refusing even to talk to his teammates. When he heard that Chapman died, he was inconsolable. A week after the tragedy, Mays took the mound again at the Polo Grounds and pitched a shutout against Detroit. He survived hoots, howls, and curses, and went on to achieve a pitching record that still brings him consideration for election to the Hall of Fame.

Speaker finally emerged from the shock of Chapman's death and, needing more pitching support, called owner Jim Dunn. "What about Walter Mails?" "He's practically on the train from Sacramento," Dunn told the manager, and Mails joined the team on August 25. By August 30, the Indians had lost 13 of 18 games and dropped to third place behind Chicago and New York. Mails was 24, built like a football player, handsome, and talkative. He had everything, including "rabbit ears." The rookie was brash and loud: "They use round bats up here, don't they!" he told interviewers.[80] He impressed everybody, for the weakness in his armor had not yet been discovered.

"Duster" Mails won his first major league game over Washington in relief. The Indians still needed to replace the departed Chapman. "We're in another jam." Speaker told Dunn, "How about that Sewell boy down in New Orleans?"[81] Joe Sewell, a college-boy shortstop at New Orleans, was needed to replace Harry Lunte, who was batting only .197 when he was sidelined with a pulled muscle. On the recommendation of Zen Scott, University of Alabama football coach, Dunn signed the 5'6½" shortstop for a hefty $6,000, as requested by New

Orleans ownership who held his contract. It turned out to be money well invested. Sewell played his first game on September 10 and was in the lineup to stay. Forty years later, Speaker reminisced that the little Alabamian, a left-handed hitter, "was without doubt the worst hitter against left-handed pitchers I ever saw. He couldn't even come close to hitting a south-paw's curve."[82] Every morning Speaker had Sewell bat against Duster Mails—Cleveland's only left-hander—until the newcomer began to gain a little confidence and proficiency, and the drill worked, for Sewell batted .329 in the season's final 22 games.

Three teams—Cleveland, Chicago, and New York—raced to the finish line in the tightest American League pennant race since 1908. All through that eventful 1920 season, there had been an unsettling, ominous undercurrent of rumor about doings at the World Series of 1919. There was *sotto voce*, persistent talk about a "fix" the previous year—a dishonest deal that had enabled the Cincinnati Reds to beat the Chicago White Sox, five games to three. These ugly rumors surfaced on September 23, while Cleveland prepared for a three-game series with the White Sox. The two were separated by 1½ games with Cleveland in first place. The White Sox won two of the three games to cut the Indians' lead to one-half game.

On September 28, the biggest scandal in sports history drove the tight American League race between Cleveland and Chicago from the front pages. Eight members of the Chicago White Sox were indicted, along with selected gamblers, for throwing the 1919 World Series. Included were two former Tribesmen, Black Sox ringleader Chick Gandil and "Shoeless" Joe Jackson. Based upon the best resources available, the fix was inspired by these eight players, who believed they were underpaid by penurious owner Charles Comiskey, and by the greed of gamblers, particularly Arnold Rothstein, a behind-the-scenes, big-time gambler from New York.

Charles Comiskey summarily suspended the eight players with three games left in the tight American League pennant race. The following August 1921, a jury returned a verdict of "not guilty" of conspiracy. This decision, however, did not influence Judge Kenesaw Mountain Landis, newly appointed Commissioner of Baseball. In November 1921, he banned the eight players from all future contact with Organized Baseball at any level.

On a bone-chilling Saturday, October 2, some 10,000 Detroiters came to Navin Field, most of them disgusted by the revelation in Chicago and ready to cheer for a Cleveland victory. Speaker called on Bagby for the 48th time that season, and the Georgian came through splendidly, allowing only one run. The Indians tallied ten runs, helped by Speaker's three singles, three runs scored, and five difficult catches in the swirling winds. Cleveland had won its first pennant in the modern era of professional baseball! Cleveland fans were ecstatic. Prayers of *The Sporting News* and baseball fans had been answered. As columnist Joe Vila remarked, "Had the White Sox finished in front, the World Series would have been both unpopular and farcical, and the game would have fallen deeper in the slough of despond."[83]

The Tribe's victory was the best outcome that baseball could have desired. The game desperately needed several players cast in a heroic, clean-cut mold to restore the image of the national pastime, and Cleveland, in large measure, answered that call. Ray Chapman, a prototype of the clean-cut, high-minded athlete, gave his life playing the game to the hilt. Jim "Sarge" Bagby won 31 games, and Cleveland native George Uhle came directly from

Rookie Joe Sewell replaced the late Ray Chapman in August 1920. Sewell excelled in his 14-year career, 11 with Cleveland, finishing his playing days with a .312 batting average. He was inducted into the Hall of Fame in 1977 (Library of Congress).

local sandlots to don a Cleveland uniform. Ray Caldwell, who had fought the bottle as well as the opposition, won 20 games for the only time in his 12-year career, rewarding Speaker's faith in him. Gutsy 155-pound Joe Sewell set the foundation for a Hall of Fame career, and one needs to check the record book to note how many teams have posted ten players who batted .300 or better in a given season, as was true of this Cleveland team.

The 1920 World Series turned out to be baseball's best reply to cynics, the best possible antidote to the poisonous Black Sox scandal. The Indians and Brooklyn Robins slugged it out, toe-to-toe, in a seven-game Series that still stands out as a classic—the next-to-the-last time the World Series was scheduled for nine games.

There were a few problems leading into the World Series. The first was perpetrated by owner Jim Dunn. The opening game of the Series had been scheduled for Cleveland, but it did not happen that way. Optimist Dunn, in order to accommodate a larger World Series crowd, began building temporary wooden bleachers in center and right field one week before the regular season ended. Due to the delayed completion of the bleachers, league officials had to move the first game to Brooklyn's Ebbets Field, which held the same approximate number of fans as Dunn Field.

A second problem was of more serious concern to the Indians. Shortstop Joe Sewell was ineligible for the World Series, for league regulations dictated that a player must be listed on a team's roster 30 days before the end of the season. In an act of kindness seldom seen in the professional ranks, and with respect to the Chapman tragedy, league officials and Charles Ebbets graciously gave Sewell permission to play.

On October 5, nearly 24,000 were on hand to watch the Series opener on a raw, blustery day. In the press box, Ebbets slipped each sportswriter a half-pint of whiskey to keep warm. One writer was so appreciative that he thanked Ebbets for the booze in his story. The problem was that Prohibition was the law. The next day, U.S. Treasury agents searched the press box and Ebbets' office, determined to keep the writers sober. They found nothing since Ebbets had been alerted about the raid and had stashed the illegal liquor.[84]

Speaker's choice to pitch in the opening game was Stan Coveleski. Wilbert "Robbie" Robinson of the Robins countered with Cleveland native Rube Marquard, who was in the twilight of his career. Coveleski threw his spitter effectively, limiting the Dodgers to only one run and five hits. Cleveland also garnered only five hits but two were run-scoring doubles by Speaker, sparking a Tribe victory.

The Indians ran into difficulty in the next two games. In Game Two of the Series, Brooklyn's ace, Burleigh Grimes, defeated Jim Bagby and the Tribe, 3–0. Grimes, too, was headed to the Hall of Fame. Brooklyn showed signs of life in the third game, when over 25,000 Flatbush fans packed Ebbets Field to see Sherry Smith outpitch Duster Mails for a 2–1 victory. Cleveland's only run came in the fourth inning when Speaker lined a hit into the left field corner and circled the bases after Zack Wheat let the ball go through his legs.

A downcast "Sunny" Jim Dunn left the Polo Grounds with Tris Speaker. Trailing Brooklyn two games to one, the owner had reason to be worried. Speaker allayed his fears, telling his boss that the Tribe would win the next four games. A first-rate soothsayer, Speaker kept his word as the Dodgers were never in the lead during the remainder of the Series. In fact, the Brooklyn team scored only two more runs off the superlative Indians pitching staff.

With a police escort, both teams hurried to the Pennsylvania Terminal to catch separate trains to Cleveland for the fourth game. When the Indians' train pulled into Union Station at 9 a.m., they were greeted by factory whistles and bells. A mass of people met them; thousands of others lined the route carrying the players to the Hollenden Hotel. A *New York Times* reporter wrote, "Here is one place where no one is talking about the crooked work in last year's World Series."[85]

The effect of the Indians' first World Series in downtown Cleveland was electric. Business in the city was at a standstill, and thousands gathered on downtown streets, seeking the last word on each Series game. It was tense for four straight days amidst good weather for early October. No newspapers on Sunday, no radio broadcasts, and no beer—at any rate, not legally. In Public Square, crowds gathered and watched the progress of each game on an 18 × 24-foot scoreboard, displaying play-by-play action. The "ball" was celluloid and "players" were represented by lozenges—diamond shaped. Only 26,000 fans could cram into "cracker box" Dunn Field.

Speaker exuded confidence. On Saturday, October 9, 25,734 fans packed the expanded Dunn Field. Fans maintained a cacophony of horns, auto sirens, and cowbells. Coveleski's spitball was working, and he easily gained his second victory in the Series, 5–1. The Series was tied at two games each. Before the game on Sunday, October 10, scalpers were selling $5.50 tickets for $30, and box seats for four were fetching $100. Rube Marquard, Game One starter for the Robins, also wanted in on the big bucks and tried to sell $52.80 worth of tickets for $300. He was nabbed by policemen and later fined $25 for ticket scalping. Ebbets was so incensed by Marquard's behavior that he traded him to Cincinnati after the Series.

Over the years, the fifth game of the Series has received more publicity and coverage

Tris Speaker crosses home plate with the only run of the sixth game in the 1920 World Series. One game later, the Indians were crowned World Champions for the first time (courtesy Scott H. Longert).

than any one World Series game. It is what journalists call a "classic." The game itself was decided in the early innings when Cleveland scored eight runs off Burleigh Grimes and Clarence Mitchell, Brooklyn's other spitball pitcher.

The first of three memorable events occurred in the initial inning with Cleveland at bat. The bases were loaded when Elmer Smith stepped up to the plate to face Grimes. Smith, a left-hander, was a local favorite from nearby Sandusky. A journeyman player, Smith had played for five teams in ten years, saving his best year for 1920, batting .315. Thin of face with a wiry, muscular build, Smith sent Grimes's fourth pitch over the 20-foot screen above the right field wall and over the temporary bleachers. His bases-loaded home run was the first ever hit in World Series play. The cheers from the astounded crowd thundered throughout the city.

Not to be outdone, with two outs and two on in the fourth inning, pitcher Jim Bagby, Sr., slammed a three-run homer into the temporary seats in right-center field. Bagby's home run was the first for a pitcher in the World Series. The editor of the *Reach Guide*, with a bit of sarcasm, described the blow: "Bagby's homer ... was merely a piece of luck, as the ball fell just inside of the temporary bleachers in right center, which seats should not have been permitted to encroach on the playing field."[86]

The climax to all of these fireworks occurred in the fifth inning. Ohio native Bill Wambsganss recorded the first unassisted triple play in World Series history. Bagby, buoyed by a seven-run lead, allowed singles to the first two batters. In Lawrence Ritter's *The Glory of Their Times*, Wamby recounted what happened next with men on first and second, and Clarence Mitchell, the Robins' pitcher—and a pretty good left-handed hitter—at the plate:

> I figured to play pretty deep for him, not especially caring whether we got a double play or not.... So I played way back on the grass. Bagby served up a fast ball that Mitchell smacked on a rising line toward center field, a little over to my right—that is, to my second base side. I made an instinctive running leap for the ball, and just managed to jump high enough to catch it in my glove. One out!
>
> The impetus of my run and leap carried me toward second base, and as I continued.... I saw Pete Kilduff still running toward third. He thought it was a sure hit ... and was on his way. There I was, the ball in my glove and him with his back to me, so I just kept going and touched second with my toe [Out two] and looked to my left.... Otto Miller from first base was just standing there, with his mouth open, no more than a few feet from me. I simply took a step or two and touched him lightly on the shoulder, and that was it. Three outs and I started running to the dugout.[87]

For all practical purposes, the Series was over for the Brooklynites. Bagby won this history-making fifth game, 8–1, although allowing 13 hits.

For the sixth game, Speaker gave the ball to left-hander Walter Mails, who deserved this opportunity after his late-season heroics. Furthermore, he had a grudge against Wilbert Robinson. With Brooklyn in 1916, "Uncle Robbie" Robinson had used Mails a mere 17 innings, then released him. Before the game, Mails spoke with bravado: "Brooklyn will be lucky to get a foul off me.... If Spoke and the boys will give me one run, we'll win."[88] A man of his word, Mails' phantom sore arm disappeared, and he pitched a beautiful three-hit shutout before 27,000 happy fans. As requested, the Indians scratched out one run in the sixth inning off pitcher Sherry Smith when Speaker singled and scored on a double by George Burns.

One of the most notable teams in franchise history, the 1920 Cleveland Indians included Hall of Famers Tris Speaker, Stan Coveleski, and Joe Sewell, plus Jim Bagby, Sr., with 31 victories (courtesy Scott H. Longert).

In modern-day baseball, "Stan the Man" was a reference to St. Louis Cardinals great Stan Musial. In the 1920 World Series, the slogan might have been "Stan Was the Man," referring to pitcher Stan Coveleski, who wrapped up the World Series in the seventh game with a 3–0 shutout in spite of three Cleveland errors. Coveleski's three Series victories matched those of the great Christy Mathewson, who won three games, all shutouts, in the 1905 World Series. Coveleski posted a 0.74 ERA for the Series.

After two decades of frustration, the Cleveland Indians were finally World Champions. As the seventh game ended, Speaker raced to the infield, grabbed the ball from Wamby, and went to owner Dunn's field box. He gave the ball to a tearfully happy old lady celebrating the victory and her 75th birthday at the same time. "We did it, Mother," he said as he hugged his biggest fan.[89] The fans celebrated in many ways for a week, ending in a civic outdoor fete at Wade Park, on the East Side, where 50,000 fans cheered their idols and fought for autographs. There was no hint of the darkness that had enveloped the 1919 classic. The players quickly departed for their respective homes with a $4,204 World Series check. Each Robin received $2,387. Besides Mails and Sewell, Kathleen Daly Chapman also received a full share.

Despite tragedy and infamy, the Cleveland franchise had a great season, and the Indians looked forward to a bright future. From here on, the ominous shadow of the New York Yankees was to lie across League Park, Municipal Stadium, and all other American League parks. Indians fans would not taste this kind of victory again for 28 years.

4

The Roaring Twenties
and New Ownership

"I will never be a bench manager."
—Tris Speaker in an interview June 1921

Celebration of the 1920 World Championship continued for days. No championship team ever had been treated more enthusiastically by employers or admirers. On the day after the World Series, the team met for a farewell in their Dunn Field dressing room. Owner Jim Dunn and Tris Speaker were ecstatic. Dunn made a short speech: "I hope ... that you will all be back with us next season."[1] He did not have to worry about holdouts, for raises were granted to nearly all players, and they immediately signed their 1921 contracts. In addition, he had given each player a bonus equal to ten days' pay. The players reciprocated with an engraved watch for Speaker and a set of diamond-studded cuff links for the beaming "Sunny" Jim Dunn.

With the announcement of additional indictments against eight "Black Sox" players, however, post–World Series stories were shunted to the back of newspapers. Meanwhile, the owners realized they had failed in management of their own affairs with a three-man league commission.

A suit had been brought against organized baseball by the Federal League in 1915. The Feds charged organized baseball with being a combination, conspiracy, and monopoly in contravention of the anti-trust laws. This issue was taken to the United States District of Northern Illinois, with future baseball commissioner Judge Kenesaw Mountain Landis presiding. The Feds doubtless chose Landis's court mindful of his reputation as a trust-buster. They did not know, or chose to ignore, that Landis was also a baseball fan.

Never one to permit judicial impartiality to interfere with his personal biases, Landis took the case under advisement and stalled making a decision for a year. Meanwhile, the Feds abjured legal reprisals against the contract jumpers to the Federal League. By then World War I had ended and the need for a court ruling was obviated.[2]

The Black Sox scandal did not deter the World Champions from preparing for a repeat performance. Management and Speaker decided to move spring training from New Orleans to a new site in Dallas. At the time, New Orleans had minimized prostitution, and liquor had become illegal, although it was still available in unsanctioned forms. However, players had lost considerable sums of money at local racing tracks in New Orleans the previous spring. In addition, a move to Dallas permitted the Clevelanders a better opportunity to fill out their spring training schedule with six other major league teams encamped there.

In the spring of 1906, John McGraw had outfitted his New York Giants uniform with the words "World Champions" written on the shirts. The Giants had disposed of the Philadelphia Athletics in five games in 1905. Dunn wanted to make sure that no one forgot that Cleveland was number one in the baseball world. When the 1921 season opened, the Tribe sported new uniforms minus the familiar block "C" on the chest. In its place were the words "World's Champions." Sportswriter "Whitey" Lewis wrote that the players believed they deserved this recognition on their "work clothes," and were not embarrassed to wear them.[3] Baseball historian Morris Eckhouse considered the uniforms "somewhat ostentatious." No doubt the uniform would annoy Tribe opponents in 1921. For the next six seasons, the Indians were unable to capture the magic of 1920, although they nearly did in 1921, posting the second-best record in club history to date (94–60).

Speaker, Dunn, and many prognosticators were convinced that the Cleveland team would repeat in 1921. This prediction would have seemed less likely had the Indians begun the season without their center fielder. Speaker, possibly exhausted by the triumphant but traumatic previous season, or perhaps wanting to leave the game while on top, planned to retire. According to Charles Alexander, Tris Speaker's biographer, Dunn talked him out of retiring. When asked if he would retire as a player but continue to manage, Speaker was adamant, "I will never be a bench manager."[4]

Before the home opener, Cleveland management publicly announced that League Park ushers would no longer bother fans about returning foul balls. Customers were expected to abide by the honor system and return the balls, but management would not make a scene about it. Fridays were designated as Ladies Day, with bleacher seats available for a ten cent "war tax."

The Indians' new uniforms did not intimidate the New York Yankees or St. Louis Browns, both seeking their first pennant. Miller Huggins, irascible yet erudite manager of the New Yorkers, quipped, "The Yankees are wonderfully equipped ... to make a hard and determined fight of it," and in a moment of candor admitted, "We fear only Cleveland."[5]

Unbeknownst to Huggins, the Indians soon experienced a sad lesson about the fickleness of fate. During spring training, Bill Wambsganss, now a well-known name in major league baseball history, broke his arm and missed a third of the season. Harry Lunte, his best available replacement, was injured and missed the whole season. Catcher Steve O'Neill broke a finger early in the campaign and could not resume catching until mid–July. A month later, backup catcher Les Nunamaker broke his leg, and Speaker, in the heat of the pennant race, twisted his knee on September 11 and was out for the season.

In addition, much was expected of pitcher Duster Mails, an important cog late in the 1920 pennant race. Self-acclaimed as "The Great," Mails soon acquired another nickname, "Rabbit Ears," bestowed upon him by Ty Cobb. The two played in a winter league in California after the 1920 season ended. Cobb began to "rib" Mails about his luck in winning seven consecutive games the previous season, about his great break in picking up all that

World Series money, and about the World Series game in Brooklyn that Ray Caldwell had to start because Mails had the jitters.

"So that's why Brooklyn let you go," chided Cobb. "You can't take it. You're a busher, Mails.... Wait until we get you back east next summer. Buddy, you'd better cover up your ears."[6] Mails now had a new nickname. His "rabbit ears" were tuned in to every bench jockey in the American League. Even with cotton in his ears, Mails could not keep from being rattled by disparaging remarks from coaches and the bench. Led by Cobb, he was driven out of the major leagues. Amazingly, he compiled a 14–8 record in 1921, but very little after that. After winning only four games in 1922, he was shipped to the minor leagues.[7]

Huggins was not aware of all the Tribe's miseries nor did he expect such a year from Babe Ruth. Sportswriter Heywood Hale Broun coined the phrase, "The Ruth is mighty and shall prevail."[8] This was an understatement for the 1921 season. Cleveland had already withstood Ruth's record-setting 1920 offensive onslaught. Ruth's 1921 season is still considered by many baseball historians as the single greatest offensive performance in baseball annals.

Ruth batted .378, hit 59 home runs, drove in 171 runs, and scored 177 runs. His slugging average of .846 is the third highest ever recorded, eclipsed by his .847 slugging average of 1920 and Barry Bond's record .863 in 2001. In addition, Ruth stroked 44 doubles (surpassed by Speaker's league-leading 52) and 16 triples, drew 144 walks, and even stole 17 bases.

The Indians struggled mightily against the first real New York Yankees juggernaut. However, in mid-season the team realized another incentive. The infamous Chicago Black Sox were found not guilty of charges of criminal conspiracy associated with the 1919 World Series. The Chicago courts were unable to bring any eastern gamblers to the witness stand, placing the prosecution in an untenable position. The Cleveland players believed that the White Sox, having been banned in the last days of the 1920 season, had prevented them from winning a clean moral victory on the field.

In spite of the late-season effort of rookie Riggs Stephenson, the injury-riddled season literally ended with Speaker being laid up. With ten days remaining in the season, the Indians held out hope and in fact were only two percentage points behind New York. Arriving in the Polo Grounds for a crucial four-game series, the Tribe lost three of the games. Only George Uhle, future pitching mainstay, was able to shut down the Yankees, who won their first of 43 league championships. The Tribe finished 4½ games behind in second place.

For the rest of his life, Speaker believed that the Tribe was the better team and should have won their second pennant. He likely would have had added that he never expected the loss of productivity of pitchers Jim Bagby, Sr., and Raymond Caldwell, whose victory production dropped from 51 victories the previous year to 20. Only Stan Coveleski met expectations with 23 victories.

The Indians' 1922 season was interrupted when on June 9, owner Jim Dunn died at the age of 57. Dunn, second owner of the Tribe, willed the team to his wife Edith. She was ably assisted by trusted and beloved Ernest "Barney" Barnard, who served as president of the team until November of 1927. Dunn had distinguished himself as a "players' owner." In the annals of Cleveland Indians history, he presented the loyal fans with one of Cleveland's two World Championships over a 114-year period.

From 1922 through 1925, ball players streamed in and out of Dunn Field as though it were Union Station. The team as a whole had aged. Twelve-year veteran Jack Graney retired in 1922. Others who left were Stuffy McInnis, Louis Guisto—still suffering from gas attacks in the recent war—Ted Oldenwald, Sherry Smith, and Pat McNulty. A major trade in 1924 sent Steve O'Neill, Bill Wambsganss, outfielder Joe Connolly and pitcher Danny Boone to the Boston Red Sox. In exchange, the Indians received infielder Chick Fewster, catcher Roxie Walters, and returning, popular first baseman George Burns. Burns, born in Niles, Ohio, had a most unusual stance at the plate. He stood with his feet together and his body ramrod straight. How he snapped out of this military stance in time to swing remained a mystery.[9] Regardless, he was a consistent .300 hitter and a valuable addition to the team.

As the Indians were breaking up, losing old-timers and acquiring new talent, George Uhle soon became the ace of the pitching staff and began to hone his pitching skills. A native of Cleveland, he developed a cross-fire pitch and a slider to go with his control and coolness on the mound. "Ukelele" Uhle, as his teammates called him, won 22 games in 1922 and 26 in 1923 before having a couple of down years and regaining his winning ways in 1926. Indeed, Uhle was Cleveland's only mainstay on the mound as the team gradually slipped downward in the standings.

The last major trade of this era was the loss of Stan Coveleski, who was sent to the Washington Senators in 1924 for two players of little help to the Indians. Coveleski ended his great nine-year career pitching at Cleveland with two losing seasons. But he was not finished. In 1925, Coveleski rallied to win 20 games and lose five, helping the Senators win their second consecutive pennant, only to lose the World Series to the Pittsburgh Pirates in seven games. A key loss was the second game of the Series when Coveleski allowed one run in seven innings before shortstop Roger Peckinpaugh's two errors in the eighth inning allowed Pittsburgh to win the game, 3–2. The unfortunate Peckinpaugh, a future manager of the Indians (1928–1933), committed a record-breaking eight errors in the World Series.[10]

After their valiant effort in 1921, the Tribe slipped to fourth place in 1922 with a 78–76 record, a disappointment to team ownership. The team had earlier acquired first baseman Stuffy McInnis from the Red Sox for offensive help, but the failure of several pitchers and injuries were too much to overcome. Only manager Tris Speaker continued outstanding hitting with a .378 average, good for third place in the race for the batting championship behind George Sisler's .420 and Ty Cobb's .401.

Cleveland improved slightly in 1923, finishing in third place, barely behind the Detroit Tigers. The team was led by George Uhle, who led the American League in victories (26), complete games (30), and innings pitched (357⅔). Speaker continued his torrid hitting with a .380 average, which again left him in third place, this time behind Detroit's Harry Heilmann (.403) and New York's Babe Ruth (.393).

Baseball in the 1920s was slowly experiencing a transition in the acquisition of future major leaguers. The existing players mainly came from scouting efforts, a small number of minor leagues, a modest number from colleges and universities, and finally, many came from the sandlots. Sophisticated farm systems, such as Branch Rickey's farm system for the Cardinals, American Legion programs, baseball academies and camps, and high-powered high school and collegiate baseball programs had not yet come on the scene. Little League and Hot-Stove League programs for youth did not take hold until the late 1930s.

Cleveland at this stage acquired three players who were privy to these forthcoming advances in baseball recruitment and instruction. First there was Riggs Stephenson, a muscular outfielder and former football player at the University of Alabama. "Old Hoss," as he was called, could hit but was an erratic thrower, with little finesse or savvy. A frustrated Speaker tried numerous ways to help the slugger throw more accurately, either in the infield or outfield. Stephenson rebelled, was released and was picked up by the Chicago Cubs. After nine seasons with them, his career batting average was .336.

In 1925, Cleveland, desperate for pitching, signed 260-pound left-hander Garland Buckeye—an appropriate name for one pitching in Ohio. He had pitched one game in the major leagues for the Washington Senators in 1918. Buckeye played semi-pro baseball for seven years while working as a banker in Chicago. He performed admirably for the Indians, posting the team's best pitching record in 1925 (13–8). The one-year wonder, no longer effective, retired after three years.

Finally, there is the success story of Joe Sewell. After the death of Ray Chapman in 1920, the Indians signed Sewell from the New Orleans Pelicans. In his first game, he made an error on the first ball hit to him and popped up to third base on his first at-bat. Sitting on the bench, watching the speed and power of the major league game, he kept repeating, "I don't belong up here."[11] The diminutive shortstop soon made certain that he did belong. He worked diligently to overcome a weakness against curve balls, particularly from left-handed pitchers. Sewell went on to play 11 of his 14 years in the majors with Cleveland. He batted .312, and most notably, struck out only 114 times in 7,132 at-bats. Sewell was inducted into the Hall of Fame in 1977.

The next two years, 1924–1925, were down years for the Clevelanders as the team finished in sixth place both years. Even the raging New York Yankees did poorly in 1925, finishing one notch below the Tribe. The Indians were beset with injuries and illnesses throughout the 1924 season. The pitching fell apart. George Uhle had a 9–15 record, and Stan Coveleski's nine-year tenure with the Tribe came to an end. Speaker continued his steady hitting with a .344 average, and Sewell led the team with 106 RBI.

For the most part, the 1925 season was a repeat of 1924, except that the team won three more games. Player-manager Tris Speaker hit one of his 12 home runs on Opening Day, helping Cleveland defeat St. Louis, 21–14, as Cleveland scored 12 runs in the eighth inning. Speaker went on to tally a .389 batting average, the best of his 22-year playing career. The rest of the season was downhill, particularly due to a lack of pitching.

The Indians' performance was such that by late July, fickle Indians fans and the influential local press began to cry for Speaker's scalp. President Barnard, a close friend of the press, resolved the issue by quickly signing the manager to a new contract through the 1926 season. Again, Speaker did not win the batting title as outfielder Harry Heilmann of Detroit eclipsed him by four points, batting .393.

The prospects for the Indians did not look much better in 1926. Speaker was determined "to right the ship" in his last year as manager of the Tribe. There had been little, if any, meaningful personnel changes except for the acquisition of Johnny Hodapp, who became an important component in the Cleveland lineup after 1926.

In many ways, this club was one of the most remarkable in Cleveland history. The pennant race did not figure to be close with a strong Yankees team ready to break out of the gate. Cleveland made a race because of two Georges—pitcher George Uhle and first baseman George Burns. Both had their career-best seasons and held the team together during the first half of the season.

The club started out well for the first three weeks, then faltered and dropped into fifth place. The team jelled in July and August and made a spirited drive to overtake the Yankees. In early August, the Tribe celebrated when manager Speaker stroked his 700th career double. The players were inspired by the accomplishment of right-hander Dutch Levsen on August 28. Pitching against the Red Sox, Levsen became the last major leaguer to pitch complete-game victories in a doubleheader. He allowed just four hits in each game without striking out a batter.

Led by Speaker, Sewell, Uhle, and Burns, the Indians were set to make a final run toward glory in a key six-game series against the league-leading New Yorkers. Dunn Field was filled to capacity for the first game, and the five-day series drew the largest successive crowds since the 1920 World Series, well over 100,000 fans.

On September 15, the Yankees increased their lead to 6½ games by defeating George Uhle, 6–4. The following day Levsen and George Myatt were superb on the mound, winning a doubleheader, 2–1 and 5–0. The Indians continued their charge, winning the next two games, 5–1 and 3–1, against Waite Hoyt and Urban Shocker, two of the Yankees' best pitchers.

The Indians were now only 2½ games out of first place. Before an overflow crowd of more than 30,000 fans, the Yankees salvaged the Sunday finale, 8–3, as Levsen was shelled hard and left in the game in the seventh inning after the Yankees had scored all of their runs. New York was led by the heart of Murderer's Row, Lou Gehrig with three doubles and a home run, and Babe Ruth with an inside-the-park home run, his 43rd of the season.

For all practical purposes, the season was over for the Tribe, who finished in second place, three games behind the Yankees. The individual Tribe stars of that season were George Burns, who with a .358 batting average, 216 hits, a major league record 64 doubles, and 114 RBI earned the Most Valuable Player award for the American League. George Uhle led the American League with 27 victories, 318⅓ innings pitched, and 32 complete games, a statistic unheard-of in present-day baseball. Meanwhile, Speaker recorded one of the worst years of his career, batting only .304. Now 38, Speaker was tired and beginning to feel the strain on his legs. He also suffered mental disappointment with the Indians' failure to win the 1926 pennant.[12]

It would be 14 years before the Indians would again challenge for a pennant. Speaker, for one of the few times in his managing career, came under serious criticism. Henry Edwards, the dean of Cleveland baseball writers, questioned why the manager left Dutch Levsen on the mound so long in the final game and why he did not start a left-handed pitcher in the crucial sixth game of the Yankees series. The reporter said, "I am told, that there was a lack of cooperation between ... Speaker and some of his veteran players," and added that "Speaker's mistakes are the result of his failure to give his job more of his time and thought."[13]

Instead of attending the World Series in which the St. Louis Cardinals upset the New York Yankees, Speaker and Ty Cobb, avid hunters, were off to the Grand Tetons for big-game hunting. Charles Alexander summarized, "What awaited them upon their return would call into question their integrity and dramatically and painfully alter the course of their careers."[14]

The baseball world was shocked when on November 2, 1926, Cobb resigned as manager of the Detroit Tigers and soon thereafter was released. One month later, Tris Speaker resigned as manager of the Tribe and indicated he was going into business with David R. Jones, a rising stamping works industrialist in Cleveland.

Baseball fans everywhere, particularly in Cleveland and Detroit, received news they preferred not to hear or read. In the fall of 1926, Commissioner Landis received a correspondence from pitcher Hubert "Dutch" Leonard. Leonard had won 139 games during his 11-year career with the Red Sox and Tigers. He had come out of a two-year retirement in 1924 to aid Cobb's depleted pitching staff, only to be placed on waivers the following year despite an 11–4 record. Cobb believed Leonard was lazy and was not impressed with his inflated 4.51 ERA. Leonard swore revenge on Cobb and added Speaker to his list when Speaker declined to claim Leonard on waivers for the Indians.[15]

Leonard's revenge took the form of revealing letters written by Cobb and "Smoky" Joe Wood, then an outfielder for Cleveland, to Leonard on a supposedly fixed game late in the 1919 season between Cleveland and Detroit at Navin Field. The White Sox had clinched the pennant, the Indians were assured of second place, and Detroit was fighting the Yankees for third place, which would mean a small share of the World Series players' pools.

After the game of September 24, Cobb, Wood, Leonard, and Speaker allegedly met under the Navin Field stands to talk baseball, and Cobb hoped the Tigers could finish in third place. Speaker was supposed to have assured Cobb that the Tigers would defeat the Tribe the next day, September 25. Wood's letter left no doubt that wagers were placed by himself and Leonard on that particular day. Speaker's name was not mentioned in either Cobb's or Wood's letter, a fact that was not lost on Landis as he investigated the matter.

The Tigers won the game, 9–5, with the *Plain Dealer* noting that "it did not seem like a real championship game ... with nothing really at stake.... If there was chicanery involved it failed, Detroit finished a half game behind the Yankees and out of the money."[16]

Landis probed Leonard's accusations cautiously, since the reputations of two legendary players were on the line. Landis was fond of both Speaker and Cobb personally, and his admiration of them as ball players knew no limits. This feeling may have entered into his decision, but from the evidence, and to the joy of fans, both men were cleared of charges.

As the details of the Speaker-Cobb travesty unfolded, Landis stormed out of his office exclaiming, "Won't these God damn things that happened before I came into baseball ever slow coming up?"[17] Landis vowed to uncover the truth of these findings from Leonard's charges. Uncovering more damaging charges and punishing two of baseball's icons was not Leonard's desire. He realized that it was in his best interests to soft-pedal his approach. The commissioner had just signed a seven-year extended contract with a salary increase of 30 percent to sixty-five thousand dollars. Even President Calvin Coolidge did not make that kind of money.

Other factors influenced his cautious moves on this highly convoluted imbroglio. First and foremost, Ban Johnson, an ailing and spiteful president of the American League, despised

Landis and tried to do anything he could to embarrass the commissioner. Landis had to protect his backside.

Secondly, Dutch Leonard failed to appear for a scheduled hearing to confront his former teammates as alleged co-conspirators. His life might have been in danger with a person like Ty Cobb on the other side. The knuckle-ball pitcher had received $20,000 in "blood money" from Ban Johnson. In no way was he going to leave his farm in Fresno, California.

Lastly, Cobb and Speaker wisely hired two reputable attorneys who demanded that Landis rescind the Johnson "order" directing Cobb and Speaker to take retirement. Behind the scenes, it was agreed that Cobb and Speaker would not manage in the major leagues again.

As the years went by, columnists like Henry Edwards, Shirley Povich, and Arthur Daley helped create the image of Landis ruling with an iron hand, determined to keep baseball free from any image of wrongdoing or scandal. Author Timothy Gay said it best:

> All the stories they [journalists] wrote about Landis made good copy, but they weren't an accurate reflection of Landis's real motivation. Nobody back then wanted to confront the game's seedy realities—not the lords of baseball and certainly not the columnists who covered it. So they went along the canard that.... Landis had saved baseball from the wretches of gambling.[18]

And so on January 17, Landis issued his official verdict: "These players have not been, nor are they now, found guilty of fixing a ball game. By no decent system of justice could such finding be made."[19] The players could have sued major league baseball for "defamation of character," as suggested by Charles Evans Hughes, chief justice of the Supreme Court. Speaker chose not to retire and was signed by Clark Griffith of the Washington Senators, and Cobb went to Connie Mack's Athletics. In 1928, both joined forces to play with the Athletics, after which season both future Hall of Famers retired from the playing field. Johnson's health began to deteriorate and the American League owners implored him to take a sabbatical in the winter of 1927. After a brief respite, he retired and died March 28, 1931.

Speaker's career was replete with outstanding statistics, one remaining as a major league record—792 doubles. At the time of his retirement, his 223 triples stood sixth on the all-time list and his 3,514 career hits and .345 lifetime batting average placed him fifth in both categories. He was elected to the Hall of Fame in 1937, a member of the second group to be selected for induction.

During the next two decades (1927–1946), the history of the Cleveland franchise is what author Henry W. Thomas has termed "a study in the consequences of failure to live up to expectations." With little knowledge or savvy about operating a major league franchise, ownership was often harassed by a knowledgeable press and cheered or booed by a loyal fan base. The millionaire owners would soon take over, and fans would need a scorecard to keep track of who was managing the Indians.

In 1927, the club lost its rudder when principal owner Mrs. Emily Dunn sold the team to a group of local real estate magnates and businessmen, and team president Ernest S. Barnard left to become president of the American League. In 19 years beginning in 1928, the Tribe would finish in the first division 12 times, neither winning the pennant nor finishing in last place.

The list of new owners read like a "Who's Who of Cleveland." The Alva Bradley family had a long history in Cleveland. Bradley's grandfather, also named Alva, had pioneered the shipping business on Lake Erie, and Bradley's father Morris continued the prosperity of the family with railroad development in the greater Cleveland area.[20] A second investor was Bradley's brother Charles. Additional owners were John Sherwin, Sr., of the Sherwin-Williams paint conglomerate, Percy Morgan, head of a lithographing company, former Secretary of War Newton D. Baker, and two brothers—Mantis J. and Otis P. Van Sweringen—who revitalized downtown Cleveland.[21] This syndicate paid $975,000 for the team, an outrageous sum in that time.

The investors believed Alva Bradley, an avid baseball fan, would be an ideal president for the franchise. He was quickly elected to that position, where he remained for 19 years. At the time of his election, he was in his early forties. Eventually, he became president of the Cleveland Chamber of Commerce. *Cleveland Press* sports writer Franklin Lewis described him as "suave, even-tempered and inclined to adopt a conciliatory view of disputes."[22] The new president would be severely tested over several headline-grabbing issues encountered by the team in the 1930s.

Bradley immediately changed the name of Dunn Field back to League Park, as it had been called before 1916. With the departure of the erudite Barnard, Bradley was in need of a general manager, but none of the board members was particularly knowledgeable about the inner workings of a major league franchise. For years, Bradley had observed with favor Billy Evans, erect and broad-shouldered, who had become dean of umpires in the American League. He was the same individual who recommended that the U.S. President throw out the first pitch to start the season. (President William Howard Taft, a baseball devotee, fulfilled this duty on April 14, 1910.)

An ambitious man, Evans signed a three-year contract at a salary of between $30,000 and $40,000 per year. Evans was the first baseball executive ever to hold the title of general manager.[23] There was rejoicing among the stockholders. Writing for the *Plain Dealer*, Henry Edwards exclaimed, "Cleveland's fondest hope—our Indians owned by Clevelanders, operated as a civic enterprise as well as a money-making vehicle, and eventually playing in a great new municipal stadium on the lake-front—came a step nearer realization.[24] Now the owners wanted their broom to sweep as cleanly as possible. A new manager was needed, and the gate to a graveyard for Tribe managers opened for the first time under the Bradley regime.

When Tris Speaker resigned at the end of the 1926 season, the Indians promoted Coach Jack McAllister to the managership. He had neither played nor managed previously in the major leagues. His one claim to fame occurred in the 1920 World Series. While coaching third base, he noticed that Brooklyn Robins second baseman Peter Kilduff would throw dirt in his glove to counter the effects of a wet ball, tipping off Tribe batters that Burleigh Grimes was about to throw a spitter.[25] The Indians tumbled from second place to sixth place in 1927 and McAllister was relieved of his duties.

After some deliberation, Bradley and Evans settled on Roger Peckinpaugh as the Indians' new manager. Peckinpaugh was a favorite for several reasons. He was a native Ohioan who had begun his career with the Indians. He was sold to the New York Yankees, where he later served briefly as manager in 1914. He finished his 17-year playing career with the Washington Senators and Chicago White Sox. A classic journeyman player, Peckinpaugh demonstrated leadership qualities of a manager in the big leagues. In later years, Bradley described his new manager as "sound and scrupulously honest in all his dealings. I never had to fear that he might get the club in trouble."[26]

Prior to the 1928 season, the Cleveland team, now under new ownership and management, prepared for better things. General manager Billy Evans, with a definite collegiate tone, signed the first Jewish player to appear on the roster of the local club, shortstop Jonah Goldman, late of Syracuse University.[27] Henry Edwards' appointment to the American League's service bureau left a vacancy in the *Plain Dealer's* sports department. Gordon Cobbledick, who had played football at Case Tech and had held several menial positions at the *Plain Dealer*, was appointed baseball reporter to replace Edwards. Over the years, the sharp-tongued reporter's reputation elevated him to the title of "dean of Cleveland sports writers."

On February 19, 1928, Cobbledick's column carried the headline, "Vanguard Will Board Rattler Late At Night."[28] A portion of the team and Cobbledick, who was making his first spring training trip, left the old Union Station in downtown Cleveland bound for New Orleans. The training camp had been moved from Lakeland, Florida. This move was a concession to the team's ownership, a few local patrons and Governor Huey P. Long, all of whom shared a common interest in certain railroads that went through Louisiana to New Orleans. The New Orleans Pelicans, the Cleveland team's primary minor league franchise, provided worthy opposition for practice games.

Early in the spring, the Tribe repeatedly beat up on the Triple-A Pelicans. The new club president beamed as he entertained Billy Evans and Roger Peckinpaugh with cocktails. It was 1928, and cocktails were illegal but obtainable if one knew a fellow named Louie, which nearly every adult did. "Gentlemen," said the abstemious Bradley, sipping delicately on his Coke. "I'm enormously pleased. I believe we've got a pretty good team." Evans's reply was prompt and emphatic. "Mr. Bradley, we've got a lousy team."[29] Early in his tenure, Evans indicated he would not be a "yes" man.

Evans was right. The Indians finished in seventh place that season—only by the grace of the Boston Red Sox. But in 1929, they bounced back up to third place, and over the next seven years were never out of the first division. In fact, the Clevelanders finished out of the first division only four times in 28 years beginning in 1929. Evans was operating head in the front office. How much credit can be given to Evans for this enviable record is, no doubt, debatable.

Evans was determined to build a more powerful team offensively. Bradley went along with this idea and even took a stab at recruiting more offense himself. The owner admitted that he knew little about the business of baseball. The New York Yankees' "Larrupin' Lou" Gehrig was holding out for a pay raise. He had hit .373 in 1927, his third full season in the major leagues. The Cleveland owner made an initial offering of $150,000 for this first baseman. He was rebuffed several times by Ed Barrow, the crafty business manager of the Yankees. Bradley finally offered $250,000 for Gehrig, an astronomical figure in the 1920s, and was again rejected. As might be expected, Barrow closed the door by signing the former Columbia University Lion.[30]

Evans had a free rein and the millionaires' checkbooks to search for additional firepower. He went to the West Coast to check talent in the Pacific Coast League, which was rapidly approaching the major league level in playing quality. Evans checked out the highly regarded outfield of the San Francisco Seals, including left-handed batters Roy Johnson, Smead Jolley, and Earl Averill. Johnson had great speed, good power, and a strong throwing arm. Unfortunately, he had made a commitment to the Detroit Tigers. Jolley was a powerful hitter who was clumsy in the outfield. He did not impress Evans.[31]

The least impressive was left-handed outfielder Averill, from Snohomish, Washington, a small sawmill town directly north of Seattle. During his childhood, Averill, who lost his father when he was two, worked in the sawmill, but he had a talent for baseball. Local sportsmen recognized his abilities and helped to bankroll his rise through the minor leagues. Married at the age of 22 and father of a son, Averill's financial situation was dire. Modest and quiet, Averill was eventually signed by Evans for $50,000 and two players. The rookie would be poor no longer. Called "Rock" by his teammates for his sinewy physique, Averill was described by sportswriter Franklin Lewis as having the body of a "watch-charm football guard." When owner Alva Bradley first saw Averill, he asked Evans, "You mean we paid all that money for a midget?"[32]

Averill had a strange batting stance. He stood with his feet fairly close together, crowding the plate, and swung his bat with his body instead of "stepping into" the pitch with a snap and lash of the wrists (somewhat like Ichiro Suzuki). It did not take long for Averill to show Bradley why he was worth the money. On Opening Day at League Park in 1929, Averill faced the Detroit Tigers' crafty left-hander, Earl Whitehill. In the first inning, with two out and no one on base, Whitehill quickly ran the count to two strikes and no balls. On the next pitch, Averill launched his Hall of Fame career with a screaming line drive over the 45-foot-high right field screen. It was the first time that an American Leaguer had hit a homer in his first at-bat. Less well remembered is the fact that Averill also hit a home run in his second game. Number two came off George Uhle, Detroit's ace right-hander. The 26-year-old rookie hit .332 for the Tribe that year, with 18 home runs and 96 RBI. "I kept two things in mind at the plate," Averill said in a 1965 interview with *The Sporting News*. "One was I was up there to swing; the other was to keep my eye on the target, which was the pitcher's cap. I always aimed for the middle. The base hits I swung for. The homers came of themselves."[33]

The "Earl of Snohomish" was one of several players who signed with Cleveland in the late 1920s and early 1930s who formed the nucleus of a good hitting team. Evans had promised Cleveland sandlot officials that he would farm out several of the best prospects from a highly ranked amateur program all-star game in order to obtain more hitting power. After picking five prospects, Evans suddenly asked his wife Linda whom she would pick. Without hesitation, she responded, "That good-looking blond Viking over there."[34] Evans agreed with his wife and signed Joe Vosmik to a minor league contract. The first generation Czech tore up the Three-I League at Terre Haute with a .397 average, and in 1930 he was called up to the "big time." The popular local had a successful career with the Indians before being traded to the St. Louis Browns in 1937. He finished his 13-year career with a creditable .307 average. Spalding's baseball guide wrote of Vosmik, "playing his first year for Cleveland, he made as good a record as any first-year player on the eight [American League] clubs."[35] He died of lung cancer in 1962 at the age of 51. A teammate, pitcher Willis Hudlin, recalled Vosmik as a good, sound batter. "But he always had bad legs, always limping. He busted his legs so easy."[36] In 1935, the outfielder led the league in hits, doubles and triples, and batted .348, losing the batting championship by a fraction of a point to Buddy Myer of Washington.

While Evans worked diligently to put together a winning team, Bradley soon realized that greater income from larger crowds was imperative for the development of expensive rookie talent. Established stars were generally unavailable, as Bradley had found out in his efforts to acquire Lou Gehrig.

In the 1920s, the city of Cleveland embarked upon an ambitious new program. For several years, there had been talk that a new stadium should be a part of the overall downtown development. In 1921, Cleveland voters decided to revitalize city government by adopting a city-manager form of governance. In 1924, this new system went into effect, and William R. Hopkins (for whom the current Cleveland airport is named) was the first to serve the city from the city-manager's chair.[37] A strong leader with a background in development, Hopkins took the next steps to fill the void on the lakefront.

Cities were not yet in the habit of subsidizing their professional sports franchises, and most baseball clubs owned their ball parks. Bradley knew that he needed a larger stadium than quaint, family friendly League Park. His initial interest in purchasing the team had been whetted by plans for a new lakefront stadium, and in 1928, to prompt the city to action, he spoke at a builder's exchange forum, informing his audience, "If the city doesn't provide a stadium as we hope it will, we will lease the land and build it.... No big city (Cleveland was still the sixth-largest city in the country) is really a big city unless it has a stadium."[38]

The city fathers, however, perceived an anticipated new stadium as a potential profit maker, and Bradley's determination to move the team to a larger stadium prodded the city into renewed action. In 1928, the City Council, with one dissenting vote, authorized a $2.5 million bond issue to be put before the voters on the November ballot.[39]

A myth has persisted that the Cleveland Stadium was built in the hopes of hosting the 1932 Olympic Games. Nothing in the literature, speeches, or newspaper clippings of the day used in the voter campaign, however, indicates that the Olympics were anything more than a minor talking point in descriptions of how versatile the lakefront facility would be. To the contrary, the stadium was built primarily to meet the specific needs of the city's professional baseball team. The city fathers wanted to demonstrate to the nation that Cleveland was anything but a second-tier metropolis, and that argument helped Clevelanders return a positive decision on election day. A 55 percent affirmative vote was required, and the issue passed with a comfortable 3–2 margin.[40] Cleveland stayed in the same "league" as Chicago and Philadelphia, which had commissioned major outdoor arenas. A taxpayer suit filed in Cuyahoga County Common Pleas Court on April 29, 1929, to block the Stadium project delayed construction. However, after one year, the suit was thrown out by the Ohio Supreme Court.[41]

Soon after the referendum passed and in spite of dark economic warnings, preparations began for breaking ground. On June 20, 1929, the first bulldozer took its initial bite out of the landfill near Lake Erie. An enormous task faced the local Osborne Engineering Company.

In some spots, the land rose just two feet above Lake Erie, in others, 40 feet above. Much of the fill was trash. A foundation had to be established that would secure the huge steel, brick, and concrete structure which was to rise above it. More than 2,500 pilings were driven into the landfill, some as deep as 65 feet.[42] Construction was completed on July 1, 1931, six months ahead of the projected schedule, at a final cost of $3,035,000, some 21 percent over budget.[43] This result was not uncommon in publicly funded projects. In view of what was about to happen to the country's economy, however, the citizenry and Bradley must have felt relieved that the project was scheduled for completion before the Great Depression struck. Historian Fred Schuld recalled that Alva Bradley boasted, "We'll fill that place often, every Sunday."[44] That was an overstatement to say the least. First of all, there were several internal flaws in the stadium. There were no lockers in the clubhouse, and the players hung their street clothes on single nails in the wall. The outfield was soggy with new landfill partly because a portion of the stadium was built over land that was formerly part of Lake Erie, and drainage was poor. A background of white shirts worn by fans in center field bothered hitters.[45]

Secondly, the Stadium was unique in many ways. An overriding factor was the wind. Old-timers, including this author, sat through many a game with the lake locked in ice to the break wall and beyond, with the wind from the lake screaming around the stadium like a storm blast from the Yukon. On January 30, 1930, a strong wind from the lake snapped cables holding a construction tower, and the scaffolding collapsed, dropping two workers to their death, 120 feet below.[46] One game was called by fog, as impenetrable and bewildering as London pea-soup. The stadium was subject to all the violent and capricious whims of weather generated by water and wind.

Then there was the field itself. It was expansive, reaching 471 feet from home plate to the bleacher wall in center field. No player ever hit a home run into the faraway center field bleachers. Early games were treacherous for batters, catchers, and home plate umpires. The first major problem with the cavernous stadium was the white background in center field, created by the white shirts of the crowds or by the concrete that was so white it hid the ball. Cleveland catcher Luke Sewell recalled, "It was so tough to see the ball while catching that you became like a prize fighter, ducking foul tips."[47] The situation was not much better for the batters or plate umpires. Officials soon blocked off the middle of the bleachers and eventually provided a green backdrop.

The expanse of the outfield provided a large area for outfielders to cover. When the New York Yankees and Babe Ruth came to town, Ruth let out a blast which was heard around the country: "The Cleveland team will have to quit this big stadium and the overall outfield distances!"[48] The distance down the left field foul line was a respectable 320 feet. The outfield quickly lengthened to 363 feet in the power alleys.[49] A wire fence was eventually installed which shortened center field to 410 feet by 1948. The designers of Municipal Stadium were "purists," believing the home run was vulgar and cheapened the game.[50] The Lakefront Stadium was designed by P. P. Evans of the Osborn Engineering Company, the foremost ballpark engineers of that era. The Osborn group had also built Yankee Stadium as directed by owners Jacob Ruppert and Cap Huston in 1922–1923. Yankee Stadium's short right field was built to accommodate Babe Ruth and was reverently called "Ruthville." Originally the distance to right field was 296 feet. This distance was lengthened to 310 feet in 1974–1975 when

Yankee Stadium was remodeled. Long-ball hitters on the Cleveland team and opponents moaned, and rightfully so, about the overwhelming Municipal Stadium outfield. Babe Ruth told the Indians, "A guy ought to have a horse to play the outfield."[51] By May 1933, the field had to be sodded with new turf for a third time.

The opening game on July 31, 1932, in the new Stadium acclaimed as the biggest and best in the baseball world, gave an indication that pitchers would reign supreme in this giant structure. The Tribe, with 22-year-old Mel Harder pitching, faced possibly the greatest left-hander of all time, Robert "Lefty" Grove, and the Philadelphia Athletics, the defending American League Champions. A near-capacity crowd of 76,989 was not disappointed when Grove out-dueled Harder, 1–0.[52] It was the last time in the 1930s the Cleveland team would fill the stadium.

In 1933, the Tribe played all of their home games in Municipal Stadium. In an early season game against the New York Yankees, Ruth tried to run down a ball hit by first baseman Eddie Morgan. When he started for the ball, which was hit to left-center field, he shouted to his fellow outfielders, "Tell [manager] Joe McCarthy I will send him a wire and tell him when I'm coming back." Later, Ruth howled to Morgan, "What's the big idea of running me ragged." Morgan laughed, "I'm still puffing myself," after touring the bases for an inside-the-park home run. "It's no cinch to get homers in this park, no matter where you hit them."[53]

Hitting in the stadium was a major problem for the Tribe in 1933. The team had developed the attitude that they could not hit in the new stadium. Dan Daniel of the *New York Times* summarized the situation: "In other years the Indians were noted for their power.... You could rely on the Cleveland team to give you a battle with the bat."[54] The team batting average dropped to .260, seventh in the league, compared to .285 in 1932. Run production dropped by 160, although the Tribe scored 52 more runs at home. This negative psychological angle was particularly difficult on Earl Averill and Joe Vosmik. Averill's average dropped to .301. He batted a credible .319 at Municipal Stadium, but only .280 on the road. Vosmik was hurt early in the season and missed the first two months. His batting average plummeted from .312 in 1932 to .263 the following year. Daniel made a good point that the poor mental angle had a deleterious effect upon the members of the local team.[55] Something had to be done, and Bradley soon made several important changes, eventually moving most home games back to League Park.

As for the stadium itself, *Sports Illustrated* many years later, called it "The Temple of Doom." To the faithful in Cleveland, this story was widely resented. *Plain Dealer* sportswriter Bill Livingston accurately described the stadium as "big, cold, majestic, and truthfully ugly. But it was ours." He added, "Cleveland's status as a major league town was nearly condemned many times, both on and off the field. The old edifice became a symbol of the city."[56] Lakefront Stadium vindicated its existence immediately after World War II, when millions of loyal fans poured into the huge, and to many, beautiful structure during what is affectionately called "The Golden Age of Sports" in Cleveland. Major league attendance records were broken, and the Tribe capped a decade (1947–1956) of winning teams with a World Championship in 1948 and an American League pennant in 1954. Sadly for many fans, the Lakefront Stadium joined the "ballpark graveyard" in 1992 when the edifice was demolished.

The nationwide euphoria of the 1920s—the feeling that prosperity and good times would continue—did not last beyond the decade, and this sentiment permeated metropolitan Cleveland. The Crash of 1929 and the subsequent Depression brought Cleveland to its knees. Industrialist Cyrus Eaton suggested that Cleveland was more badly hurt by the Depression than any other city in the United States. "That assertion," journalist George E. Condon, Jr., wrote in 1967, "is plausible enough to people who remember the exuberant, dynamic Cleveland of pre–Depression days and who can compare it with the somber, convalescent city that walked with a dragging gait and a querulous expression."[57] Everything that could go wrong did: unemployment quickly rose to 25 percent, soup kitchens became commonplace, and blue chip stock sold for fewer than five dollars a share. Few signs of improvement were imminent.

Bradley did not believe in retaining a public relations firm for the team, reasoning that a winning team would sell itself. If the record was a losing one, he argued, "I don't care what you do; you cannot interest the fans in seeing a lot of poor players."[58] The fans would soon see that the Indians had a lot of good players. The Tribe played their games exclusively in Municipal Stadium through the end of the 1932 season, winning 19 of 31 games. Bradley was tight-fisted and was not happy that during the 1933 season, the average attendance per game at the new stadium was only 5,817, about a thousand fewer than could have been expected at the old League Park. It didn't help that Ruth called Municipal Stadium a "cow pasture" and Connie Mack informed Bradley that the greatest place in the world to play baseball was none other than League Park.

By 1934, the Cleveland team returned to League Park for their weekday and Saturday games. There were no night games in the major leagues until 1935. League Park never had lights during its existence. Bradley explained his rationale for this move: "We are cancelling our lease…. We lost $80,000, the players are complaining and I resent that Mayor Ray Miller said he gave us an easy contract.[59] Over the winter, Bradley calmed down and softened his position. The Indians didn't move out entirely in 1934, remaining a part-time tenant and playing at the Stadium on Sundays and holidays. By now the grand "lady by the lake" was being identified as the city's "white elephant."[60]

As if things weren't bad enough, Bradley decided to cancel all radio broadcasts of Tribe games, believing they hurt game attendance. This viewpoint was strongly shared by others, particularly Ed Barrow of the New York Yankees and Charles Stoneham of the neighboring New York Giants. General manager Larry MacPhail of the Brooklyn Dodgers, however, favored radio and finally in 1939, with his persuasion, radio broadcasts came to New York City.

The Cleveland franchise had been a pioneer in radio broadcasts, partly due to the charisma of one Thomas "Red" Manning. Born on the near west side of Cleveland, Manning early on became the dean of sportscasting in Cleveland. Winning a contest at Euclid Beach for the newsboy with the loudest voice led to his career as an announcer. Red-haired and Irish, his eyes ice-blue, his tones rasping, he was jocular and effusive. Jimmy Dudley, later the "Voice of the Indians" on WHK, aptly described young Manning's effect upon his audience: "For most people he was their first attachment to baseball. What had been cold newsprint, Tom brought alive. And the great part of this town simply took a siesta, with a radio on their cot, when he stepped behind the mike."[61] One pundit described his voice as "the second loudest noise in Cleveland, the first being the foghorn off Whiskey Island."[62]

In the early 1920s the Cleveland team hired Manning, who used a four-foot megaphone with an amplifier, to shout the lineups to the press box and the batters to the fans. In 1928, Billy Evans hired him to be the first voice of the Indians on station WTAM. In 1931, another station obtained broadcasting rights for the Clevelanders' games and Manning was released. He picked up other piecemeal assignments, including nine World Series, many with Graham McNamee, and three heavyweight championship fights. In addition, he announced Ohio State football games for 30 years.[63]

The Indians would not be without broadcasts for long. Evans asked former Cleveland outfielder Jack Graney if he would like to try announcing. Graney agreed, Evans took him to the radio booth at League Park, introduced the former player, and Graney was on the air. "I was ready to jump out the windows."[64] Graney rapidly overcame his mike fright and went on to become a legend in Indians broadcasting history.

John Gladstone Graney was born in St. Thomas, near London, Ontario, in Canada. An excellent left-handed pitcher, he was purchased by the Cleveland Naps in 1908. Graney was determined to make an impression in batting practice: "I wasn't content to just lob the ball up.... I wanted to put something on it, show the boys what I had." The result was that each hitter was up there about 15 minutes before he got four or five pitches that could be reached. Graney was that wild. Up came manager Nap Lajoie to hit. Graney remembered, "I was pretty cocky and had a crazy idea I could strike Lajoie out. So I wound up, reared back and cut loose with a fast ball that was supposed to go past him before he ever saw it. But it didn't. Though Larry tried to duck, the ball hit him above the left ear, and he went down like a load of bricks. Instead of striking him out, I knocked him out."[65]

That evening, Lajoie called Graney to his room and the wild pitcher found him with an ice bag against his head. Graney tried to apologize but Lajoie stopped him. He said, "They tell me the place for wild men is out west. So you're going west, kid, so far that if you went any farther your hat would float. Here's your railroad ticket."[66] Graney was sent to Portland in the Pacific Coast League. In his first workout, he hit six batters, and according to a newspaper at the time, Graney was switched to the outfield "for humanities [*sic*] sake."

In 1910, he was brought back to Cleveland, where he played for the next 13 years. In 1916, he became the first twentieth-century major leaguer to wear a number on his shirt, which was "16." He was also the first batter to face pitcher Babe Ruth in the major leagues. Graney was Ray Chapman's roommate at the time of the shortstop's death, and was the first former major leaguer to become a baseball announcer.

When he began announcing in 1932, Graney became one of the first, if not the first, broadcaster to recreate away games for the Indians. Baseball broadcasters generally did not accompany a team on road trips. He broadcast from Kane Motor Company in a Ford agency which Graney had co-owned in nearby Brooklyn. As a former player, he was extremely adept at describing an away game as though he was at the park in a live setting. He used various audio props and always started a game with "Here's the windup ... here's the pitch." He commented, "I used to tell when the ball took a bad hop, and so forth, in my accounts of the games." Asked for the reason for his radio announcing success, Graney explained, "I tried to follow the ball, stay with the play and leave the fancy words to others."[67]

Graney had the advantage of being a former major leaguer and understanding the game from an "insiders" perspective. Added to this asset, Graney's salty staccato voice and enthusiastic manner made him the most popular broadcaster in Cleveland baseball history with the possible exception of Jimmy Dudley. Tennis commentator and Cleveland native Bud Collins best summed up Graney's impact upon his listeners: "You could worship from afar … taking the scripture in the paper, or listening to games on the radio, whose bull-frog voice, former Indian Jack Graney, took a few liberties in those days before television. Very little was routine that happened before the eyes of the imaginative and histrionic Graney."[68]

Bradley's fallacious supposition that canceling broadcasts would boost attendance was not unlike Ed Barrow's unwarranted fear that night baseball would be harmful to baseball. In 1933, the Indians' attendance was 80,000 fewer than in 1932. It is difficult to ascertain how many fans listened to Graney's broadcasts. There is little doubt that this number was significant, and like the three daily newspapers, important in stimulating interest in the only major league team in town.

Other distractions thwarted improvement in the Indians' attendance—besides a mediocre team. Most importantly, by 1933, the United States was in the throes of the country's worst-ever Depression. President Franklin D. Roosevelt took office on March 4, 1933, and reassured the citizenry that "the only thing we have to fear is fear itself."[69] Long-distance travel by automobile was uncommon during the 1930s, especially to see a major league baseball game. Blue collar factory workers averaged approximately $30 a week in take-home wages (for those who had a job). Gasoline was ten cents a gallon; a loaf of bread eight cents; a new car $700; and a new home $4,000.[70] Fans who went to see the Cleveland team play at League Park paid $1.50 for a reserved seat. The decade-long Depression brought Cleveland to its knees. Condon decried that "the Cleveland the world knew from 1930 to 1955 was a hurt town and it showed in many ways." The popular columnist emphasized, "There was a disposition toward petty bickering among … civic leaders on petty issues, while the large issues … went unattended and the sprawling downtown area turned gray and shabby."[71] The Indians' player payroll was trimmed by $70,000. It had cost the team $80,000 to play in the new Stadium for the remainder of the 1932 season.[72]

The financial situation was not good for the Tribe. After 1932, the new ownership endured five straight seasons in the red. Bradley never took a cent of salary, and everyone from Billy Evans to the office staff suffered cuts in income. During the Depression and after, Bradley never negotiated with the players about their salaries. After discussing a given player with the manager and general manager, the front office determined the figure the club would pay. The first figure was the final one.

In this regard, Bradley was particularly upset with two of his pitchers—Willis Hudlin and Wes Ferrell: "I am personally thoroughly disgusted with both Hudlin and Ferrell. Any fellow who does not want to take an $8,000 and $12,000 job better sit home and find out how hard it is to accumulate this much money to pay them. I would rather throw my baseball interest in the wastebasket than let two fellows of this caliber lick me."[73] The economic situation in 1933 was unfortunate for Ferrell, who was in the midst of a great career. He had just completed four consecutive 20-win seasons (92 wins). Ferrell won 23 games and lost 13 in 1932. The right-hander eventually signed at the club's terms, but a sore arm handicapped him adversely in 1933. The next year he was offered $5,000 and a bonus arrangement which would pay him $1,000 for every victory over ten. Ferrell rejected the offer flatly, and the Indians sold him to the Boston Red Sox.[74] He garnered two more seasons with 20 or more wins.

This dispute with Bradley's two ace pitchers was only the beginning of his ownership troubles during the Great Depression. The 1933 season had not gone as well as was expected. Attendance was disappointing in the new stadium and Cleveland was off to a poor start, lodged in fifth place in mid–June.

On June 9, the managers' graveyard opened for the second time in six years, when Bradley removed Peckinpaugh from the post. Although well liked by the media, Peckinpaugh had a low-key personality. Bradley claimed the team "lacked pep" and "play[ed] loosely." He added the time-worn cliché: "We only hire the manager, the public fires him."[75] Little did the neophyte owner know that the press would have much to do with the removal of the next candidate for the graveyard.

5

Filling Up the Tribe
Managers' Graveyard

*"Over a period of some 15 years from the late 1920s into the
1940s the history of the Cleveland franchise is a study in
the consequences of failure to live up to expectations."*
—Henry W. Thomas, *Walter Johnson, Baseball's Big Train*

As the Great Depression droned on, the 1930s were depressing for citizenry in general, and for Cleveland Indians fans. Although finishing in the first division consistently during this time period and usually winning more than 80 games each season, only rarely had the team posed a serious challenge to claim a pennant. From 1929 to 1941, the frustrated Tribe posted 11 winning seasons and finished in the first division ten times. Four managers were released. From 1900 until 1942, the average tenure for an Indians manager was 2.8 years.[1]

During those years, the competition for "scoops" and inside information was fierce among three dailies. Until the mid-twentieth century, the Indians were covered primarily by Stuart Bell, Franklin Lewis, and Frank Gibbons of the *Press*. These journalists were inspired by Louis Seltzer, a highly competent, influential firebrand editor. Harry Jones, James E. Doyle, and Gordon Cobbledick wrote for the *Plain Dealer*, and Ed McAuley and Ed Bang wrote for the *News* until the paper closed shop in 1960. Hal Lebovitz, Russ Schneider, and Bob Dolgan followed soon thereafter, writing for the *Plain Dealer*. Outstanding cartoonists Lou Darvis of the *Cleveland Press* and Fred Reinert of the *Plain Dealer* added to the mix. For the most part, these men were competent, in the 1940s and 1950s, and many readers bought all three papers in order to compare notes on what had been written about their team. While the journalists' rivalry was keen, there was an element of cooperation when needed. Bell of the *Press* had a drinking problem and on occasion he was so inebriated he could not write his column after a game. He was known to persuade Cobbledick of the *Plain Dealer* to write his column so he would not lose his job. On one occasion, Cobbledick wrote such a good column that Seltzer sent Bell a memo declaring him one of America's great sportswriters.[2]

Baseball writers carried considerable influence with team management—probably too much—and fans, and Cleveland was certainly no exception. Writers and fans asked the perennial question that became as noteworthy as the beer that made Milwaukee famous,

"What's wrong with the Indians?"[3] The cry resounded in 1930, when during mid-season the team lost 20 of 23 games and fell out of the pennant race. Letters besieged the sports departments of the three dailies during the next two years, and finally Bradley yielded to public pressure.

The new ownership had been patient with Peckinpaugh. In his five-year tenure, the former shortstop had won 490 games and lost 481 for a .505 percentage. Upon Peckinpaugh's departure, Bradley defended his deposed manager: "Roger Peckinpaugh has worked hard and done everything in his power to make a winner."[4] Cleveland brass decided to go with an outstanding baseball celebrity as their next manager, and on June 9, 1933, Walter Johnson, arguably the greatest pitcher of all time, was named as the new Cleveland manager. Henry W. Thomas, Johnson's grandson, who wrote an excellent biography of his grandfather, commented, "An outsider like Walter Johnson didn't stand a chance."[5]

After completing his illustrious 21-year pitching career for the Washington Nationals in 1927, Johnson was hired as manager of his home team. Evaluations of his performance during his four-year tenure were mixed. He compiled the best record of any manager in the 84-year history of the capital team's major league tenure. His club won 71, 94, 92, and 93 games for a .562 percentage with finishes of fifth, second and third twice. On the debit side, his record was often discounted on the grounds that the talent under his direction was better than his management of it. This argument was supported by the fact that the Nationals won the pennant the year after his departure, in 1933, under the tutelage of 26-year-old Joe Cronin.

Several members of the Senators and friends of Johnson, particularly third baseman Ossie Bluege and coach Al Schacht, flatly declared him a failure particularly in his handling of pitchers.[6] Shirley Povich, guru of baseball journalism at this time, defended Johnson, arguing that the "Big Train" had done as well as could be expected, considering his chief competitors were powerhouse teams, the New York Yankees and the Philadelphia Athletics.[7]

Johnson soon found the Cleveland press to be a thorn in his side. Their proprietary attitude was made clear to him soon after his arrival in Cleveland. One reporter cheekily said, "Come down to the office and we'll get together on the situation." Johnson asked, "What situation?" "Well," the reporter answered, "two heads are better than one. We'll talk over ... running the team."[8] This invitation was rejected outright, ending Johnson's honeymoon with the press before it began.

Understandably, Thomas was not sympathetic with the local press. He wrote, "The often-poisonous atmosphere surrounding [Tribe] teams were the efforts of local baseball writers to run the club with their typewriters, backing favorite players and second-guessing management without regard for its effect on team harmony."[9]

There was more than an element of truth concerning reporters and their close relationship to the players. Times were different in the 1930s. Teams traveled by train and it was inevitable that reporters would fraternize with team members during a two-or three-week road trip. Journalists spent long evenings with other journalists or with players until the midnight curfew. Few night games were scheduled until the end of World War II. The availability of prop airplane travel after 1945 and jet travel soon thereafter adversely affected player-press relations, formerly congenial. Cobbledick recalled, "There [was] no wandering into a club car for a modest pre-dinner libation. There [was no] leisurely dining car meal with good talk or friendly ribbing. There [was no] card game, no chess or checkers, no swapping of atrocious lies. You learned to like some of them [players] and to avoid others. But you knew them."[10]

Players generally were immune to severe criticism when caught breaking training rules. Often flagrant acts of behavior were covered up by the press. In the case of Babe Ruth and his aberrant behavior, he was so adulated by fans that his meanderings were swept under the rug. The press treated President Franklin D. Roosevelt much the same way, giving little publicity to his physical liability or romantic trysts. Present-day technology inhibits players' efforts to live a private life devoid of potential negative publicity.

The odds appeared to be stacked against Johnson and his efforts to bring a winner to Cleveland. The great right-hander, who had been a beloved idol in Washington, D.C., was not a worldly individual. Johnson had given little evidence in his previous managerial assignments that he possessed a magical wand to shake the Cleveland team out of their mediocre record. More importantly, Billy Evans was not particularly enamored with him and had signed him only under pressure from the owners. Evans made it plain to newspaper friends that he would not be responsible for the new manager's actions.[11]

Bradley, however, left little doubt that Johnson was the boss. He believed that the new manager's pitching accomplishments and calm demeanor would help generate better attendance. Johnson soon ran into trouble with his pitchers. One was hot-tempered Oral Hildebrand, one of the Indians' mainstays. On July 31, 1933, with the Indians playing the Browns in St. Louis, Johnson hurried to the mound after the right-hander had walked three batters. Hildebrand, who was having his best year with the Tribe, demanded to be left in the game. Johnson told him to go to the showers and take the first train back to Cleveland. Hildebrand later told Evans that he didn't believe any pitcher could work for Johnson and satisfy him. He later reconsidered and apologized for his behavior, returning to the team in good graces and finishing the season with six shutouts and the team's best record of 16–11.[12]

Hildebrand's initial defiance was in response to Johnson's apparent impatience with his pitchers. A more serious altercation with Wesley Ferrell, Cleveland's number one pitcher, reached a climax during Johnson's tenure as manager. The Great Depression was putting a strain on the Cleveland franchise to retain its top-flight players. Ferrell was a prime example. Beginning in 1929, the right-hander won 20 or more games in each of his first full four seasons. Not only was he an outstanding pitcher, he also showed great talent as a hitter. Joe Williams of the *New York World-Telegram* wrote, "You can add Mr. Wesley Ferrell to your list of supremely self-confident athletes.... Mr. Ferrell is good, knows it and admits it."[13] John Kieran of the *New York Times* wrote that the late Miller Huggins only had to watch Ferrell twice before declaring him the best young hurler he had seen since [Mathewson].[14]

Ferrell had a mind of his own. According to fellow hurler Willis Hudlin, "Ferrell was one of the best short-fused pitchers there ever was. When he got knocked out of the box, which didn't happen very often, he'd take that glove and tear it and bite it and sometimes he'd just sail it into the stands."[15] On September 12, 1932, he was fined $1,200 and suspended for ten days by easygoing Peckinpaugh for insubordination. This fine was significant on a salary of $18,000. The right-hander won 23 games but near the end of the season showed symptoms of a sore arm.

Bradley knew baseball business would be terrible in 1933 as the Great Depression set in, and he had no choice but to reduce player salaries. Ferrell's salary was reduced by a third to $12,000 for the coming season. In normal times, a pitcher who had completed his fourth straight season of 20 or more victories would get a raise. "I'm not asking [for] that, but I don't think I should be cut," Ferrell complained.[16] How long the Ferrell brothers—Rick, a catcher with the St. Louis Browns was also a holdout—were out on strike became a moot question as tragedy befell the family. Before spring training began in 1933, Wesley and Rick were visiting their brother Marvin Ferrell's home when a fourth brother, Ewell, committed suicide. This tragic incident was rarely discussed by the family.[17]

Wesley Ferrell had little choice but to sign his contract with the Indians. He did have a sore arm and suffered through an 11–12 season. After the season, the handwriting was on the wall for Ferrell and he was traded to the Boston Red Sox on May 25, 1934. He recovered and posted a 14–5 record that season, adding two more 20-win seasons to his record in 1935 and 1936. In 1937, he was traded to the Washington Nationals. Ferrell's six 20-win winning seasons matched the number accrued by Bob Feller, the Indians' soon-to-be pitching star. Manager Johnson was blamed unfairly for the loss of the Tribe's premier hurler to the Red Sox.

When the country was deeply entrenched in the Depression, the ownership badly needed to recover some cash. The trade had been ill-fated, even though the franchise received $25,000 in cash and two journeymen players, pitcher Bob Weiland and outfielder Bob Seeds, from Boston in place of Ferrell. Seeds played only 61 games with Cleveland, batting .247 in 1934 before being sold to the Tigers. Weiland posted one win and five defeats before being traded along with infielder Johnny Burnett to the St. Louis Browns for outfielder Bruce Campbell. Only Campbell proved to be a valuable asset, although just for the next five years.[18]

Ferrell's departure was echoed by Cleveland's poor management decisions in the first decade of the 2000s. In 2008 the Tribe traded 2007 Cy Young Award winner CC Sabathia to the New York Yankees for four players of questionable potential. In 2009, the management traded another Cy Young Award winner, Cliff Lee, to the Philadelphia Phillies for right-handed Carlos Carrasco.[19] Retention of high-quality players is more difficult today due to free agency and prohibitive salaries which have escalated into millions of dollars. Small market franchises find it difficult to keep much-sought-after players. Sabathia pitched for the World Champion New York Yankees in 2009 and Lee pitched well for the pennant-winning Phillies in 2009 and the Texas American League champions in 2010.

Nineteen thirty-four was a critical year for Johnson. He made player fitness a priority in spring training. According to his biographer Jack Kavanagh, "It had been his way of getting ready and he ran his players ceaselessly." The manager was quoted by the *Cleveland Press* as "favoring married players, provided they were wed to a good woman. A bad wife can ruin a good ballplayer faster than anything else."[20]

Johnson agitated several of his players, continually feuding with Oral Hildebrand, and when the team floundered, mostly in fourth place, the press increased their criticism of Johnson. Ed Bang, sports editor of the *Cleveland News*, lashed out at Johnson. "Johnson showed anything but mental alertness and managerial ability. Truth be told, he fell so far short of

Hall of Fame pitcher and manager Walter Johnson giving instructions to his Cleveland team in early 1934. Johnson was manager for a little over two years, compiling a respectable 180–168 record, but he had difficulties with his players.

what a wide-awake manager should do, that fans who were wont to cheer him in days gone by as a great pitcher, groaned in despair and booed him."[21]

Soon thereafter, the fiery *Cleveland Press* ran a critical story topped by an eight-column headline which challenged Tribe ownership: "The Indians, Without Leadership, Have Flopped, What Are the Owners Going to Do About It?"[22] Nothing was done at the moment, however, and the season dragged on. In September, the team finished strong, winning 21 games and losing only ten to finish in third place, one notch above their 1933 finish.

In spite of the overall disappointing finish, in Bradley's opinion Johnson had done several things right. Most importantly he had added $100,000 to Cleveland's financial bottom line. He had disposed of veteran hangers-on and reduced the coaching staff by coaching at first base himself and using a benchwarmer to coach at third base.

Bradley also received flak from the press, possibly unfairly, for the decision to move the team back to League Park. Municipal Stadium was looked upon as a "white elephant" by the franchise, city fathers and fans. The smaller League Park was more fan-friendly and less expensive to maintain. This move did not alter home attendance figures significantly— 387,936 in 1933 compared to 391,338 in 1934.[23]

League Park, the original major league ball park, built in 1891 and rebuilt in 1910 to become the fourth major league concrete and steel park. It was home for the Tribe until abandoned by Bill Veeck in 1946 (author's collection).

The 1935 season opened optimistically with an Associated Press poll predicting a pennant for the Cleveland team. Five weeks into the season, the team had given evidence of realizing this prediction, trailing close behind the Chicago White Sox and New York Yankees. In May 23 came the coup de grâce for the beleaguered manager. Throughout his managing tenure at Cleveland, Johnson had shown more than a tinge of jealousy toward a few veteran players on the team, among them Willie Kamm, the popular third baseman, and catcher Glenn Myatt. Johnson claimed, "They were no longer useful to me as players and I felt they were an antagonizing influence upon the club."[24] This decision incensed several of the sports writers, particularly Cobbledick, who added fuel to the fire when he wrote a letter to President Bradley published in the *Plain Dealer* on May 26, 1935. In it, he analyzed the situation from the players' standpoint and cited possible jealousy as the motivation for Johnson's actions. By and large, Cobbledick was supportive of Kamm as a valuable asset to the team's success,

> He's a great hand with the young fellows because he not only knows his stuff but he knows how to put it over. Maybe Johnson resents this. Maybe he doesn't like it when a kid infielder comes to the bench at the end of the inning, walks past the manager, sits down besides Kamm and asks, "What's wrong with me on that play?" Johnson is only human and jealousy is a human emotion. But I can't see why Kamm should be the goat.[25]

Johnson was not particularly popular among the Cleveland players, especially the fan-favorite third baseman Willie Kamm and catcher Glenn Myatt. Although Earl Averill stood up for Johnson, saying, "I'm 100 percent for Walter.... The boys found Walter is on the level and has plenty of guts."[26] Yet there was a feeling of unrest during the early weeks of the 1935 season. While the team was in Philadelphia for a series in mid–May, Johnson told the media that he discovered an "anti–Johnson" faction on the team. The ringleaders were Myatt and in particular Kamm.

The Kamm issue was a mystery. An excellent veteran fielder and consistent hitter, Kamm had tried on his own to help several young players improve their skills. Obviously there was a clash of personalities. Johnson created a firestorm of protest in the Cleveland press with the release of Kamm and Myatt on May 23.[27] In view of the outcry from the press, Johnson might well have displayed more diplomacy in handling this issue.

A predicted player revolt against Johnson's authority failed to materialize when the team returned in early June from a losing road trip. *The Sporting News* reported, "Anti-Johnson Bomb Turns Out to be a Dud." Cheering for the embattled manager drowned out scattered boos at the first game back in Cleveland in June. At the same time, 21 members of the Indians team placed an ad in all three dailies which stated in part, "We want fans to know that we are not a team split wide open by dissension arrayed against our manager."[28]

In order to clear his name, Kamm pleaded his case to Commissioner Landis. After a hearing, the commissioner issued a statement that disciplinary action was an internal affair that should be handled by team management. Bradley did just that. Kamm was appointed a scout for the Cleveland team, and Myatt signed with the New York Giants. Kamm never played another major league game. He led third basemen in fielding in the American League for eight of his 13 seasons, including three with Cleveland (1932–1934). Kamm managed the San Francisco Seals in the Pacific Coast League in 1936 and 1937. Myatt finished his 16-year playing career with the Detroit Tigers in 1936. The departure of Kamm and Myatt evoked little sympathy anywhere but from the local press, and in late June a winning streak brought the club within two games of first place, relegating the dismissal of the two veterans to the back page.

From that point, the team took a nose-dive, losing 15 of 19 games. The morale of the team was not much better. The loss of Averill for six weeks only added to the despondency in the dugout. During a Fourth of July celebration, a firecracker had exploded in his hand. Bradley and Evans fretted as the team dropped into the second division and attendance fell off even more. A Detroit newspaper column asked the question, "Is Johnson Being Persecuted?"[29]

Shirley Povich of the Washington *Post* vehemently defended the soon-to-be-deposed manager: "[Johnson] is under fire as manager of the Cleveland club, the target of fourth-wit Cleveland fans and newspaper writers who have been heaping abuse on Johnson because he has failed to win a pennant with a fourth place club."[30] *Baseball Magazine* had earlier jumped into the fray with an attack on local sportswriters:

> Owner Bradley, while admitting that Walter Johnson had made some mistakes, pointedly asked, "Who was free from mistakes?" He allowed it to be known that the Cleveland club was not being run by local sports writers. This irresponsible fraternity, entirely lacking in business experience, are quite out of their province when they attempt to coerce the owner in the selection of a manager.[31]

Years later Cobbledick, older and wiser, wrote an article defining a sportswriter's responsibility in handling news about a team's inner workings. Readers had questioned whether sportswriters had the duty to censor news in an article or column by determining to publish only what is advisable for the readers to know. Cobbledick took the position that such a policy was not wise because for the most part, sports writers are not wise enough to be entrusted with such decisions. Cobbledick concluded, "It is a great waste of time to try to kid the public about its ball club. The baseball writer who makes [this] effort only lowers his standing and that of his paper in the minds of the cash customers. The ball club belongs to the public and it is the baseball reporter's duty to chronicle all the news fit to print."[32]

Regardless of what the reporters or public thought, the axe fell on Johnson on August 5, 1935, as Bradley announced Johnson's "voluntary resignation." The great right-hander's managerial record with the Indians was 180 victories, 168 defeats and a third-place finish in 1934. Johnson never managed again either in the major or minor leagues. Although the 1935 season had begun with high hopes, steady attacks by fans, newspaper criticism, and clubhouse problems with several of his players, the dismissal of Willie Kamm, and disappointing results in the standings were too much even for his friend Alva Bradley.

Cleveland was swept by the soon-to-be World Champion Detroit Tigers on the road before Johnson officially threw in the towel. Herman Goldstein of the *Cleveland News* described Johnson's last mile as a manager:

> When the train pulled into the [Cleveland] terminal, everybody hurried off but Johnson.... He stood and stretched, fiddled with his necktie, stood around.... He was walking toward the guillotine. I finally left the train feeling very sorry for Walter Johnson. A great ballplayer, he was far from a great team manager, very nice guy."[33]

Thus the gate to the managerial graveyard in Cleveland opened for another deposed manager.

Did the Cleveland franchise have enough firepower to launch a serious challenge to win the pennant during the Peckinpaugh-Johnson tenure (1928–1935)? The general feeling is no—it would have been difficult for the Indians to overcome Connie Mack's juggernaut (1929–1931), Mickey Cochrane's Detroit pennant winners of 1934-1935 and Joe McCarthy's first of eight pennants with the New York Yankees in 1932. Possibly the pennant winning New York Yankees of 1928 and the Washington Senators of 1933 might have been vulnerable. But at no time during this eight-year period did the Tribe finish any better than 12 games out of first place.

What kind of talent did the Clevelanders possess to challenge the front-runners? In 1929 the team claimed seven .300 hitters, led by the "Earl of Snohomish" Averill and first baseman Lou Fonseca. Averill in his rookie year batted .332 with 18 home runs and 96 RBI. Fonseca was the American League batting champion with a .369 average and 103 RBI. Other .300 hitters were reserve outfielder Dick Porter (.328), second baseman Johnny Hodapp (.327), third baseman Joe Sewell (.315), and right fielders Eddie Morgan (.318) and Bib Falk (.309). The pitching crew was led by 21-game winner Wes Ferrell and Willis Hudlin.

The 1930 team also possessed seven .300 hitters and additional quality pitching in the form of native Nebraskan Mel Harder, who toiled his entire 20-year career with the Cleveland franchise, winning 223 games. The hitting remained strong with four regulars hitting

Earl Averill hit a home run in his first at-bat in 1929, one of his 238 for the Tribe. He still leads the Indians in six offensive categories. A popular player with fans, Averill frequently clashed with the front office. He was elected to the Hall of Fame in 1975 with a career .318 batting average (National Baseball Hall of Fame, Cooperstown, New York).

over .300 in 1931, the year Cleveland native and power hitter Joe Vosmik arrived on the scene. He was an important cog in the team's immediate future. The number of .300 hitters dropped off significantly in 1932 and 1933 as did the team batting average. In late 1933, first baseman Hal Trosky arrived at League Park to become one of the all-time great sluggers in franchise history. In 1934 future Hall of Famer Averill continued his better than .300 seasonal average. In this season Trosky dominated the Indians' offensive output with outstanding offensive statistics. The move back to League Park appealed especially to batters hitting from the left side of the plate.

Years after Johnson's removal as manager, in an interview with McAuley, Bradley confessed that "Walter was not a good manager."[34] It distressed him to say so, for he had thought highly of Johnson: "I tried so hard to figure out why so fine a man couldn't understand mediocrity," Bradley reminisced, "I think there is only one answer. He had been so good himself he couldn't understand less than excellence. He had no patience with players who had to struggle to master the game, and he saw absolutely no excuse for a pitcher ever developing a sore arm."[35]

Bradley did not countenance favoritism only among field managers, and he subtly forced out Billy Evans from his duties as general manager in November of 1934 when profits declined to $70,000. Asked to take another pay cut, the disgruntled Evans rejected the cut and turned in his resignation, which was accepted.[36] Bradley asked Cyril "Cy" Slapnicka to take over with the new title of "assistant to the president."[37]

Slapnicka—"Slap" or "Slapsie" for short—was one of the most successful and controversial management figures in Cleveland baseball history, primarily as a scout. The right-hander was a spitball pitcher—it was legal at that time—of some renown in the minor leagues, particularly the American and Southern Associations.

Slapnicka was called up to the major leagues twice, first with the Chicago Cubs in 1911 and then with the Pittsburgh Pirates in 1918. His cumulative record in the big time was one win and six losses. A crony of his during his ballplaying days described him as "stubborn as a span of Missouri mules and as mean as a caged bobcat with a toothache ... and he had more guts than ten guys."[38]

Like his competitors, Slapnicka lived by the unpleasant axiom that there is more than one way to skin a cat. He preferred the direct method. For example, when he was pitching in the old Central Association in the early twentieth century, his pitching arm "went dead." He literally could not throw a ball from the pitcher's mound to the plate. Instead of going back to the dry goods store and calling it quits, he showed up several years later in spring training with a glove for his right hand, calmly announcing that he now was a southpaw. The ambidextrous pitcher had spent the winters teaching himself to throw left-handed, and he was ready.

He did not become a Rube Waddell or a Carl Hubbell, but he attempted to gain a fair measure of success using the simplest of pitching strategies. "You knocked the batter down with the first pitch, broke the second across the outside corner, knocked him down with the third pitch and so on until you retired the batter," he recalled.[39] His record indicates that his ambidexterity was not successful. His success as a "headhunter," or a scout, was another story. Sly Cy discovered and signed more than 30 major leaguers for the Cleveland franchise. The most highly recognized were Hall of Famers Bob Feller, Earl Averill, and Lou Boudreau. Other notables included Mel Harder, Hal Trosky, Odell "Bad News" Hale, Jeff Heath, Ken Keltner, Bobby Avila, Jim Hegan and Herb Score.[40]

That Slapnicka was one of the shrewdest judges of baseball talent cannot be denied. When he evinced interest in a minor league or sandlot player, said player's value was enhanced in the eyes of other ivory hunters. When he turned thumbs down, his rivals were prone to back off and reconsider. The crafty scout seldom erred in his estimate of a young prospect. The "sly one" did miscalculate on one Hall of Fame pitcher—Vernon "Lefty" Gomez, often called "Goofy" or "The Gay Castillian."

In August of 1929, Gomez showed his pitching talent when he won his 11th straight game for the San Francisco Seals. Scouts began to make a beeline to the Bay City to talk to Charley Graham, part-owner of the Pacific Coast League club. Scouts held back on signing Gomez because of his slight build, less than 150 pounds.

Cy Slapnicka arrived first and secured a ten-day option for Cleveland to purchase Gomez's contract for $50,000 plus three other players. It turned out that Lefty's weight was not the only physical attribute that would work against him. Noted San Francisco *Examiner* sportswriter Abe Kemp recounted:

> I'm sitting up in the tower talking to Charlie Graham, Slapnicka ... comes in and he says, "Charlie is it all right if I go down to the clubhouse where the players are dressing?" Charlie said, "Sure." After Slapnicka left, Graham says to me, "What the hell do you suppose he wants to go to the clubhouse for?" I told Charlie I had no idea.[41]

About a half-hour later, Slapnicka returned and said, "Charlie, I'm going to forfeit my option on Gomez." Graham asked him why he would change his mind, "Well," Slapnicka said, "I'll tell you, Charley. I just saw Gomez undressed in the clubhouse and anybody who's got as big a p—k as he's got can't pitch winning ball in the major leagues."[42]

Slapnicka ducked out and the writer began to laugh. When Graham asked him what was so funny, he said, "This is the best God damned story of my life, and I can't write a word of it."[43] Gomez never knew about Slapnicka's option until he read about it in Chicago sports writer Jerome Holtzman's 1973 book, *No Cheering in the Press Box*. "I had to laugh," Gomez said, "Abe Kemp only tells the story when I'm sixty-three years old. But Abe [wouldn't] write about it when I'm twenty and it would have made a big difference on my road trips."

In 1928, Slapnicka had already signed the talented Averill, who would finish his career with a batting average of .318. In his home state of Iowa the savvy scout uncovered two gems who made every effort to lead the Tribe to pennant contention. The first of these Hawkeyes was Harold Arthur Troyavesky, better known as Hal Trosky—the family name was shortened prior to his entry into the major leagues. Trosky was one of a significant number of pre–World War II players who as sons of immigrants made their mark in the major leagues. Reduced quotas of foreigners in the mid–1920s inhibited the potential for additional first generation immigrants to compete in the "big show." *The Sporting News* on March 25, 1937, proclaimed in a headline, "League of Nations! No, It's the Majors—America's Melting Pot." By 1936, 27 nationalities were identified as participants in the American League.[44]

Norway, Iowa, Trosky's birthplace, produced more than its share of immigrant sons who competed in the major leagues. Mike Boddicker, cousin of Trosky, won 134 games for four major league teams. Catcher Bruce Kimm spent a short time in the big leagues, primarily as catcher for Mark "The Bird" Fidrych of the Detroit Tigers. Trosky's son, Harold, born in Cleveland, had a cup of coffee with the Chicago White Sox, winning one game in the three innings he pitched.[45] He later moved back to Norway to attend school.

Senior Trosky gained his strength and athleticism on his father's 420-acre farm, milking eight cows by hand, morning and night, until he was 17 years old. Both he and Jimmie Foxx attributed some of their iron grip to this farm chore. Slapnicka delighted in snaring young prospects out in the so-called "sticks." In fact, the wily scout observed young Trosky hitting corncobs with an axe handle against his dad's barn. At the time, Trosky, then right-handed, batted cross-handed. "Why don't you keep your hands the same way on the bat and merely turn your body around and bat left-handed?" suggested Slapnicka. Trosky was amenable to this suggestion, and the results were more than gratifying.[46]

The Indians scout fought off efforts by the St. Louis Cardinals and Philadelphia Athletics to sign Trosky, and he soon became the property of the Cleveland team. Slapnicka switched the Iowan from pitcher to the outfield so he could play regularly, and the rest is in the record book. After two seasons in

Harold "Hal" Trosky: One of Cleveland's outstanding sluggers, with a league-leading 162 RBI in 1936. Hampered by migraine headaches, Trosky finished his short career with 228 home runs and a .302 batting average.

the minor leagues, the husky lad reported to the Indians in 1934. The club released first baseman Eddie Morgan, who had hit well over .300 during his six-year tenure with the Tribe. In contrast to Trosky, Morgan had been an excellent fielding first baseman but management deemed that Trosky would now take over these duties in spite of his inexperience.[47]

An even-tempered player was never labeled "colorful." He let his bat speak for him. Playing in every game in his freshman year, Trosky batted .331, stroking 45 doubles and 35 home runs and driving in 142 runs. His offensive statistics exceeded those of both Lou Gehrig and Jimmie Foxx in their initial year in the major leagues. Dan Daniel, veteran sports writer for the New York *World-Telegram* and *Baseball Magazine*, called Trosky's first year "amazing" and selected Trosky for the "Rookie of the Year" award, edging out runner-up Paul "Daffy" Dean, winner of 19 games for the St. Louis Cardinals.[48]

In 1935, Trosky suffered from a so-called sophomore jinx, batting .271 but still driving in 113 runs and connecting for 26 four-baggers. Now a more graceful fielder, but not a Joe Judge or Bill Terry, he prepared for the greatest offensive year of his career in 1936. First basemen had to compete for acclaim against the likes of Gehrig, Foxx, and Hank Greenberg of the Detroit Tigers—all in the same period—but he met the challenge and then some. Trosky batted .343, and connected for 42 home runs and an astounding 162 RBI. *Baseball Magazine*, using 12 categories for offensive statistics, ranked the Tribe's first baseman third overall in the American League, trailing only teammate Averill and Gehrig. He began to make believers of long-time observers of the game. Connie Mack designated him as heir apparent to Babe Ruth's slugging crown.[49]

Ed Barrow, successful general manager of the New York Yankees, predicted that Trosky would overtake the accomplishments of Lou Gehrig. "He is a much greater ball player than Hank Greenberg," commented Barrow. "He will develop much faster than [the Tigers first baseman] and someday will rank as the greatest hitting first baseman in his league."[50]

Unfortunately for Clevelanders, Barrow's prediction did not materialize, although Trosky experienced several more noteworthy seasons. The rapid improvement of Trosky and the steady play of Averill provided a foundation for a potentially powerful offensive unit. Local favorite Joe Vosmik had one more productive year left before a constellation of injuries forced management to trade him to the St. Louis Browns. Outfielders to replace Vosmik included hot-tempered Jeff Heath, Roy Weatherly and Bruce Campbell. The infield, more than adequate, consisted of Trosky, Odell Hale, Billy Knickerbocker, and Roy Hughes, with diminutive Frankie Pytlak behind the plate. This lineup matched up favorably with that of the 1930 team.

What about pitching? Again, Slapnicka rose to the occasion. First, he traded 19-game winner Monte Pearson and rookie pitcher Steve Sundra to the New York Yankees for another hot-tempered pitcher, Johnny Allen, who had won 20 games in 1936. Still more pitching help was needed, and Slapnicka came to the rescue.[51] He traveled back to his home state to pluck a 16-year-old phenom out of the corn fields in Van Meter, a few miles southwest of Des Moines, named Robert William Edward Feller, soon to be more accurately called "Rapid Robert." Little did Slapnicka and the Feller family anticipate a controversy over Feller's signing which eventually reached Commissioner Landis's desk. Nor did Cleveland ownership anticipate such a tumultuous period of discord for the next five years, both on the playing field and in ownership offices. And the manager's graveyard continued to receive new members from Tribe management.

In his autobiography, Louis B. Seltzer, legendary *Cleveland Press* editor, wrote, "We reflect our times. If times are bad, we think they will be forever bad. If times are good, we think they will be forever good. Neither happens."[52] During the mid–1930s, it was difficult to persuade the average U.S. citizen that good times were just around the corner. A blue collar worker was fortunate to earn $25 a week. Many young men—often married—who worked in government-sponsored programs might have been paid only $30 a month. Minimum prices were the only savior for these laborers. Picnic hams cost 16 cents a pound, pork sausage 25 cents a pound, rib steak 21 cents a pound, pork and beans five cents a can, and coffee 15 cents a pound.[53]

So it was with the citizens of Cleveland and surrounding Cuyahoga County in 1936. In an effort to provide locals and visitors with relief from the dreariness of the Depression years, the city fathers organized the Great Lakes Exposition for the summer of 1936 and 1937. This exposition celebrated the centennial of the incorporation of Cleveland as a city.[54]

The downtown Mall was transformed into a grand entrance with brilliantly lighted pylons and a promenade leading toward Lake Erie. "Streets of the World" featured 200 cafes and bazaars representative of Ohio's 88 counties. Included in the popular Exposition were many historical and industrial exhibits, such as the Court of Presidents, a Hall of Progress, an Automobile Building, an art gallery, a marine theater, and horticulture gardens. On August 5, 1936, the Indians promoted a special day at Municipal Stadium—Lakefront Stadium in its early years—that was the only game played in the stadium that season. A crowd of 65,345 fans watched the Indians tie the New York Yankees, 4–4, after 16 innings of play.[55]

In this game, many fans feared they had witnessed a repeat of the Ray Chapman tragedy 16 years earlier. Many were spread throughout the center field bleachers, wearing light-colored shirts. There had been persistent efforts to block off the middle section of the bleachers with a green background, so batters could more easily see the pitcher's delivery. Nothing was done about this situation until years later.

The massive crowd was sickened and stunned as right-handed Yankees pitcher Monte Pearson, having the best year of his career, zoomed a pitch out of the white shirts toward catcher Frankie Pytlak, a five-foot, seven-inch, 160-pounder. He turned his head a trifle, because the previous pitch had missed him by mere inches. But this pitch caught the gritty catcher on the side of his face. Blood spurted from his mouth and he staggered as Yankees catcher Bill Dickey and Joe Vosmik, who was in the on-deck circle, grabbed him. He was rushed to the hospital, where x-rays revealed a triple facial fracture, ending his season, and his .321 batting average was sorely missed.[56]

The injury-prone Pytlak gained a measure of notoriety on August 28, 1938, when he, along with the Tribe's third-string receiver, Hank Helf, broke what was then called the "altitude catching record" in front of an estimated 10,000 fans gathered at Cleveland's Public Square. Both caught baseballs dropped from the top of the 708-foot-high Terminal Tower, the tallest building in Ohio. Mathematicians estimated the balls were traveling 138 miles per hour when they landed in the catchers' gloves. "For a while, I didn't know if the ball was going to hit me in the head or my glove. When I caught it, it stung more than Bob Feller's fastball." Pytlack reported. The two catchers were credited with breaking a record set 30 years earlier by Gabby Street and Billy Sullivan, who caught balls from the top of the 550-foot-high Washington Monument in the nation's Capital.[57]

When the Exposition season ended in 1936, nearly four million visitors from throughout the nation had attended, and gratified sponsors decided to carry the show over to the next year. The extended exposition season opened with a new attraction which was extremely popular. The Great Lakes Exposition gave its city and its visitors—seven million—a kind of Coney Island and miniature World's Fair jumbled together. It was the most marvelous diversion offered locals and visitors throughout the long years of the Great Depression. Even the jobless could occasionally scrape up enough dimes and quarters to take in the expo and admire its many shows. President Franklin D. Roosevelt visited the Exposition on August 14, 1936, and was given an enthusiastic reception. An aquacade featured water ballet shows and starred Olympians Eleanor Holm and Johnny Weissmuller. By the end of the second season, an additional three million visitors poured through the turnstiles. Nearly $70 million was spent by attendees.

In a 1991 article on Cleveland's self-image, John Fleishman described the pre–World War II city: "Questions of cultural or moral rankings could be only addressed by symphony conductors and preachers. For many Clevelanders, the only standards that mattered were posted at the financial exchange or the ball park."[58] From the entry of Cleveland's American League team in 1901 until the end of World War II, baseball was the preeminent national game. News of professional, semi-pro, and amateur teams filled sports pages from spring until fall. Newspaper coverage and radio broadcasts reached much of the country. Beginning in 1947, television, the emergence of professional football and basketball, and new marketing techniques brought major changes to the sporting world. In the United States, Cleveland's permanent move to Municipal Stadium, the integration of both the military services and baseball, and the forthcoming movement and projected expansion of franchises from the original eight-team leagues inspired a "whole new ball game."

From 1901 to 1946, the Cleveland team enacted the seasonal ritual of professional baseball: The yearly cycle of the winter "hot stove league," spring training, exhibition games, Opening Day, streaks and slumps, an All-Star Game break, the pennant drives to the finish, a World Series and the post-mortems sustained the public's interest throughout the year. Publicity flowed continuously from club headquarters and the American League service bureau, which was established in 1932, and soon thereafter from the National League service bureau.

With moderate success, the Cleveland franchise worked hard to promote the team during the Great Depression. The club had no full-time publicity agent, and the three local newspapers filled the void with extensive coverage of off-season activities and spring training. Opening Day, usually around April 15, was a festive affair. Pre-game activities featured the introduction of celebrities, a band and vocalist, flowers for the managers, and a parade of the teams to center field for the flag-raising. The Cleveland mayor, or possibly the governor—if he was from Cleveland—threw out the first ball. Frank J. Lausche, mayor of Cleveland during World War II, five-time Ohio governor, and two-time U.S. Senator, enjoyed displaying his talent. He had been a star third baseman in Cleveland's amateur baseball program and was a former minor league player.

Although several club owners resisted radio broadcasts of their games, broadcasts of Cleveland games proved to be a great incentive to fan interest and game attendance. Jack Graney's gravely voice became synonymous with Cleveland baseball. Graney had a style of his own. In the 1930s, there were not many broadcasters to emulate. His delivery is best described by Clevelander Bud Collins, noted tennis commentator: "You could worship from afar ... taking the daily scripture of the paper, or listening to games on the radio, when ... Graney took a few [liberties] in those untelevised days. Very little was routine before the eyes of the imaginative and histrionic Graney."[59]

His broadcasts were partially financed by the Standard Oil Company founded by fellow Clevelanders, the Rockefellers. The cereal maker General Mills marketed Wheaties, the "Breakfast of Champions," and helped sponsor baseball broadcasts nationwide except in Boston. By 1939 all 16 clubs were receiving a million dollars yearly for radio rights.[60]

Indians spectators were usually young and middle-aged males. The promotion of Ladies Day proved popular in the 1930s, particularly at Municipal Stadium. Three days after 25,707 women had attended a doubleheader, the *Plain Dealer* ran a feature on team bachelors.[61] By 1938 ladies filled the upper deck and provided additional customers for concessionaires. Scorecards consisted of only four pages, with only a few advertisements. The leading advertisers in the 1920s were banks, followed by hotels and sporting goods stores in the late 1930s.[62] Subsequently cigarette and beer ads claimed the most advertising space.

Management tried its hardest to draw fans into quaint League Park and, on special occasions, to Municipal Stadium. The late Bob Boynton, a native Clevelander, saw many games at the wooden structure on Lexington Avenue. He recalled,

> League Park was really a dump, with wooden flooring in the upper deck, a section of original wooden slat bleachers in left-center field that had never been replaced, unsavory sanitary facilities and a primitive scoreboard mostly operated from the back. The ball-strike numerals were inscribed on one side of each of seven motor-driven rotating metal plates and were controlled from the press box. Sometimes a number would spin crazily in the wind. The bottom of the tall right field wall, only 290 feet at the foul line, featured an irregular concrete surface that followed the contours of the vertical steel beams within, from which hits would ricochet at unpredictable angles.
>
> The top half of the structure consisted of chicken wire strung between beams, which extended forty feet from ground level. If one sat along the right field foul line at just the right angle, you could see the screen was replete with indentations from having been struck by thousands of baseballs during batting practice and games. If a ball hit the screen directly, it would drop almost straight down, but if it hit one of the beams over which the screen was stretched or beyond the point where the chicken wire ended, it might go anywhere, in or out of the park.[63]

The right field wall was an inviting target for sluggers like Babe Ruth, Lou Gehrig, Tris Speaker, Earl Averill, Hal Trosky, Jeff Heath, and many others. League Park served as the Cleveland team's primary home field until September 21, 1946. From that point on, cavernous Municipal Stadium took over as the facility which provided fans with entertainment both in professional baseball and football.

Cy Slapnicka, one of the earliest major league scouts to scour the hinterlands, was now an assistant to President Bradley in 1936. He had been an "ivory hunter" for the Clevelanders for 13 years. Rough around the edges, Slapnicka had become an extremely successful scout. Now he was in a position with much more power in making team decisions.

Upon Walter Johnson's dismissal, popular Steve O'Neill had become the Indians' 13th manager. The paunchy, rough-hewn Irishman had been a reliable catcher for Cleveland from 1911 through 1923. O'Neill was the most successful of four brothers who played in the major leagues. He saved his best season for the 1920 championship year, compiling a .320 batting average and 50 RBI. Charlie Grimm once remarked that "shaking hands with [battered old catcher] Steve O'Neill is just like grabbing into a bag of peanuts."[64]

When O'Neill took over the reins, Bradley couldn't resist commenting, "I really can't understand why anyone would want to manage a ball club. It's such a thankless, nerve-racking job, and every fan is your boss." O'Neill merely laughed.[65] The president acknowledged that he had only the average layman's understanding of the playing end of the game. "One newspaper story," he recalled, "tried to build me as a baseball man. The writer said that I had a .450 batting average at University School [in Cleveland]." Judge Ben Wickham corrected the reporter saying that "Alva may have had a fielding average of .450 but not a batting average with the same numbers."[66]

O'Neill, who had been third base coach for Johnson, led the Tribe to a successful conclusion of the 1935 season. The team won 36 and lost 23 games to move up to third place in the final standings. O'Neill experienced two critical events during the remainder of that season. In the first, Bruce Campbell, a 25-year-old outfielder, was stricken with a form of spinal meningitis and collapsed. Upon his recovery, he resumed playing in 1936 but collapsed again months later in Boston. Campbell was laid up for a month and went on to bat .372 in 76 games.[67] The gritty outfielder played well for Cleveland and ended a 13-year career with the Detroit Tigers and the Washington Senators and a creditable .290 lifetime batting average.

In the second instance, Joe Vosmik lost the 1935 American League batting championship to Washington's Buddy Myer by less than a full percentage point. Going into the final day, Vosmik retained a three-point margin. The leftfielder, to protect his safe lead, sat out the first game of a doubleheader against the St. Louis Browns. He received word that Myer had gone four-for-five in his game, which put his average ahead of Vosmik's. Vosmik played the second game and laced out one hit in three at-bats. However, he was victimized when the game was called after the sixth inning due to darkness, and his hitting opportunities suddenly ceased.

O'Neill had inherited the youngest infield in the history of the game, namely Trosky (22), Boze Berger (24), Billy Knickerbocker (23), and Odell Hale (26). O'Neill added 25-year-old Roy Hughes from Cincinnati.[68] It was a reasonably solid infield defensively, still young and with considerable offensive clout as well.

Hale was nicknamed "Bad News" by opposing pitchers, who credited him with using his head on the field in more than one way. Willis Hudlin, one of Cleveland's starting pitchers during the 1930s, described one of the most unusual plays involving Hale that he had ever seen:

> We were playing Boston [September 7, 1935] in a doubleheader.... Joe Cronin was [their] manager. In the ninth inning they had the bases loaded and nobody out. Cronin was the batter and he hit a line drive at Odell "Bad News" Hale on third. The ball went through Hale's glove and hit him in the forehead. Then the ball, without ever hitting the ground, caromed over to shortstop Bill[y] Knickerbocker who caught it [in the air] for the first out. Bill threw it to Roy Hughes at second for another out and he whipped it over to Hal Trosky at first for the third out and a triple play.[69]

It may have been the strangest triple play in baseball history. The Tribe won, 5–3.

Slapnicka soon became the most widely publicized club executive in the major leagues with the exception of Larry MacPhail, the Barnum of the Brooklyn Dodgers. The newest member of Cleveland's inner sanctum was variously portrayed as a "hopeless dope, a meddlesome busy body, a scheming Machiavelli, and a pop fly that fell foul by a foot."[70]

The truth of the matter is that the cliché "got the job done" applied to Slapnicka, and without doubt his proudest acquisition was Robert Feller, who had been groomed by his father William to become an outstanding major leaguer. The fact that Slapnicka was from Iowa and understood the state and its rhythms had given him instant credibility with Feller's father. A contract was drafted and signed by the father and his son in early 1936. Feller's bonus called for one dollar and an autographed ball from the parent team. He was scheduled to report to Class D Fargo-Moorhead in North Dakota. His salary was set at $500.[71]

However, Feller never reported to Fargo-Moorhead nor to the Double A New Orleans Pelicans, an Indians' farm team in the Southern League. The reason for his failure to report was a so-called "sore arm" and the need to graduate from high school. Since Feller had never spent a day in the minor leagues, Slapnicka and the Indians essentially violated the rule which prohibited the signing of a sandlotter to a major league contract. Meanwhile, Slapnicka raced back to Cleveland to meet with the franchise's Board of Directors, whom he assured, "Gentlemen, I've found the greatest young pitcher I ever saw. I suppose this sounds like the same old stuff to you, but I want you to believe me. This boy ... will be one of the greatest pitchers the world has ever known."[72]

During this time, Feller—now 17—continued to be shuttled around. The youngster arrived in Cleveland in June 1936, where he pitched for the Rosenblums, a high-powered amateur team in the nationally recognized Cleveland Baseball Federation program. The crafty Slapnicka was not interested in sending the young phenom to the minor leagues. However, the management wanted to see what young Feller could do against top-flight competition. An exhibition game was scheduled against the St. Louis Cardinals during the All-Star break. As Feller warmed up, players from both teams stopped to watch in fascination. They saw one pitch shoot over catcher Johnny Bessler's head and into the stands, shattering the back of a $1.50 seat. Frankie Frisch, the Cardinals manager and second baseman, summoned reserve outfielder Lynn King: "You ever played second base?" King said no. "You're playing second base today," Frisch retorted. "I'm too old to risk my life against that wild man."[73]

It was Feller's first appearance in a major league park, and the fireballer struck out eight of the nine batters he faced. The Indians left that game to launch an eastern trip to Philadelphia. Feller did not accompany the team, for a 17-year-old could not suddenly be expected to pitch against the best hitters in baseball. Possibly after two or three years of training in the minor leagues he would be ready, it was thought.

In the mind of manager Steve O'Neill, however, an idea refused to die: There would be occasions when an opposing team would have the winning run on third base with one or no outs in the last of the ninth or in an extra inning. Why not bring the kid east just for that purpose? If he lost, well, the probability was that they would have lost anyway. And he just might save a couple of games.[74] Feller was sent for, and the minor leagues never saw his pitches. Neither would many of the batsmen against whom he fired the most fearsome assortment of fast balls and curves that any hitter of any generation had known. Perhaps a handful of pitchers could have thrown a ball as fast or faster, but few if any could mix it with such an explosive curve.

In the fall of 1936, the Cleveland franchise and Feller found themselves in difficulty with the Commissioner's office. And who was in the middle of the imbroglio but sly Cy Slapnicka! The issue came to a head when Lee Keyser, owner of the Des Moines Class A team in the Western League, filed a complaint, claiming that he had attempted to sign Feller but that Slapnicka had signed him first. This *fait accompli* was a violation of a major league-minor league agreement on how amateur players were signed. The Des Moines owner added that Feller had worked out at his club's ballpark and had been offered $7,500 to sign a Des Moines contract.[75]

Occasionally, Commissioner Landis would crack down on a flagrant violator, but this practice of so-called poaching was so widespread that airtight policing was impossible. The Commissioner sent a letter to Bradley informing him that there would be an investigation. Slapnicka wanted to keep the young pitcher, as did the somewhat naïve Bradley, so he concocted a story and brought it to Bradley. The Indians chief responded to his administrative assistant after reading the fable: "'Slap,' if you tell that story to Judge Landis, he won't say a word. He'll just walk over to his window in his office and raise it. Then he'll pick you up and drop you out. And it's a long fall to the pavement."[76] Slapnicka relented because he still had an ace in the hole: The Fellers, father and son, wanted to stay in Cleveland. Landis called the Fellers to his office and asked several difficult questions. When Landis pointed out that he might take Feller away from the Indians, the young man blurted, "I don't want to play anywhere else. I want to play for Cleveland." His father added a warning word: "My word is as good as my bond and so is my son's. If you don't let him play for Cleveland, we'll take you to civil court and see what prevails, the laws of the land or baseball rules."[77]

Landis knew well that he had a tiger by the tail. Without a change in the agreement between the major and minor leagues, the freeing of Feller would allow wealthy franchises to run the bid up for the fireballer's services, and all minor leaguers would rally to seek free agency.

On December 10, 1936, Landis called Bradley to his office to announce his decision. He told the Indians president that Feller wanted to stay with the Tribe so badly that he had lied to him in the hope that he would allow him to remain in Cleveland.[78] Landis continued,

> Alva, nobody lies to me. Club owners, general managers, players, umpires—when they stand across from my desk and see this bony finger pointed at them, they tell the truth. Yet that 17-year-old boy had the nerve to stand there and tell me the blankety-blankest lie I've ever heard. I almost laughed in his face. But if he wants to stay in Cleveland as bad as all that, I think I'm doing the right thing by letting him stay.[79]

Feller signed a 1937 contract for $10,000, far more money than any ballplayer of his age had ever been paid.[80] Feller was now officially a member of the Cleveland Indians, and he remained loyal to the Tribe for 18 seasons as a team member and literally until his death.

Feller had hoped to be the oldest living member of the Hall of Fame at the time of his death. *USA Today* incorrectly reported that he was the oldest when he died on December 15, 2010. In fact, Bobby Doerr of the Boston Red Sox, six months older than Feller, was still alive as of that date.

Slapnicka's free and loose method of signing ballplayers, and helping effect their transfers throughout the minor leagues to the majors, caught up with him during his tenure as general manager. He was well known for contract manipulation. This is not to say that Slapnicka was the only one working the system. Scouting was and is an extremely competitive field, and taking shortcuts was more or less the norm. This practice would not be remedied until the introduction of an amateur draft in 1965. Additionally, one must note that the

Bob Feller, the greatest pitcher in Cleveland history, with 266 victories and nine pitching records. He pitched only for the Indians (18 years) and served in World War II for four years, receiving eight battle stars. He was elected to the Hall of Fame in 1962 (author's collection).

farm system was in its infancy during Slapnicka's early years in the field; the kinks had to be worked out. The Feller case, however, focused major attention on the Cleveland organization.[81] Slapnicka was frequently disciplined by Landis. One source claimed, "Slap spends so much time on Judge Landis' carpet as to be practically indistinguishable from the nap."[82]

Tommy Henrich recounted how he signed up with the Bronx Bombers of New York rather than with the Tribe. The left-handed hitter had shown considerable talent, and general manager Billy Evans signed him in 1934. However, Indians management, including Slapnicka, kept his abilities under wraps. He had a great year in 1936 with the New Orleans Pelicans, batting .346. When he was promoted to Triple-A Milwaukee in 1937 rather than to the parent team, he was naturally disappointed.[83] Instead, Cleveland management brought young Roy Weatherly up to the majors, believing he might become the next Joe DiMaggio.[84]

Evans, earlier dismissed by the Tribe, had no particular affection for Slapnicka. In an article for the *Saturday Evening Post* concerning the value of "baseball flesh on the hoof," he observed casually that New Orleans had a young outfielder named Tommy Henrich, who if he were a free agent, could easily sell himself for $15,000, a conservative figure.[85] In fact, Cleveland management had fatally neglected to record their ownership of this budding star formally, and had essentially "kept him in the closet."[86] This was the most common of devious dodges employed by baseball executives to circumvent the rules which forbade franchises to "owner control" more than 40 players. Most clubs considered that 200 young prospects undergoing development in the minors were not too many, and clubs might conceal 160 or more recruits. Judge Landis did not approve of this ruse.

Henrich asked Landis to look into his predicament. The judge determined that Henrich had been sold to Milwaukee by New Orleans. The Indians believed they owned Henrich and ordered the transfer, and Landis promptly declared the baseball vagabond a free agent. In April 1937, Henrich signed with the New York Yankees, in a deal worth at least $45,000, including the winner's share of the next three World Series won by New York.[87]

Gordon Cobbledick recalled his encounter with Henrich at the late Colonel Jacob Ruppert's Victory Dinner after the Yankees had destroyed the New York Giants in the 1937 World Series. The grand ballroom of the Commodore Hotel was teeming with beautiful women and a lot of men. A name band was playing, and champagne flowed. The pink-cheeked, wide-eyed Henrich took in the whole glittering scene with a gesture and grinned, "Next time you see Slapnicka, tell him I said thanks for all [of] this."[88]

According to Franklin Lewis, the Indians' front office believed that future Hall of Famer Billy Evans had "blown the whistle" by secretly advising Henrich of his rights. Henrich makes no mention of this issue in his autobiography, and in any case, nothing came of Bradley's threat to institute a civil suit against his former general manager for "breach of ethics." Instead, Slapnicka was again called on the carpet by Landis, who laid down the law regarding his exceedingly bad press throughout the country. Slapnicka's only reply was to shrug and comment, "We've still got Feller and those other guys haven't got anything but a headache."[89] Slapnicka suffered a heart attack in 1937 but continued to scout for several teams during the next 20 years.

Henrich was the only important Indians casualty of Slapnicka's maneuvering in the never-ending war between Landis and the men he tried to keep honest. On the other hand, the judge raided the St. Louis Cardinals in 1937 and made off with more than 60 young rookies; snatched 90 players away from Detroit in 1939 in a wholesale cover-up purge; caught the Cincinnati Reds cheating several times and cracked down with more or less vigor on virtually every club.[90]

In conversations with Henrich, he revealed that he had really wanted to stay close to home. However, like many youngsters of his era, he had been enamored of the exploits of Babe Ruth and Lou Gehrig as described on radio. It was not unlike the attachment of young and old in the 1930s to Notre Dame football, later glorified in the movie *Knute Rockne, All-American* (1940). Henrich, a true gentleman, soon became known as "Old Reliable," a tenacious hitter (much like Jorge Posada) who repeatedly came through in the clutch for the Yankees. He was proud of his accomplishments, and although modest, he believed he deserved strong consideration for the Hall of Fame.[91] Tommy Henrich died December 1, 2009, in Dayton, Ohio, at the age of 96.

The Indians' 1936 season started with high hopes. Unfortunately, the new manager needed a change of personality. Much like his two predecessors, the affable O'Neill was too lenient with his players. He was faced with five team members noted for their rowdiness and explosive tempers: two returning players, Frankie Pytlak and Sammy "Bad News" Hale and three newcomers, Johnny Allen, Roy "Stormy" Weatherly and Jeff Heath. Catcher Ralston "Rollicking Rollie" Hemsley, a free spirit with a drinking problem, would join these players in 1938.

O'Neill knew of Allen's hot-headedness but believed the right-hander could help the Tribe. Cobbledick described an example of Allen's competitiveness early in the 1936 season in a game against the St. Louis Browns. In the 16th inning, the score was tied at 7–7, and the Indians filled the bases with no outs. Allen was on second base. Second baseman Roy Hughes tapped a bouncer straight back to pitcher Jim Walkup, who flipped the ball to Hemsley at home plate for a force out, and the catcher relayed his throw to Jack Burns at first base for a double play. The *Plain Dealer* sports writer described with flair what Allen unexpectedly pulled off:

> But wait a minute. There comes Johnny—forgetting that pitchers aren't supposed to exert themselves unduly on the bases, forgetting everything except that his ball game is at stake, knowing there isn't going to be any seventeenth inning.... So here he comes carrying the mail. His thick legs are pounding and his great jaw is jutting belligerently as he rounds third and sets sail for the plate. Pitchers don't do that.... And pitchers don't do what Allen did when he reached a point ten feet from the plate. He left his feet in a head first dive and hit Hemsley a gosh-awful lick just as ... Burns' hurried throw landed in the catcher's mitt.
>   Umpire Lou Kolls jerked his arm in the signal that ... a triple play had been completed ... then as Hemsley was catapulted backward by the impact of Allen's 190 lb. body, Kolls ... reversed himself, spread his palms down as a sign that Johnny was safe. Allen, his face coated with a thick layer of League Park dirt, leaped to his feet and grinning broadly dashed for the runway to the dressing room.[92]

There was more to come with the fiery Allen. Meanwhile, after Henrich had been declared a free agent and no longer with the Cleveland franchise, Cleveland management had already decided to sign free agent feisty Roy "Stormy" or "Little Thunder" Weatherly, an outfielder, whose rave notices elicited comparisons with Joe DiMaggio. He was even better on the radio, where play-by-play announcer Jack Graney transformed the speedy outfielder into a Gulliver with a glove, a racing, leaping and diving maker of impossible catches, and sprinting almost to Willoughby [a suburb of Cleveland] for some of them. He would steal innumerable hits from the enemy, never making a routine out. A DiMaggio he was not, however he was an excellent defensive center fielder, an umpire-baiter, and hit over .300 in three of his seven seasons with the Tribe. He finished his ten-year career with a respectable .286 average. According to the *Cleveland News*, Weatherly had come about his umpire baiting naturally. Weatherly's father had attended a game at League Park early in the 1936 season, and witnessed his son being called out at first base by umpire Brick Owen on a close play. The elder Weatherly stormed out of his field box to register his protest with the startled arbiter.[93]

Weatherly may have been the first and only major leaguer to be granted a bonus for *not* being thrown out of single game during a season. Early in the 1940 season, Weatherly was ejected by Bill McGowan, one of the best umpires of all time, and allegedly the center fielder was "blacklisted" by the American League. Bradley promised the sleek outfielder $500 at the end of the season if he stayed out of trouble. Weatherly succumbed to his owner's wishes and received the check.[94]

There were few positive highlights for the 1936 season. O'Neill's efforts at team improvement were stymied by pitching woes. Mel Harder had arm trouble; Willis Hudlin suffered from bone chips in his elbow; Oral Hildebrand and Lloyd Brown experienced sub-par years. The always optimistic O'Neill endured the season with an injury-ridden pitching staff. The one bright star was newcomer Johnny Allen, who won 20 games, 11 of them after undergoing an emergency appendectomy in June.

On August 23, the Indians trotted out young Bob Feller for his first start, the beginning of a legendary career, to face the lowly St. Louis Browns, managed by Rogers Hornsby. The 17-year-old made an auspicious start, striking out 15 batters, only two short of Rube Waddell's American League record set in 1908. Feller won the game, 4–1, and began to command headlines on the sports pages. A few days later, "Rapid Robert" struck out 17 A's, tying the major league mark set by Waddell and Jerome "Dizzy" Dean in 1933. Feller finished his first season with carefully scheduled assignments and compiled a 5–3 record, then returned home to Iowa and completed his high school education.

Compelling as Feller was, without a doubt, the premier player on the 1936 team was Hal Trosky, the "Bohemian Bomber." He faced awesome competition from rival first basemen Lou Gehrig, Jimmie Foxx, and Hank Greenberg—who was out most of that season with an injury. Trosky was the league leader in total bases (405) and runs batted in (162), and second in home runs (42, a club record), and slugging percentage. *Baseball Magazine* put together a statistical analysis of the top offensive leaders in the American League for 1936 which showed that Trosky finished third behind the indomitable Lou Gehrig and Trosky's own teammate Earl Averill, who batted .378.[95] Trosky's firepower, however, was not enough to elevate the team above fifth place, and the Tribe finished with a record of 80–74, 22.5 games out of first place, but only three games out of second place.

Slapnicka, firmly settled within the hierarchy of team management, began to wield a broom in preparation for the 1937 season. He swept away several team members who had been integral to Billy Evans' team. In a major trade, he acquired outfielder Julius "Moose" Solters, shortstop Lyn Lary, and pitcher Ivy Paul Andrews from the St. Louis Browns. In return, the Tribe traded away popular Joe Vosmik, Billy Knickerbocker and Oral Hildebrand. Slapnicka made a frivolous and likely unnecessary trade when he pawned off Thornton "Lefty" Lee for Earl Whitehill, from Cedar Rapids, Slapnicka's home town. Whitehill and he were good friends.[96] But Whitehill was ineffective in his two years with the Tribe, for his best years seemed behind him.

To make matters worse, in 1937 Feller developed "house maid's" elbow and could not win until a "mechano" therapist—called a chiropractor today—snapped the ulna back in place, after which Feller steadily improved over the remainder of the season. Again, the star of the pitching corps was Allen, who fashioned a phenomenal string of 15 straight wins and was undefeated until losing on the last day of the season to Detroit.

The volatile Allen exploded after this game. He had desperately wanted to win in order to tie the American League record for consecutive victories held by four hurlers. His anger was directed toward third baseman Odell Hale, often called "iron glove." In the first inning, after Detroit's Pete Fox doubled, Hank Greenberg slashed a hot grounder to Hale. The ball slipped by him, and the home town scorer credited the slugger with a hit. Allen fumed. After the run, he pitched scoreless ball and suffered his first and only defeat, 1–0. Tigers journeyman pitcher Jake Wade allowed the Indians only one hit.

Franklin Lewis of the *Cleveland Press* explained what happened next.

> Allen was irate in the clubhouse, accusing Hale of sloppy fielding. Only O'Neill's intervention stopped a fistfight. Returning to Cleveland on the train that night Allen started yelling at Hale in the dining car. Just when blows seemed inevitable, O'Neill got between Allen and Hale and shouted, "You've popped off enough, now shut up." The pitcher yelled, "I ought to kill him, any bush league third baseman would have made that play." Again O'Neill ordered Allen to pipe down. "Listen, John," Steve eventually offered, "If you'll only shut up and forget it, I'll buy you gasoline for [your] trip back to St. Petersburg [Florida] (Allen's home). That's about twenty-five bucks. Good enough?" Allen agreed and the trip continued without incident."[97]

Midway into the 1937 season, the Indians surrendered first place to the perennial champion Yankees, and continued their descent to fourth place, a familiar spot for the Tribe. Fans grumbled, and Slapnicka had little confidence in O'Neill. He was not an O'Neill man. To top it off, Ed McAuley, a young baseball writer for the *Cleveland News*, addressed an open letter to O'Neill. "Get Mad, Steve," read the headline.[98]

In spite of a strong finish by Cleveland, the vultures began to circle over League Park. Feller came of age and finished with a 9–7 record and a 3.38 ERA. The team won 40 of their last 61 decisions for a .656 percentage. It wasn't good enough. O'Neill was the victim of the worst curse of all, finishing fourth for the fourth time during Bradley's tenure as president of the team. At the end of the season, the graveyard opened, and O'Neill relinquished managerial reins. "We hire the manager and the public fires him," Bradley reaffirmed again.[99]

O'Neill's career as a player, coach, and manager spanned more than a half-century. His gentle touch was his downfall. Bradley argued that the former catcher had tolerated insubordination and had failed to curb the violent behavior of several of his players. Gordon Cobbledick described O'Neill as a good person, a devoted husband and father, warm in his friendships, and a solid citizen in his community.[100] He stayed on with the Cleveland team as a scout and coach until 1943. The Detroit Tigers hired him as manager in 1944 where he enjoyed success for several seasons, winning the World Championship in 1945 and finishing second three times. O'Neill was fired in 1949. He continued to manage in the 1950s, first with the Boston Red Sox, where he followed manager Lou Boudreau in 1952, and finally the Philadelphia Phillies. The veteran manager died in Cleveland in 1962 at the age of 71.

Bradley must share a portion of the blame for the Cleveland team's less than successful performance during his tenure as owner. He hired a succession of managers for whom the chief criticism was their lack of fire and dash that could inspire a team to do a little better than its best when the occasion demanded it. After O'Neill's departure, Bradley attempted to lure manager Bill McKechnie away from the Boston Bees (Braves), who could not afford to pay him what his proven talents were worth. McKechnie wavered for several weeks between offers from the Indians and the Cincinnati Reds, and finally chose to stay in the National League with Cincinnati.

Bradley and Slapnicka agreed that their new manager must be the antithesis of Peck-inpaugh, Johnson, and O'Neill: He had to be volatile, effervescent, and fiery. His personality must preclude his team ever going to sleep on the field, as it had sometimes been accused of doing under previous managers. Slapnicka suggested that Oscar Vitt, whom he knew only casually, was such a man. Vitt had just won the International League pennant as manager of the Newark Bears, a farm team of the Yankees, by a margin of 25 games. Indications were that he possessed something more than a bubbling personality. Immediately after the 1937 World Series, the Indians president invited Vitt to Cleveland. Bradley was so impressed that he signed him without delay to a two-year contract—the first long-term agreement he had made with a manager. Bradley and Slapnicka were both smitten with their new manager.[101] The fans screamed, "Who's Oscar Vitt?" after Bradley introduced the Californian to replace the popular O'Neill. Who, really, was this man? The fans and players would soon find out!

6

The Tumultuous Tenure
of Oscar Vitt

*"I don't know much about this team, but I can tell you one thing.
We'll have the damnedest fighting team you ever had here.
There'll be no loafing. Ol' Os will see to that."*—Oscar Vitt,
quoted in Franklin Lewis' *The Cleveland Indians*

"Ol' Os," as he called himself, was a bandy-legged, gray-haired little man with a toothy smile who had made it to the major leagues as a banjo-hitting third baseman for the Detroit Tigers and Boston Red Sox. His playing career extended from 1912 through 1921, his first seven years with Ty Cobb of the Tigers. His career batting average was .238.[1] Vitt was a hustler, outspoken and proud of having played with Cobb during his heyday.

After signing a contract with Cleveland, Vitt returned to his home in San Francisco. Unbeknownst to the new manager, he was followed west by Stuart Bell, sports editor of the *Cleveland Press*, who hoped to interview the man who was to lead the Indians out of the baseball wilderness. Bell accomplished his mission, and within weeks, seeds of the Slapnicka-Vitt feud were sown. Vitt told Bell for publication that he would be "double-damned" if he would stand for any front office interference from Slapnicka. Specifically, he meant to pitch Feller in turn and not make a Sunday pitcher out of "Rapid Robert."[2] At this point, Slapnicka began to entertain some misgivings about his managerial choice.

Personal feelings aside, Slapnicka did work hard to give the new manager the makings of a pennant contender. Of all his transactions in 1938, the most expensive was the acquisition of third baseman Ken Keltner. The purchase price was between $35,000 and $50,000, a considerable sum during the Great Depression, depending on how one evaluated several players sent to Milwaukee in partial payment of Keltner's contract.[3]

The general manager picked up infielder Oscar Grimes, son of major leaguer Ray Grimes. Oscar had shown great potential with his play in northern Ohio amateur baseball circles. And he signed at no cost to the team. In mid–1938, Slapnicka picked up controversial catcher Rollie Hemsley from the St. Louis Browns in exchange for fan favorite infielder Roy Hughes and catcher Billy Sullivan. At the same time, in one of his biggest coups, Slapnicka snagged Lou Boudreau, a member of the University of Illinois whiz kids basketball team, from under the noses of the two Chicago teams.

In March 1938, the on-field atmosphere was definitely different when spring training began in New Orleans. Vitt had made it clear that a lack of effort or sloppy play would not be tolerated. Upon his hiring, he had declared, "I don't know much about this team, but I can tell you one thing. We'll have the damnedest fighting team you've ever had.... There will be no loafing.... Ol' Os will see to that."[4] Soon thereafter, at a meeting of team owners and directors, Bradley proclaimed, "I have every reason to believe we will have a fighting, peppy ball club in 1938. Our team should reflect the personality, the desire to win, the animation of our new manager."[5] Little did Bradley know what the next three years would bring in regard to the success and failure of his team.

In contrast to O'Neill, Vitt was inept at applying the basic principles of Psychology 101. If he detected lack of hustle, for example, players would hear about it loudly and abrasively, and an undercurrent of uneasiness began to rise among them. The players had been privately warned of Vitt's abrasive personality by friends who had been on his pennant-winning Newark team the year before. Bluntly, they said that the Tribe's new manager was obnoxious.

Vitt worked individually with certain players, particularly Feller and Trosky. He wanted the fireballer to lower his kick when winding up, but Feller was uncomfortable with this change, and dubbed Vitt the "Drill Sergeant." Yet Feller knew that something had to be done about his inability to hold runners closer to the bases. Vitt ordered left-handed Trosky to hit more to the opposite field rather than trying to pull the ball for power.[6] The hard-driving manager prohibited clubhouse poker, banned "intemperate" drinking and enforced a strict curfew on the road. "Rollickin' Rollie" Hemsley soon drew Vitt's ire after a drinking binge late in spring training that drew a week's suspension for the catcher. Further, Vitt threatened any team member caught carousing with Hemsley with a $500 fine, a significant loss to the pocketbook.[7]

In the first half-season, the Tribe was a sensation with a .632 winning percentage. But in spite of the club's fast start, Vitt was prone to pull players for the slightest miscue. To him, a losing streak or unforgiveable errors meant immediate lineup changes. He benched outfielders "Moose" Solters for Jeff Heath and then Roy Weatherly; he benched Bruce Campbell and replaced him with Heath, and he jerked veteran shortstop Lyn Lary from the lineup in favor of Jimmy "Skeeter" Webb. The entry of Webb, a son-in-law of former manager Steve O'Neill, into the starting lineup was out-and-out nepotism. In a 12-year career, Lary had a career batting average of .269 and 526 RBI. In contrast, Webb survived 12 years in the major leagues with a .219 batting average, including four seasons under .200, and only 166 RBI.

In Vitt's opinion, when a player missed a sign, he was not hustling. He was not hustling when he failed to think—and fast. Weatherly, for example, brought on the manager's wrath when he tried to stretch a single into a double in the ninth inning with his team three runs behind. The speedy outfielder was thrown out, thereby provoking a lecture from Vitt on the insignificance of an extra base. In Vitt's view, Weatherly should have played it safe under those circumstances.[8]

Vitt could only hope that the team would take to his high-strung, abrasive and sometimes embarrassing management. However, the older players, used to the softer demeanor of three previous managers, were not in touch with Vitt's gung-ho approach to the game. For the most part, with the exception of Averill (36), the regular lineup was under the age of 30. In spite of festering animosity between most of the players and their manager, the Indians continued to stay up with the leaders well into June. Feller began to hit his stride and along with Mel Harder won 17 games for the season. Heath, Trosky, Averill, Keltner, and Hemsley all hammered the ball with authority. The infield was erratic at times but adequate.

But there were ominous signs that the Tribe would begin to falter. Joe McCarthy, manager of the Bronx Bombers seeking their third consecutive pennant, commented, "The Indians will fold up.... They always do."[9] The first serious indication took place at Fenway Park in June. The agitator was the egregious Johnny Allen, who had done little to corral his volcanic temper.

In the first inning, Allen began to complain to plate umpire Bill McGowan about his calls, leaving neither of them in a good mood. McGowan was considered the best ball and strike umpire in the American League. In addition to complaining volubly, Allen was irritating Red Sox batters, slinging the ball with a sidearm delivery while wearing a long-sleeved sweatshirt with a three-inch tear near the cuff, which made the shirt flap in the air with a distracting effect. Batters complained to McGowan.

At the start of the second inning, McGowan walked to the mound and told Allen to remove the ragged shirt. Allen refused, complaining, "You can't show me a thing in the rulebook that says it is illegal." McGowan retorted, "Well it's not legal to me. It's got to come off or you're out of the game." "That's okay with me," Allen shot back.[10] He stormed to the bench and sat in the dugout, refusing to pitch.

Vitt had no choice but to remove him from the game. For his insubordination, Vitt fined him $250—causing Allen to display more anger. "No pitcher of mine can walk off the rubber without me telling him to," Vitt added. "You and McGowan can both go to the blazes," replied Allen.[11] The shirt incident became a *cause célèbre*, and photos of the shirt soon graced the sports pages of national newspapers.

Bradley gathered all the evidence of the incident and came up with a brilliant idea. He bought the shirt for $250, returned to Cleveland with the soiled and tattered garment, and had it mounted in a glass showcase in a men's furnishing department of the fashionable Higbee Company. It was more than coincidental that Charles Bradley, Alva's brother, was president of Higbee Company. The Allen shirt story spread throughout the country, and the shirt was later displayed at the Hall of Fame in Cooperstown.

From that point on, Allen's career went downhill. Supposedly, he slipped in his bathtub the night before the All-Star Game in July in Cincinnati. With an injured elbow, Allen pitched three innings with bone chips in his elbow, allowing one run in a losing cause. The elbow eventually required surgery and the right-hander was never the same on the mound.[12]

In 1943 Allen went to the extreme. Now pitching for the Brooklyn Dodgers, he was suspended after charging and shaking umpire George Barr because of a balk call. Manager Leo Durocher tackled the pitcher and broke up a fight. Allen later was traded to the New York Giants. After the 1944 season, he decided to hang up the glove for good. In a bit of irony, Allen actually umpired in the minor leagues in the late 1940s and early 1950s. He died at 54 in 1959.

Allen's sore arm and run-ins with umpires may have denied his entry into the Hall of Fame. His 142–75 record and .654 winning percentage compare favorably with Dizzy Dean's record of 150–83 and .644 winning percentage, and with Sandy Koufax's 165–85 and .655 percentage. All three pitchers had their careers cut short by arm injuries.

As the "dog days" of August approached, the atmosphere in the Cleveland dugout became poisonous. Vitt attempted to motivate his charges with sarcasm and insults, but the team played tighter, afraid of making mistakes. Then, as if Vitt had not encountered enough adversity, Bob Feller, his star pitcher, began to lose confidence in his ability. Knocked out in the third inning at Boston in late July, Feller confided to Ed McAuley of the *Cleveland News*, "I'm not sure what it is.... All I know is that I don't seem to be able to throw the ball fast anymore." "Do you mind if I print that?" asked McAuley. Feller replied, "No, why not?" "It's true," noted John Sickels, Feller's biographer.[13]

McAuley's story caused an uproar in Cleveland. *Cleveland Press* sports editor Stuart Bell thought the young pitcher was just "excited." He resisted pressure from his bosses to rewrite the *Press* game-day story to exclude Feller's comments. Bell finally gave in to pressure but not before predicting Feller would pitch well in his next start. Bell said he would resign his position if he was made to look bad. "You may know more about your business than I do," Bell told his superiors, "but I know more about young baseball pitchers."[14]

Another skeptic regarding Feller's so-called arm trouble was Bill, his father. Dad took a train back to Cleveland to console his son after a disastrous road trip. "Look here son.... It's like driving a fast car. After you ride in it awhile, it doesn't seem to be going as fast as it was in the first place." *The Sporting News* noted, "Some observers believe Feller has sacrificed speed for accuracy, but not many rival batters ... endorse that opinion."[15] To be sure, Feller had greatly improved his ability to hold runners, and his poise on the field under pressure had become that of a veteran.

In his next start, the fireballer proved both his father and Bell correct, as he fanned ten Athletics in a complete game for a 4–2 victory. However, the Indians could not claim the same success as a team, and as the season drew to a close, they made Joe McCarthy's prediction a reality. Injuries did not help their cause. Allen's elbow injury forced him out of action, and Harder was sidelined with a broken finger. Vitt tried everything from lineup changes to changing batting orders in order to rejuvenate the team, but with little success. The Tribe finished in third place, one notch higher than in 1937 but 13 games out of first place. They ended the season with an 86–66 record, only slightly better than the previous year. The Yankees went on to win their third consecutive World Championship, defeating the luckless Chicago Cubs in four games.

October 2, the last day of the season, provided more than usual excitement for baseball aficionados. There was drama in the air. The Detroit Tigers' premier slugger, Hank Greenberg, had stroked 58 home runs, only two shy of Babe Ruth's record 60. There was a record broken that day but it was not Ruth's—it was Dizzy Dean's strikeout record. It was young Rapid Robert who took center stage.

Feller said it was one of those days when everything felt perfect: his arm, his coordination, and his concentration. The crowd of 27,000 in Municipal Stadium was solidly behind their pitcher, even though Feller lost 4–1 due to seven walks. Entering the ninth inning,

Feller had registered 16 strikeouts. He struck out two men in the ninth inning, including outfielder Chet Laabs for the fifth time on a called third strike. He had broken Dean's record with 18 strikeouts, while suffering defeat. Only 19 years old, Feller led the American League with 240 strikeouts. Young Robert had arrived! This final game mirrored brilliant flashes of success dimmed by the frustration of players and manager. There was grousing in the dugout, and players complained about Vitt. Perhaps the off-season months would bring about a change of heart in both adversaries.

In *1939, Baseball's Tipping Point*, Talmadge Boston quotes Malcolm Gladwell's definition of "The Tipping Point" in his introduction. Gladwell had suggested that "Though most change occurs gradually, every so often there comes a special time, a dramatic time, [when] things seem different than they were before."[16] For American baseball, 1939 was, indeed, a tipping point, associated with the celebration of baseball's so-called centennial year and the invention of baseball by Abner Doubleday. Subsequent research has, for the most part, discounted any theory that Doubleday "invented" baseball in 1839 in Cooperstown, New York.[17] The consensus of baseball historians is that Doubleday was the wrong man, Cooperstown was the wrong place, and 1839 was the wrong year. Likely the game evolved from a British game called rounders and modified activities evolving from earlier forms of "ball." In 1965, Branch Rickey seemed to close the case succinctly when he commented that: "The only thing that Doubleday started was the Civil War when he answered confederate General P. G. T. Beauregard by firing the first shot from Fort Sumter."[18] Since 1900, baseball had moved along at a steady, if not sluggish pace. Noted scientist Stephen J. Gould defined this period of time as "punctuated equilibrium," and the centennial year provided opportunities for celebration and an increase in the game's popularity.

The United States Post Office joined in the celebration on June 12, 1939, with the issuance of a three-cent stamp commemorating the so-called 100th anniversary of the sport. President Franklin D. Roosevelt may have had some influence on the stamp issuance, not only because he was an inveterate stamp collector, but also as a dedicated baseball fan. Attractive pennants were distributed throughout the country. Most importantly the Hall of Fame opened in Cooperstown, and five giants of the game—Ty Cobb, Babe Ruth, Honus Wagner, Walter Johnson, and Christy Mathewson—were the first players elected to the Hall of Fame.[19] Over the decades, the museum has become an excellent showcase for baseball's bountiful history.

Moreover, the major leagues of this era featured many stars who would eventually enter the Hall of Fame. One of the greatest in the game's history was Lou Gehrig, affectionately known as the "Iron Horse," who was struck down with a rare disease called amyotrophic lateral sclerosis, more commonly referred to today as "Lou Gehrig's Disease." The Yankees first baseman was forced to retire on May 2, 1939, after playing in a record 2,130 consecutive games. This record held up for 56 years, until Cal Ripken of the Baltimore Orioles set a new standard playing in 2,632 consecutive games.[20] The revered Gehrig died on June 2, 1941, at the young age of 37.

Other future Hall of Famers who excelled during this era included outfielders Ted Williams of the Boston Red Sox, the "Yankee Clipper," Joe DiMaggio, and two years later Stan "The Man" Musial of the St. Louis Cardinals, and pitchers Feller and Leroy "Satchel"

Paige, one of several great African American players unable to show their wares in the major leagues as yet due to segregation. His time would finally come in 1948 with the Tribe at the twilight of his career. For the younger generation, Carl Stoltz founded Little League baseball in Williamsport, Pennsylvania, in the summer of 1939.[21]

In many ways, 1939 was also a "tipping point" in the history of the Cleveland franchise. Subtle events suggested that "the beginning of the end" of the Bradley regime approached. Even with a new manager, attendance had increased by only 11,000 from 1938 to 1939. Management tried to determine how many games to play in the confines of friendly League Park and how many in the cavernous Municipal Stadium. Rental costs at the stadium rose year by year. Now management seriously considered the prospects for night games.

In the early 1930s, Bradley had had much ownership support in his opposition to night baseball. Frank Navin, longtime owner of the Detroit team, had proclaimed "[night games] will be the beginning of the end of Major League baseball."[22] (He did not have to worry about this issue because he died on November 13, 1935.) In fact, Detroit was the last American League team to begin playing night games. The most vociferous critic of night baseball in the 1930s was Ed Barrow, general manager of the New York Yankees: "I am more convinced than ever that there is absolutely no future in electric lighted play." Several years later, he reiterated his conviction: "Night baseball is a wart on the nose of the game."[23] In a 1934 editorial, *The Sporting News* vehemently opposed night baseball. When the first night game was played in Cincinnati on May 24, 1935, National League president Ford Frick commented, "Night baseball is just a step above dog racing."[24]

Bradley likewise viewed night baseball negatively. For him, baseball was a "day game," even though he knew that night baseball would generate additional profits. He recalled, "When we played all our games in daylight, everyone could get all the baseball he wanted even if he worked all day. There were 12 Sundays, 12 Saturdays and one or two holidays at home. How many fans see more than 25 games a season?"[25]

By 1937, however, Bradley had changed his mind. Indeed, he became known as the "Apostle of Night Baseball" in the American League. The Cleveland owner knew he had a tough fight to bring night baseball to the Junior Circuit. Ed Barrow continued his strong opposition, but Bradley gained the support of Connie Mack of the Athletics. The proponents needed another vote, and a bit of chicanery won the day. Washington owner Clark Griffith wanted to sell first baseman Zeke Bonura to the New York Giants for $20,000. Bradley and Mack refused to waive Bonura unless Griffith joined them in a vote for night baseball, and Griffith yielded to their request. In late 1938, the league voted 5–3 in favor of night games.[26]

Later, Bradley admitted, "You can't sit back and say, 'This thing is bad for the game so we are not going to let the fans have it even if they holler for it.' We are here to cater to ... popular tastes and ... popular demand."[27] The League approved seven night games for each team for the 1939 season.

Cleveland played in the first American League night game against Connie Mack's A's in Shibe Park on May 16, 1939, before 15,000 fans. Roy Weatherly was the first batter, and the A's went on to triumph, 8–3, in ten innings. Meanwhile Bradley had lights installed in Municipal Stadium, and the first of seven scheduled night games was played at the Stadium on June 27, 1939, against Detroit with Bob Feller pitching. Unaccustomed to lights, the Tigers were virtually helpless before Feller's slants in a 5–0 shutout. He struck out 13 batters on his way to pitching his third one-hitter. A possible no-hitter was ruined by Earl Averill, the former Indians favorite who had been traded to Detroit two weeks earlier.[28]

The night games boosted Indians attendance figures by a factor of three: For the seven games, the Indians drew 35,000 fans per game in contrast to 12,000 for day games. In spite of the boost in attendance, however, the Indians' overall attendance dropped 90,000 from the previous year (564,000 in 1939 from 652,000 in 1938). But attendance figures would rebound in 1940, missing by 10,000 the team's attendance record of 1920, the Indians' only world championship season.[29]

Attendance may have decreased in 1939, but fan interest remained high through the voice of Jack Graney, whose voice and imagination were magnetic, increasing listenership year after year. More stations in communities surrounding Cleveland and in the neighboring states of New York and Pennsylvania with increased transmission power carried all the action of the Tribe's games.

Graney was said to have a whiskey voice. Whatever, the broadcaster intoxicated his listeners with descriptions of Tribal feats that could not be challenged by other forms of communication. The quality of TV reception of major league games did not improve until the early 1950s. Graney's listeners could hear the ticker-tape clicking in the background giving him the barest of details. He made the dullest plays glow vocally, painting masterpieces.[30] His imaginary broadcasting was not unlike that of future president Ronald Reagan, who broadcasted Chicago Cubs games in the early1930s from Des Moines, Iowa.

Graney transformed 5'7"centerfielder Roy "Little Thunder" Weatherly into a Gulliver with a glove, a racing, leaping, diving maker of impossible catches, sprinting almost to Willoughby (a neighboring community) for some of them. Or he might say, "the center fielder's riding the Flying Red Horse (sponsor Mobil gasoline's trademark) back for the fly ball ... he's got it!"[31] When Graney broadcasted away games with one of his early radio partners, "Pinky" Hunter, he added little touches to make it sound as though the two men were broadcasting from the site. He even added the roar of a crowd via a vinyl recording of crowd noise.

At times, when the ticker-tape said the pitch was a called strike, Graney would say, "Look out, Pinky, here comes a foul ball." Then he would slap the desk to make it sound as though the ball hit the press box. "That was a close one, Pinky," Graney would say. "We were corny, but it was fun," Graney recalled years later.[32] By means of his detailed description, the listener could smell the rosin in the dugout and hear the clean crack of balls against the bat. After a broadcasting career of 21 years, Graney retired in 1953. He and his wife, Pauline, of 70 years, moved to Bowling Green, Missouri, to be near their daughter. The Graneys lost an only son during World War II. The veteran broadcaster died April 20, 1978, at the age of 91.[33]

In 1939, Oscar Vitt began his second year at the helm, already feeling the heat. The manager had not been happy with the Indians' performance in 1938. Cy Slapnicka was not happy either. The general manager was developing an intense dislike for Vitt, whose personality had begun to adversely affect the Indians' performance in 1938.

Slapnicka's decision to trade popular Earl Averill to Detroit in June 1939 created a firestorm with the fans. Reporters and Slapnicka believed the one-time star outfielder was slipping. In 1938, he had played in 134 games, hitting .330 with 93 RBI, clearly a strong year at the bat. It was more likely the 37-year-old was traded due to a disagreement over a bonus he thought he was owed. When one considers that the Depression still lingered, that attendance had dropped precipitously, and that the owner was tight, a bonus was unlikely. Averill was beginning to become a clubhouse distraction, and the groundwork was laid for a trade.[34] Unfortunately, the Indians made a poor exchange, receiving Tigers pitcher Harry Eisenstat, who was of little help to the team.

Afterwards, President Bradley defended the trade: "Earl was dissatisfied.... He went on record early in the season that he would like to be traded."[35] Management's logic was sound, but the press and angry fans reacted in unison, ripping the move. They were unhappy to see their longtime star traded to the rival Tigers, and the trade did little to alleviate the acidic clubhouse atmosphere. (This trade presaged one of the Rocky Colavito trade fiascos.)

In 1975, Averill was inducted into the Hall of Fame, the 11th Cleveland Indian honored. His lifetime batting average was .318. When he passed away in August 1983, in Everett, Washington, he was extolled by an editorial tribute in the Cleveland *Plain Dealer*:

> The death of Baseball Hall of Famer Earl Averill brings back boyhood memories of old League Park ... and the athletes who were our heroes. Averill was one of the brightest stars, a batter with enormous power in what appeared to be a modest frame. It was said you never could understand his strength until you saw him with his shirt off. He was a graceful athlete with a unique swing but suffered from a misfortune that plagues many. He reacted the same way to a home run or a strikeout. To fans this looks like indifference. Yet, sometimes these athletes are extremely intense, burning inside. Averill was a great player who looked like he didn't care.[36]

What a contrast to many of the players in today's game, who stand at the plate after a home run in an adulatory position. As an aside, Averill's son, Earl, Jr., played in the major leagues for seven years. He did not approach his father's accomplishments.

The 1939 season began dreadfully for the Clevelanders, with numerous rainouts and more defeats than victories, and the team did not extricate themselves from seventh place until late in April. May was a month of .500 ball with little gain on the leaders. The season was saved by two events: the first night game in the Stadium and a late-season desperation maneuver to increase action at the box office.

In June, as the season continued to move forward in a ho-hum fashion, the Indians were unable to move very far above .500, while the Yankees were on their way to a fourth straight World Championship. To add to Vitt's travails, after the season ended Slapnicka made several personnel changes that led to controversy and more agitation with the manager. The most controversial took place December 15, 1938, when he sent Denny Galehouse, a Doylestown (Ohio) native, to the Boston Red Sox for outfielder Ben Chapman. A right-hander with average talent, Galehouse started only 12 games for Cleveland in 1938, compiling mediocre overall numbers (7–8 record). Galehouse became an important figure in Indians lore ten years later. The Tribe believed they had enough pitching strength with Feller, Harder, Allen, left-handed Al Milnar, and two youngsters, Joe Dobson and Bill Zuber.

The trade for Ben Chapman was another story. At first, it looked to be a good trade because the Boston outfielder had hit .340 in 1938 and he was expected to improve a sagging hitting attack. Offensively, Chapman was an asset. He batted .290 with 101 runs scored and 82 RBI. The speedster stole 18 bases, the most of any player on the team. Why was Chapman problematic? The main reason was his rancorous behavior in the dugout. Ed Linn, well-known Boston scribe, wrote about Chapman's behavior in Boston: "Chapman goes down in the annals of baseball as the quintessential clubhouse lawyer—good ball player but a bad guy to have on the club." He added, "He second-guessed [manager Joe] Cronin endlessly. The joke ... was that Joe had to play him because he was afraid Ben would lead a mutiny if he left him on the bench while Joe was out in the field."[37]

Umpire Ernie Stewart recounted a run-in with Chapman, who was a big Tennessean, built like a giant, a great ballplayer but an ornery bastard. He was the first major leaguer Stewart threw out of a game. When Chapman was playing for the Washington Senators, he faced knuckleball pitcher Roger Wolff who was pitching for the Philadelphia A's. According to Stewart,

> He threw Big Ben a knuckler. Strike One. Nothing said. Another knuckler. Strike two. A third beauty. Strike three. Ben never moved his bat. He turned around and said, "You pretty boy son of a bitch." I said, "Ben, you are through for this day." "You're not putting me out!" I said, "No, I've already put you out. Get out!" Manager Bucky Harris came over to home plate. "What's the matter, Ernie?" I told him. [He said] "Good boy" and went back to the bench.[38]

On September 16, 1942, player-manager Chapman of Richmond in the Piedmont League slugged umpire I.H. Case and was suspended for the 1943 season.

Vitt's relationship with his players continued to erode. The beleaguered manager was under fire from the press and fans for constantly juggling his lineup, belittling players in public, and generally alienating them. In plain words, the players despised him. Gordon Cobbledick of the *Plain Dealer*, attempting to be fair on the issue, insisted that [Vitt] had proved himself a sound tactician, that in his strategic moves including the handling of pitchers, had guessed rightly more than wrongly.[39] Upon being reminded that he was unpopular with certain players, Vitt's only comment was, "I guess it can't be helped. I'll just go along doing the best I can ... and the boys will have to like it."[40]

He was rewarded with good play from several unexpected sources. For example, Ken Keltner continued to perform well at third base. A fine defensive player, he batted .325, stroked 35 doubles, and accumulated 97 RBI, playing in all 154 games. Feller as well came into his own with his best season to date. Hemsley and outfielders Bruce Campbell and Chapman gave workmanlike performances. Roy Weatherly was an outstanding defensive center fielder and batted .310. Feller received pitching support from Mel Harder (15–9) and local pitching prospect Al Milnar with a 14–12 record.[41]

However, two of Vitt's key players—Trosky and Heath—did not perform up to expectations. Hal Trosky was a stalwart in the starting lineup, with the potential to become a Hall of Fame candidate, but he fell into a horrendous hitting slump, at one time without a hit in fifty-seven times at bat. In desperation, in a meaningless game, the left-handed hitter turned around and batted right-handed; he lined a single to left field, then returned to batting left-handed and ended his slump. Trosky analyzed his batting slump: "doing a little something wrong ... that spoils [one's] perfect timing.... Mine was due to having my rear foot turned too far."[42] Of more serious consequence for Trosky was the onset of severe migraine headaches. "I know the fellows are counting on me," Trosky told the *Cleveland News*. "I know that I can't always make good for them. I'm all right until I get on that field. Then my head starts hammering."[43]

In spite of these impediments, the all-star first baseman had a solid year, even though he played in only 122 games. He batted .325, drove in 104 runs, and clouted 25 home runs and 31 doubles. A leader in the clubhouse, the Iowan would soon lead his dispirited team members in an overt rebellion against manager Vitt.

In deference to Vitt's many problems with his players, one must point out they were not the most angelic group of men. Throughout his three-year tenure as manager, Hemsley, Chapman, Roy Weatherly, Johnny Allen, and Jeff Heath were a pain in the neck for Vitt. Heath was a particular thorn in Vitt's side. He had an uncontrollable temper. Although the power hitter displayed potential to be the greatest Canadian-born player of his time, too often he was his worst own enemy. Heath so impressed Vitt when he first saw him in the batting cage in 1938 that he called the rookie "the best natural hitter I've seen since Joe Jackson."[44] A handsome, muscular athlete, Heath had come off of two outstanding years in the minor leagues. Later, in 1938, Slapnicka reiterated Vitt's opinion of Heath. Former manager Roger Peckinpaugh added, "If every man on the ball club had showed [*sic*] the determination and hustle that Jeff has showed me ... we'd be so far ahead you'd think we were in another league."[45] Heath's seasons ahead, however, would not particularly demonstrate these attributes.

Heath performed more like a veteran than a rookie in his first full year in 1938, batting .343 with 21 home runs and 112 RBI. He eventually would be one of only three players to hit a home run in every major league park of this period. The other two were Harry Heilmann and Johnny Mize. Flaws soon appeared in his performance and temperament, and Heath and Vitt grew to hate each other.

In 1938, Heath was benched for not hustling. In 1939, Vitt's feud with the left fielder came to a head when he fined him $50 for failing to run out a ground ball. On another occasion, Heath and pitcher Johnny Broaca fought in the dugout, though as it turned out, the confrontation had been staged for Vitt's benefit. The pair had hoped Vitt would intervene, with Heath planning to land a punch on his manager. Heath's temper reached a boiling point when Ed McAuley of the *Cleveland News* suggested that he ought to be a better team man. He added that the outfielder should give 100 percent all the time. Heath relayed a message that he would physically throw McAuley out if he ever showed his face in the locker room or dugout again.[46] McAuley dutifully reported Heath's retort in the *News* the next day, then went to the dugout just before game time. A horde of reporters was on hand, but no blood was shed nor punches thrown, and Heath greeted McAuley with a big grin and handshake.[47] Later, word leaked that Bradley had sent a message to the clubhouse: "Tell Heath that if he touches one hair on McAuley's head, I will see to it that he never plays one more inning in organized baseball."[48]

To add to this dysfunctional mixture in the dugout, by now Feller had shed the early shyness exhibited when he first joined the team. Often described as the BMOC (big man on the club), he had gained more confidence. However, the hurler was not the most popular player on the team, for he could be brusque to others, including his teammates, and sometimes spoke his mind without considering the repercussions of what he said. This tendency plagued Feller throughout his life.

Further, a cadre of teammates was jealous of his success. Feller was aware of this negative feeling toward him, and remarked, "There's a whole dugout full of players on the other side trying to pin my ears back.... What difference do a few more make even though they wear Indians on their chest?"[49] The farm boy "took the bull by the horns." The youngster had recorded a modest record of 31 wins and 21 defeats in his first three years. In 1939, he "arrived," as the saying goes, winning 24 games and losing nine. He led the league in complete games (24), innings pitched (296⅔), and strikeouts (246), and posted a respectable ERA of 2.85. Lefty Grove led the American League with a 2.54 ERA. Feller also led the league in walks (142).[50] He finished third in the MVP voting and would have easily won a Cy Young Award (this award didn't begin until 1956). In addition, Feller recorded his second and third one-hitters and was the youngest pitcher to date to win 20 games in a season.

However heroic, Feller could not lift the Tribe into contention for the pennant against the Yankees, and the best Bradley could get in 1939 was a second-place finish. In the 20 years starting in 1921, when Cleveland had finished second to the New Yorkers, who claimed their first pennant, the local team finished ahead of the Yankees only twice. The first time was in 1925, and the second would be in the coming year: 1940.[51]

Cobbledick, trying to allay the constant drum-beating to fire Vitt, commented, "I don't think Cleveland has any kick coming against the kind of baseball it has seen in the last two seasons. It has been far better than the average in other major league cities. And I don't think Vitt is going to be fired."[52]

Vitt wasn't fired. Bradley did not want to add another manager to the graveyard. On August 12, 1939, the lead story on the front page of the *Plain Dealer* proclaimed that Vitt had been rehired, and talk of his ouster was silenced. The owner was pleased with Vitt's performance, considering the obstacles he had overcome, and underscored his support by adding that the players "have got to know who the boss is." Further, he said, "and they may as well know ... that Vitt will be giving the orders again next season. Naturally, I will back him up in whatever action he may see fit to maintain discipline."[53]

Responding to the owner's decision, Cobbledick wrote with an even hand: "Vitt's patience with his team was better and his tendency to ridicule team members in public was less noticeable. His strategic moves, including the handling of pitchers, proved right more often than not." The veteran scribe concluded, "Criticism of [Vitt] by [his] players is to be expected.... Probably no manager ... ever escapes private criticism by the men under his command."[54]

The second of the two player transactions pulled off by Slapnicka—as referred to earlier in this chapter—had more of an impact on the Tribe's future than most of his previous endeavors. In 1939, attendance remained stagnant in spite of new stadium lights. The Indians were literally out of the pennant race. Slapnicka decided to bring up Lou Boudreau and Ray Mack, two young phenoms from Buffalo. In comparison to several other club executives, Slapnicka was considered only a minor law breaker. Notwithstanding his relative innocence, suspicions arose about his decisions. Often he was mercilessly blasted when in reality he took the rap for someone else. The Lou Boudreau–Ray Mack promotion was a good example. Scouts were pronouncing the duo as the finest second base combination since Jack Barry and Eddie Collins of the Philadelphia Athletics. The two were members of Cleveland's primary farm team, the Triple-A Buffalo Bisons in the International League. During the early weeks of the season their sensational progress was chronicled by the local press.

Slapnicka was panned for rushing a pair of promising youngsters into a situation that would be above their ability. Had he done this in order to sell a few extra tickets? Outraged reporters asked Vitt if he thought this move was a bit premature. Vitt agreed that it seemed unwise, but he could do nothing but make the best of the situation. The story came out later that Vitt had wanted Boudreau and Mack against Slapnicka's better judgment, and this disagreement did not enhance the relationship between these two protagonists.[55] Neither realized that his days with the Cleveland organization were numbered.

The arrival of Boudreau and Mack on the parent club was not an easy matter. The New Orleans Pelicans of the Southern Association, managed by former Indians manager Roger Peckinpaugh, had a working agreement with the Tribe. The Buffalo Bisons were managed by Steve O'Neill, another former Indians manager. The question was how to assign two second-base combinations from the minors, Boudreau and Mack, and two other youngsters, shortstop Frank Scalzi and second baseman Jim Shilling.[56] O'Neill told Slapnicka he preferred Scalzi and Shilling because he wanted to make a good showing in Buffalo and they looked to give more immediate help. Boudreau and Mack, however, were two raw collegians with only a portion of a season in the minor leagues under their belts. Peckinpaugh also wanted Scalzi and Shilling, but because he possessed seniority, he won the decision, and Boudreau and Mack started the 1939 season in Buffalo.[57]

In mid–July, Slapnicka contacted O'Neill and informed him that management desired to bring the two young players up to the "big time." O'Neill, in a tight pennant race, wanted to keep the phenoms, and the players also wanted to stay in Buffalo. Slapnicka won out because the parent club was looking for a solution to a middle infield that was in disarray. Meanwhile, Scalzi never made it to the majors and Shilling came up in late 1939 for a brief stay.[58]

The Boudreau and Mack move was an instant hit. On August 7, in a night game, these two new players helped the Tribe defeat St. Louis, 6–5, before 16,000 fans in the Stadium. Boudreau broke in with a triple and single. He had been an outstanding athlete in basketball and baseball at the University of Illinois and was an integral part of the 1939 "whiz kids" Illinois team which tied the University of Minnesota for the Big Ten basketball championship. Playing third base, Boudreau with the Illini also won the Big Ten baseball championship that year.

Boudreau's athleticism caught the eye of scouts from the Chicago Cubs and the Tribe. Scout George Zrelan of the Indians struck first. He offered Boudreau $1,000, $500 each for mother and stepfather, and $500 for his father. In addition, Boudreau's mother would receive $100 per month until her son graduated from the university. It was an oral agreement and Boudreau did not sign any papers. Boudreau was young and naïve. Unfortunately, Boudreau's stepfather, not a very nice person, wanted all of the $1,000. Boudreau said no to this request. In retaliation, and in order to spoil the young player's chances, his stepfather sent a letter to

Major John L. Griffith, then commissioner of the Big Ten, telling him of Boudreau's arrangement with Cleveland.[59]

Major Griffith forwarded the letter to the University of Illinois Athletic Board, asking for an investigation and ruling. Three of the seven members voted for Boudreau to be allowed to retain his eligibility so long as his parents returned the money to the Indians. Three other board members voted that Boudreau should be declared ineligible. The seventh member of the board, Athletic Director Wendell Wilson, for whatever reason abstained.

That meant the decision had to be made by the Big Ten athletic directors, who, of course, did not want this outstanding athlete to compete against their teams, so Boudreau was declared ineligible the first semester of his senior year.[60] Boudreau's case became a *cause célèbre* in Chicago. Three nationally known sports columnists supported Boudreau. Jim Enright, John Carmichael, and Wendell Smith wrote that the Big Ten had made the wrong decision and was hypocritical.[61]

When Slapnicka offered to renounce the Indians' claim on Boudreau, he could have become a free agent, legally able to sign with any team. He later remembered, "I could have gone out and sold my services to the highest bidder but I didn't feel that was the right thing to do. There was more loyalty in those days."[62]

Mack's offensive shortcomings were offset by solid defensive work at second base. He was an important asset in developing a formidable double-play combination. Boudreau, in particular, caught the eye of the press and fans. Franklin Lewis wrote, "From the moment he trotted out to shortstop for infield practice, Boudreau had the crowd in the palm of his hand.... He had the movements of a natural athlete." Cobbledick concurred. "You had to be there to believe it. Halfway through the first inning, the kid from the bush was running the team and everybody [on] the field and in the stands knew it."[63]

The decision to rehire Vitt for a third year seemed to calm the team. The two rookies gave the troubled team a lift in the last weeks of the season. The Tribe made a strong finish, winning 36 of their final 56 games, and the team finished in third place for a second straight year with a record of 86 victories and 67 defeats, a one-game increase in victories over the 1938 season. On the debit side, the Tribe finished 20½ games behind the Yankees in 1939 as compared to 13 games in 1938.

Optimism permeated the press box and the Tribe nation. Could this team, which looked to be formidable, mount a credible challenge to win a pennant in 1940 after a 20-year hiatus? Could the Tribe, with a solid lineup, play to their capacity, in spite of Vitt's abrasive managerial style? As it happened, the 1940 season would develop into one of the most tumultuous, exciting, and disappointing seasons in Cleveland franchise history.

In a satirical fashion, the following ditty by the author sums up the atmosphere in the wigwam as the Tribe prepared for spring training in 1940.

> The hitters had better hit or Vitt will not be able to sit.
> The batted ball had better end in the mitt,
> Otherwise there will be a conniption by Vitt.
> Mental errors will not cause Vitt to quit,
> But you can bet the Skip will have a fit.
> Any effort less than the best,
> Will ensure Vitt a trip to the Wild West.[64]

7

Tempest in a Teepee

*"I do not want to be a hero, and I would hate like hell
to be a cry-baby."*—Lou Gehrig, quoted from
Geoffrey L. Ward and Ken Burns, *Baseball*

Often defined as America's national pastime, baseball has had a special place in the hearts of the public and for decades in the 20th century outdistanced the popularity of other team sports. Baseball has generally reflected social change, and in any case, has certainly not been isolated from social change. As it developed, baseball moved forward with positive changes, though sometimes at a slow pace, as in the advent of night baseball and radio broadcasts. To its credit, the sport eventually took a leadership position in racial integration; only in labor relations and league expansions did owners drag their feet.

Historian John Rossi considered these changes in racial fairness the most revolutionary in the game's history. Advancements were initiated by a basically conservative institution which was often profoundly suspicious of innovation. He noted, "each change was an important symbol by which baseball defined itself to the sports public. These changes helped save the National Pastime."[1]

During the 1920s and 1930s, Cleveland took the lead in promoting baseball on all levels. The Forest City was recognized for its outstanding Amateur Federation baseball program. The city fathers, led by the entrepreneurial Van Sweringen brothers, provided the city with an up-to-date rail system, which in turn brought fans to downtown Cleveland and the new Municipal Stadium along the lakefront. At this point, this stadium held more patrons than any other stadium in the major leagues.

Because Jack Graney's broadcasts of Cleveland Indians games had a dramatic impact on a growing number of "dyed-in-the wool" fans, Bradley was eventually brought to see the wisdom of night baseball, and Cleveland became the second club to schedule the seven games allowed each season until 1946, when the number of night games increased. Without doubt, the Cleveland baseball team was the main sporting attraction in Cleveland through the beginning of the fourth decade of the twentieth century.

The excitement of the approaching 1940 season was tempered by war clouds over Europe and Asia. The Nazi blitzkrieg raced through Denmark, the Netherlands, Belgium, and soon thereafter France. Japan made repeated forays into China and Southeast Asia. For the most part, the United States resisted direct involvement, although lend-lease materiel were shipped to a desperate England. President Franklin D. Roosevelt was constrained by an impending election, and the populace was split on foreign policy by strong lobbying of isolationists led by Charles Lindbergh, the country's air hero.

Against this backdrop, to Clevelanders, however, baseball was in the air as the Tribe returned from spring training in Ft. Myers, Florida. International tensions did not diminish the cry of "Play Ball." Optimism prevailed along the shore of Lake Erie. Possibly, it was hoped, the local team could finally derail the four-time World Champion New Yorkers. The Tribe had finished ahead of the Yankees only once (1925) since winning their World Championship in 1920.[2]

Scribes at the three dailies in Cleveland, led by Gordon Cobbledick, Franklin Lewis, Ed Bang, Frank Gibbons, and Ed McAuley, chose the Indians—partially out of loyalty—to finish first or second. The team featured veterans Trosky, Keltner, Chapman, Weatherly, Heath and Hemsley. Hemsley was a bigger asset after having joined Alcoholics Anonymous the year before. In a heartwarming story, Hemsley called the local scribes together during the 1940 spring training season. The catcher had been sent home the previous spring by Vitt for drunkenness. He told the reporters, "it has been a year since the most wonderful thing happened to me.... I didn't have a drink all last season. Alcoholics Anonymous did that for me."[3] The reformed catcher had a creditable year, batting .267 in 119 games. He remained Feller's personal catcher until December 4, 1941, three days before Pearl Harbor Day. The pitching staff of Feller, Harder, and Milnar was augmented by the acquisition of left-hander Al Smith from the Philadelphia Phillies.

In spite of acrimonious feelings toward manager Oscar Vitt, there was a cautious air of optimism among team members. Bob Feller was determined to start the season with a bang. Prior to the advent of television and league expansions, Opening Day of a 154-game schedule took place approximately in mid–April. The players and fans hoped that spring had arrived and cold, rainy weather was about to abate. All teams in both leagues were located north of the Mason-Dixon Line and east of the Mississippi River, with the exception of two St. Louis franchises on the west side of the mighty river.

However, the weather did not cooperate in Comiskey Park on April 16. At game time, the temperature was 40 degrees, with a raw wind coming off Lake Michigan and sweeping through center field. The Indians faced chunky left-hander Eddie Smith, who would post a 14–9 record that season. Graney, beginning his ninth season behind the mike, sat in a warm studio at WHK in Cleveland, ready to describe all the action. The incessant wind bothered both pitchers. In the second inning Weatherly dropped a fly ball in center field. Feller walked the next two batters to load the bases. The right-hander settled down to fan third baseman Bob Kennedy.

The Tribe was having its own troubles with Smith. The visitors broke the ice in the fourth inning. Jeff Heath scored on a two-out triple by Hemsley. Meanwhile, starting in the third inning, Feller retired the next 20 batters. Tension grew in the Indians' dugout. Could the Indians' ace pitch a no-hitter after having pitched three one-hitters in his short career? The Tribe still held a 1–0 lead when Feller faced the meat of the White Sox order in the ninth inning. To that point, he had struck out eight batters, and he retired the first two batters.

A big hurdle remained in future Hall of Famer "Old Aches and Pains," Luke Appling. Notorious for making a pitcher work by fouling off pitches, this shortstop was one of the toughest batters to retire in baseball. Appling fouled off several pitches. The battery mates finally decided to walk the pesky pitch-spoiler. Feller recalled later that he had a feeling Appling was going to stroke a hit.[4] Appling claimed one of his foul balls hit the chalk, but third base umpire Lou Kolls did not see it that way.

Feller now faced another nemesis, right fielder Taft Wright. Twice while playing for the Washington Senators, he had delivered clutch hits to hand Feller tough defeats. After taking a ball, the left-hander smashed the next pitch between first and second base. Second baseman Ray Mack made a brilliant play, ranging far to his left, almost behind first base. He made a diving stop and while on the ground, threw to Trosky to retire Wright by a half-step.[5] Joyful teammates descended upon Feller. The full-bloomed star had pitched the first and still the only Opening Day no-hitter in the major leagues. A meager crowd of fewer than 16,000 gave Feller a standing ovation. Gordon Cobbledick of the *Plain Dealer* captured the moment: "The thing that had to happen sometimes happened.... [T]his chilly afternoon ... the Iowa hurricane rapped at the door of baseball's mythical Hall of Fame ... for the fourth time during his brief and meteoric career ... and was finally admitted."[6]

Feller's electrifying heroics gave little inkling of the disturbing and disappointing season which was about to unfold. Much like the storm clouds which enveloped Walter Johnson's tenure as Indians manager, a repeat performance was about to take place, and Bradley was most concerned that another player-manager uprising would derail the team's chances for a highly successful season. Unfortunately, Vitt's abrasive personality continued to affect team morale adversely. Game mistakes brought on a tirade. The manager commented publicly on issues players thought should be discussed in the clubhouse, and the press fed on this increasingly despotic atmosphere. Out-of-state reporters mimicked the carping of local writers with critical comments. Several suggested the beleaguered manager be fired, while others came to his defense.

However, the team continued to play well in the early going. They bounced in and out of the top spot with Boston and Detroit during April and May. But tensions continued to increase, and players spoke to Vitt only when necessary. Willis Hudlin, veteran pitcher for the Tribe, recalled, "Vitt wasn't tough to play for, but he'd go to other people and run [down] his own players. He'd talk about them to other managers, other players, and the press."[7] Feller recalled Bradley admonishing Vitt: "Oscar, you talk too much. It's going to get you in trouble someday."[8] Upon being reminded of his shortcomings, Vitt commented tersely, "I guess that can't be helped. I'll just go along doing the best I can ... and the boys will have to like it."[9] Feller added that, in his opinion, "Vitt's decision to manage from the dugout [instead of third base] ... hastened the [impending] blowup.... Out on the coaching lines he could yell and release his emotional steam. In the dugout, he paced up and down and delivered sarcastic remarks. It was our feeling that he produced tension."[10]

As the season moved into June and a road trip to Boston, the atmosphere in the dugout was oppressive. On June 11, Feller had a rough day in Fenway Park, losing to the Red Sox, 9–2. While he struggled, Vitt complained to the rest of the team in the dugout, griping, "How can I win a pennant with him? He's supposed to be my ace."[11] Feller heard him but said nothing. He was not what one would call a veteran yet and chose not to cause a scene. One day later the veteran Mel Harder, probably the most popular player on the team, was routed and lost to the Red Sox, 9–5. Vitt complained afterwards, "When are you going to start earning your salary? It's about time you won one, the money you're getting." Harder shot back, "I gave you the best I had."[12] Picking on Harder only intensified the players' anger. Vitt's remark to Harder was one too many to take.

At the end of the Boston series, a group of older players decided to take their complaints to Frank Gibbons, highly respected baseball writer for the *Cleveland Press*. He described their visit:

> The players loitered near Hotel Kenmore. "Let's take a walk up the street," Trosky said. "Something we want to talk to you about." We went down Commonwealth Avenue, a short distance and into a downstairs bar. Trosky, Harder, Keltner, and Johnny Humphries were there, as I recall. Trosky did the talking. "We think you are a pretty good guy," Trosky stated and might have added ["for a reporter."] "You work with us in the spring and play cards with us. We want to talk and we don't want it in the papers." All right, I said.
> "We're going to get rid of Vitt and we wonder what you think of it?" Trosky continued. I asked for details. "He's knocking us in the papers, to other teams, and he blows his top in the dugout during games. We're going to Alva Bradley with it and we're going to get him fired! What do you think?" I told them I didn't think they could win and their charges in the paper would seem childish.[13]

For weeks the rumors had floated that the team was on the verge of rebellion. That night on the New York Central back to Cleveland, a larger group of players held a secret meeting to determine their strategy. They planned to meet Bradley the next morning (June 13). Not all of the key players would be in attendance for this showdown. Trosky's mother had died, and he was on his way to Cedar Rapids, Iowa. In his haste to fly home, he neglected to contact Gibbons, so the *Press* reporter did not know of the team's plans for a meeting until too late.[14]

Neither Lou Boudreau nor Ray Mack attended the meeting, for the veteran players had decided to leave the young newcomers out of the impending revolt. The future Hall of Fame shortstop Boudreau remembered Ben Chapman taking them into a men's room on the speeding New York Central train: "We are not including you two in our petition, not even mentioning your names in the matter. You're both too young in baseball, just starting out and if this should backfire, it could ruin your careers."[15] Boudreau considered this decision a generous gesture on the part of Chapman, Hemsley, and the others. He believed that had the veterans asked him and Mack to join forces, they probably would have done so, for the twosome did want to be part of the "gang." But they appreciated the protection offered to them since they were only in their early twenties and more vulnerable than the others.

Several other team members did not participate. Outfielder Beau Bell, newly acquired from the St. Louis Browns, was excused. Weatherly, somewhat of a rebel from Texas, turned his back on the protest. Young Cleveland native Mike Naymick, Clarence "Soup" Campbell, Hank Helf, and Al Smith were also excused.

In 1940, the players had no union for support or to negotiate with management. With rare exceptions, players did not have an agent. Negotiations were primarily on a one-to-one basis, with management holding the upper hand. The press was the most likely source for breaking news. Television and advanced techniques of communication had not come on the scene as yet. Radio stations had limited staffs to follow up on breaking news and behind-the-scenes activity in the clubhouse.

Several local reporters were aware that something was amiss in the Indians' camp. However, they had only fragments of the story. Gordon Cobbledick alone put the pieces together. Before the team departed from Boston, the *Plain Dealer* reporter sat in the lobby of the Hotel Kenmore, which was empty of players. Even the most inveterate lobby-sitters among them were absent. Suddenly a dozen players appeared at once. The veteran writer deduced that something was awry, and "I nosed around," he remembered, "and finally got the story as we headed back to Cleveland."[16]

On the morning of June 13, a dozen teammates went to owner Bradley's office at 8:30 a.m. Bradley had thought only Harder was meeting with him, possibly on personal business, and although his door was always open to his players and employees, he was taken aback to see so many players. "Well, come in. What's this all about?" he asked. Harder stated the players' position: "We think we've got a good chance to win the pennant, Mr. Bradley," he began, "But we'll never win it with Vitt as manager. If we can get rid of him, we all feel sure of this."[17]

The veteran pitcher summarized the team's general complaints: Vitt sneered at his players on the field; he was double-dealing with [the players], praising or belittling first one, then another according to his immediate whim; he held them up to ridicule before the press; he held grudges and undermined their confidence. During this meeting, the telephone rang. The owner answered. "Mr. Bradley, this is Hal Trosky [in Cedar Rapids, Iowa]. I want to tell you I am 100 percent in favor of the story you are now hearing. These are my sentiments without qualifications."[18]

Bradley was stunned when he heard the players' arguments for dismissing Vitt. "I think he was flabbergasted in the beginning," Harder remembered, "but then realized we were serious." When Bradley saw Bob Feller in the group, that made a lot of difference. "Alva Bradley was a good friend of mine," Feller reminisced. "He knew if I was there it wasn't just for tea and crumpets."[19] When the players were about to leave the owner's office, Bradley warned them, "If this story ever gets out, you'll be ridiculed for the rest of your life." He turned to his secretary, Katherine Kelley, and lamented, "Miss Kelley, those boys don't know what they're starting." And he was right.[20] An hour later, just before noon, Bradley received another dreaded call, this one from Cobbledick, who repeated almost word for word the complaints the players had voiced to the owner. "Is that what they said?" Cobbledick asked.[21] Bradley had to admit to the near word-for-word accuracy of the reporter's question.

For a journalist, to report an exclusive scoop is like winning a Pulitzer Prize. Cobbledick stayed away from League Park the next afternoon while he wrote an account of the rebellion. In order to allay suspicion, a substitute reporter was sent to the press box to deliver the message that "Cobby is tired and was given the day off."[22]

His magnum opus was kept out of next morning's early edition of the *Plain Dealer*, so that printers could not leak the breaking news and radio stations would be unable to pre-empt the story before it hit the streets. News of the Tribe's rebellion was held back until the final edition was delivered on June 14, 1940. The headlines screamed the story and, for the moment, pushed the German conquest of Paris to a secondary level. Rival reporters, caught completely unaware, later inquired of Bradley, "Is this story true?" The Indians boss confirmed its truth: "It couldn't be more factual if Cobby had been hiding under the table during the meeting of the players."[23]

In the late summer of 1993, this author spent an afternoon with Bob Feller and Russ Schneider in Municipal Stadium. The Indians were playing a rare doubleheader. I often kick myself for not asking Feller who had been the informer, but it is likely that he would not have told me. I interviewed several key individuals for an answer, with no success. Neither of Cobbledick's sons, Bill or Dorn, could come up with an answer, nor did Schneider, longtime baseball writer for the *Plain Dealer*. Lou Boudreau surmised that it had been Hemsley who spilled the beans. He recalled, "To be honest ... I don't know how the Vitt story was leaked. [Cobby] scooped everybody including me and a lot of the players."[24]

At the time of his retirement, Cobbledick was asked to name the informant but declined. He responded, "Only three people know, the player, myself, and my wife."[25] Feller recalled that one of the other reporters could have had the story before Cobbledick, but he was too busy in a bar bending elbows.[26] Trosky, one of the more vehement rebels, was ruled out because he had been in Iowa. The two most likely informants were Hemsley or quiet, dignified Mel Harder. There was speculation that Hemsley, referred to as "Deep Throat" by author Bill Gilbert, was the one because he wanted Vitt's job. Others often named Harder since he and Cobbledick were close friends and were known to go hunting together on occasion.

Cobbledick's death in 1969 prompted colleague and sports humorist James E. Doyle to reflect in his own column,

> A scoop was a scoop in that baseball era of long ago.... It was Cobby ... who came up with one of the hottest scoops in all baseball history. It was the story of the tempest in the teepee ... in which Cobby had sat ... until it was time for the setting in the *Plain Dealer*.[27]

Whenever there is a player-management disagreement or players are upset by what a writer puts in print, there is the potential for retaliation. Often, players have little recourse when a writer displays his cleverness at the defenseless athletes' expense. In contemporary society, athletes often refuse to give interviews to the press for fear that their remarks might be misconstrued. In collegiate sports, and particularly in football, players often speak when they should refrain from responding to questions from the press. In the 1940s, the maligned athlete occasionally spoke up when it would have been well to remain silent. A good example was the contentious exchange between young Ted Williams and the Boston press.

Cobbledick, tough but fair, visited the Indians' bench after writing an objective but not flattering column about a player. His policy was to face the player immediately: "Give them their shot at you," he said.[28] On one occasion, after Cobbledick had taken a seat on the bench, a player said angrily, "I read what you wrote." Cobbledick responded, "I wrote it to be read."[29] The nonplussed player was completely disarmed.

One columnist not a member of the Cleveland press corps in the 1940s was Terry Pluto. He came along later, first writing for the Cleveland *Plain Dealer*, then the Akron *Beacon-Journal*, and finally back to the *Plain Dealer*. Winner of numerous journalism awards, Pluto wrote from a fresh perspective. Writing in 1999, his reflections about Vitt are deserving of a hearty laugh. If you recall, Vitt was a member of the Yankees organization who had managed the 1937 Newark Bears to a runaway title in the International League. The Bears won the pennant by 25½ games. Journalist Robert W. Creamer called the Bears probably the best minor league team of all time.[30] Vitt replaced easy-going Steve O'Neill. Pluto wrote, "So you bring a guy with Yankee arrogance to Cleveland, a guy who thinks he's going to set all the hayseeds straight. He had about as much tact as the gout."[31]

Feller told Pluto that Vitt's wife was an astrology fan and that Ole Os consulted her (and the stars) when it came to making out his lineup and pitching rotation. Whether true or not, when the team was not going well, Vitt would harken back to his Newark days and claim that the Bears had been better than the Indians. This harangue no doubt did not sit well with All-Stars like Feller and Harder.

Sportswriters suggested that a major league player with a name like Ossie would grow up with a chip on his shoulders. This might be particularly true if he were one of those feisty infielders who had made it to the "big-time." Managers like Leo Durocher, "Sparky" Anderson, Dick Williams, and Ozzie Guillen come to mind. Pluto believed Vitt was of the same ilk. He described Vitt as a pain in the backside and a bowl of green oatmeal. His players implied that Vitt wasn't a manager but, instead, "nails dragged across a blackboard" or a "dentist's drill."[32]

Pluto went so far as to suggest that Vitt hated his players: "The players certainly wished he'd awaken one morning and gargle with battery acid so they'd never have to hear his voice again." He concluded that for a supposedly bright guy, Vitt could be a total "stonehead," adding, "[Vitt] was stunned that all his vile words uttered in what he thought was in 'strict confidence' continued to make it back to the players whom he attacked."[33] The fans didn't like Vitt either—not because he had all the tact of an IRS agent with a migraine but because the Indians were underachieving. Vitt was booed regularly, but that would change the day after news of the revolt reached the papers.

Hal Lebovitz, long-time sports writer for the *Cleveland News* and *Plain Dealer*, succeeded Cobbledick as the sports editor for the *Plain Dealer* in 1964. Years later, while cleaning out his office, Lebovitz came across the original statement signed by the players, which declared, "We the undersigned publically desire to withdraw all statements referring to the resignation of Oscar Vitt. We feel this action is for the betterment of the Cleveland Baseball Club."[34] Bradley had persuaded the team to release this statement. The letter was signed on June 16, 1940, three days after the blowup.

Twenty-one members of the 25-man roster signed their names. The four players who didn't sign were Roy Weatherly and Ben Chapman, who were unavailable, and Jeff Heath and Roy Grimes, who were away with injuries. The letter was given to the *Plain Dealer* that night (June 16). It was printed on the sports pages the next morning. This retraction was too little too late. The damage had been done—three days earlier. According to historian Fred Schuld, this statement in no way meant the players had changed their minds. To the contrary, insiders on the team called the present situation an "armed truce," likely to continue for the rest of the season.

Vitt met with Alva Bradley and had his authority confirmed. "Mr. Bradley told me I'm still manager of this team." It was hard to feel sorry for the hard-nosed and arrogant Vitt, but his managerial situation was untenable. He admitted to being hurt by the rebellion and, in particular, he could not understand how the young stars like Keltner and Feller were involved. He spoke of Feller as "The greatest kid in the world ... like a son to me."[35]

Feller did not reciprocate the warmth of Vitt's remarks. The outstanding pitcher, for those who knew him well, was reserved but could speak his piece. His increasing self-confidence developed into a desire to voice his mind, not always diplomatically. In 1956, the year Feller retired from the mound, *Cleveland News* writer Ed McAuley asked him pointblank if he truly had disliked Vitt or if he had been anxious for the respect of the older players: "I hate[d] his guts," Feller replied directly, "and I don't care who knows it." The twirler had told other reporters, "Oscar makes us nervous. I wouldn't want to play for him [another] year."[36]

Feller, who lived in Cleveland until his death in 2010, recalled this issue. "I remember signing that [document]. It was ... Bradley's idea. But it didn't work. Vitt's trouble was he talked too much. It's everybody's trouble, I guess. The man is dead and I don't want to say any more."[37] Two other players who signed the retraction statement, still living in Cleveland in the late 1970s, gave their reaction nearly 40 years after that dreadful event. Clevelander Al Milnar, who had an outstanding season in 1940 with an 18–10 record, recalled he had gone along reluctantly with the rebellion: "I had my best years under Vitt," he remembered, "My feelings were good toward him. I was young (27). I felt the same as Roy Weatherly did. But I went along with the other fellows—the team—while he didn't."[38]

Southpaw Harry Eisenstat commented,

> I was very much against the revolt.... It's not that I favored the way he handled the players because he did talk out of both sides of his mouth. It simply was that I wasn't in favor of striking out against a manager. But I didn't have much to say because I was in the hospital at the time. I was involved in a collision while covering first base and broke a blood vessel. The guys kept me informed by phone. Hemsley, Trosky, Johnny Allen, Jeff Heath, and others and I tried to tell them to cool it. I was in favor of sitting down with Vitt and talking things over, but I had little influence.... After my experience in industry, I know I was right.... The whole thing hurt our concentration. I don't know if it lost the pennant for us but it certainly didn't help. It put us all on edge.[39]

By and large, the Cleveland press tended to handle the Vitt situation with caution. Franklin Lewis insisted in the pages of the *Cleveland Press* that Vitt resign, but Lewis realized that the Tribe couldn't fire Vitt because it would establish a precedent that would restrict every future manager of the organization. Most of the local scribes refrained from ripping the players or the manager, an indication they agreed with most of what the players had to say.

Soon after the dust settled, Cobbledick asked, "Is Vitt a good manager?" and then answered the question. "Recent events suggest the answer is 'no.'"[40] Not all sportswriters agreed with Cobby. Jim Schlemmer, respected columnist for the nearby rival Akron *Beacon-Journal*, viewed the players' action as mutinous: "To permit a group of high-priced players to throw out their manager is to give in to a revolutionary move which can only hurt baseball."[41]

Schlemmer's comment about high-priced players is questionable. It is ludicrous to compare salaries of twenty-first century professional athletes and wages of typical 40-hour-a-week employees. The comparison of salaries with the year 1940 is somewhat less bizarre, for inflation was minimal then. What was a high-paid salary in 1940 in relation to the clerical or blue-collar worker at the twilight of the Great Depression? Most players negotiated directly with parsimonious owners since there was no players' union. One or two star players on a team would meet the category of highly paid. Feller's salary was $26,000 in 1940.[42] In the same year, Trosky, who had six consecutive seasons of 100 or more RBI, drew a salary of $19,000. Joe DiMaggio's salary in 1940 was $32,000.

Franklin Lewis of the *Cleveland Press* pointed fingers instead at the front office. "I think the officials of the baseball club should get together and hide in shame for allowing such a putrid situation to develop right under their nose." He added in his column that if they didn't know of this approaching revolution ... they are not capable of operating a base-ball team in the major leagues. If they did know of the inevitable and allowed such a con-dition to develop, words fail me."[43] Long-time sportswriter Ed Bang of the *Cleveland News* wrote that, to win the players' respect, Vitt had "to be more patient with their shortcom-ings."[44]

On June 18, 1940, Judge Landis, responding to a letter from Bradley regarding the Cleveland situation, seemed to take the players' side as suggested by the facts and circum-stances relayed to him: "The players did not act without reason," he wrote, "and ... with the pennant biting them ... the team was not being strengthened by such goings on."[45] Landis wondered if Vitt was keeping day-by-day incident records concerning the team members. Writing more like a psychologist, Landis concluded,

> Maybe, after all [the uprising] was a good thing.... Emotions and sentiments naturally present in such a development had better be let out than kept depressed.... [T]he English government for many years has afforded accommodations in Hyde Park for all discontented persons to air their views, their theory being that the fellows who do that won't dynamite anyone.[46]

To date, no evidence has been uncovered to suggest that Vitt kept any kind of book as questioned by Landis, detailing his actions or those of the players.

Regardless of what the players, press or fans thought about the internal turmoil, Bradley chose not to act; he was not about to change managers in the middle of the pennant race. The situation settled down somewhat. The players had to move forward. The manager became more subdued and spoke to his men only when necessary. Harder reflected that Vitt became a quieter manager.

The "Vitt Rebellion," as well as the prologue and epilogue, was to that date easily the most comprehensively covered sports story ever to startle the readers of Cleveland newspa-pers. Eleven years later, Ed McAuley of the *Cleveland News* confirmed that Bradley's hasty decision to keep Vitt cost him the only chance he ever had to win a pennant in his 18 years as owner of the Tribe. He wrote that Bradley remembered:

The players who asked me to fire Vitt didn't demand that I replace him with Luke Sewell (a former Indians great and later coach). They only said they thought Sewell would be a good man for the job. I turned my chair toward the window and looked out over the lake. I could see the entire picture. I honestly believe that if I had fired Vitt then and named Sewell manager, that 1940 team would have won the pennant by 20 games.[47]

Bradley went on to explain, "I simply couldn't do it. I had to act for the good of baseball.

If my players could order a change of managers, then so could the players of every club in the business. I decided right then that, whatever my investigation might disclose, Vitt would be our manager the rest of the season."[48]

Bradley was an early supporter of radio broadcasts. In a discussion of baseball and the radio with Ed Bang, Bradley recalled that when his group bought the Indians in 1928, he had commented that "progress is progress" and that baseball was in the middle of a big changeover. He told Bang that as far as Cleveland was concerned, the broadcasting of games started when general manager Billy Evans told Bradley that Cleveland station WTAM wanted to pay the franchise $2,500 for broadcast rights for the last half of the 1928 season. "Billy said it looked to him like getting $2,500 as a gift. And besides the broadcasts might be good publicity." Bradley added," They certainly were ... but when I read about $3,000,000 in budgets [in 1950] I wonder where all the progress is going to end."[49]

The records showed Cleveland on a rampage, winning 19 of 27 games from just prior to the team revolt and up to June 25. The club remained in first place, two games ahead of the Tigers, and the usually conservative Bradley publicly predicted a pennant for his team.

James E. Doyle of the *Plain Dealer* wrote a daily column called the "Sports Trail." The humorist was the *Plain Dealer*'s effort to provide parody reminiscent of the redoubtable Ring Lardner. He added his two cents to the serious analysis of any given game or sporting event in Cleveland. The Indians-Yankees encounters always brought forth his best rhetoric: "Play ball," bellowed David Boone Doggler, just after hard-hitting rain had brought a cessation of hostilities. "them Yankees shouldn't mind the rain. They're all wet, anyway." The columnist concluded, "That [remark] was rather out of line, but it does seem certain they've reached the end of their reign, boys. The league is full of Yankee clippers this year."[50]

In spite of a winning record on the field, all was not well in the dugout. The team met the bellow of "CryBabies" in city after city and even in their own hometown. The scene was not pleasant, especially when coming home to one's own fans. Before the start of the first home game at League Park after the team uprising, the majority of the 18,000 fans cheered manager Oscar Vitt and booed their home team. Sports writers from opposing cities were no more humane than the fans. Shirley Povich of the Washington *Post* wrote that the Indians were a club of prima-donnas and ridiculed Bradley's business acumen. More than one writer pointed out that Vitt had a better record than Cleveland's previous "nice guy" managers, Walter Johnson and Steve O'Neill. The "writing heads" simply implied that the club lacked the guts to succeed. Feller did not agree. Even though there was an "us against them" atmosphere, Feller believed the label helped down the stretch. "The tag helped.... Otherwise I don't think we would have gotten as close ... as we did."[51]

Trosky had a different view. When he returned from his mother's funeral, the captain of the team, for which assignment he received $500, was greeted with boos: "The biggest shock of my life was coming to the ballpark and hearing myself practically booed out of the stadium," Trosky said. "That was one of the saddest days of my life. They [had] me down."[52] It did not help that the Iowan suffered from those migraine headaches which would shorten his potential Hall of Fame career. A few weeks later in New York for a series with the Yankees, Trosky chased a jeering fan up a flight of subway stairs. There is no record whether or not the first baseman caught the heckler. The slugger was burning when it was over.

In the next week, the maligned Clevelanders won five games in a row. It was not the humidity or hot woolen uniforms worn in 1940 that sent mild-mannered Trosky into a rage after one game. He stormed into the clubhouse: "I sure would like to meet a couple of those grandstanders. When I got through, the league would have all my money in fines and I might be washed up for the season."[53] It was that way game after game as the team traveled from city to city, and even when they returned to their home park. As July approached, the atmosphere in the clubhouse and dugout remained subdued. The club was trying desperately to win their first pennant in 20 years. A majority of the players had signed the so-called truce for Mr. Bradley, but they did not believe what they signed nor did they act as if they were repentant. For the most part, silence was the order of the day.

Two players gave Vitt more headaches than any others: Johnny Allen and Jeff Heath. Both had been perennial troublemakers since they joined the franchise in 1936. On July 4, 1940, the Indians were playing Detroit in a crucial doubleheader. Vitt called in Johnny Allen for a relief appearance. The manager was talked out of the move by captain Trosky, who suggested that Allen be saved for the second game. Trosky's strategy seemed to make sense. The problem was that Allen had already arrived on the mound after warming up in the bullpen. He walked haughtily back to the dugout, embarrassing Vitt.[54]

Heath was another matter. This young man had played only 32 games with the Tribe in 1936 and 1937. When Vitt joined the club as manager in 1938, he called Heath "the best natural hitter I've seen since Joe Jackson."[55] As it turned out, this remark was premature and exaggerated. Flaws soon appeared in his performance and temperament. Unfortunately, 1940 was his worst season in a 14-year career and the press blamed him for the demise of the Tribe's drive for a pennant. Heath and Vitt argued consistently. There was no love lost between the two, and Vitt shuddered, "Those eyes. Lock the door. You never know what he will do."[56] What Heath didn't do well in 1940 was perform, batting only .219 with 50 RBI.

In early August, Vitt asked Slapnicka to bring up an outfielder from the Louisville farm team. Slapnicka still had no use for Vitt. It had been rumored that the general manager had encouraged, if not actually instigated, the earlier team uprising. He could not or just did not acquire the requested player for Vitt.[57] Still the team had not given up. The Tribe won 12 of 16 games in early August, and by August 22 was solidly in first place, 5½ games ahead of Detroit, eight ahead of Boston, and nine ahead of New York. As baseball fans know, however, no lead is secure as teams head into the final month of play. Witness what happened in 1951 when the Brooklyn Dodgers were ahead of the New York Giants by 13½ as late as August 15 and lost the pennant to the Giants in a three-game playoff. In 2011, the Boston Red Sox, although in second place, were 9½ games ahead of the Tampa Bay Rays on August 20. The Red Sox went into a tailspin; Tampa Bay rallied and won the playoff spot. Much the same happened to the 1940 Indians but to a lesser degree. September looked to be a classic "down the home stretch race." The Indians and Tigers were scheduled to meet 11 times during August and September. In early September the Tribe lost six straight games. The Yankees were also moving up in the standings, only a game or two behind whichever team was in second place.

After the six-game losing streak, several players met in Johnny Allen's room. The team leaders, Allen and Hemsley, decided the team wasn't using their hit-and-run strategy enough.

The hitting attack was in a slump. Reporters found out the next day the players had decided that a second set of signals would be used to stimulate the struggling offense, ignoring Vitt's signals. Vitt was oblivious to what was happening behind his back. Later, Vitt maintained that only two or three players were guilty of such subterfuge. One can be reasonably sure that two of the players were the irascible Allen and Heath. The Tribe, in dire shape and with short tempers, faced the last two weeks of the season fighting for their lives. Feller was worn out as a result of several starts with three days' rest and relief assignments between starts. His season ending statistics give evidence of why he should be fatigued, but he was willing to start and relieve for the rest of the season if it would help the team.

The Indians arrived in Detroit for the last time on the night of September 19. According to Lewis, no group was ever received with a more diversified bombardment. When the team walked up the ramp and through the railroad station, they were hit with tomatoes, eggs, lemons, and other edibles. Shouts of "CryBabies" came from everywhere. The next afternoon, September 20, Tigers fans put a baby buggy in the Tribe's dugout. Where were the Detroit security officers? Baby bottles bearing nipples were dangled from the upper deck of Briggs Stadium. Indians outfielder Ben Chapman placed his bat in the buggy and rolled it out when he went to the plate.[58]

None of these shenanigans seemingly bothered the Indians. Harder, who had experienced an up and down season, was "on" this day and had things well in hand through seven innings, allowing only three hits. Taking a 4–1 lead into the bottom of the eighth inning, he gave up a walk and a bloop single. Vitt, faced with a tough decision, made the wrong one,

The much maligned Cleveland "CryBaby" Indians in 1940, with Manager Oscar Vitt (front row, fourth from right). They lost the pennant in the final series against the Tigers (courtesy William Cobbledick Collection).

which in many ways was the coup de grâce for the manager. Certainly the reporters thought so. The manager called on his workhorse, Rapid Robert, but Feller was no longer so rapid: He was plain tired. In three weeks, he had made seven appearances and pitched 45 innings.

Vitt supporters rationalized that even if the feared Hank Greenberg hit a home run, the game would only be tied. But Feller did not have his stuff. Big Hank promptly singled. Two more hits followed, and Feller was finished. By the time Joe Dobson put out the fire, the Bengals had scored five runs, eventually winning 6–5.[59] Detroit now led by one game. The Tigers won again the next day, and the situation was critical.

One week later, Detroit came to Municipal Stadium for a season-ending three-game series. It was do-or-die for the local team. The Tribe trailed the Tigers by two games. They had to win all three games to claim the pennant. Not surprisingly, Feller would pitch the first game. Detroit had more latitude in its pitching selection. The league leader's pitching guns included veterans Bobo Newsom, Schoolboy Rowe, Hal Newhouser, and Tommy Bridges. Tigers manager Del Baker, in consultation with his key players, determined it would be folly to put a front-liner against the Indians' ace. Why not start a little-known "rookie?" He settled on Floyd Giebell, a 30-year-old right-hander with a career record of 2–1. This was his second year in the major leagues. Giebell, at the age of 83, remembered the circumstances of his unlikely start:

> I had a working agreement with Buffalo [Double A Tigers farm team], even though I belonged to Detroit. Steve O'Neill, former Indians great and manager of the Bisons, told Baker I wouldn't walk a lot of men. O'Neill is probably the reason I got my start. I was called up to the majors around September 19 and pitched against the Philadelphia Athletics, beating them 12–3. I knew there was a possibility I'd get a start but I didn't know for sure until that day [September 27].[60]

A Ladies Day crowd of 45,553 arrived at Municipal Stadium. The ladies were armed with fruit and vegetables in retaliation against Tigers fans for their treatment of the "Cry-Babies." The women held their fire until the bottom of the first inning, and then, as Greenberg circled under a fly ball in left field struck by Weatherly, the irate ladies pitched their goodies. Somehow in the shower, Greenberg managed to hold onto the ball, but left field resembled a garden patch. Plate umpire Bill Summers stopped the game until the area was cleaned up. He and manager Vitt grabbed the public address microphone near the Indians dugout and pleaded for order.

In the top of fourth inning of a scoreless game, future Hall of Famer Charlie Gehringer walked. Rudy York, a left-handed slugger and one of a handful of players with a native–American background, lofted a lazy high fly ball down the left field line. A strong wind was blowing across the field, from left field to right. The spheroid stayed fair by a foot.[61] It appeared to be nothing more than a routine out. Left fielder Chapman went back and back and back until he was up against the wall and could not go back any further. He leaped as high as he could. The ball tipped the top of his glove and dropped into the bleachers, just inside the foul pole, 320 feet from home plate. Municipal Stadium, with the exception of the two foul lines, was considered one of the toughest parks in the major leagues in which to hit a round-tripper. York's devastating two-run shot was one of only three hits given up by Feller in this classic pitchers' duel.

The ladies struck again in the sixth inning, strewing fruit and vegetables on the field. Worse was to come. Frank Gibbons of the *Press* reported what happened next:

> In the Tigers' bullpen along the left field line, catcher Birdie Tebbetts, Schoolboy Rowe and a couple of other pitchers were sitting down. In an upstairs box directly over the bullpen sat an ice peddler. He had come to the park with a basket of bottles and fruit. The misguided soul calmly dropped the groceries over the railing. The missiles struck Tebbetts, temporarily knocking him unconscious.[62]

George Pipgras, umpiring the bases, remembered, "I thought Tebbetts was dead. I thought they had killed him."[63]

The police led the culprit out of the stadium. By now, Tebbetts—regaining consciousness—raced after the assailant and confronted him in the clubhouse where police had taken him for identification, and slugged the man in the jaw. Meanwhile, plate umpire Summers again grabbed the microphone and warned the fans if another incident occurred, the arbiter would forfeit the game. The malicious activity ceased. During the season, Indians games were halted at least 12 times to clean up debris.

The crowd regained its proper behavior. The Indians struggled desperately to plate some runs. Throughout the game, Giebell had a plan. A control pitcher, he possessed a slider and a changeup. He teased the power hitters with a slider on the outside corner of the plate, followed with a fastball or changeup. Beau Bell and Ken Keltner singled with two outs in the fourth inning, but Giebell struck out Ray Mack.

Hemsley singled in the fifth, and Feller walked with one out. Giebell struck out Chapman and Boudreau with a variety of changeups. In the seventh inning, Mack nearly decapitated Giebell with a line-drive single up the middle, and Hemsley again reached base, this time on an error by the most reliable Gehringer. Giebell struck out Chapman for the third time. The Indians did not threaten in the eighth or ninth innings. Giebell had pulled it off. What a catastrophe! The Indians were eliminated from the pennant race. Giebell pitched two complete games in 1940, winning both. He ended his career at the end of the 1941 season, hurling a total of 39 innings in relief. His overall record was three wins, one defeat.

The Indians won their last two games and finished in second place, one game behind Detroit. The Tigers played the last two games without much robustness, losing both games on purpose. Tigers manager Baker wanted Cleveland to finish ahead of the Yankees. Finally, the Tribe finished ahead of the Bronx Bombers for only the second time in 20 years.[64]

It was small consolation to the fans and a tremendous disappointment to team members. The players knew they should have won the pennant. No one was more disappointed than manager Vitt. He, too, knew the team should have won. When the last game ended, he walked back to the clubhouse. The about-to-be-deposed manager silently shook hands with each player including Feller, Harder, Trosky, and Hemsley, the men Vitt knew hated him, and left. He and his wife departed in his automobile for their home in San Francisco. His wife had been a strong force in the manager's battles.

Vitt was relieved of his managerial duties on October 8, the same day the Cincinnati Reds clinched the World Championship over the Tigers by a score of 2–1 in the final game of the World Series. The Tribe's failure to win the pennant deprived Buckeye fandom of a first all–Ohio World Series. Ironically, in Vitt's three-year tenure as manager, the Tribe posted a 262–190 record for a respectable .580 winning percentage. Of the Tribe's 40 managers, only Al Lopez's winning percentage of .617 exceeded Vitt's.

Vitt is included among those 27 managers who were fired or quit after three years or fewer. These numbers give evidence of why the Cleveland franchise is often referred to as the "graveyard of managers."[65] The attendance for 1940 was 902,576, an improvement of 338,650 over the previous year. It was the largest seasonal attendance since the world championship in 1920. Vitt managed in the Pacific Coast League for three years and retired from baseball in 1943. He suffered a stroke in late 1962 and died on January 3, 1963, at the age of 71. His 13-year major league career—ten as a player and three as manager—was besmirched by the 1940 debacle.

Gordon Cobbledick and Sabermetric guru Bill James may have analyzed the situation most accurately. Cobbledick theorized that "a ... manager's success depends about 10 percent on his tactical soundness and 90 percent on his ability to handle men to win their respect if not their affection and to keep them hustling."[66] James observed, "What happened [in Cleveland] is something that any school teacher can relate to. Sometimes a class just gets away from you."[67]

Fans, team members, management, and the press all believed the Cleveland team had the fire power to win the pennant. Many believed the players blew their chance and thought if the team had followed their manager's instructions without so much vitriol, they might have overcome a negative atmosphere. Not all agreed with this subjective thesis. Disregarding the popular hypothesis of Indians superiority, author Bill McMahon argued that Detroit had the better team. Using Bill James' Pythagorean projection measure (don't ask me to explain it), one calculates a .605 winning percentage for the Tigers, or 93 wins, and for the Indians, .554 or 85 wins. Since the Tigers won 90 and the Indians won 89, McMahon argues that the Tribe had played slightly over their heads, indeed, had done well to come as close as they did.[68]

In support of his thesis, McMahon noted that Detroit had a better hitting team with a .286 average compared to the Indians' .265 average. Further, the Tigers had outslugged the Indians by 44 points (.442 to .398) and had scored 178 more runs than the Tribe. The Indians had a weaker bench and had been impeded by injuries, one of which kept slugger Jeff Heath out for a third of the season. Since Vitt did not use his bench much, the regulars may have been more tired than the Detroit regulars during the pennant drive in September.[69]

McMahon acknowledged that Cleveland, playing in a better pitcher's park, may have had an edge in pitching. It is true that the Indians staff allowed fewer total runs, 637 to 716; much of this difference was due to Feller's superlative year. He was the league leader in wins (27) against losses (11), ERA (2.61), innings pitched (320⅓), strikeouts (261), and complete games (31), an extraordinary figure that is unthinkable in the twenty-first century. The right-hander was named "1940 Player of the Year" by the Baseball Writers' Association of America.[70] Later in Feller's career, researchers would eventually have fun with statistics which this pitcher put together for his five most productive seasons, 1939–1941, 1946, and 1947 (the break due to nearly four years in military service). Comparisons began to be drawn between Feller and the great pitchers of the past, notably Walter Johnson, Grover Cleveland Alexander, and Christy Mathewson. (Their five best years of pitching were: Johnson 198–63;

Alexander 148–63; Mathewson 158–53; and Feller 124–56. Their cumulative winning percentages were: Johnson .599; Alexander .642; Mathewson .665; and Feller .621. The missing factor is that Feller, in all likelihood, would have won 70–90 games during the four years of competition he missed during his war years.)

An additional circumstance may have entered into the final standings. In his first full season at shortstop, Boudreau had a good season, hitting .295 with nine home runs and 101 runs batted in. The brilliant rookie led American League shortstops in fielding percentage, the first of eight seasons he would do so. He was voted the American League's Rookie of the Year by the Chicago Chapter of the Baseball Writers' Association. However, as he played the last two weeks of the season, he ignored what was thought to be a pulled muscle in his stomach. It turned out that the "injury" was an inflamed appendix. Soon after the season ended, Boudreau's doctor removed his appendix and informed the shortstop that had he ignored the pain any longer, he might have died a promising young major leaguer.

A book, rather than a chapter, could be written about the 1940 season. It was the year the Indians lost the pennant by one game. Those who played in it often wondered if the outcome might have been different (a) had they been able to dispose of Oscar Vitt as manager, and (b) had they not rebelled against him in the first place. No one will ever know, for the team's uprising against their manager was unsuccessful. Owner Alvin Bradley was more succinct in his analysis. He told *The Sporting News* later in 1944, "Our players ... kicked it away. The players were literally booed out of the championship.[71]

None of these post-mortem analyses could allay the disappointment for two 12-year-old boys, tennis whiz Bud Collins and this author. Collins summed up the feelings of a 12-year-old youngster as the pennant slipped out the window. He wondered why a strapping 30-year-old man in a gray flannel knickerbocker suit, glowering and towering at 6'2½", would make 12-year-olds cry!

"He was only doing his job," his mother replied, trying to console her son. Collins lamented, "But why did Floyd Giebell, nothing more than a nondescript right-hander on that September afternoon in 1940, do something that he had only done twice before and would never do again? Did he have to beat Bob Feller ... and squash my beloved Indians' last gasp bid for the pennant?"[72]

For Collins and other faithful fans, the words of John Greenleaf Whittier may have assuaged their disappointment:

> For all sad words of tongue or pen,
> The saddest are these: "It might
> Have been!"

There was only one recourse: The fans must rise up to cry out the time-worn refrain from "Dem Bums" in Brooklyn: "Wait 'Til Next Year!"

8

Boy Manager, Bradley and the Burrhead

"I was not a war hero. Heroes don't return from war."
—Bob Feller, commenting on his military career

As the harsh winter of 1940-1941 descended upon Cleveland, city fathers reflected on the town's status. What had the Great Depression done to their beloved metropolis? Where had the good times gone? The once exuberant, dynamic city now moved with a dragging gait. George Condon wrote, "In an effort to survive, the major issues of Cleveland's future went untended. The sprawling down-town area turned gray and shabby."[1]

As the fifth decade of the twentieth century began, Cleveland faced potential decentralization. Although it remained the sixth largest city in the nation, a rapid movement of families from the inner city to the suburbs could not be ignored. Accordingly, a 1941 report by the Cleveland Chamber of Commerce stated succinctly, "It is evident that most people who live in Cleveland are anxious to move outside the central area [economic status permitting]." The reasons for their desire to move, according to this report, ranged from smoke and dirt to congestion, vice and crime, deterioration, and finally, the proximity of races having a depreciatory effect on [property] values.[2]

The character of the city was changing. Natives and a large number of foreign-born whites—mainly European—were leaving the inner city for fast-growing suburbs, particularly Brooklyn, Lyndhurst, Mayfield Heights, Maple Heights, South Euclid, and Parma, to be replaced by a large influx of Appalachian whites and southern blacks. At the same time, migrant workers from Puerto Rico arrived in large numbers. The most significant increase was in the black population, which grew from 85,000 to 148,000 in the 1940s.[3] This major development affected the future of the Cleveland baseball franchise from 1941 onward.

Fortunately just before 1940, the city had been favored with forward-thinking politicians. Cleveland, not unlike other large cities, was infested with rapidly expanding crime syndicates. In the 1930s, a number of gangsters, particularly from Chicago and New York, had infiltrated the city. Reform-minded Mayor Harold Burton, elected in 1935, replaced a corrupt administration, combining independent ideals with Republican practical politics. Burton's first appointment was Eliot Ness as Safety Director of Cleveland. Ness had confronted gangsters in Chicago during the Prohibition years, and his efforts, with the help of the U.S. Treasury Department, brought an end to the reign there of the notorious Al Capone and other gangs.

From his Cleveland office window, Ness looked down at the oily, yellow Cuyahoga River flowing out to an increasingly polluted Lake Erie. Cuyahoga, a Native-American term meaning "crooked," applied to crime ridden Cleveland and neighboring suburbs in the 1930s.[4] Ness demonstrated his commitment, exerting diplomacy and a strong hand. With the assistance of 2,500 policemen—excluding members found guilty of graft and removed from the force—Ness rapidly cleaned up the crime-ridden city. His escapades were later popularized on a televised show called "The Untouchables."

Concurrently Ness was assisted by a young first generation Slovenian named Frank J. Lausche (pronounced to rhyme with "how-she"), who held the position of Cuyahoga County Common Pleas Judge. Occasionally, the Judge accompanied Ness on his raids, and in prosecuting the criminal element or running them out of town, he was a major asset to Ness.

In 1940, Ness and Lausche were the hottest team in Cleveland. For restoring a sense of dignity to a beleaguered community, John Patrick Heather, executive secretary for Thomas A. Burke, future mayor of Cleveland, recalled of Ness, "There never was anything like him in Cleveland. He was given hero worship like no other city official. Eliot missed a golden opportunity. He should have run for mayor in 1941 against Lausche who was a comparative unknown with a hard name to pronounce."[5]

They soon parted ways. Ness fell upon hard times at the same time that the popular Lausche was elected mayor in 1941. In 1942, Ness was embroiled in an acrimonious divorce and suffered additional bad publicity from a hit-skip auto accident. Under considerable pressure, Lausche had no choice but to remove him from office, and Ness never recovered from this debacle.[6]

At the same time, Lausche provided strong leadership in the mayor's office during the war years. In mid–1943, he organized a high-powered post-war Planning Council to coordinate planning for all levels of community well-being. He instructed the council "not only to build the bridge from war to peacetime production, but also to lay plans for making Cleveland's industrial advantages so patent that we can keep all the industries we have and attract new ones."[7] Soon thereafter, the forward-thinking mayor laid the groundwork for dealing objectively with inter-racial relations, appointing a panel to define areas where problems existed—in housing, recreation, health, and employment practices. Proactive measures rather than reactive actions would be necessary. In 1944, after Lausche left office to become governor of Ohio, the new mayor, Thomas Burke, established a Cleveland Community Relations Board. This board's mission was "to promote amicable relations among the racial and cultural groups in the community."[8] These issues would have direct relevance to the Cleveland Indians' new ownership in 1946 and soon after.

In 1941, baseball fans experienced what noted baseball writer Robert W. Creamer described as the "best baseball season ever."[9] What did Creamer mean by his proclamation? Perhaps Joe DiMaggio's 56-game hitting streak. Perhaps it was young Ted Williams, only 22 and in his third full season in the majors, who scaled the mountain by hitting over .400, a figure that since 1941 has not been surpassed. In addition to Williams' sensational batting binge, he stroked a game-winning three-run home run in the bottom of the ninth inning to

win the 1941 All-Star Game. Perhaps Cleveland's own Bob Feller, completing his third consecutive 20-win season with a 25–13 record and league leadership in strikeouts for the third
consecutive year.[10]

On the negative side of this "greatest season," however, was the impending loss of talent
to the draft as United States involvement in World War II was about to expand. Increased
U.S. registrations for the military draft and dramatic international tensions strongly suggested
America's likely entrance into World War II. Nevertheless, by 1941, fans and players tried to
put worldly affairs in the background. Clevelanders were anxious to discard the disappointment of the previous season and move on to better days on the diamond. The city's loyal
baseball followers were still crushed by the 1940 calamity. The general feeling of local writers
was that catcher Luke Sewell, former Indians great, would be the next manager. As a coach
under Vitt, he had been a player favorite, but it was not to be. On November 12, 1940,
Bradley invited baseball newsmen and radio personnel to a luncheon for an announcement
of a new manager. Frank Gibbons of the *Cleveland Press* noted that when the announcement
came, "it was so quiet that you could hear a herring drop."[11]

The ultra-conservative Bradley did not make a national search for a manager, much
more common in present-day hiring of new managers in the major leagues. Instead, he
selected Roger Peckinpaugh, whom he had fired eight years earlier, as manager of the Indians.
Peckinpaugh, born in Wooster, Ohio, and now 50 years old, was considered a loyal company
man, the perfect antidote to the jitters resulting from the Vitt fiasco. He had worked with
Slapnicka to improve a team that had lost the 1940 pennant by one game.

Privately, Bradley implied that Sewell had been passed over because of his association
with Vitt as a coach. However, the former catcher stayed on with Peckinpaugh. Later in the
season Sewell was selected to manage the lowly St. Louis Browns. He turned the fortunes
of that club around, guiding the Browns to their only pennant in 1944.[12]

The general feeling among writers and fans suggested that the Cleveland club needed
to do some rebuilding. Slapnicka and Peckinpaugh did not agree, but a bit of fine tuning
was in order. Although Weatherly was the only Indian to hit .300 or better in 1940, the
Clevelanders had six team members selected for the 1940 All-Star team. Slapnicka picked
up pitcher Jim Bagby, Jr., whose father had won 122 games for Cleveland from 1916 to 1922,
including an American League-best 31 wins in 1920. Although the young right-hander did
not match his father's achievements, he managed two 17-win seasons in 1941 and 1943 and
led the American League with 273 innings pitched in 1943.[13] Slapnicka, in his last year at
the helm, also acquired catcher Gene Desautels and outfielder Gerry "Gee" Walker. The
team gave up pitcher Joe Dobson, veteran catcher Frank Pytlak, and fan favorite Odell Hale.

The 1941 Indians, which Bradley had thought good enough to win the 1940 pennant
by 20 games, looked even more formidable as Opening Day neared. Peckinpaugh echoed
his boss's optimism: "We should win the pennant," the manager told the reporters off the
record. "We've got the best team in the league."[14] The Indians began the season as though
they intended to validate their manager's prediction. The team won 16 of their first 20
games and took over first place on April 29. Feller was pitching well for the third straight
year. Jeff Heath had rebounded from a disappointing season. By May 25, the Tribe was 28–
12 and well out in front. Everyone liked Peckinpaugh much better than Vitt. Heath, the

temperamental Canadian, was hitting .370 by the first of June and slammed a gigantic home run into the upper deck of Cleveland's enormous Municipal Stadium, the first time hit one into that area. Feller won ten games before the end of May. All seemed right in the tepee. But there were storm clouds on the horizon.[15]

The New York Yankees started to put their act together. Joe DiMaggio began to hit consistently. Joe Gordon returned to second base, and the Yankees gained ground on the Tribe. In early June, the New Yorkers, although only four games above .500, began to make their move. On June 1, before 52,000 fans in Municipal Stadium, New York swept the Tribe in a doubleheader. It was an ominous sign.

The Tribe refused to give in and, with the exception of a couple of days, hung on to first place for two months. Bob Feller carried the pitching load. By June 26, his record was a magnificent 16–3. But he showed signs of fatigue, as DiMaggio continued to hit in game after game. On June 29, the New Yorkers took over first place for good, and the Tribe began what reporters disparaging called their "swoon song."

A contributing factor causing the Tribe's downward slide in the standings was the migraine headaches suffered by slugger Hal Trosky, at one time headed for an outstanding career. During his first six full seasons with the Tribe, he had averaged 126 RBI per season. Bothered to some extent with headaches for several seasons, Trosky still garnered 93 RBI and 25 home runs in 140 games in 1940.

In 1941, the headaches intensified. "He had those headaches every day of his life from the time he was sixteen," related Hal, Jr., his son. "They were pounding headaches, headsplitting. The Indians tried everything to help him. They sent him to every clinic and hospital. He tried molasses and vinegar. Nothing helped."[16] Teammate Mel Harder remembered, "He'd be down in the trainer's room and then go out and play.... He was really a nice person, a good family man, a good hustler, and not a bad fielder. Lord knows how far he would have gone ... if it wasn't [sic] for the headaches."[17]

Migraines also affected his vision. In one game with a runner on first base, Trosky asked pitcher Mel Harder not to throw to first to hold the runner on base. "I'm afraid I won't be able to see the ball," Trosky exclaimed.[18] In his brief career, the first baseman had also been hampered by a broken finger, stomach ailments, leg injuries and shin splints. Hal Trosky, Jr., continued, "On another occasion, a pitcher threw a fast ball under his chin and [Dad] never moved. The umpire told him the ball almost hit him."[19] Trosky was relegated to spot appearances for the rest of the season, playing in only 89 games.

For the next three weeks into July, the Tribe desperately hung on with mediocre pitching in spite of the loss of Trosky. Interest in baseball all over the country turned to one person, Joe DiMaggio, the season's best road attraction. On July 16 the Yankees and Joe DiMaggio arrived in Cleveland for a three-game series. In the opening fray of this series, DiMaggio garnered three hits off "Lefty" Al Milnar and Joe Krakaukas. Now his hitting streak was at 56 games.

On July 17, 67,467 fans poured into giant Municipal Stadium, the largest night game attendance in baseball history to that point. With tension on every pitch that DiMaggio faced, his first at-bat was against left-hander Al Smith, adept at throwing a screwball.[20] DiMaggio smashed a ground ball down the third base line, almost directly over the bag.

Third baseman Ken Keltner, playing deep and near the line, stabbed at the ball backhand—à la Brooks Robinson—as it went by in foul territory. He set himself, making the play "after the ball was past him" and threw a bullet to first baseman Les Fleming just in time to nip the straining Californian. Amidst boos, Smith walked "Joltin' Joe" the second time at bat.

In the seventh inning, DiMaggio pulled another hard grounder down the third base line and again Keltner made a fine play, grabbing the ball and nipping DiMaggio at first by less than a step. DiMaggio came to bat for the fourth and last time in the eighth inning with the bases loaded and one out. Right-hander Jim Bagby, Jr., took over pitching as DiMaggio made his final bid to keep the streak intact. The center fielder hit a scorcher to shortstop Boudreau that took a bad hop. Boudreau threw up his hands to protect his face, then snatched the errant ball with his bare hand and started a double play, ending the inning and the streak.[21]

Indians fans booed Smith when he walked DiMaggio because, while they wanted the Indians to win, they also wanted to see DiMaggio hit. Entering the last of the ninth, neither wish was likely. Behind 4–1, the Tribe rallied with two runs and had a man on third base with no one out. Fans figured if their team scored the tying run and no more, the game would go into extra innings, DiMaggio might bat again, and the Indians could win the game later. The runner stayed on third while Trosky grounded out. The next batter hit back to the mound, and the runner on third base was hung up between third and home and tagged out. The next batter grounded out. The game was over, and so was the streak.

Mike Seidel, author of *Streak*, later wrote that the Yankee Clipper "spoke carefully after the game." Seidel recalled that Atlanta Braves pitcher Gene Garber, who had stopped Pete Rose's 44-game hitting streak in 1978, was angrily chastised by Rose for pitching "like it was a World Series." According to Creamer, years later DiMaggio, although outwardly gracious, was still simmering at the way Keltner had played his position the night the record was broken. "Deep? My God, he was standing in left field."[22] He swallowed his disappointment, relieved the ordeal was over, but he had wanted the streak to go on as long as it could.

In most of the write-ups of the two plays by Keltner, the word "sensational" served as an appropriate adjective to describe his fielding gems. Rusty Peters, utility infielder for the Tribe, watched the plays from the dugout. He disagreed with the writers' praise of Keltner's play:

> [DiMaggio] hit a couple of one-hoppers right down the line.... He hit the ball good, but all Keltner had to do was reach over and backhand the thing.... They made a big deal out of what great plays they were.... They were just run of the mill plays. If it had been anyone but DiMaggio, they wouldn't have had anything to say about it.
>
> The play of the night was a play that Boudreau made.... DiMaggio hit a ball to Boudreau and it took a bad hop. Lou had the quickest hands I ever saw. He made a great play, leaping up and barehanding the ball. He made it look halfway ordinary, and he turned it into a double play! Lou was probably the only shortstop in baseball that could have made that play.[23]

Later interviewed by John Drebinger of the *New York Times*, DiMaggio said, "That play Ken made on me in the first inning, when he went behind third for a back hand stop of that hard smash, was a beautiful piece of work. When they take them away from you like that, there's nothing a fellow can do about it."[24] Regardless of whose account of the play was more accurate, over the last seven decades the play of great fielding infielders such as

Ozzie Smith, Brooks Robinson, Graig Nettles, Omar Vizquel, and others have made such plays commonplace.

When the streak ended, the red-hot DiMaggio registered a batting average of .408 for those 56 games and connected for 15 home runs, four triples, 16 doubles, and 56 singles.[25] The unhappiest person in the ball park after the streak was stopped was Lefty Gomez, the Yankees' colorful left-hander. He complained, "I'm gonna find that cabbie who brought me down to the park. That dirty heel said DiMag would be stopped tonight."[26]

Bob Feller applauded DiMaggio, ever graceful in both action and reaction:

He didn't kick the bag at first base or argue with umpire Joe Rue, and if we had been using batting helmets in those days, he wouldn't have sailed his back to the dugout like a Frisbee.... He simply trotted to the edge of the grass where the infielders and outfielders used to drop their gloves on the way to the dugout after an inning on defense. He picked it up and continued running out to center field like the thoroughbred he was.[27]

Of all things, DiMaggio immediately started another streak after being stopped by the Tribe, and he hit in 16 consecutive games before being halted a second time. He lifted his batting average to within 20 points of Williams's. In later years, Feller said with disarming frankness, "You know, Joe had a little luck in his streak." Creamer editorialized, "Sure he did, but in seventy-two out of seventy-three games?"[28] As DiMaggio slowed during the rest of the season, Ted Williams kept on hitting at a .400 clip and finished the season with a remarkable .406 average, a league-leading 37 home runs plus 135 RBI. It has been over 70 years and counting, and neither Williams's nor DiMaggio's record has been eclipsed.

Concurrently, the Yankees in typical fashion went on a torrid streak, winning 42 of their last 50 games as August arrived. The Indians hung on precariously for three more weeks, and then the pennant race was over. Feller wore out, winning only six games in the last two months of the season. Trosky's broken thumb did not help. Mel Harder experienced elbow trouble and had to have surgery at the end of the season. Finally, opposing pitchers discovered a weakness in the heralded hitting ability of second baseman Ray Mack, who had hit .283 as a rookie the season before but dropped to .228 in 1941.

On August 12, Cleveland trailed the Bronx Bombers by 14 games. The situation only worsened, and by September 4, the Yankees had clinched their fifth pennant in six years. Feller staggered to the finish line but still put together creditable numbers. He led the American League with 25 victories, 343 innings pitched and 260 strikeouts. Later, Feller reflected on his third straight outstanding season:

One thing that pleased me ... was that I led the league again in innings and games pitched. Those stats have always meant something to me. They show that a pitcher is taking his turn every time in ... the rotation, that he's willing to work when he's tired or has the flu or some nagging aches or pains or problems at home.[29]

The workhorse added, "A pitcher isn't helping his team enough if he's not out ... working hard every fourth or fifth day doing his best to help his teammates.... I had my share of controversy in my 18 years as a major leaguer, but nobody ever accused me of saying no when the manager handed me the ball."[30] During the preceding three-year period, Feller made 112 starts, completing 83 of them, and averaged 320 innings per season. Jeff Heath finished with a .340 batting average, fourth in the league behind Williams, Cecil Travis of the Washington Senators (.359), and DiMaggio (.357). The left fielder led the league in triples (20) and finished with 123 RBI.

In many ways, the saddest aspect of the 1941 season was the unfortunate demise of Hal Trosky, at least as far as the Indians were concerned. Relegated to sporadic duty late in the season, Trosky spent some unhappy moments. No man ever played baseball for a living without his share of heartaches, without wondering occasionally why he had left the farm. To the fan, baseball looked to be a glorious vocation, but not always to a player. Trosky may have been unhappier than some of his fellow players but that was because the Iowan was somewhat sensitive. Franklin Lewis wrote, "Trosky is a worry wart who can't give his best efforts if he is upset.... World affairs worried him. He fretted [over] imperialism in Germany." He became a neurotic who was caught between a mental fog and a physical fog. Eventually, he quit baseball in 1946. Headaches, stomach ailments, leg injuries, shin splints, etc., figured in his final decision.[31] Terry Pluto's comment that Trosky played first base with all the grace of a blacksmith strumming a harp likely did not bring a smile to his face. He wasn't made for light-hearted laughter. Certain teammates used to teasingly call him "Little Sunshine" because no other nickname would have been less descriptive of his nature.

Pluto, sportswriter for the *Akron Beacon Journal* and, later the *Plain Dealer*, described Trosky best:

> He was right there, standing on the cusp of greatness, and it all fell apart. He returned to [his farm in Norway] angry about not making an All-Star team, as he could never beat out [Gehrig,] Foxx [or] Greenberg for a shot. He seethed over being one of the "CryBabies." ... He asked the Lord why all the headaches, which sometimes made him feel nearly blinded at home plate. His guts churned with every boo from the stands.[32]

Trosky was declared 4-F during World War II. He worked near his home at the Amana Refrigeration Company, where he assembled an amateur baseball team which he managed. Two players on his team were Emlen Tunnell of pro football fame and infielder Jack Dittmer. In spite of his headaches, in 1944 Trosky was lured back by the Chicago White Sox partly due to a shortage of major league players. However, he was a mere shadow of his former slugging self. After sitting out in 1945, he concluded his career for good in 1946. Those last two subpar seasons lowered Trosky's lifetime batting average to a still respectable .302. All in all, he amassed 1,561 hits, 1012 RBI, and 228 home runs.

In 1962, at the age of 50, Trosky purchased a small farm, raising purebred Angus cattle, and hogs. During this time, he made an amazing discovery. Having drunk milk and eaten butter for most of his life, Trosky suddenly stopped consuming dairy products for two days. He exclaimed to his wife Lorraine, "I don't have my headaches any more."[33]

In 1977, he suffered a major heart attack, and his physician advised family members that he would not survive two weeks. Instead, he lived two more years and passed away on June 18, 1979, at the age of 66. He is buried on the left side—naturally, for a left-hander—of a cemetery on a rolling hillside on the north side of his home town. Those of German descent and Catholic were buried on the left side of the cemetery. The Norwegians, mostly Lutheran, were buried on the right side of the picturesque countryside.[34] Suffice it to say, had Trosky's career extended to a reasonable conclusion, he likely would have been elected to the Hall of Fame.

Immigrant sons like Trosky faced obstacles in professional baseball which resulted in under-representation on major league rosters until the mid–1930s. In 1910, no major league rookie was of southern or eastern European stock. In 1920, two Italians, two Bohemians, and no Jews nor Poles represented the 133 first-year players.[35] The four superlative first basemen—Gehrig, Foxx, Greenberg, and Trosky—playing at the same time in the 1930s in the American League were representative of the increasing influx of second generation European immigrants. Success in baseball allowed these immigrant sons to display prowess and gain status.

Progressive reformers supported second-generation interest in baseball because they considered the national pastime second only to public education as an agent of Americanization. Playing baseball did not necessarily lead to acceptance by the core society but it did loosen the ties of ethnic identity. Attacks on Hank Greenberg and his Jewish heritage were commonplace. On bad days at the park, fans implored Trosky to "Go back to Russia" or asked, "Why don't you quit baseball and drive a truck?"[36] President Calvin Coolidge signed the National Origins Act of 1924, which set restrictive quotas on immigrants. In doing so, the president added fuel to the fire, imploring "America must be kept American."[37]

Similarity in ethnic heritage and success in the major leagues were not the only comparable elements associated with these four sluggers. Each in his own way encountered serious adversities. The tragedy of Gehrig's life shortened by an incurable disease is well documented. Although Foxx's playing career spanned 20 seasons, he battled a drinking problem in his later playing years. An army hitch of three and one-half years interrupted Greenberg's short 12-year career. And there were Trosky's migraine headaches. All but Trosky are in the Hall of Fame. Interestingly, of the four premier first sackers, only Greenberg lived past the age of 70. Gehrig died at the age of 37, and Foxx was 59 when he choked to death on a piece of meat.

Trosky and his fellow professional players were an important part of the second and third generation European immigrants who loved baseball. At this time baseball was unquestionably the most popular and well-regarded professional team game in America. Long after their playing days, these players represented a symbol of yearning and hope. It was a time of simplicity and tradition, a time of innocence and wonder, when any youngster without the advantages of a more modern society could reach the pinnacle of success.

The time had arrived, far too late for other elements of American society, particularly African Americans and Hispanics, to enter the playing field. In the coming years, baseball prospects from many other parts of the world broke barriers to join rosters in the major leagues. World War II served as an impetus for cultural and racial change on the diamond.

By October 1941, the disappointing season was over for the Tribe. Manager Peckinpaugh's early season prophecy fell flat. They didn't win. Instead, they finished in fourth place, tied with the Detroit Tigers and 26½ games out of first place. The final record was 75–79, 14 wins fewer than in 1940. Possibly the frustration over the team's poor showing was best exemplified by the behavior of Bob Feller. Future tennis guru Bud Collins had always wanted to obtain Feller's autograph. He came close late in the 1941 season. Collins stood by the clubhouse door where the players left. Feller came out and approached his car at the curb. The nervous young 12-year-old proffered a notebook and pencil. As he remembered, he asked, "May I please have your autograph, Mr. Feller?" Feller blasted back, "Get the hell out of the way, kid, or I'll run you over." Upon hearing the story, Collins' mother commented, "At least you two had a conversation."[38] As Feller later reasoned about the season, "We couldn't blame [Oscar] Vitt for that season. We had the individual talent, but we ... didn't work together as a team."[39] Attendance dropped from 902,000 in 1940 to 746,000 in 1941. The Yankees would go on to win their fifth World Series Championship in six years. This time the cross-town rival, the Brooklyn Dodgers, were the Series opponent, the first time the two teams had met in a World Series.

One might imagine what happened next in the Indians' front office. The Bradley-Evans-Slapnicka-Peckinpaugh regime was about to take a flip-flop. The result was a dramatic move by Bradley after an insistent plea from Tribe board member George A. Martin.

Within a few weeks after the end of the season, Cy Slapnicka resigned as general manager and assistant to President Bradley. Although he was only 55, his six years with the club had been grueling. He had overcome one heart attack, and the three years with Vitt had been demanding. In Franklin Lewis's opinion, although a superior judge of player talent, Slapnicka had never mastered the art of public relations.[40] Meanwhile, Peckinpaugh was not about to let the public get to him again. He readily accepted Bradley's offer to assume the general manager's position, little realizing that he would start spring training in 1942 without one of his key players. At the same time, the front office and Cleveland fandom were confident that they would start the 1942 season with their star pitcher and a blossoming young shortstop. But who would be the new manager?

The truth of the matter is, with no false self-confidence, Lou Boudreau believed he was as qualified to manage the Indians as some of the earlier managerial appointments. When the news broke that a vacancy existed, Boudreau consulted with his former University of Illinois coaches. Boudreau had exerted leadership from his early days of competition and throughout his college years, he had been a "natural-born leader." After deliberating with his coaches and at their suggestion, he sent a letter of application. In all likelihood, he would receive a nice letter saying "Thanks but no thanks." Two days later he received a call from Bradley requesting that he come to Cleveland for an interview. His coaches urged him to interview, for it would be good experience, but not to expect an offer.

A nervous and excited Boudreau took a train to Cleveland to meet with Bradley and the Indians' Board of Directors. Bradley did not want Boudreau for manager but yielded to the board's insistence that they meet with the 24-year-old shortstop. Bradley wanted Ohio native Burt Shotton, who was not managing at the time. Bradley had consulted with Branch Rickey for advice concerning selection of a manager, and the famous double-talking executive recommended elderly, smooth Burt Shotton, then in his winter home in Florida. Bradley had sent Peckinpaugh to Florida to offer Shotton the job while he was interviewing Boudreau.

During the interview, Boudreau impressed 85-year-old Martin, board member and chairman of the Sherwin-Williams Paint Company. Franklin Lewis remembered that Bradley and Martin, golf cronies day after day, discussed their team's potential managerial candidates from tee to green. "Boudreau is the greatest shortstop in the world," argued Bradley. "I'm not going to ruin his career by burdening him with the problems of managing." Martin snorted, "He's practically been the manager right along ... he was the captain or leader of every team he ever played on. That boy's a natural."[41]

Later, Martin told Boudreau that the first vote by the board had been 11 "no" and one "yes," and he was the "yes" voter. He explained to the board that Cleveland had become the "graveyard of managers" and that it might be best to turn to a young manager and let him build something.[42] Bradley acquiesced, and Boudreau became the 16th manager in the 42-year history of the Cleveland franchise.

The setting was a dramatic contrast to the fancy offices in modern-day ballparks. The League Park offices hadn't had an after-dark visitor in years. Often only a night watchman, two cats, and an occasional stray executive might have frequented the dingy offices. The baseball reporters were surprised when Alva Bradley summoned them to a press conference on November 25, 1941. With the Indians, the potential announcement of a new manager was old hat. The scribes were in an outer office. The door opened and Bradley stepped out, wearing his best smile. "Gentlemen, meet the new manager." Behind him stood 24-year-old Louis Boudreau, Jr.[43] Managing a major league team had been considered a job for a mature man, especially if he was also playing.

There were two major exceptions. Bucky Harris and his Senators won the AL pennant and the World Series in his first year as a playing manager in 1924, when he was 28 years old. His team won the pennant again in 1925 but lost the World Series to the Pittsburgh Pirates. That year Harris managed from the bench.

Joe Cronin took over the reins of the Washington Senators in 1933, replacing deposed Walter Johnson, who soon thereafter became the Tribe's field manager. Cronin was 26 when he assumed his managing responsibilities. Like Harris, he also won the AL pennant his first year, losing the World Series to the New York Giants, under new manager Bill Terry. Terry took over for John McGraw, the New Yorkers' long-time managerial icon. McGraw died a few months later on February 25, 1934. Amazingly, Harris and Cronin captured the only pennants—three—ever to hang in Griffith Stadium.

And so the "Boy Manager," as he was reverently called, knew he had a lot to learn. Boudreau later recalled, "perhaps because of my youth and inexperience, I didn't really anticipate any problems. Looking back ... I realize how naïve I was. I'm not saying I was in over my head, but ... I didn't really become a good player-manager until after that first or perhaps second season."[44]

The reporters weren't as surprised as one might imagine. They had seen Boudreau play through two full seasons and had been impressed. The shortstop had not only developed as a masterful shortstop, but also a dangerous batter and sterling competitor. Boudreau was a key man on the field from the moment he first wore a Cleveland uniform in August 1939. He was a magnet drawing to him all the responsibilities that would befall a manager.

Not unexpectedly, in the early stages of Boudreau's appointment, Bradley made it clear that his shortstop had not been his first choice. Later, he commented, "I never regretted making ... Boudreau our manager. My fear that added responsibility might affect his play adversely was entirely groundless. The fact is he got better every day."[45]

But Bradley did make one stipulation. He chose to assign two older veterans to Boudreau to give more experience to the coaching staff. Bradley called Shotton, his original choice for manager. Bradley recalled:

Burt said he would take the job on two conditions. First, Boudreau himself would have to tell [Shotton] he wanted him. Secondly, Shotton must never be expected to express an opinion that would be contrary to Boudreau's opinion. If he differed with the manager only Lou would know about it.[46]

This arrangement was satisfactory with Boudreau. While getting ready for spring training in February 1942, Boudreau officially hired Shotton, who was happy to return to the major leagues. He had managed the Philadelphia Phillies from 1928 to 1933, and later, in 1947 and 1949, led the Brooklyn Dodgers to National League pennants. Del Baker, who had guided the Detroit Tigers to the gut-wrenching pennant over the Indians in 1940, was added to the coaching staff in 1943. Boudreau later extolled Shotton for the four years he coached for the young manager. "There were times I got the impression that he wasn't as happy as the rest of us when we won," and added, "Perhaps it's because I got the job he had wanted, that he had expected to get."[47]

The young leader received valuable support from former manager Steve O'Neill and general manager Roger Peckinpaugh. Roy Weatherly and Jeff Heath, the "rebellious twosome," were effusive in their support of and desire to play for Boudreau. These were two of a dozen or more players who graced the Indians lineup since Alva Bradley took over ownership and often made headlines in an unsavory manner. Frankie Pytlak, Rollie Hemsley, Johnny Allen, Lyn Lary, Roy Hughes, Oral Hildebrand, Wes Ferrell, Eddie Morgan, and Jim Bagby, Jr., are a few dissidents who come to mind for old-time Cleveland fans.

Throughout the nation, some newspaper comments on Boudreau's appointment bordered on the bitter or facetious but did not outdo more favorable comments. It was inevitable that there would be expressions of disapproval and dismay by the press since Boudreau was so young and inexperienced. Soon after the appointment, one Cleveland writer wrote, "Great! The Indians get a Baby Snooks for a manager and ruin the best shortstop in baseball."[48]

The most acerbic comment floated across Lake Erie from the Motor City, which still hated the Tribe from their "cry baby" days during the Vitt Rebellion. The Detroit *Free Press* wept openly on the editorial page: "Being made manager of that outfit after two years in the majors and having to face the irascible Cleveland public and a press box full of second guessers is enough to warrant calling out the Society for the Prevention of Cruelty to Children."[49] Bradley came in for criticism, as journalists implied that the tight-fisted owner was trying to save on salary by combining the jobs of shortstop and manager.

The world of major league baseball became hectic for the new manager. Soon after the announcement of his appointment, he met with reporters who flooded him with questions. One asked Boudreau if he would be intimidated by what had happened to Oscar Vitt. The "Boy Manager" responded, "We'll start from scratch. I think the boys have forgotten the Vitt incident. I'll never ask anybody to do anything except hustle for me.... Any one who doesn't hustle won't be long with the club."[50] Bradley commended Boudreau on the way he handled the press, and Boudreau headed back to Harvey, Illinois, to receive the congratulations of family, friends, and his mentors at the University of Illinois. Little did he realize that his prospects for a successful managerial debut were about to take a serious blow. His path to Illinois would almost collide with his premier pitcher.

On December 7, 1941, Bob Feller, owner of a brand new 1941 Buick Century, was driving from Van Meter, Iowa, to Chicago. He was scheduled to meet with Slapnicka and Peckinpaugh to discuss his 1942 contract. As he crossed the Mississippi River, his car radio—an expensive item in pre–World War II days—blared out a "flash" that the Japanese had bombed Pearl Harbor. Feller had considered enlisting in the service at the end of the 1941 season but had hesitated because of his father's terminal illness. He now made an immediate decision to join the Navy and drove on to Chicago to tell the Tribe brass of his decision. He took the oath and joined the Navy two days later on December 9—the first major league player to enlist in the military after the U.S. declaration of war on December 8.[51] The young man had just turned 23.

Feller reported to Norfolk training camp in Virginia where he took the oath from Lieutenant Commander Gene Tunney—former world heavyweight boxing champion—and waited for assignment. A patriot and a "hawk" in political terms, Feller commented, "If you have any appreciation for the country ... you're ... going to do whatever you can." Like many young inductees with little fear, he expressed his hope that, "I don't care where I'm sent as long as I can get in the middle of the fight."[52] Feller's pay went from $40,000 a year with the Indians to $1,188 with the Navy.[53] In reality, the young sailor could have received an exemption from military service as his family's sole provider. The native Iowan went on to see much more combat duty than most major leaguers in the service.

Boudreau's military status was a different issue. He was immediately declared 4-F because of one arthritic ankle, and the other ankle was weak. The poundings on the basketball floor and a basketball injury had taken their toll. He was often referred to as the only great athlete who walked on the outside of his ankles. The weak ankles would dog the All-Star shortstop throughout his playing career.

Faced with the loss of Feller, Boudreau encountered a real challenge to achieve better results than those of the 1941 team. Before he knew it, Boudreau showed his innocence in two somewhat laughable situations. As he prepared for spring training, he believed a touch of the old "college rah-rah" spirit would inspire his troops. The day before spring training, he had signs put up in the locker room with sayings like "Have a will to win and a passion to score," "He who refuses to be beat, can't be beat," and other well-known slogans of encouragement. Within 24 hours of the players' arrival, the signs were torn down and defaced with tobacco spit. The new manager decided not to put such signs up again.[54] In 1941, far fewer major leaguers had gone to college or understood the concept of collegial camaraderie. It just wasn't done at the professional level.

The second incident was far more embarrassing. Soon after spring training began, Boudreau called his first press conference. The purpose was to have some understanding of manager-press relations with the three dailies, the *Cleveland Press*, *Cleveland News*, and Cleveland *Plain Dealer*. The sports pages were important to the vitality of the newspapers. These writers were experienced and well-known in their profession. Boudreau suggested to the writers that in the future they show him their stories before they went to press. He continued, "In that way nothing will appear in the papers that will be detrimental to the ball club." Gordon Cobbledick choked on a piece of herring. "Look, Lou," Cobbledick admonished, "You run the ball club, we'll write the stories, and while we're on the subject, we all wish you would quit referring to us as 'your newspapermen!' We work for our newspapers, not the Cleveland Indians."[55] Boudreau later wrote that "Cobby" had put him in place in a hurry.

In spite of the loss of Feller and Trosky, as always, there was excitement in the wigwam as the Indians opened their first wartime season. The Indians began the season with a 5–2 victory over the Detroit Tigers. Boudreau showed the way with a double and single. The hitting star was rookie first baseman Les Fleming, who had replaced Trosky. He pleased the local fans with a home run, double, and single. Jim Bagby, Jr., pitched eight innings for the victory.

The Boudreau-led team lost their next three games, and then went on a 13-game winning streak, arousing wartime fans' interest. The honeymoon came to a halt in late May. From that point on, the season was like a roller-coaster ride. The team finished in fourth place again, 28 games behind the winning Yankees with a 75–79 record, the same as the previous year. It was a disappointing season for the "Boy Manager." However, the playing manager's personal record was better. He batted .283, playing in all but seven games. A personal highlight for Boudreau was playing all nine innings in his third consecutive All-Star game. He hit a home run off Mort Cooper of the St. Louis Cardinals and handled nine chances in the field as the American League won, 3–1.

A few days later on July 7, a second "all-star" game was played at Municipal Stadium before 62,094 fans. This game pitted the American League All-Stars against a team of major leaguers who were in the service. The American League won, 5–0. Bob Feller, pitching for the service team, did not have his stuff and was routed in the third inning. The proceeds—$120,000—went to the Army-Navy Relief Fund.

With the war accelerating in Europe and in the Asian Pacific Theatre, baseball officials pondered the fate of wartime baseball. Commissioner Landis was not an admirer of President Franklin D. Roosevelt and kept his distance relative to a White House decision. He knew that Clark Griffith, owner of the Washington team and friendly toward the president, would signal that baseball would be a strong supporter of the war effort. Roosevelt, a fan of baseball, replied with an official letter to Commissioner Landis. He gave baseball what was widely hailed as a "green light" approval.[56]

Baseball players were under the same military obligations as the general public, and teams would have to cope with wartime restrictions on travel and materials. However, at no time did baseball face the complete shutdown that occurred during World War I in 1918. The total of minor league teams who stopped play increased year by year during the wartime period. Only ten of the upper level minor leagues remained in operation by the end of the 1944 season.

With the acceleration of the war, the country enjoyed full employment. Wages were higher, and in spite of gasoline rationing, game attendance held steady during the war years. In 1942, the major league owners voted to allow 14 instead of the usual seven night games. Bradley never changed his conservative attitude about night baseball. On January 27, 1942, he wrote to American League president William Harridge: "I do not know whether we should play fourteen night games. I do not know [if] there is a demand for that much night baseball in Cleveland and we certainly don't want to kill the goose that laid the golden egg."[57]

The purpose of more night games was to give workers coming off the "graveyard shift" an opportunity to attend some more games.

Between 1941 and 1942, attendance at Cleveland games dropped by over 300,000 patrons, with the 1942 season attendance of only 460,000. This drop in attendance was considerably greater than the overall average decrease of six percent in the American League and eight percent in the National League. The local team's lackluster record did not help. Attendance for the Tribe stayed relatively stable for the remaining war years—439,000 in 1943, 475,000 in 1944, and 558,000 in 1945.[58] The seven additional night games elevated the daily average attendance for those seasons.

There is no doubt that the quality of play in the majors deteriorated during World War II. It was inevitable, for by 1943, over 100 major leaguers and over 1,400 minor leaguers were in uniform. By spring of 1945, some 60 percent of the men listed on big league rosters four years earlier were in the armed forces. Baseball writers gibed that various service teams actually made up a "third major league."[59] Bill James, in his *Historical Abstract*, estimated that only 40 percent of wartime players were of major league quality. Only 22 of the 64 National League starters—not including pitchers—of 1945 were regulars in 1946.[60]

Younger players were recruited during wartime. One was Joe Nuxhall, a schoolboy from Hamilton, Ohio, who had to obtain a note from his principal for permission to pitch. He was 15 years, ten months, and 11 days old—a bit younger than Bob Feller when he signed. The left-hander pitched two-thirds of an inning for the Cincinnati Reds in 1944. He did not pitch again in the majors until 1952 when he again joined the Reds. Nuxhall ended his 16-year career with a creditable 135–117 record and continued his long baseball career as a beloved broadcaster for the Reds.[61]

Another pick-up player was Pete Gray. The young boy had lost his right arm in a farm wagon accident at the age of six in the anthracite coal region of Pennsylvania. As a child, Gray learned how to hit one-handed. Playing outfield, he wore a tiny glove which he discarded in order to throw. He played for Memphis in the Southern Association in 1944 and was signed by the St. Louis Browns in 1945, batting .218 in 234 at-bats.[62] That was the extent of his major league career.

Even several old-timers donned uniforms to fill roster gaps. Pepper Martin, Babe Herman, Jimmie Foxx, Al Simmons, and the Waner brothers, Lloyd and Paul, took a few more swings before hanging the gloves up for good. Wearing major league uniforms for the first time were assorted policemen and sanitation workers, to say nothing of Eddie Basinski, a violinist with the Buffalo Philharmonic, who played sporadically from 1944 to 1947. This infielder, nicknamed "The Fiddler," put on the uniform for 203 games, batting .244, and although not a drummer, he even banged out four home runs.[63]

Senator Albert "Happy" Chandler from Kentucky, ever the politician and a friend of baseball, gave support to wartime baseball, insisting that "Baseball should have the right to use rejects if that would mean keeping the game going. Playing baseball is the most essential thing most of those fellows can do."[64] Chandler may have had a premonition about his own future in baseball.

In the fall of 1944, Commissioner Landis was in St. Luke's hospital in Chicago, and the annual winter meeting was shifted from New York to save the ailing judge the trip eastward. On the morning of November 25, William Harridge, president of the American League, sent Bradley the following telegram: "Sorry to tell you that Judge Landis passed away early this morning. There will be no funeral."[65] Landis was 78.

One week earlier, Bradley had written to the stricken commissioner, "if my memory serves me right, Monday (November 20, 1866) is your birthday. I congratulate and wish you many more years of happy birthdays. Over the many years I have known you, I know you are tough enough to fool them all."[66]

Bradley was not surprised by Harridge's announcement that there would be no funeral. He recalled, "The Judge and I attended Phil Ball's funeral in St. Louis—Ball was former owner of the St. Louis Browns. It was a disgrace almost like a parade. We got back to our hotel, the Judge said; 'Alva, I've just made a decision. When I die, there will be no funeral.'"[67] Bradley told the Judge he was overly tired and he would change his mind when he had a little rest. "No, Alva," he answered, "Just wait and see. Within twenty-four hours of my death the president of the league will notify [you] of the occurrence. That will be all. There will be no funeral."[68]

With the death of the capricious and despotic Landis, Chandler was in the right place at the right time. He was appointed commissioner of baseball in March 1945. His happy-go-lucky, ebullient personality was a far cry from that of his predecessor. For the next few years, the names of Chandler, Branch Rickey, Bill Veeck and Larry MacPhail would dominate the headlines of major league baseball for one primary reason: Integration of the game.

There had been whispers about the inclusion of black players in the major leagues ever since Moses Fleetwood Walker became the first black person on a major league roster. A native of Mt. Pleasant, Ohio, he played in 42 games for Toledo in the American Association in 1884. When Judge Landis became commissioner in 1920, the game remained lily-white, with mostly negative innuendos toward any possibility of integrating the game. A classic example was the racist attitude of Larry MacPhail, general manager of the Brooklyn Dodgers. Under severe pressure, Judge Landis began, at least publicly, to relent on this issue within his tenure as commissioner. He emphasized, "Negroes are not barred from organized baseball by the commissioner and never have been in the 21 years I have served. There is no rule in organized baseball prohibiting their participation and never has been to my knowledge."[69]

But Jim Crow was still prevalent in the country. MacPhail was the major figure lobbying for the separation of the races in baseball. He berated Landis for his conciliatory remarks. He put down his list of reasons for keeping the game segregated:

First, there is no real demand for Negro baseball play(ers).

Second, how many of the best players in the Negro circuit ... would make the American and National Leagues? Very few.

Third, why should we raid [the Black circuits] and ruin their games?

Fourth, I have talked to some of the leading Negroes. Ask them what they think of breaking down the customs.

Judge Landis was not speaking for baseball when he said there is no barrier: there has been an unwritten law tantamount to an agreement between the major league clubs on the subject of the racial issue.[70]

These statements certainly seem bizarre and unrealistic in the twenty-first century. Once Jackie Robinson was admitted to the National League in 1947, all teams had signed at least one black player by 1959. At one point late in the twentieth century, 20 percent or more of the players were African American. (This figure did not include Hispanic ballplayers.) Early on, *The Sporting News* was of little help on this issue. In its August 6, 1942, issue, the lead editorial headline read, "No Good from Raising the Race Issue."[71] Members of both the black and white race, the paper argued, "prefer to draw their talents from their own ranks and both groups know their own psychology and do not care to run the risk of damaging their own game."[72]

Americans began talking openly about the injustice that saw blacks dying for their country in service but still shut out from organized baseball. "I can play in Mexico," Negro Leagues pitcher Nate Moreland was quoted as saying, "but I have to fight for America where I can't play."[73] The new commissioner left little doubt where he stood. Asked shortly after taking office whether he favored lowering the color bar, Chandler unhesitatingly replied, "If a black boy can make it on Okinawa and Guadalcanal, Hell, he can make it in baseball."[74]

We know Branch Rickey's long-held position on this issue, as he became the first general manager to sign an African American player. It is a well-established fact that during World War II, baseball owners, with the exception of Rickey, were slow to search for outstanding black players. Rickey was different. In his youth, the Dodgers' general manager had given strong evidence of his racial conscience. To Rickey, the question was not whether integration should occur in baseball but when and how. Lee Lowenfish, in his excellent biography of Rickey, explores how Rickey's social conscience led to his history-making efforts.

During the early years of World War II, Rickey secretly moved forward on his project. At times, he seemed to take a sideways step, perhaps even a backward one in his movement toward racial equality in baseball. Two events eased the way for him. The first was the death of Commissioner Landis. Although Landis had died with a more than creditable legacy, he had fervently opposed Rickey's farm system and most any proposal initiated by him. Landis' prior actions suggest he would also have opposed Rickey's efforts to breach the color line in baseball.[75]

The second breakthrough was a piece of legislation passed in the state of New York. A new law took effect in July 1945 stipulating that employers were subject to a fine of $500— a considerable sum in 1945—or jail term up to a year for employers who refused to hire an individual on the basis of race.[76] Requiring integration of the armed services—the edict by President Harry Truman—in 1947 only put the icing on the cake. Thus Rickey, with careful planning, contacted UCLA three-sport star Jackie Robinson. The rest is history.

While Rickey carried out his plan, much has been written about whether Bill Veeck, soon-to-be owner of the Cleveland team, tried to buy the Philadelphia Phillies in 1942. His plan was supposedly to sign a number of black players and help the long-suffering Phillies to rise up, phoenix-like, to a respectable position in the National League standings. Veeck's story appeared credible in view of his later accomplishments in ending the color ban in the American League. In his best-seller autobiography, *Veeck ... as in Wreck*, he verified that, indeed, he had tried to buy the Phillies primarily for the purpose of racial integration.[77]

But this story really isn't buried in cement. It is well known that Veeck was a consummate raconteur and that he might have stretched the truth a bit on given occasions. In a well-researched article by three reputable baseball historians—Larry Gerlach, John Rossi, and David Jordan—the authors challenged Veeck's account as described in his autobiography.

"The major difficulty with the oft-told story, is that it is not true," the authors wrote. The research evidence is solid, particularly the hypothesis that if Veeck had done as he said, someone would have written about it before Veeck did in 1962.[78]

These critics suggested that writers and historians had been careless in accepting Veeck's account without "the most rudimentary research to see if it checked out." They pointed out that the "burrhead," as Veeck was affectionately depicted, had made several fundamental factual errors, such as confusing Doc Young, who was sports editor of the Cleveland *Call and Post*, with Chicago *Defender* black sports editor Fay Young.[79]

Noted historian Jules Tygiel, author of the highly acclaimed *Baseball's Great Experiment*, was a bit more cautious in his observations. In 1996, he publicly doubted the Veeck story: "Most of us who have worked in the field of baseball integration," Tygiel commented, "have always mainly and even professionally, taken Veeck at his word, although his report was totally unsubstantiated by supporting evidence." In 2007, he added that although Veeck was a master story teller, often prone to exaggeration, the controversial Jordan, et al., article in "a rush to judgment ... offers yet another cautionary tale of relying on an absence of evidence and overreaching one's resources in drawing conclusions."[80]

As might be expected, Veeck loyalists were less sympathetic to the research conclusion of Jordan et al. In a letter to *The National Pastime*, published by the Society for American Baseball Research, member Mike Gimbel responded, condemning the publication for "printing this scurrilous article and the authors for their mean-spirited attacks on Veeck."[81]

And so the controversy continues. But there was no doubt that Veeck was interested in purchasing a major league franchise. None seemed to be available. From 1944 until 1946, there were rumors the Cleveland franchise might be for sale. Time after time Bradley was asked if the team was for sale. But to all of them he gave the same answer: "The Cleveland club is not for sale." The war was the paramount issue commanding public attention.[82]

But a strange thing happened one day in June 1946. As Bradley left his box next to the Indians dugout, he was stopped by general manager Roger Peckinpaugh. "Alva," said Roger, "take a look at that big fellow in the back row of [the] stands—the one with the curly hair and the open shirt. You know who that is, don't you?" Bradley squinted into the shadows of late afternoon, but even in the poor visibility there was no mistaking that striking figure: Bill Veeck had come to Cleveland.[83]

But the Veeck era in Cleveland was still a few years away. In 1943, Boudreau began his second year as manager realizing he had learned a lot about player-manager relationships. He knew he had made needless mistakes. He remembered that, "I wasn't always alert enough to be thinking an inning or two ahead, which a good manager must do. It was probably because I was concentrating on playing my own position." To Boudreau, one of the toughest jobs as manager was knowing when to replace a pitcher. "It's something I felt I never did well until after I managed a couple years."[84]

There was also the issue of his relationship with teammates. Boudreau was a very competitive individual. He played with determination, aggressiveness, and the will to win, all admirable traits. What bothered the young manager was why his players didn't play with the same intensity. He commented, "There were times I was intolerant of my players for that reason, though I did my best to keep it within me, and not let it out publicly."[85]

Another problem concerned appropriate personal relationships with his teammates now that he was the manager. His older coaches, Shotton and Baker, who had been through the mill as managers, strongly urged Boudreau to set himself apart from his teammates. It just wouldn't work if he were seen to be friendlier with certain players at the expense of other teammates. He regretted that he couldn't socialize with the players; he set his course and stuck to it. This modus operandi was hard on Ray Mack, his minor league pal and second base sidekick. Boudreau's relations with Mack actually reached the stony-silence stage at one time.[86]

Little did Boudreau or Mack realize that an observation by Cobbledick in 1942 would become a reality to the detriment of Mack, and would indirectly bring an end to his tenure with the Tribe. During the 1942 All-Star Game at the Polo Grounds, second baseman Joe Gordon, then with the Yankees, was Boudreau's partner in the middle infield. Cobbledick wrote the next day, "If Boudreau and Gordon could play together for a full season, they would overshadow every pair from Tinker and Evers down to the present. Their double play in the first inning was faster than the lightning that had been flashing around the Polo Grounds a few minutes earlier."[87] Cobbledick's wish became reality five years later when Gordon joined the Cleveland club. Ray Mack hung up his glove the same year (1947) with a lifetime batting average of .232.

As Boudreau and the Indians entered spring training in 1943, the texture of the game changed significantly. A mass exodus of players who had been drafted into the service induced sports commentators to lament that the caliber of play approached Triple-A at best. That wasn't all: Commissioner Landis had decreed that all major league teams had to train above the Mason-Dixon Line. Landis was not going to take the chance of photos in the newspapers showing players enjoying the beaches in Florida.

As the 1942 season came to an end, two little-known players were gaining experience in the service—Jim Hegan and Bob Lemon. Military obligations took them away from Cleveland until 1946, but after the war the two would become important players in the Indians' future success. Cleveland management was fortunate to contract with Purdue University in West Lafayette, Indiana. The university had a huge field house where the Indians were able to train. They were not alone. Buzzing here and there was a company of sailors and collegiate track men preparing for the Purdue Relays. Young Cleveland pitcher Allie Reynolds recalled, "Spring training at Purdue was tough." He added, "Working on the soft ground outside and hard ground inside gave me a beautiful case of shin splints. Because so many players were going into the service, several of us worked out at two positions. My second position was center field."[88]

In 1941, Oris Hockett, a young outfielder and native of Amboy, Indiana, left the Indians to take a job as a tool maker in Dayton, Ohio. He had thought of giving up the game. After exploring all angles, he said, "I decided my place was with the team.... If I had thought by leaving my workbench to play ball I was depriving the army or navy so much as a single round of ammunition, I'd have stayed in the factory.... I knew I could be replaced."[89] Hockett played throughout the war years with the Indians and retired after playing for the Chicago White Sox in 1946.

The foul spring training weather had Boudreau worried about his team's conditioning.

National League president Ford Frick, a Wawaka, Indiana, native, agreed. "There is no use pretending," he said. "A team cannot get in shape in weather like this. A team must be outside, really playing baseball, to get into proper condition."[90] The Cleveland team continued to train in West Lafayette until 1946.

As the 1943 season was about to begin, fans and players had more adjustments to make as the war continued. A full schedule was played despite crowded trains and lack of gasoline for cars and buses. Players were occasionally bumped from trains to make room for military personnel. Broadcasters and reporters were warned not to mention weather in their city, lest the information somehow might be relayed to the enemy. Selective night games were played, despite frequent strategic blackouts and energy shortages. Bradley believed that these wartime conditions and the declining caliber of players beyond a certain threshold should put baseball on hold. "If we ever reach the point where we'd have to put catchers in the outfield, I'd be in favor of suspending the [season]."[91] The owner believed firmly that the war effort should be subordinated to all other business.

Of the first three war years, 1943 was the best for Boudreau and the Tribe. As usual, the team started out on a high note, moving into first place in late May, and then skidding to seventh place before recovering their winning ways. With the pitching of Jim Bagby, Jr., and Al Smith, the team rallied in August to take over second place temporarily. They faltered in the last two weeks, losing out to the Washington Senators and finishing in third place. The New York Yankees won the pennant again, their seventh in eight years. To most American League fans, it was most discouraging.

For Boudreau, the team would post the best record (82–71) credited to the "Boy Manager" in his first three years at the helm for the Tribe. He posted a solid year as a player, batting .286 with 67 RBI. No one on the team had as many as 79 RBI, with the exception of Jeff Heath.

The 1944 season for the Indians was much of the same except for their manager. In a year when most batting stars were in the service, Boudreau won the batting championship with a .327 average. The young phenom batted .392 in September to edge out Bobby Doerr of the Boston Red Sox, another future Hall of Fame member. Boudreau also set a new fielding record with a .978 percentage and combined with teammates to register 134 double plays, the most ever by a shortstop to that date.

The season, however, was a disappointment to Boudreau. The team climbed to fourth place in the standings and but for only two weeks in late July. The Indians finished in a tie for fifth place with the Athletics with a dismal record of 72–82. It is fair to say that only because of wartime conditions was Boudreau able to retain his managerial position. Certainly the highlight of the season was the St. Louis Browns, who fought off the Detroit Tigers to win their only pennant in the 53 year history of the franchise. Manager Luke Sewell, former Indians great, engineered this unlikely triumph.

Meanwhile, Bradley corresponded with his star pitcher as best he could during wartime. But Feller was on the move. For several months, his main responsibilities were to drill recruits in physical conditioning and to play baseball for various military all-star teams. Feller wanted to see combat duty, to be a fighter pilot, but he didn't qualify. His high-frequency hearing was deficient in his opinion, from growing up in proximity to so many noisy tractors and hunting guns.[92] He selected a naval gunnery school, qualified as an anti-aircraft gun crew chief, and was assigned to a combat post far from the shores of his native country. Before he departed, his father died of cancer in early January 1943. Home for the funeral, he handled the expected passing as well as could be expected. Feller had been close to his father, who had molded his son's life as the personification of an All-American athlete, patriot, and soldier.

A few days later, Feller tied the knot with his fiancée, Virginia Winther from Cleveland, and after a brief honeymoon, he returned to join his ship for two years of combat duty. Feller had requested assignment on his home state ship, the USS *Iowa*, but in spite of his notoriety, Feller was bypassed and instead was assigned to the USS *Alabama*, a 44,000-ton floating fortress manned by a crew of more than 2,000 sailors. Feller's responsibility was to serve as chief of a crew of 24, manning one of the .40 millimeter anti-aircraft mounts on the aft of the superstructure. The *Alabama* left Norfolk on February 13, 1943. After brief training, the battleship sailed to the North Atlantic corridor to help escort convoys toward Europe. A few months later, when conditions improved in the Atlantic, the *Alabama* was transferred to the Pacific theatre, and the powerful ship saw more than a year of hard fighting before returning to Seattle in January 1945.

Soon thereafter, Feller, who never shied from giving his opinion on most issues, wrote a letter to Ed McAuley of the *Cleveland News*. He complained about rumors that baseball would be shut down for the 1945 season, making the point that such rumors were having a negative impact upon the morale in the military. "The most obvious and biggest peeve among servicemen," Feller wrote, "is directed against those who are attempting to scuttle competitive athletics."[93]

After a leave in January 1945, Feller was assigned to the Great Lakes Naval Training Station in Chicago. He took over as manager of the training station's baseball team, which included several major league players. He replaced future Hall of Famer Mickey Cochrane. The former Tigers manager was a lieutenant commander whereas Feller was an enlisted man. The Navy was evidently impressed with Feller's leadership skills, and he not only managed but also pitched in preparation for his discharge from the Navy.

As the war came to a close, Feller wrote to Bradley on July 3, 1945:

> Dear Mr. Bradley: I have been intending to write to you for some time, but thought it would be best to wait until I had given my arm a thorough tryout before making any comments. I can truthfully say that I have my old stuff and can let out in a prewar fashion as the occasion demands.... I am looking forward to returning to Cleveland at the earliest possible moment and take up where I left off, if at all possible.[94]

Feller's remarks were good news for the somewhat beleaguered owner.

The United States dropped an atomic bomb on Hiroshima, Japan, on August 6, 1945, and a follow-up bomb on Nagasaki three days later. A reluctant Japan surrendered on August 14, and the long Second World War had at last come to an end. A week later, on August 21, Bob Feller was discharged from the U.S. Navy. He had survived! Feller served for 44 months, close to the top in length of time served by major leaguers in World War II.

Although Feller was proud of his military career, as well he should have been, he did not view himself as a war hero. "Heroes don't return from war," he poignantly remarked.

"It's a roll of the dice. If a bullet has your name on it, you're a hero. If you hear a bullet go by you, you're a survivor. There are millions of survivors."[95] Feller was awarded five campaign ribbons and eight battle stars during his tour of duty. Meanwhile, at the ballpark, the Indians, or at least Boudreau, expected to do better in 1945, but it was not to be. Unfortunately, the team started the season in poor fashion and got worse before getting better overall. There were several good reasons.

Ken Keltner entered the Navy and Ray Mack was drafted into the Army in 1945. Jeff Heath, who wanted to be traded, and catcher Buddy Rosar were both holdouts for the first six weeks of the season. Veteran Mel Harder did not pitch a game until July 1. He had been working in a war plant until that time. To top it all off, the manager was reclassified and ordered to report for a physical on June 15. Boudreau failed again because of his subpar ankles.

There was another major issue. The team had been shuttled between League Park and Municipal Stadium. Forty-two of the 77 home games were scheduled for the Stadium. Certain home games were switched from League Park to Municipal Stadium at the last minute if an attractive opponent projected that there would be larger attendance.[96]

Obviously the Indians pitchers liked the Stadium with its expansive outfield. Before 1947, there had been no interior fences. On the other hand, friendly League Park was paradise for left-handed batters, only 290 feet to the right field foul pole. The players seemed always to be in a hectic hurry-up situation without a true feeling of a home park. Boudreau dealt several stiff fines in June to three or four players for not hustling. The manager's action seemed to help as the team moved up in the standings from seventh to fourth place and above the .500 mark.

A crushing blow occurred on August 13, one day before the Japanese surrender. In a double-play effort, big Dolf Camilli of the Boston Red Sox slammed into Boudreau, and Boudreau's right ankle snapped and was broken. The manager's season was finished. Boudreau had a creditable year, batting .307 and making only nine errors while handling over 500 chances.

Ten days after war's end, Bob Feller returned to the team and pitched his first game, a night game August 24 in Municipal Stadium. Only six members of the team when he had left in 1941 were on hand to welcome the veteran back into the fold—Boudreau, Jeff Heath, Mel Harder, Al Smith, Gene Desautels and Jim Bagby, Jr. Feller, now 26, was emotionally more mature, more engaging, and more vocal. Hostile fans and snoopy reporters no longer presented a threat to the young star. Years later, he put his own feelings in perspective, reflecting that "After coming out of war, you realize that sports are insignificant. Sports are only a game. A lot of people don't understand that. It's only a damn game."[97]

It was likely more than a game when Feller returned to the mound on that Friday evening. A happy and enthusiastic crowd of 46,477 fans were on hand for the game. A lower deck reserve seat along the first base line cost $1.50. Pre-game festivities included presentation of a Jeep to Feller to take back to his farm in Van Meter, Iowa.

Feller and the Tribe were opposed by Hal Newhouser and the Detroit Tigers. The Detroiters were headed for the world championship, eventually defeating the Chicago Cubs in a seven-game World Series. It remains the last time the Chicago Cubs played in a World

Series. Newhouser, Most Valuable American League Player in 1944 and 1945, was a formidable opponent for Feller. Ironically, in the first inning Feller faced Hank Greenberg, the second ball player to have been drafted into the military service during the war. The fans gave Greenberg a grand ovation for his contribution to the military effort. Feller fanned the Tigers slugger in the first inning, and Greenberg went for the horse collar in four at-bats.

After a rocky three innings, Feller settled down and was the pitcher of prewar years. The fireballer faced only 22 more batters and allowed no runs after the third inning, striking out 12 Tigers. The Tribe went on to win the game, 4–2. Feller was aided by expert calling of pitches by catcher Frank Hayes. Certainly this game was the high point of an otherwise drab and disappointing season for Cleveland. Ed McAuley of the *Cleveland Press* summed up the evening: "It's the Same Feller, a Winner."[98]

On September 19, Feller again faced Detroit in League Park. This time he pitched a one-hitter, the sixth of his short career as Cleveland won, 2–0. The fourth season under Boudreau's tutelage found the Tribe finishing with a 73–72 record and a fourth-place finish, 11 games out of first place. An encouraging aspect of the season was an increase of 80,000 in attendance from the previous year.

Behind the scenes were rumblings of a potential change in the Indians' ownership. The name of William Veeck was mentioned as one interested in buying a franchise. And there was change in the city of Cleveland. The metropolis was about to experience one of the most exciting and dramatic sporting eras in the city's history. Although the forthcoming decade was fraught with social issues, particularly racial, these problems were overshadowed by what is respectfully described as the "Glory Years." We shall see why the coming years merited this laudatory description.

9

The Cleveland Franchise
Takes on a New Look

*"Create an aura in your city. Make people understand that unless they
come to the ballpark, they will miss something."*—Bill Veeck

The year was 1946. The war which had taken nearly a half million American lives was over and ongoing foreign affairs were fraught with tensions and serious ideological differences, particularly with Russia, a former ally. But the American public was much more concerned with domestic matters—economic issues, labor uprisings, race relations and related social concerns. Housing shortages and congested highways were serious problems. Multitudes of troops returned home, exacerbating the situation. The 1944 G. I. Bill of Rights prompted thousands of veterans to pursue a college education. A shortage of all kinds of goods, including tires, automobiles, nylons, and dozens of other items, did not please the populace. The crime rate escalated significantly.

Months elapsed before industries switched from wartime production to peacetime assembly lines. Inflation threatened to explode under the pressure of price hikes and wage demands. The cost of living rose 18 percent from the beginning of 1945 through 1946.[1] In the first four months of 1946, strikes occurred throughout the country, particularly in large industries. John L. Lewis, czar of the United Mine Workers, ordered his workers to strike, and that was followed by a railroad stoppage against the government causing the country's economic growth to halt for a few days. Once these immediate postwar problems subsided, however, inflation decreased and prosperity swept the American landscape. *Fortune* magazine described the latter 1940s and into the 1950s as "the dream era ... what everyone was waiting through the blackout for ... the Great American Boom."[2]

Meanwhile, the major leagues faced a serious threat in 1946 from the Pasquel brothers, Jorge and Bernado, south of the border. Jorge, a powerful liquor baron, began luring major leaguers to the Mexican League. He envisioned a challenge to American supremacy in the baseball world through Pan-American competition against American teams. The haughty baseball enthusiast corralled 18 major leaguers, caustically called "Mexican jumping beans." Baseball commissioner Albert "Happy" Chandler banned these players, in effect preventing them from returning to the states and playing in the major leagues. For a variety of reasons, including disenchantment with life south of the border, however, players soon tired of a failed effort to increase their salaries.[3] Bob Feller was one player who turned down a lucrative offer from the Pasquels, telling the press, "no chili con carne baseball for me."[4] Feller had already signed his highly publicized contract with the Indians for $50,000 plus a bonus based on final season attendance figures.

Financial troubles and Jorge Pasquel's death in late 1947 contributed to the Mexican League's disbandment, and by 1949 the southward migration of errant players was over and players petitioned to return to their American teams. Several players filed anti-trust suits and owners instructed Chandler to lift the blacklist. Player suits were settled out of court.

For the stay-at-home major leaguers, the most pressing issue was better player-owner relations. Players were particularly concerned about unfair salaries and lack of pensions. They demonstrated restiveness with the antiquated and autocratic manner in which owners conducted their business, and had observed how successful other unions had been in improving the benefits for their employees.

Players expressed strong feelings about the need to improve their unique role as so-called employees. The owner-player method of arbitration had changed little since the leagues were organized in 1900. Their grievances originated from the 1922 reserve clause ruling which gave owners unlimited control over the fortunes of their players. There was little recourse but to hold out, an action which often proved to be deleterious to all concerned.

One postwar faux pas drove a further wedge between players and owners. When players returned from wartime duty, most, if not all received the same contract—in financial terms—they had held before entering the service, and they were not happy, to say the least. War veterans believed there was a complete disregard by owners concerning their contributions to the war effort.

Of the 480 players signed to play in 1946, only 15 players received $20,000 or more in straight salary. Five players signed a contract that gave them additional funds if home attendance surpassed an agreed-upon figure. The five players were Bob Feller, Ted Williams, Joe DiMaggio, Hank Greenberg, and Stan Musial. At the other end of the spectrum, 19 National Leaguers and 31 American Leaguers signed contracts of $5,000 or less. In view of contemporary salaries and disregarding inflation, the overall disparity in 1946 is difficult to fathom.[5]

Two of the unhappy players were the DiMaggio brothers, Joe and Dominic. Joe had held out for a higher salary before World War II and continued to threaten a holdout throughout his career. Dominic's postwar contract automatically called for $10,000, the same as he received before the war. He was not pleased. Dominic had served in the Navy for three years, four months, and 19 days. Before his discharge, the veteran consulted with a Navy lawyer to ascertain free agent status. He received minimal help and eventually realized that he possessed little leverage to alter his contract. Dominic eventually signed for $15,000 and an attendance clause similar to that of other higher paid players.[6] The seeds were sown to bring about a unified player organization to demand arbitration. The threat of unionization of players continued to take shape. On opening day of the 1946 season, Robert Murphy, a former examiner for the National Labor Relations Board, formed the American Baseball Guild. Among its demands were an end to the reserve clause, the establishment of a minimum

$7,500 annual salary, pay for spring training, and the initiation of a policy giving players 50 percent of their purchase price when they were sold from one team to another.[7] There was no demand for a pension plan for retirement.

As expected, the owners responded indignantly. Clark Griffith, owner of the Washington Senators, countered, "Such a move would ruin the reserve clause; it would wreck baseball; knock it flat on its face."[8] Players were dismayed with their conditions but hesitant to move too fast. Murphy saw his opening in August and attempted to persuade Pittsburgh Pirates team members to have his guild serve as their negotiating agent. The Pirates owners, led by President William Benswanger, were deathly afraid of player unionization. He had promised concessions to his players in July. Not unexpectedly, the hesitant players voted 15 to 3 against the guild, the remaining members abstaining. Murphy continued unsuccessfully to attempt to unionize players, however, and in 1947 dropped his efforts. Bitter over his failure, Murphy told reporters, "The players have been offered an apple, but they could have had an orchard."[9]

At war's end, many major leaguers were now more aware of the economics of the game. The union movement in America had made significant strides since passage of the Wagner Act in 1935, and older players began to ask how they could bring about more equity to their profession. Of the 636 major leaguers in 1946, 38 percent (243) were returning veterans who had missed the 1945 season or more.[10]

To the fans, however, baseball was one of the most stable institutions in the country. How would fans respond to player strikes and disruption of play? Baseball was intrinsically bound up with the seasons. Winter brought on the "Hot Stove League," as fans gathered around pot-bellied stoves to discuss the game and analyze the recent World Series. They contemplated potential trades that might help their favorite team and wondered about salary issues, potential holdouts, and the prospects for their team in the forthcoming season. Each spring, baseball was reborn, and Opening Day was like a national holiday. By the time summer officially arrived, the season of 154 games was in full bloom and attendance increased, particularly for contenders vying for the pennant. The pennant races became increasingly exciting, with more riding on each victory or defeat. By the first week of September, fans and even football aficionados were drawn to the final days of the season.

Baseball, not football, was king of the American sporting world in the 1940s. The fall classic took place as pennant winners battled for the all-important World Championship. It was the most exciting time of the year for sports fans. By December, the process repeated itself for the following season. In spite of impending player-owner strife, Roger Angell, one of baseball's most respected chroniclers, wrote, "Baseball is everybody's game, still the American pastime."[11] Certainly this was true in northeast Ohio, where Clevelanders prepared for their season opener. Early in the season, inclement weather was always a major factor for the Forest City team located along the shores of frigid Lake Erie. The 1946 season began in what musical terms would be described as a soft ballad, and ended with a crescendo. Unbeknownst to local fans, the crescendo would be the announcement of new ownership of the Cleveland franchise.

After three years of spring training in a northern collegiate field house at Purdue University, the Indians greeted the Florida sun with smiles, this time training in Clearwater. Not even the wildest of fanatics who lived and died with the Indians in prewar pennant races were foolish enough to suggest the Indians would be a pennant contender in 1946. This departure from the usual custom of false optimism was welcomed. The lack of pressure meant Boudreau could begin his first peace-time season with an anvil off his shoulders. Or so he thought.

His managerial status was a rare entity. An extremely popular player and individual, his player statistics were outstanding. The same could not be said for his managerial record. In four wartime seasons his teams won 302 games, lost 314 and finished in fourth, third, and fifth place twice. At no time during this period were his teams a serious challenger for either first or second place. Boudreau knew that 1946 would be a critical year for his managerial future. The return of Feller would be a major asset for a possible successful season. The team lacked offensive power. Only roly-poly outfielder Pat Seerey, who would stroke 26 home runs and drive in 62 runs in 1946, possessed a home run threat, stroking one-third of the Tribe's 79 round-trippers this season. With the exception of Feller, the pitching was not much better. Other than the potential of hard-throwing Allie Reynolds (18 victories in 1945), there was little hope for an improved pitching staff when Steve Gromek turned out to be a big disappointment. His record dipped to 5–15 from a superlative 19–9 record in 1945. The team floundered in the second division throughout much of the season.[12]

One significant achievement brightened the dismal start of the 1946 season. Feller was out to prove that he retained his prewar capabilities. The hard thrower opened the season with a 1–0 victory over the Chicago White Sox. Feller continued his triumphant return against the Yankees in the "House that Ruth Built" on April 30, pitching his second no-hitter. The circumstances were considerably different from Feller's first no-hitter against a weak-hitting White Sox in April 1940. The Yankees were still the Yankees with an intimidating lineup which included Joe DiMaggio, Joe Gordon, Phil Rizzuto, Bill Dickey, Tommy Henrich, Charlie Keller, "Snuffy" Stirnweiss, and Nick Etten. One after another of these Yankees went down before Feller's slants. However, Feller wasn't invincible, for he walked five, and one error was committed behind him.

No one had thought of a no-hitter in the first inning. Boudreau, in typical fashion, made a miraculous pickup of a deflected ground ball to throw out Stirnweiss. In the ninth inning, second baseman Ray Mack, in his anxiety to make the final out, stumbled on a smash by Keller and fell to his knees but recovered in time to throw him out by an eyelash. Feller was off to a great start. He completed his fourth straight outstanding season, dominating pitching statistics in seven categories, including 26 wins, ten shutouts, and 348 strikeouts.

The subdued musical sounds predominant in the early weeks of the season picked up to a fervid beat in mid–June. There had been rumblings in the press that the more powerful members of the team's board of directors were interested in selling the team. However, prospects for the sale were dimmed over the years as the team struggled to compile a winning record, faced poor attendance, and made frequent managerial changes. Bradley was hesitant to sell the team. He had made guarded overtures on April 19, 1944, when he suggested that the board should consider selling the team. At that meeting, the president summarized his 15 years as the franchise's owner. "In the last ten years ... Cleveland's overall attendance has been fourth highest in the league. The last years have shown a net profit of $734,349." Bradley added, "I do not know at this particular time if it would be possible to change own-

Bob Feller pitching to Joe DiMaggio in Yankee Stadium as Feller pitched a no-hitter on April 30, 1946 (one of three by Feller). Catcher Frankie Hayes hit a home run in the ninth inning to win the game (author's collection).

ership.... I do know that it is possible to change the president and I think ... the stock holders should give consideration to this change."[13]

Two years later to the day, April 19, 1946, Bradley was more upbeat about the fortunes of the Tribe. The president told the Board of Directors, "I do not wish to sound too optimistic.... We are going to have one of the biggest years we have ever had at the gate."[14] He was correct but unfortunately for him, this season would signal the termination of his ownership of the Tribe.

Fearing that Bradley would stubbornly refuse to sell the team, several board members moved stealthily to try to unload the team. Two of these members were the Sherwin brothers, owners of the Sherwin-Williams Paint Company. The brothers and their late father owned a major portion of the franchise stock. They had lost their father and believed this was the time to sell the franchise. The ever-inquiring Cleveland press corps, eager to garner a scoop on their competitors, suspected something was afoot. When they inquired, the brothers slyly replied, "there is no offer on the table."[15]

Meanwhile, Bill Veeck, Jr., 300 miles to the west in Chicago, was on the prowl to gain ownership of a major league team. The 32-year-old had the proper credentials. Veeck's father, William Sr. was born in Boonville, Indiana, not far from Evansville. He began working as a printer's devil and then as a pressroom helper for the Boonville *Standard.* He learned the trade by selling photographs on the road and then became an itinerant newspaperman. He eventually found a job with the Louisville *Courier-Journal,* where he spent four years as a police reporter. During this time frame, William married Grace DeForest, his childhood sweetheart and daughter of a local physician.[16]

The insufferable summer heat of Louisville along the Ohio River forced Veeck, Sr., and his family to search for new opportunities in Chicago. After short stints with the Chicago *Inter-Ocean* and Chicago *Chronicle,* he landed a job with the notorious William Randolph Hearst and his Chicago *Evening-American.* This position included coverage of the Chicago Cubs and Chicago White Sox.[17] For the rest of his life, baseball was his bread and butter. His job meant he would meet club owners, particularly William Wrigley, Sr., chewing gum and baking soda magnate—and the Chicago Cubs' new owner.

Writing a sporting column for the Chicago *Evening-American* under the pseudonym of "Bill Bailey," he criticized the operations of the northside Cubs. In one column in 1918, he decried the Chicago team's offense, proclaiming "My new son [Bill Veeck, Jr.] can throw his bottle farther than the team can hit." On November 19 of the same year, Wrigley, now one of three men with controlling interest in the Cubs, called a board meeting. Veeck, among others, was invited to the meeting. He asked a pertinent question regarding the group that had previously run the team. "Could you do any better?" Wrigley challenged Veeck. The journalist responded, "I certainly couldn't do any worse."[18]

Veeck was hired on the spot as vice president and treasurer of the franchise and received stock ownership. For the next 13 years he was a key figure in the fortunes of the Chicago Cubs. At the same time, Wrigley was positioned as the real owner of the team. Veeck initiated a number of innovations relative to ball park management, promotion, and physical makeup of Wrigley Field. The players responded with improved performances, culminating in league championships in 1929 and 1932. Fan interest was at an all-time peak.

In the World Series of 1929, the Chicagoans lost to Connie Mack's powerful Philadelphia Athletics, four games to one. In fact, Mack's team is still considered one of the greatest of all time. In 1932 the Cubs again met a superior team, this time the New York Yankees, led by the one-two combination of Babe Ruth and Lou Gehrig. This Series is most notable for a controversial gesture made by the incomparable Ruth. In the fifth inning of the third game in Wrigley Field, before stepping into the batter's box, Ruth supposedly pointed toward center field, implying that he was going to hit a home run off pitcher Charlie Root. That he did, to break a 4–4 tie. The New Yorkers overwhelmed the Northsiders in four games.[19]

A dignified gentleman and self-educated, Veeck met people well. He was eventually promoted to president of the Chicago organization, demonstrating a flair for implementing innovations in management and promotion. He resurrected Ladies Day, which had its beginning decades earlier. The number of women at games increased to the level that 30,476 women packed Wrigley Field on Friday, July 6, 1930, forcing late-arriving patrons with tickets to be turned away at the gate.[20] This event continued for many years and club attendance soared, while Wrigley and the stock holders made a respectable profit.

On June 1, 1925, WMAQ in Chicago became the first radio station to broadcast all home games, an innovation that Bradley had resisted for Cleveland games. Veeck maintained a respected and friendly relationship with his players, minimizing salary confrontations and holdouts. His understanding of human nature was evident, as well, in his treatment of women employees. Margaret Donahue, who had been the club's bookkeeper for several years, was nominated by Veeck to become franchise secretary. She was elected by the board of directors, becoming the first female who rose from the ranks to a major executive position. She held this position for 40 years and eventually was appointed to a full vice presidency.[21]

In the fall of 1933, young Bill Veeck's father was stricken with leukemia, an almost unknown disease at the time. Doctors informed the son that his father had no hope of recovery. Young Veeck was given a tip that the last thing a dying person can hold in his stomach is wine. Prohibition had just ended, and the bootleg supply was drying up. At the time, the legitimate wineries were not yet in full production.

A ballpark junkie, Veeck had met some of Al Capone's gang who liked to attend the games when they didn't have anything more important to attend to. He knew Ralph, Capone's brother and a loyal Cubs fan, and was confident that the mob would have some good wine and champagne stored away. Veeck made haste to Al Capone's headquarters and explained his father's condition, and every morning during the last days of his father's life, a case of champagne was delivered to his hospital room.[22] William L. Veeck, Sr., lapsed into a coma and died on October 5, 1933. One might wonder, since he had consumed so much alcohol, whether he may have lapsed into a drunken coma. He was 57 years old.

Young Bill was 19 when his father, "Daddy" to his son, passed away. Young Veeck was spared early grief in his life when Maurice, an older brother, was accidentally killed at the age of seven. It was a familiar scene of a loaded gun left unattended. Maurice's young friend shot him in a game of "warrior," not realizing there were bullets in the gun. Bill had not yet been born.[23] Bill's mother, Grace, never fully recovered from this tragedy. For whatever reasons, young Veeck was never particularly close to his mother, possibly because, as Bill later wrote, "I'm the only human being ever raised in a ballpark."[24] Obviously his father was his closest parent. When William, Sr. became president of the Cubs, his son followed him everywhere. Young Bill gained an understanding and appreciation of the game of baseball. Often working as a "go-fer," Veeck learned the intricacies of club and ballpark management.

Bill Veeck, Jr., could best be described as living in the fast lane long before his time. His formal education was marginal, partially due to his flamboyant behavior. He got into trouble while in elementary school in Hinsdale, a suburb of Chicago, where he was fearless and carefree to the point of carelessness but also very smart. Scott Jones, a neighbor in Hinsdale, described him as "absolutely afraid of nothing and 'the devil incarnate.'"[25] At the same time, Veeck, urged on by his father, became an inveterate reader, and absorbed nearly everything he put his hands on, particularly the classics.

It is difficult to keep track of Veeck's schooling, fragmented as it became. He had been sent away to Phillips Exeter, a highly regarded, elite private school in Andover, Massachusetts, but he became so homesick that he returned to Chicago after a semester. The young man was beginning to show his rebellious nature. He matriculated to Hinsdale High School for two years. Veeck loved football and played without a helmet. An excellent baseball player, Veeck played sandlot baseball, since Hinsdale High School did not have a baseball program.

After two years of public high school, Veeck's parents sent him to Los Alamos County

Ranch School located in Los Alamos, New Mexico. The highly expensive school emphasized rigorous outdoor living and a classical education. Veeck recalled that he was a square peg in a round hole. "I was known as that 'public school rowdy,' a description that put me just one rung above a loin-clothed savage. I got into a lot of fights. Someone would make a wisecrack and I'd pop him." He added, "I departed the Ranch School for Easter vacation with the understanding that I would not be coming back."[26] In other words, he was kicked out of this prestigious school.

Veeck never graduated from high school, but he did try formal education one more time. A good blocking-back at Hinsdale High School, he attracted the interest of several small colleges. One was Kenyon College in Gambier, Ohio, approximately 100 miles south of Cleveland. At that time, the English-type boys-only college was an average liberal arts institution that fit Veeck's "playboy" needs. The year was 1932. The effervescent Veeck passed the College Board Exam, and the small college was never the same again. In his autobiography, Veeck described his freshman year: "It tells something about the [college] ... that I was elected president of the freshman class, quite possibly on capacities having little to do with my capacity for study.... I was a pro among amateurs. I had studied this course with big-leaguers."[27]

Unfortunately the climax of his college "fun days" ended at a freshman dance. "Somewhat" inebriated, Veeck fell four stories from a dormitory ledge to the ground, breaking both legs. One could surmise that it was not a pleasant ride back to Chicago for Veeck and his parents. Veeck returned to Kenyon College in the fall of 1933 for his second year of "study" and football, but only for a few weeks. When he received word of his father's serious illness, he returned home immediately. He was about to step into a position that would presage the direction his career was about to take.

Two years earlier in 1931, William Wrigley, Sr., had died and his son Phillip K. had taken over the reins of the Chicago Cubs. When Veeck returned to Chicago, he immediately went to Mr. Wrigley's office to seek a job, and he was hired as office boy for $18 a week.[28] For the next eight years young Veeck learned many phases of club organization and management. Few if any future team owners possessed the background from the inside out that Veeck gained to oversee a major league franchise properly.

Veeck's first job with the Cubs began with operation of the switchboard. The apprentice worked with the ground crew in the winter at Wrigley Field, where the Chicago Bears then played their National Football League games. He next took a position with the Chicago Cubs advertising agency, where he ran the commissary and worked with the ushers. Veeck also learned the tricks of the trade at the ticket office, an important facet of the club business. He found concessions to be a little world all of its own and an important component of the total ballpark operation. A well-groomed ballpark included clean and attractive rest rooms and even meant the eventual growth of attractive ivy along the inside of the outfield walls which enclosed Wrigley Field.[29] As the years went by, Veeck moved up the administrative ladder to the offices of treasurer and assistant secretary, was promoted to secretary and became a member of the executive staff. Thus he could attend the National League winter meetings. At the same time, he began to realize that his dream to become Cubs' general manager was not likely to materialize.

In spite of his baseball duties at Wrigley Field, Veeck's social life did not suffer. His cavorting ceased when he reunited with Eleanor Raymond, a former classmate from Hinsdale High School and a fashionable, well-educated socialite. Their prospective marriage made headlines on the society pages. She held the unlikely position of elephant trainer for the Barnum and Bailey Circus and jumped a horse side-saddle through a ring of fire. It seemed like a perfect match for Veeck's penchant for Barnum and Bailey–like acts at the ball park. The couple was engaged in December 1934, and married one year later on December 8, 1935. Veeck was only 21 years old. Shortly after the marriage, Eleanor remarked in an interview, "When I got married I thought I was through with circuses. Apparently I was wrong."[30] The marriage resulted in the eventual expansion of the family with two boys, William L. III and Peter Raymond, and a girl, Ellen. Nearly 45 years later, Veeck reminisced about his divorce in 1949: "The divorce was my fault. I couldn't leave baseball alone.... In the end we parted on very good terms, which ... is the saddest way.... Politeness is the end of passion."[31]

Veeck also recalled that when he was 12 years old, "I decided I was going to own a baseball team.... I had other plans.... But my life was going to be centered on baseball. It was inevitable."[32] Veeck was a prophet regarding his prospective career. On June 23, 1941, at the age of 27, Veeck, with the kind of financial manipulation he was famous for, purchased the Triple-A Milwaukee Brewers, then in the American Association. Operating with the kind of high finance that had given John Ponzi a bad name, he put together a plan for purchase of the Brewers. Veeck claimed that he did not invest any of his own money in the team ownership. Rudi Schaffer, his long-time business associate, challenged Veeck's statement, stating that he had, indeed, put about $40,000 of his own money in the investment.[33]

What had Veeck purchased? After watching the team for a few days Veeck exclaimed, "My Brewers were absolutely the worst Triple-A team I had ever seen."[34] The new owner and his staff, with the help of 100 cleaning women, went to work to change the fortunes of his team and renovate a neglected wooden park. The facility had not received a fresh coat of paint in 17 years.

For the next two years, Veeck exhibited his promotional magic that impacted the baseball world for years to come. He greeted fans as they came through the turnstiles and during the games. The impetuous owner traded players as though they were baseball cards. In fact, at the end of his first season, he had retained only two original players. He staged all kinds of giveaway programs, often without advance announcements. There were special days for recognizing local businesses, lodges, or other significant organizations that supported the team. Musical combos roamed through the stands playing popular music. At other times, a band made up of office staff and manager Charlie Grimm "performed" while cavorting through the stands. Veeck did not endear himself to other owners with his questionable game-time strategies. Examples included moving outfield fences in and out based on the hitting prowess of his opponents or his own weak hitting team; placing heavy sand on basepaths to slow down opposing speedsters; or his ballplayers wearing miners' lamps in ballparks with poor lighting.

The overall results were positive and brought about major newspaper coverage. During Veeck's second year in 1942, his team finished second and attracted 273,000 fans, 200,000 more than in his partial first season.[35] The owner was honored as minor league "Executive of the Year." In spite of a few bumps along the way, the remaining three years of Veeck's tenure as owner of the Brewers proved to be a gold mine for him and his investors. His team won the league championship three straight years (1943–1945). Attendance remained strong during the wartime years, and stockholders received a profitable return on their investment. Veeck became a genuine American celebrity, appearing in three noted American magazines. *Look* magazine dubbed him "Baseball's Number One Screwball."[36]

In late 1943, the ever restless Veeck decided he wanted to serve his country and joined the Marine Corps even though being married and now with three children made him eligible for exemption from the service. Now 29, he believed his family would be all right while he was away. The soon-to-be Marine was sworn in on November 27, 1943. He did not want a commission and went in as a private with a salary of $50 a month, saying he would be "happy to be sent into battle within six weeks."[37] Many baseball owners and critics hoped that as a Marine, he would encounter a strong dose of discipline. R. G. Lynch of the Milwaukee *Journal* had known Veeck well as owner of the Brewers and had observed him for three years. He commented in his column, "[Veeck] is just a little too high pressure for most of the people he deals with. He does just as he damn pleases, in public and private, and the devil takes anyone he doesn't like."[38]

Be that as it may, Veeck was not a braggart. Sent to Camp Elliott in San Diego, and although older than the typical recruit, he excelled in his platoon. He was one of the first to scale an obstacle course and to qualify as an expert swimmer, and was "Honor Man" of his platoon. Only the firing of an M-1 rifle bothered him. He claimed that he had never fired a gun. He loathed guns because of the accident that had taken the life of his older brother he never knew. He overcame his reservations with practice, however, and posted a score of 302 out of 340 to qualify officially as a sharpshooter.[39] PFC Veeck was shipped to the South Pacific in March 1944. After a brief stay in New Caledonia, he and his battalion were sent to Guadalcanal and then to Bougainville. Part of the British Solomon Islands, Bougainville was a tropical hellhole infested with jungle insects and the potential for sickness from nearly anything in or near the jungle. Now a corporal and receiving no special privileges, Veeck's responsibility was to move heavy, 23-pound 90 MM antiaircraft gun shells with speed and dexterity. While loading ammunition, Veeck was struck in the right foot by the recoil of an anti-aircraft gun or possibly the premature firing of an artillery piece—medical reports on the exact cause were unclear.[40]

His right foot had already been weakened from assorted injuries suffered at Kenyon College. Within days, he was evacuated and subsequently transported to San Francisco. He had been overseas for nine months. This injury would haunt Veeck for the rest of his life, necessitating operation after operation and eventual amputation of most of his right leg. No one can calculate the pain and discomfort this World War II veteran experienced for the next 40 years. In the mid–1980s, this author interviewed Veeck while sitting in the right field bleachers at Wrigley Field. One could not help noticing his autographed artificial leg.

When the war came to an end in August 1945, Veeck still had his heart set on owning a major league team. But he knew his first order of business was to save his failing marriage, which had been unraveling before he went into the service. The couple agreed that he would sell the Milwaukee Brewers and use the money to buy a ranch outside Tucson, Arizona. With her equestrian background, Eleanor loved ranch life and riding. Veeck also loved to ride but his injuries and a bad case of jungle rot ruled out riding. This lifestyle no longer fit his daily regime, and the marriage continued to deteriorate. The irascible veteran could not adjust to the quiet ranch life: "I couldn't take the complete separation from baseball," Veeck admitted in his autobiography.[41]

His discontent led him to search for a major league franchise. Veeck sought the help of men like Harry Grabiner, long-time vice-president of the Chicago White Sox and an astute operator with figures. Others included Louie Jacobs, who had run the concessions for the Milwaukee Brewers during the Veeck years, and Rudi Schaffer, his business manager forever.

After due research, he considered two franchises: the Pittsburgh Pirates and the Cleveland Indians. For a number of reasons, Veeck settled on Cleveland. Although Pittsburgh was an attractive franchise with a strong history, Cleveland seemed more appealing to Veeck and his cohorts. Cleveland was the country's sixth largest city with a strong business and industrial foundation. The team had a loyal fan base but had been woefully under-promoted by the Bradley group and had not won a pennant in 26 years. When Veeck saw the largest stadium—78,000 seating capacity—in the major leagues with box seats behind home plate selling for a dollar, his mouth watered.

Bradley and Veeck negotiated in a surreptitious manner to bring about a deal. Through their lawyers, the Tribe's controlling stockholders, the Sherwin brothers, cleared the sale of the franchise.[42] Bradley was unaware of this financial maneuvering. Meanwhile, Veeck and his colleagues worked feverishly to come up with the appropriate funds. Several financial contributors could well have been of questionable character or had connections with the underworld. One such individual was a wealthy Cleveland attorney named Sammy Haas.[43] He had made his money in many ways, often attached to long-time local politicians, hoodlums, and gamblers. Stockbroker in a major Cleveland bank, Haas gave the okay for a $150,000 loan to Veeck, opening the door for the potential buyer. With the help of a cadre of friends, including Clevelander Bob Hope, Veeck put together a financial plan to purchase the Indians. The final purchase price has been disputed by several sources, but the most accurate figure seems to have been between $1,550,000 and $1,600,000.

Hal Lebovitz, then a young reporter for the *Cleveland News*, recalled first seeing Veeck on Euclid Avenue that historic June day in 1946:

> [Veeck] had no money of his own and he needed working capital, too. I saw that head with short blonde, wiry, curly hair giving rise to the nickname "Burrhead" bobbing up and down ... and like a house detective I followed him. He went into one bank, then another and I shadowed a few hundred feet behind. Ah, he was seeking the final loan. His visits in the banks were short, meaning I thought, he was being shut out. Then he went into City National Bank. He stayed a long time. He came out smiling. I had the story. The deal had been consummated.[44]

Veeck's experience as an officer with the Chicago Cubs in the 1930s had served him well in his negotiations. He knew financial figures and it was important to Veeck to become the majority stockholder so he could operate without interference. Veeck and Grabiner formed a syndicate and then secured a $1 million loan to seal the deal. By developing a then unusual debenture/common stock scheme, Veeck now owned 30 percent of the stock, making him primary stockholder among the ten new major stockholders.[45]

When the stockholders gathered to consider Veeck's offer, Bradley belatedly attempted to retain the franchise himself by forming a new syndicate, but he was squeezed out by the impatience of existing majority stockholders. "I asked them for time and an option," Bradley later revealed. "I wanted to keep the team in the hands of Clevelanders. Why did they want to sell to ... Veeck interests? ... My guess is because it was the first good offer they received."[46]

A few weeks later, information leaked that Veeck, a financial wizard in many ways, had purchased the Cleveland franchise for even less than the announced figure of approximately $1,600,000. The new figure was estimated to be closer to $1,200,000. Depending on how one evaluates $1,600,000 on the market, this final sale price was ridiculously low. Ed Bang, sports editor of the *Cleveland News*, heralded Veeck as a combination of the greatest "David Harum" and financial wizard in Cleveland brokerage circles. (*David Harum* by Edward Noyes Westcolt (1898) is a novel. Harum was an inveterate horse trader, whose version of the Golden Rule was: "Do unto the other feller the way he's likely to do unto you, and do it fust.")

The new owner had bartered so that the final sale price included $100,000 to $400,000 in cash reserves for the Veeck syndicate. This amount was dividend money for the existing owners, but by the time dividend checks were sent out to club investors, the amount had dwindled significantly due to personal income taxes.[47]

Veeck did not find a happy city along the shores of Lake Erie. The downtown area was run down, and the mood of residents troubled. The people were quarrelsome and impatient with one another and with the city where they resided. There was anticipation that the Indians and their colorful new owner would give the city favorable national visibility and something to cheer about. Popular but often obnoxious sports writer Franklin Lewis of the *Cleveland Press* expressed the hope that Veeck's well-known flamboyance would make a difference. And so the postwar era of Cleveland baseball took on a new look when Bill Veeck limped onto the scene and took over ownership of the Indians. George Condon, journalistic icon in the Forest City, summarized Veeck's eventual departure: "[Veeck's] reign in Cleveland was short—a mere 3½ years—but neither the Indians nor the old sport were quite the same thereafter. Neither, for that matter, was the city."[48]

Condon continued:

> The day—June 22—never will be forgotten in Cleveland! It brought Bill Veeck, bizarre and boyish into ... full and uncluttered view. The most ambitious and resourceful showman in the history of baseball [is on the] loose ... likely the American League shivered ... in its official boots. This is the same Willie Veeck who turned baseball in Milwaukee into a three ring circus, who might have an elephant or a two-hundred pound cake delivered to a customer in the middle of a ball game.[49]

The change in ownership, while uncomplicated in a legal or business sense, presented a contrasting picture of the two sets of owners, old and new. The former owner and stockholders had been conservative, calm, patient, and hesitant to try innovations in the game. For them, baseball was strictly a business. The new owner, in a direct contrast, was a gladhander, a congenial individual, an extrovert, who had what fans would term "the common touch." With rare exception, Veeck never wore a tie, not even when the closing papers for ownership of the Tribe were signed. He always wore an open-throated sports shirt, slacks, and when cooler weather required additional clothing, a sports jacket.

One of the first things he did was to sit in the bleachers at League Park with the fans. He told them to stop calling him "Mr. Veeck" and call him "Bill." He would listen to anyone who would talk Tribe baseball: cab drivers, fans in bars, washroom attendants, anyone who had a complaint or idea about the team. He found that Cleveland fans loved their team but felt the club ownership had cared little for them. To present-day team owners, it would seem unreal not to have the following: radio broadcasts, Ladies' Day, electronic means of reserving tickets, and posting of major league scores. All of these were implemented by Veeck in a matter of weeks. In fact, in late June, four Cleveland stations were carrying the Cleveland games with Jack Graney again behind the mike. Veeck told the stations there would be no [need for a] contract for the rest of the season. The new owner added, "If you get [the Indians] sponsored, pay me what you think [is] a fair proposition."[50]

The immediate issue would be the future for manager Lou Boudreau. Doubtless, Veeck believed Boudreau was a great shortstop, but he seriously questioned his managerial ability, and Boudreau was reasonably sure that an axe hung over his head. Shortly after Veeck closed the franchise deal, he called Boudreau for a dinner meeting in his hotel and initiated the conversation: "We know about your playing ability. But we have some doubts about your managerial ability."[51] Veeck assured the manager that he would continue to be at the helm for the remainder of the year. He planned to wait and see. The team was in fifth place with a 26–33 record at the time of their initial meeting (June 21), 17 games behind front-runner Boston. It did not help Boudreau to hear rumors that Veeck had made an overture for a new manager, possibly Casey Stengel. Veeck ended all speculation on June 24 and quashed rumors: "We are not going to change managers. Make it nice and emphatic. Boudreau's staying on through 1946."[52] The new owner emphasized that Boudreau needed some help and he would do his best even though the trade limit was in effect.

Boudreau had already made some sweeping changes during the off-season. He had traded away two veterans, Jim Bagby, Jr., to the Boston Red Sox and Jeff Heath to the Washington Senators. Boudreau had not cared for either of them, and in June he released catcher Frank Hayes as well, another player Boudreau did not particularly appreciate. Although a light hitter, Jim Hegan had earned his spurs to be the Indians' number one catcher.

The trading wheels really began to turn with Veeck at the helm. He released pitcher Tom Ferrick to the St. Louis Browns and obtained first baseman Heinz Becker for Mickey Rocco. Becker, a native of Germany, was hitting .400 for Nashville when he was called up. He batted .299 for the Tribe for the rest of the season. However, after two at-bats at the beginning of the 1947 season, he was gone. Soon Veeck optioned southpaw Vic Johnson, whom the Indians had acquired in a trade for Bagby, Jr., to Baltimore. In one way or another, Veeck proved to be successful in his trading endeavors, and it took him only two years to do so.

This action was in contrast to what Boudreau had hoped to do with his so-called five-year plan—true optimist, thinking he would last that long as manager.[53] The evidence indicated that there was little chance that Boudreau could put together a different line-up that would be more effective than what he had already sent out on the field. The question was how to put together a team whereby the younger players developed before the veteran players were over the hill.

It did not take Veeck long to increase crowd attendance. As in Milwaukee, Veeck spruced up the Stadium. The most visible change was a revamping of the role of ushers. All members of the crew were dressed in blue coats and trousers with gold stripes, white shirts, and blue neckties. They were to be clean-shaven with their shoes brightly polished and were told to treat customers with courtesy.[54] As Veeck and other owners had learned, concessions were often the lifeline to a good feeling about going to a game. Particularly important were hot dogs and peanuts—always associated with a baseball game. Hot dogs had to be fresh and locally produced, and Cleveland became famous for its ballpark mustard, a little on the dark side with a touch of horseradish.[55] To create more good will, Veeck overturned an unpopular policy held by Bradley whereby foul balls hit into the stand had to be returned. The Veeck policy allowed the fans to keep the balls for souvenirs.

Veeck began in earnest to turn the ship around. Like any successful executive, he had learned that one is only as good as the people one puts in place—staff, players, and employees combined. Besides Grabiner and Schaffer, Veeck hired Harold "Spud" Goldstein as the team's traveling secretary, or "keeper of the coins." Such a person was critical with the free-wheeling Veeck at the helm. Goldstein had proper experience, having chaperoned the cast for the *This Is the Army* show during World War II. Marsh Samuel, Veeck's old schoolmate at Hinsdale, was hired away from the Chicago White Sox to become the franchise's public relations agent.[56]

Veeck's new hires and the retention of a couple of former staffers saw the office force grow from Bradley's meager six members to over 30 employees. Two "keepers" were groundskeeper Emil Bossard, with his highly regarded sons, and trainer Max "Lefty" Weisman. Bossard was recognized as the best groundskeeper in the major leagues, and his two sons would eventually move on to comparable positions with other major league teams. Weisman had been trainer for the Cleveland team for 25 years. Extremely popular, he was known for his constant singing, corny jokes and memorable quips. On one occasion, when Feller joined the team in 1936, the young pitcher claimed his cap was too big. Weisman replied, "Make sure it stays that way."[57]

In 1947, a night was held to honor the trainer for his many contributions to the team's well-being. The special night drew 65,000 fans. Veeck boasted, "It was a super-duper evening which Abner Doubleday of Cooperstown, New York, would have difficulty recognizing as a baseball game."[58] Weisman almost "broke" his back lifting a wheelbarrow full of $5,000 in silver dollars. Veeck hauled the prize away in a tow truck for Weisman.

Throughout his tenure in Cleveland, Veeck continued the special nights. He put his experience in Chicago and Milwaukee to good use. The turnstiles kept turning with many more fans arriving at the ballpark. While the new owner admitted that his successful promotional activities in Milwaukee would not succeed in the major leagues, he conceded: "You can't substitute vaudeville for victory."[59] Veeck soon forgot those words and so did Indian fans. In July 1946, six-column advertisements in three Cleveland dailies proclaimed, "We're giving the Indians back to the fans." Slogans such as "Bring the Papooses—Reduced Rates" and "New Teepee for a Whooping Tribe" all added to the fun.

On the night of July 23, over 25,000 people came to watch the Tribe play the Athletics—a game that would normally draw 7,000. Fans did not know what to expect. A 15-piece band, attired in Indian costumes and housed in a teepee surrounded by a temporary fence in center field, played "Three Blind Mice" when the umpires appeared on the field. Veeck capped off the evening with a spectacular fireworks display. Veeck came by his love of entertainment naturally. He had always loved fireworks and circuses. "My tastes are average so that anything that appeals strongly to me is probably going to appeal to most of the customers."[60]

To the chagrin of traditionalists, Veeck had many great moments. He coated bats, balls, and gloves with phosphorescent paint, turned the stadium lights off, and lit the infield with fluorescent lights for baseball exhibitions. He hired midgets to drive kiddie cars and an orchestra to serenade the fans, and shot off enough fireworks after a game was finished to wake the dead.

The enterprising Veeck did not miss a trick. He put in a day care center for young children whose parents wanted to enjoy the games, and provided hired nurses and toys to keep the young ones entertained. He held baseball clinics for women and went out of his way to make them loyal fans. He went overboard for the women on one occasion. Veeck remembered some of his father's Ladies Day events. On August 1, reacting to the feverish postwar demand for nylon stockings, he gave nylons to the first 20,000 women to arrive at the ballpark. The popular item had been introduced by DuPont on the eve of World War II. During the war, when nylon was needed for parachutes, tires, and other wartime items, the company took them off the market. After the war ended, DuPont could not keep up with the demand for the hosiery.

On the scheduled day, 21,372 ladies participated in the giveaway of pairs of nylons presented directly by Veeck and vice president Harry Grabiner. This game against the Boston Red Sox was played in the Stadium—that number of women would have nearly filled League Park with a capacity of 27,000. "To this day," Rudi Shaffer recalled five decades later, "I still don't know where he got the nylons."[61] Knowing Veeck's business background, one suspects he may have had a black market connection.

Two of the most entertaining extra-curricular functions at the ballpark were the appearances of Max Patkin and Charlie Price. These two characters and their antics appealed to larger and larger numbers of working class fans that came to the ballpark. Veeck hired Patkin—the "Clown Prince of Baseball"—as a coach. A thin, tall man with a rubber face and large nose, Patkin was a born clown with an ability to contort his body in a most excruciating manner. He had picked up his clown reputation during the war while pitching for the Navy in Honolulu.[62]

Patkin had been released by the Indians farm team in Wilkes-Barre, Pennsylvania, due to a sore arm. Since the Indians weren't going anywhere in the pennant race, Patkin was assigned to first base as a coach. He would pretend to faint over a close or disputed call, falling over backwards while remaining as straight as a tree. It was only one of his quirky acts, and Boudreau approved of the diversion. Later in the game, Patkin would work the crowd and then return for two innings in the coaching box. He received $650 a month.

A second act may have brought more laughs, if not victories. Veeck acquired Jackie Price, a weak-hitting shortstop who had played for him at Milwaukee. Veeck signed him up not to play but to entertain the fans as a baseball trickster. It was what he could do with the ball when not hitting that astounded Veeck and the fans. This he did for the rest of the season. Price would throw two balls at once, a curve ball to one catcher and a fast ball to a second catcher. He could hit the ball while hanging suspended upside down over home plate. Price rode a jeep around the outfield catching fungoes en route even if he had to climb out on the engine hood to make the grab. "He's no comedian," Veeck commented. "He simply can do things with a ball, a bat and a glove that nobody else in the world can do."[63] However, by the end of the season, the acts of Patkin and Price became stale and less entertaining.

As the saying goes, Jackie Price "cooked his goose" during a spring training trip in 1947. The Indians and Chicago White Sox were aboard a train to Los Angeles for an exhibition game in San Diego. A group of Tribe players shared a Pullman car with women bowlers on their way back to the West Coast from a bowling tournament. Ever the prankster, Price, who carried several snakes with him as part of his show at ballparks, released two of his snakes. Max Patkin reported, "The women began screaming, with some of them hanging on to the baggage racks, standing on the seats. The panic caused the conductor to halt the train momentarily ... while order was restored." Boudreau was in another car playing cards when the conductor remonstrated him. The manager knew Price was responsible, ordered him off the team, and put him on a train back to Cleveland. Boudreau wired Veeck: "I thought I was ... manager of a big league ball club, not a circus."[64]

Veeck gave Price a tongue-lashing and sent both him and Patkin on a tour of the club's 17 farm teams. The two men continued to carry on their clown acts but only as pre-game performers, and not necessarily in Cleveland. Price kept performing until he retired in 1959 and lived until 1967, when he took his own life. Patkin, who died in 1999, kept performing until his retirement in 1995, having given more than 4,000 performances. In his crowning achievement, he played himself in the romantic comedy classic movie, *Bull Durham.*[65]

Meanwhile, Boudreau decided to get into the act. What he did pleased Veeck. The "kid manager" decided to employ a strategy in 1946 to slow down Ted Williams, known as the "thumper." Williams was in his first season after returning from the war. It was in early July, the Indians were struggling and Williams generally had a field day against the Tribe. This was particularly true in League Park with its short right field. As Boudreau poignantly stated, "[Williams] was beating the brains out of everybody."[66] It was no secret the slugger wanted to be known as the greatest hitter of all time. Boudreau later commented that Williams truly was the greatest hitter.

The Indians went to Boston on July 14 for a doubleheader at Fenway Park. In the opener Boudreau went 5-for-5—four doubles and a home run for 12 total bases. The five extra-base hits were a record at that time. But Williams went 4-for-5 with three home runs, all to right field, and drove in eight runs. The Clevelanders lost, 11–10.

That did it for Boudreau! He came up with the "Boudreau shift," or as writers called it, the "Williams shift." He established a C-formation on the field. It worked this way. Second baseman Jack Conway went back on the grass in short right field. Boudreau moved over from his regular position to play a deep second base. Third baseman Keltner moved directly behind second base on the outfield grass. Speedster George Case was the only player on the left side of the field and covered left and center fields. He moved into short left field, 30 feet closer than usual. Center fielder Pat Seerey moved to deep right center field, and right fielder Hank Edwards backed against the wall in extreme right field.[67]

The charts Cleveland kept on Williams showed that 95 percent of his hits against the Tribe were hit into right field. Boudreau wanted to force the Boston slugger to hit to left field or maybe even bunt. To hold him to a single or double would be better than another home run. But the manager also knew Williams's disposition. It was important for Williams to face a challenge head-on, which meant he would continue to hit to right field.

Surprised by this astonishing shift, he backed away from the plate, stepped out of the batting box, turned to umpire Jim Moyer, and exclaimed, "What the hell is going on out there ... they can't do that." Moyer chuckled and told Williams, "As long as they have nine guys on the field, and eight of them are inside the foul lines, they can play anywhere they please."[68] Williams would show the Indians' manager. He swung at the first pitch and grounded to Boudreau, who threw him out. The next two times, he walked. Boudreau recalled later that "After we instigated the shift we were thirty-seven percent better in retiring Williams than we were prior to the shift."[69] The ploy worked at times; however, no one would entirely stop Williams.

The 1946 season was all but over for the disappointed Tribe as they plodded through the "dog days" of August into the final month of play, with one exception: "Rapid Robert" Feller. He brushed aside any concern that four years of military action had diminished his effectiveness and finished the season with his fourth consecutive year of Cy Young Award-worthy statistics. His most impressive statistic was a supposed record-setting 348 strikeouts. It was thought that Feller had broken the strikeout record. A discrepancy in Rube Waddell's record which recorded 343 strikeouts was corrected. The discrepancy arose from Waddell's box scores in his 46 games in 1904. The *Baseball Encyclopedia* now credits him with 349. The all-time record is held by Nolan Ryan with 383.

However, researchers later determined that Rube Waddell continued to hold the season record with 349 strikeouts in 1904. In addition to most strikeouts, Feller led the American League in wins (26), complete games (36), shutouts (ten), innings pitched (371⅓), and walks (153).

After the season ended, Feller went on a barnstorming trip that lasted 30 days. The tour members traveled cross-country but not below the Mason-Dixon Line due to segregation issues, for the team included white and black stars, including the redoubtable Satchel Paige. Little did Paige realize that within two years, he would be Feller's teammate. The players entertained the fans before, during, and after each game. Even Jackie Price, the great trickster and crowd pleaser, was part of the show. The tour was lucrative for players and profitable for promoters. Stan Musial of the St. Louis Cardinals made approximately $3,500 playing in the 1946 World Series. This figure was just over one-third of the $10,000 he received after completing the tour with Feller.[70] The advent of television and the integration of the major leagues, however, meant the demise of barnstorming.

Veeck knew he would need to generate more money if he was going to provide Cleveland with a winner. One avenue was to renegotiate for a new stadium contract with the city fathers. This was done with the promise that all home games in 1947 would be played in Municipal Stadium. In September 1946, Bill Veeck had decided to vacate venerable League

Park. Originally built in 1891, this park had been rebuilt in 1910, a precursor to Fenway Park in 1912 and Wrigley Field in 1916. It was later renamed Dunn Field, in honor of owner James Dunn, until 1927. League Park had been the Tribe's home until 1946. Dunn Field was often referred to as a "schizophrenic ballpark" because of its weird layout from foul line to foul line. Veeck had his eyes on much larger crowds at Municipal Stadium. The Indians faced the Tigers in a meaningless last game, losing 5–3. Only 2,772 fans showed up. There was no ceremony, speeches, or 24-gun salute. The park was locked that night, never to serve as the Indians' home field again. Most of the park was torn down in 1950, and presently the grounds serve as a public park.[71] This closing was a far cry from the emotional celebration of the "retirement" of Cleveland Municipal Stadium in 1993.

The Cleveland Indians finished the 1946 season with a 66–86 record, solidly embedded in sixth place, by far the worst record in Boudreau's five-year tenure as manager. The new owner was not a "happy camper." On the bright side, however, home attendance jumped dramatically to 1,057,000 fans, an increase of 498,000 over the preceding season. This total marked the first time Indians attendance had reached a million. Thereafter, the Tribe registered ten straight years of over a million fans.[72]

Veeck's promotions were not very popular with Commissioner Chandler, a portion of the press, and most of the other owners. They regarded Veeck as a dangerous maverick who had little respect for the traditions of the game and the integrity of baseball. The Cleveland owner noted, however, "I never noticed any of the owners ... looking quite that insulted when I handed them their share of their receipts."[73] He knew that the most important thing for his fans was to put a winning team on the field. "If your ball club can win games, your patrons will go for anything you give them.... But if you have a bum team, all the sideshows in creation won't get them out, and keep them coming out."[74]

As much as Veeck admired Boudreau as a player, he continued to have serious reservations about his management skills. He believed that the superb shortstop relied too much on managing with "hunches" rather than using standard baseball strategy, so he tested the waters regarding the removal of Boudreau as manager. Newspaper reports suggested that he favored Casey Stengel as the new Indians manager. The young owner underestimated the popularity of Boudreau in Cleveland, evidenced by the outcry among Indians followers when word leaked out. In reality Boudreau held most of the cards. In spite of his mediocre managing record, Boudreau was tremendously popular with fans and the press, and his outstanding playing contributed to the team's success. Furthermore, his charismatic personal demeanor left Veeck with little choice.

The owner called Boudreau to his office for contract negotiations. Both men believed that the Tribe would fare better in 1947. Boudreau held out for a two-year contract so that he would not have the pressure to provide a winner within only one year. Reluctantly, Boudreau accepted with the stipulation that he surround himself with several veteran coaches to counter his tendency to manage with impulsive hunches. The most important coaching addition was 60-year-old Bill McKechnie, whose credentials included 25 years as a manager in the National League. His record included two pennants and one world championship while he managed the downstate rival Cincinnati Reds, defeating the same Detroit Tigers who had edged out the "crybaby" Indians in the never-to-be-forgotten 1940 pennant race.

The other two additions to the coaching staff were veteran catcher George Susce and former Indians coach Oscar Melillo. Boudreau later recalled that McKechnie became like a father to him: "He knew baseball as well as anybody I ever met and had a great influence on me and my career from that point on."[75]

Lest it be forgotten and in support of Boudreau, likely his best personnel move occurred late in the 1946 season. The player in question was Bob Lemon. After returning from the Navy, Lemon, a third baseman, reported for spring training in 1946 in Clearwater, Florida. Boudreau switched Lemon to center field. He had a strong throwing arm and was an excellent fielder, but unfortunately his hitting did not measure up for an outfielder—although it certainly did for a pitcher. Veteran hurler Mel Harder suggested to Boudreau that he give the young man a trial as pitcher. Boudreau asked New York Yankees veteran catcher Bill Dickey his opinion. Indeed, Dickey had seen Lemon throw in the service and believed he had potential. Boudreau broke Lemon in slowly during the remainder of the 1946 season. At the same time, the right-hander developed one of the best sliders of his era.

In the spring of 1947, Boudreau turned Lemon over to McKechnie for additional tutelage. Several days later McKechnie went to Louie (he always called Boudreau "Louie") and proclaimed, "You've got yourself a pretty good pitcher.... Lemon is ready."[76] The rest is history. After a 4–5 record in 1946, Lemon went on to compile ten straight seasons with a winning record. This record included seven 20-win seasons before his retirement with the Tribe in 1958, and his sustained outstanding performance ensured his election to the Hall of Fame in 1976.

The author and his oldest son, Tom, had a running debate concerning who was the better pitcher, Lemon or Early Wynn, who spent ten years with Cleveland. There was no doubt that Wynn was also an outstanding pitcher with 300 victories and entry into the Hall of Fame in 1972. With due respect to Wynn, I said Lemon, and Tom insisted Wynn was the better of the two. In an interview with Bob Feller in the spring of 2008, we asked him which of his teammates had been the better pitcher. Without hesitation, Feller replied, "Lemon."[77] For once, dad was right.

At the end of August 1946, Veeck, in a conversation with Frank Gibbons of the *Cleveland Press*, remarked that the Tribe needed six solid players to ensure a winning team in 1947.[78] He began his quest in October with a "blockbuster" trade. Veeck, the master wheeler-dealer, offered Larry MacPhail, president of the Yankees, the hard-throwing Red Embree for New York's third baseman, Snuffy Stirnweiss. MacPhail, a shrewd operator, said "No" but countered by offering second baseman Joe Gordon, just as Veeck had hoped. Gordon had had a major flare-up with MacPhail, who had accused the All-Star of quitting on him and had ordered manager Bill Dickey to take Gordon out of the lineup. The manager erupted at this suggestion and was soon relieved of his duties.

MacPhail wanted to check with Joe DiMaggio and Tommy Henrich concerning which pitcher would be better in exchange, Embree or a young, roundish Allie Reynolds from Oklahoma. Reynolds had pitched for four years with the Indians and was projected to have a promising future. Both DiMaggio and Henrich said there was no doubt: "Get Reynolds."[79] Both owners got what they wanted, and the deal was consummated. Boudreau and Gordon developed into an outstanding double-play combination for the exciting years ahead.

Reynolds gave the Yankees eight solid years on the mound and compiled an impressive 7–2 record in six World Series. The astute Cobbledick of the *Plain Dealer* supported the trade, which had been bitterly debated among Cleveland locals: "Reynolds is a pitcher and ... as a defensive unit ... the Indians were a hopeless team because they could not make runs in sufficient numbers to reward good pitching with victories. They need offensive power and Gordon may supply it."[80]

A few weeks later, Veeck made what was considered a "minor" trade with the Yankees but turned out to be a bonanza for the Tribe. He traded away Ray Mack and catcher Sherman Lollar, neither of whom figured in Cleveland's plans, and received outfielder Hal Peck, who had been a Veeck favorite from his Milwaukee days. Peck, a left-hander, was a decent hitter and had a respectable season in 1947. Also obtained was left-handed pitcher Al Gettel, who won more than he lost in 1947 (11–10) but shortly thereafter was released. The icing on the cake was a little-known minor league pitcher with a developing knuckleball. This was Gene Bearden, whose name is etched into the annals of one of Cleveland's most glorious baseball seasons. Veeck, who was as close to being a Yankees hater as one can be, bragged about this trade: "We beat the Yanks on that one."[81] There would be more trades after the first of the year.

The finish of the 1946 season meant the end of the 19-year reign of Alva Bradley. Fred Schuld, a native Clevelander and historian, studied Bradley's tenure as owner and concluded that Bradley had been baseball's last renaissance owner.[82] Bradley had held firmly "to the proposition that baseball is a sport rather than a business." It was a sentiment appropriate for the times. He would not be confronted with interlocking entities that would invade his concept of what team ownership was all about. It would have been difficult for Bradley to absorb the impact of television, expansion, a players' union, agents, inflated salaries, longer seasons, and playoffs.

Bradley told Howard Preston of the *Cleveland News*, "I've always been a conservative man. Fireworks and free nylon stockings ... are novel.... Our old organization couldn't have done it. Different people have different ideas."[83] In 1951, he suggested to Ed McAuley that the biggest question today is, "How many people are in the ballpark? Get them in somehow. Play all your games at night. Give the fans souvenirs. Get them in the park."[84]

McAuley's exhaustive research into Bradley's voluminous papers produced only one letter addressed to Veeck (1946): "Dear Mr. Veeck," wrote Bradley. "I am sorry that you had your leg amputated. You have my sincere wishes for a speedy recovery."[85] After leaving his League Park offices in 1946, Bradley never attended another game in Cleveland until 1948, when the Tribe won their second world championship. He died on March 29, 1953, of a heart attack. The former owner was 69 years old. *The Sporting News* wrote that "Bradley brought to the National Pastime, calmness, dignity, and honesty of purpose which helped us through some of the most dangerous times, the long years of the [Great] Depression and of World War II."[86]

Meanwhile, "Barnum" Bill Veeck traveled throughout Ohio and neighboring states during the winter months of 1946-1947, promoting a rejuvenated Indians team. For the next two years the fans would be treated to excitement never experienced before in the Forest City. Cleveland would not be referred to as the "mistake by the lake" for years to come.

10

Team Integration
and the Glory Years

In his classic *The Theory of the Leisure Class* (1899), Thorstein Veblen wrote, "The addiction of sports ... in a peculiar degree marks an arrested development of man's moral nature."[1] Had Veblen visited Cleveland in the late 1940s, he could have stumbled upon what he might have interpreted as an amoral society. He even may have questioned whether sports had replaced organized religion as the individual's moral compass. In Cleveland, Veblen would have observed citizenry reading one of three viable dailies which devoted fully one-fifth of their column space to sports. New electronic media soon would devote large segments of airtime to sports. But in local homes, offices, factories and automobiles, fans listened to radio announcers Jack Graney and Jimmy Dudley, who brought the action of Indians games to listeners.

The chamber of commerce no longer considered sports a mere adjunct to normal development and growth of the local economy. Rather sports came to be seen as symbolically linked to the social, political and economic fortunes of post-war Cleveland. A citizenry that had lived through a wartime period, when material growth had slowed and leisure-time activities were few, was ready to have fun. Plants reopened, work forces expanded, and more people moved into the city proper and to suburbs. By 1946, the value of goods produced by industries in Cuyahoga County amounted to $2,673,300,000, more than 2.5 times the value of production in 1939. The labor forced increased by a factor of 1.6, and the industrial payroll grew to 2.8 times the 1939 level. In 1950 the city population reached an all-time high of 914,000.[2] Of this population growth, a large proportion emanated from Appalachia and the South, seeking jobs.

After World War II, large and rapidly growing metropolitan regions contended with potential interracial issues. The white population had an increasingly difficult time adjusting to a large influx of African Americans. In many cases, there had been little to no interaction between the races. Soon thousands, white and black, would attend Cleveland Indians games. The impact of less-than-educated migrants from the Appalachian region did little to improve the cultural well-being of city environment. Long-time residents, many from the highly cultivated Northeast, feared a disruption to the quality of their lives and fled in increasing numbers to suburbs surrounding the inner city.

By 1950, 148,000 or 16 percent of the city population was African American.[3] In most cases, housing for these newcomers was substandard at best. There were obvious signs of potential trouble. Former mayor Frank J. Lausche, in a 1943 speech launching the Postwar Planning Council, protested that there were slums with "living conditions unfit for human beings."[4] The city had expanded carelessly, and the mansions that remained on Millionaires Row—Euclid Avenue—now rubbed shoulders with billboards, car-wash lots, tourist homes, and factories. The problems associated with this suburban growth were reaffirmed by *Architectural Forum* in 1955: "the parasitic situation reaches an extreme.... Suburban chauvinism in Cleveland is more than a political and financial problem. It is a social problem."[5]

City fathers, now led by popular mayor Thomas A. Burke, anticipated potentially serious racial and ethnic issues. The city formed the first municipal community relations board in 1945, and passed fair employment legislation in 1950. The political leaders, black and white, used various options to mitigate the obvious effects of racial bias. Veeck, along with other leaders in the sports world, tried in their own ways to alleviate racial disparities.

There was great energy in the city, a surge of struggling humanity. Cleveland emitted a large roar, the metallic-electric hum of power in action. Newly located migrants were caught up in the thrill, the life, the movement, and the strength of the city. Cleveland was the nexus of a world of finance, art, sport, journalism, and politics. Bill Veeck wanted to be a part of these phenomena.

To the average Joe, these social problems could be handled later. The war was over; it was time to return to prewar life styles—back to normal. "Normal" meant *real* baseball with their favorite team. In 1946, the Tribe was the main sporting attraction in the city along Lake Erie.

Cleveland celebrated its 150th birthday in 1946 with pageants, parades, and entertainment, drawing national attention. Columnist L. H. Robbins, writing in the *New York Times Magazine*, presented a favorable impression of the city and its people: "Clevelanders display an exuberant enthusiasm for their town and their way of life such as you don't ever recall noting in any city east of the Alleghenies.... It really is remarkable, their town boosting, their local pride and contentment."[6] In 1946, it still ranked as the sixth largest city in the nation. The Chamber of Commerce promoted the slogan "Cleveland: The Best Location in the Nation."[7]

The sports community of the city, including the newspapers, proclaimed Cleveland the "City of Champions." The pundits were a bit ahead of themselves as far as their favorite team, "The Tribe," was concerned. Other local professional teams had already begun to foster a following.

Following the departure of the 1945 National Football League champion Cleveland Rams to Los Angeles, a new team was assembled, the Cleveland Browns. The franchise immediately joined the year-old All-American Football Conference. The team was led by Paul Brown, highly successful high school coach (Massilon, Ohio) and college coach—The Ohio State University. The Browns became a juggernaut in the All-American Conference and won the league championship four straight years (1946–1949).[8] This team entered the National Football League in 1950. The Browns were led by five future Hall of Famers: quarterback Otto Graham, end Dante Lavelli, kicker Lon Groza, fullback Marion Motley and lineman Bill Willis. The last two—both black—were members of the National Football League at a time when few blacks were playing.[9]

In their first season, the Browns demonstrated that they were not to be taken lightly, showing their mettle by winning the National Football League championship. Cleveland upended the recently departed Los Angeles Rams, 30–28, in one of the great pro football games of all time.[10] The Browns continued their winning ways with Coach Paul Brown at the helm, capturing back-to-back league championships in 1953 and 1954. As the years went on, more and more Cleveland sports fans adopted the Browns as their favorite local team.[11] The legions of dyed-in-the-wool Tribe fans would soon have their opportunity to celebrate victory.

To complete a winning atmosphere throughout the year, the minor league Cleveland Barons dominated the American Hockey League. The Barons brought the Calder Cup Trophy home in six of eight seasons, beginning in 1944 through 1951, and became the New York Yankees of minor league hockey. The Calder Cup testified to the Barons' superiority in the elite minor league of professional hockey. Indeed, many hockey experts expressed the opinion that the Cleveland team would have held their own in the National Hockey League. Playing in an up-to-date Cleveland Arena, the Barons consistently drew 10,000 fans or more for home games. The arena had been built during the Great Depression in 1937 and was hailed as "an All-Sport Palace." The Barons were scheduled to become the seventh member of the National Hockey League in 1952 but the deal fell through.

Cleveland had another champion during the mid–1940s, one more closely associated with the National Pastime. This team was the less publicized Cleveland Buckeyes, an all-black professional baseball team. Earlier, Cleveland had had a number of African American clubs, but most of these teams had lasted only a year or less. This pattern changed in 1943 when the Cleveland Buckeyes were organized by Ernest Wright, a hotel and night club owner in Erie, Pennsylvania. Wilbur Hayes, a local sports promoter, served as executive manager of the team.[12]

The Buckeyes began playing in Cleveland in 1943, with several members of former black teams on the roster. They featured pitcher Willie Grace and a better known outfielder, Sam Jethroe, one of three black players given tryouts in 1945 by the reticent Boston Red Sox. Ironically, these same Red Sox became the last major league team to sign an African American. Another member of the team was all-star catcher Quincy Trouppe, who reached the major leagues briefly in 1952, playing six games for Cleveland.

The Buckeyes finished in the middle of the standings every season of their existence (1943–1950) except for 1945 and 1947. In 1945, the Buckeyes became another member of the "City of Champions." The team won the Negro American League title with an overall record of 53–16. The local heroes earned a spot in the Negro World Series against the famous defending champions, the Homestead Grays. The Buckeyes, unafraid of the Grays, defeated them in the first game in Municipal Stadium and then moved to League Park to win the second game. The Buckeyes went on to sweep Homestead, located just outside Pittsburgh, to claim another World Championship for Cleveland.'[13]

In many ways, Sam Jethroe was the most notable player in the Negro American League. Sam "The Jet" had been scouted by several major league teams, including Cleveland, and had left the league in 1948 to play for the Dodgers' farm team in Montreal. In 1950, Branch Rickey sold Jethroe's contract to the Boston Braves, and he became the first black player to wear a Braves uniform. He was named "Rookie of the Year," the oldest rookie (32) to receive this award. The speedster led the league in stolen bases with 35, batted .273, slammed 18 home runs and scored 100 runs. Don Newcombe, Brooklyn Dodgers pitcher, remembered that when he and Jethroe were teammates in Montreal, he declared Jethroe was the fastest human being "one had ever seen." Buck O'Neil added that when Jethroe came to the plate, "the infield would have to come in a few steps or you never throw him out."[14]

Again in 1951, Jethroe pilfered a league-leading 35 bases and slugged 18 home runs. He retired in 1954 with the Pittsburgh Pirates. Although Jethroe did not command the headlines of a Larry Doby or Jackie Robinson upon his retirement, he did strike an important legal blow for African American players. In 1994 he filed suit in federal court against major league baseball and its players association, arguing that baseball's segregationist policies before 1947 had kept Jethroe and other National League players from receiving a major league pension. The suit was dismissed but in 1997 Major League Baseball established a yearly plan to compensate Negro League veterans.

Major league baseball first offered pensions in 1947. A player needed four years in the majors to qualify. However, black players were restricted from receiving a pension. (The modern agreement states that players only need to play one day in the majors to qualify.) Jethroe completed three years and 17 days with Boston and Pittsburgh, falling just short of the required four-year minimum.

However, although his suit was dismissed on October 4, 1996, major league baseball decided to grant pensions to Jethroe and dozens of other Negro players in 1997.[15] He received his pension before dying on June 16, 2001, at the age of 83 in Erie, Pennsylvania.

The accomplishments of the Cleveland Buckeyes received major coverage from a black weekly named the Cleveland *Call and Post*. The team's fortunes were also covered in the three Cleveland dailies. The Buckeyes' success was another feather in Cleveland's hat, as the city now bragged about being the "City of Champions."

Veeck knew that 1946 was but a prelude and that 1947 must bring improvement in the standings. The National Pastime had been more conservative in high finance than the groves of Academe. In fact, Bradley and Company epitomized a laissez faire business. Under their sober direction and cautious counsel, a simple game had been turned into a complicated game clothed in traditional gray flannel and encumbered with excessive strategy and statistics. For many onlookers, this civilized restraint produced a game that was about as exciting as a Sunday outing of the Watch and Ward Society.[16]

Veeck realized that the bells and whistles entertainment must cease to focus fan attention on the playing field. Laughter would have to make way for cheers. In the words of the old admonition, "faith without work crashes." He knew that the fans' faith must be justified with a more effective baseball machine. The owner explained his view of this matter in his autobiography:

> We did not draw crowds simply by putting on a show. Cleveland has been without a pennant
> for twenty-six years, the longest of any American League city and we communicated our
> desire to produce one. I agree with the conservative opposition that you cannot continue to

draw people with a losing team by giving the fans bread and circuses. All I have ever said—and I think proved—is that you can draw more people with a losing team plus bread and circuses than with a losing team and a long still silence.[17]

So Veeck went to work—retooling his team, letting players go, and bringing in new and used replacements. But before he could do any player shopping, he entered the Cleveland Clinic on October 24, 1946. His pain had increased, and this was his third hospitalization in three months. The primary diagnosis was osteomyelitis, an acute bone infection. A prescribed new drug had been effective for only so long. On November 1, he lost not only his right foot but a major portion of his right leg. This surgery would be the first of many operations and much more misery. He left the hospital on November 18 and headed for the winter baseball meeting in Los Angeles. A reporter asked him if he was religious. Veeck responded, "I believe in God, but I'm not so sure about those other things."[18] On another occasion, as he tried to get used to his wooden peg leg, he stumbled and took a spill. Reporter Hal Lebovitz, walking with him, asked, "Do you want me to get a doctor?" He replied, "No, but you can get me a carpenter."[19]

As the months went by, there would be more operations and another portion of the leg removed. No one knows for sure how much he suffered, but it was considerably. After one operation, he insisted that "I'm a cripple but I'm not handicapped." He neither sought nor accepted sympathy. "Suffering is overrated," Veeck stated. "It doesn't teach you anything."[20] So he moved forward, always on the move. To Veeck, life's natural state was activity: "I always hate to go to sleep," he once said. "I'm afraid that something fascinating is going to happen and I'll miss it."[21]

One thing he never missed was a good trade if he could make it. Most turned out well, but in the winter of 1947 he traded outfielder Gene Woodling to Pittsburgh for veteran catcher Al Lopez. Soon thereafter, Woodling was traded to the New York Yankees, where he performed well for years and was an important cog in five straight world championships for the Bronx Bombers. Conversely, Lopez played only 61 games for the Tribe. In the back of Veeck's mind, he eventually hoped to appoint Lopez as the Indians' manager. That reality did not take place until 1951, after Veeck sold the club.

A few weeks after the winter meetings, Veeck made one of his rare trips to his guest ranch outside of Tucson. Veeck knew his marriage was irreparable, and he admitted that his forthcoming divorce was his fault from beginning to end. After his frequent operations and while at the ranch, he would spend a couple of hours soaking his amputated leg, reading everything, newspapers, magazines, and books, and listening to classical music and jazz.

The Tribe owner was a vagabond in the sense that he liked to wander and could not stay in one place for long. Veeck liked people and liked to be around them, whether at a ballpark, bar, or a bench at the Public Square in downtown Cleveland. He remembered while at the ranch, "I couldn't take the complete separation from baseball. I have spent most of my life in a ball park.... There is nothing more beautiful than a stadium filled with people."[22]

As expected, Veeck's three children from his first marriage—William III, Peter, and Bernice—saw little of their father. This was one of the dark spots in the life of this otherwise highly admired human being. When Hank Greenberg, a close friend, wrote a laudatory article about Bill Veeck for *Reader's Digest*, he made no mention of his first family. Bernice summed up her relationship with Veeck: "Bill was a warm and loving person. It was sad because my first thought was, here we had a wonderful father and didn't have a chance to know him. Other people probably knew him much better than his own children did."[23] In an interview with biographer Gerald Eskenazi, his wife Eleanor reflected on the failed marriage: Speaking of her children, she said, "I'm proud of them. I think I was very lucky." Eskenazi asked, "You did it on your own?" "Well that's for sure," she responded. Choosing not to say anything derogatory about her former husband, she stated: "He was public property and they think a lot of him. He's gone now. Let the public keep their image."[24]

Veeck thought that one way to allow him more time in Arizona would be to move the Tribe to Tucson for spring training. In 1946, the Cactus League was not yet in full bloom. Cleveland would need another team to challenge for exhibition games. The only other teams training west of the Mississippi River were the two Chicago teams. The Chicago Cubs proposed that the Indians contact owner Horace Stoneham of the New York Giants. Veeck and Stoneham agreed to meet at the popular Westward Ho Hotel in downtown Phoenix. The desert city's population at this time was approximately 90,000. Tom Fitzpatrick, Pulitzer Prize–winning columnist for the Chicago *Tribune*, recalled that Veeck grinned at the memory of what transpired at the meeting.

> The mayor of Phoenix [Ray Busey] came along to meet with us. By the time the mayor and I got to the bar, Horace [known to tip a few] was already totally bombed.... Since I had to have somebody in Phoenix to play ... games with, there was no way to wait until later in the day to settle the deal. I remember the ... mayor and I just put the contract under Horace's nose ... and I put my hand on Horace's and signed for him.[25]

Later, Veeck and Stoneham drove to the airport with the mayor as both owners were headed to Chicago. "When we got to Chicago," Veeck remarked, "Stoneham came to life. He seemed surprised to see me. 'Hey Bill, it's good to see you. Why don't we get together and work out a deal for me to come to Phoenix.'" Veeck grinned at the memory of one of his great "hustles." "Horace," I told him, "You and your Giants are all set in Phoenix. You've already met the mayor. You've signed the contract. You're really gonna love it there."[26]

These two teams and many others began to fancy Arizona. The Indians and Giants were the first two of several teams to take up spring training in the southwest. Several teams had come to Arizona prior to 1946 for exhibition games, but Cleveland and New York initiated the Cactus League. In 2014, 16 teams held spring training in the greater metropolitan Phoenix area. The other 14 teams continue to train in Florida in the Grapefruit League. Cleveland shifted to Florida for a short time in the 1980s and 1990s before returning to Goodyear in western Phoenix in 2008. Unfortunately, Tucson no longer hosts a major league team. Hi Corbett Field, where the Tribe trained for years, now serves as the home field for the Arizona Wildcats, 2012 NCAA champions.

It has often been written that Veeck worked 24 hours a day, 365 days a year. That declaration is obviously an exaggeration, but he did work hard at his job in spite of his ailments. Excuses were not in his vocabulary. This meant he had to meet the fans and sell his product. He spoke from church pulpits, in bars, and once from a coal mine.

Often, Veeck stopped in a particular town and invited a friend for a ride. The next thing the friend knew, he was on a three-day jaunt to the hinterlands. Veeck wrote, "I liked to have someone with me, not only for company but because I [didn't] carry money. Occasionally, I'd run into one of those embarrassing situations where an innkeeper either didn't know me or *did* know me and wouldn't take a check. That's something that will deflate you when you get to thinking that you're riding on top of the world."[27]

To Hal Lebovitz, Veeck was magnetic, fascinating and good company. The young sports writer, at that time with the *Cleveland News*, often volunteered to drive for Veeck on snowy nights to small hamlets all over Ohio. Many communities had as few as 2,000 residents who crowded into the city hall to hear Veeck. He would tell them whiskered baseball stories and they loved it. Lebovitz concluded, "after the visit to this or that hamlet, we'd drive back."[28]

Lebovitz would drop Veeck off in uptown Cleveland, where Veeck would drink beer with a group of socialites, including selected sportswriters known as the Jolly Set. After the party broke up, he would sit around with Shonder Birns and other suspicious characters on the fringe of the law. Birns was one of Cleveland's most notorious criminals. A Hungarian national and never a U.S. citizen, Birns several times announced his forthcoming retirement from the rackets. He never had the chance: On March 29, 1975, he was killed by a bomb planted in his automobile. No one was arrested for his murder.[29] Veeck loved characters on the fringe of the law.

In late February 1947, the Cleveland club departed by train for Tucson. Along the way, teammates who lived near the rail line were picked up. After a two-day trip, the team arrived in Tucson, a true western city at that time. Most of the team had never been there, and they were unaware that the westernmost Civil War battle had taken place at Picacho Peak, a few miles north of Tucson. There was also still a touch of the south in this cactus cow town. Players knew the region only through cowboy movies. The distinctive landscape included cacti, palo verde trees, and sand surrounded by four impressive mountain ranges. It was a different atmosphere from smoky and polluted Cleveland. Instead, the air was clear and dry, cloudless, hot in the sun and cold at night. The lush, emerald green grass manicured by the Bossard family at Hi Corbett Field awaited the squad.

When the players descended from the train, there were no cabs or buses. Cabs would arrive eventually. "The hell with it," said Harold "Muddy" Ruel, "Let's go." Ruel, 57, a slightly-built coach, once had caught the fabled Walter Johnson's fastball.[30] He picked up his suitcase which appeared to weigh more than he did, and began a brisk forward march to the hotel. Without a murmur all the players followed: Lou Boudreau, Bob Feller, Joe Gordon, Ken Keltner, Dale Mitchell, and Jim Hegan among them. All carried huge bags stuffed with clothes to last the entire spring. The small army walked the half-mile non-stop to the Santa Rita Hotel, the team headquarters. The players slept there, usually two to a room, and ate together in the dining room. In 1948, all team members would be housed in the Santa Rita Hotel, except one teammate. He was black. His name was Larry Doby.

During the final days of spring training in early April, the team boarded a train headed for Phoenix. There the Indians joined the New York Giants, and the two teams traveled northward, playing in towns along the way to their home bases. Often, late winter weather interfered with scheduled games.

In mid–April as the season was about to begin, the Cleveland chapter of the Baseball Writers' Association held their annual "Ribs and Roast" banquet. The honored guest was

Bill Veeck, Cleveland's 1946 "Man of the Year" in baseball. The young president was extolled for his deeds in reviving the fortunes of and interest in the Tribe. The dignitaries present included new commissioner A. B. "Happy" Chandler and American League president William Harridge. Veeck, humbled by the honor and many gifts, responded, "the Indians will be strengthened whenever possible and the aim of the present owners is [to win] a pennant and World Series."[31] Time would tell.

An extrovert, Veeck had great rapport with the local press. The three dailies were plush with quality writers. The title of this gathering promised some ribbing of the guest by press row. This banquet was no exception. The following exchange is an example of the repartee that took place:

> ED McAULEY (Cleveland *News*): Mr. Veeck. We were just wondering about a big story for tomorrow.
> VEECK: Just call me Bill. Or old Will. I've got a great story for you. I also have sandwiches and something to drink.
> THE PRESS: What's the story?
> VEECK: I've traded Bob Feller.
> THE PRESS: Traded Feller.
> GORDON COBBLEDICK (*Plain Dealer*): What did you get for him, Bill? Ted Williams, Tex Hughson, and Boo Ferris?
> VEECK: Better than that! What a trade! Best I ever made. You fellows have your typewriters hot?
> PRESS (poised at typewriters): Go ahead. Shoot.
> VEECK (Triumphantly, after dramatic pause): I have traded Feller for the biggest damned firecracker in the world.[32]

Cobbledick and other Cleveland writers developed an immediate liking for Veeck. As Cobbledick wrote, "People are talking about ... Veeck as though he were a magician.... He has convinced people that he is trying to do something. If he ever does it ... the city fathers are going to wonder how they could ... have been so short-sighted as to build so small a stadium on the lake front."[33]

A treatise on Veeck's success in Cleveland cannot be complete without an understanding of the impact of the media. By media one is referring to newspapers, including sports cartoonists, and radio. In the late 1940s, the city was treated to a rarity—three newspapers vying for readership. The *Plain Dealer*, founded in 1842, was the oldest paper and was delivered in the morning. The *Cleveland Press*, a Scripps-Howard paper, and the *Cleveland News* were afternoon papers, hitting the streets after 1:00 p.m.

The competition was fierce and, with few exceptions, amiable among the sports writers of the three dailies. The *Cleveland Press* rose to a position of competiveness in journalistic circles due mainly to the efforts of one home-grown individual, Louis Seltzer, editor of the *Press* for 38 years. During his last 15 years, he was the single most powerful political force in Cleveland. Seltzer, a self-made individual, was much like Veeck: He possessed charisma, was known as "Little Bromo" to his critics and "Mr. Cleveland" to his many admirers. Despite no formal education, Seltzer became a king-maker, a mayor-maker, by combining native shrewdness, cunning, prodigious energy, and a large ego with a phenomenal sense of timing.

He did it almost entirely himself, with the constant encouragement of Marion, his quite charming wife. This description of Seltzer aptly resembled that of Veeck.

The fireball editor knew sports pages were an important element of a vibrant paper, and accordingly he hired well-respected writers. During the Veeck era, his main sports writers were Franklin "Whitey" Lewis, author of a popular but non-refereed history of the Cleveland Indians (until 1949), Frank Gibbons, and Bob August. These three were primarily responsible for coverage of the Tribe.

Veteran Ed Bang, a founder of the Baseball Writers' Association of America, and Ed McAuley covered baseball for the *Cleveland News*, property of the Forest City Publishing Company. Baseball coverage for the *Plain Dealer* was spearheaded by Gordon Cobbledick, dean of sportswriters in Cleveland. Others included long-time sports humorist James E. Doyle, writers Frank Gibbons, Hal Lebovitz, and Bob Dolgan, and writer-broadcaster Harry Jones. Later on came encyclopedic Russ Schneider, who covered the Tribe for 14 years.

Respected columnist Don Robertson of the *Cleveland Press* maintained that Cobbledick, Bob August, a graduate of the College of Wooster, Frank Gibbons and James E. Doyle consistently produced literate copy. For the most part, these writers gave the profession equable and judicious appraisal, sadly lacking in modern-day sports journalism. These men understood that reporters are not shills for the team and were free of sophomoric yea-saying in the post-war era. The journalist reported what happened: he gave his readers the facts; the reader could draw his own conclusions.[34]

These writers felt comfortable with Veeck, as he did with them. Jimmy Dudley, long time Indians announcer, claimed that "Veeck was closer to 'Cobby' than any of the other Cleveland writers." This was a testament to Cobby.[35] In an interview with Veeck 18 months before his death, the former Indians owner recalled, "When I was in Cleveland, I was at Cobbledick's home once a week. Cobby was a pretty good poker player and we would have games at his home." Veeck added, "When I left Cleveland, I always called him before I would give a story out. He would be ready for it."[36]

This group of writers was central to Veeck's social life. Their setting was a restaurant called Gruber's, located in a fashionable shopping center in Shaker Heights. Max Gruber was the owner and his restaurant from early in the evening to late at night attracted social leaders of the city, gossip columnists, local entertainers, and assorted other celebrities.

Veeck and Gruber were in charge of social activities. The group was soon named "The Jolly Set" by Bill Roberts, a *Cleveland Press* cartoonist. He would run a cartoon, sometimes on page one, portraying the conversation of the Jolly Set. "In the Jolly Set, we had parties," Veeck related. "The parties celebrated our birthdays and anniversaries. We had parties to celebrate a Cleveland victory.... We had parties just because nobody could think of any good reason *not* to have a party." Gruber added, "The Jolly Set was a group of people hell-bent for fun."[37]

If the fun life in Paris during the 1920s resided in the salons with the patronage of the Fitzgeralds, Hemingways, Gertrude Stein, and many others, so did Cleveland society, as the underworld, the sporting fraternity and fun seekers came together at Gruber's night club after World War II.

Sports writers were wooed by Veeck in a positive way. The new owner set up a Wigwam

Room, a dining facility for the press and radio personnel at the Stadium. In one case, Veeck's charitable acts toward the press backfired so far as Cobbledick was concerned. When the joy of the 1948 World Championship subsided, Veeck perpetuated a predicament. An always generous person, Veeck had been lavish with gifts to the sports writers. After the series ended, the Tribe owner had new television sets delivered to Herman Goldstein and McAuley of the *News*, Lewis and Gibbons of the *Press*, and Cobbledick. The editors of the *News* and the *Press* requested their writers return the sets, and they complied. Paul Bellamy, son of Edward Bellamy[38] and Cobbledick's editor, asked Cobbledick to do the same.

Cobby bowed his back and rejected this request. Bellamy remained silent. Cobbledick, in a fit of anger, insisted that a television set could not buy him off and "if [the editor] thinks that, you can get rid of me."[39] The long-time staff member resented the inference that he could be "bought off" by management of a professional sports team. He was the only one of these reporters who did not return his television set. The issue never came up again.

Cobbledick defended the thesis that covering the Tribe as representatives of their respective newspapers did not make the writers shills for the franchise. He explained, "In the eyes of these writers, it is news when a pitcher declaims in public that 'he doesn't like the manager and wants the world to know it,' just as it is news when the manager replies that ... 'he doesn't like the pitcher any better.'"[40]

Writers are aware that publication of such "behind the scenes" activities probably does not do the club much good, but these activities are legitimate news, and newspapers print it. Ball players are public figures, and the public wants to know all about them. Fans are interested not only in runs and hits but also in how well players respond to criticism and how they get along with each other.

Cobbledick compared a baseball writer to a drama reviewer: He or she tells not only what the play is about but also how well the company and its performers have presented a given production to the public. The award-winning writer concluded, "One of the first lessons I learned was the [realization] that it is a great waste of time to try to kid the public about its ball club. The baseball writer who makes this effort only lowers his own standing and that of his paper in the mind of ... cash customers."[41] The veteran writer believed the local team belonged to the public and that it was the baseball columnist's duty to chronicle all news fit to print.

In addition to baseball writers, sports cartoonists and baseball broadcasters promoted the popularity of America's national pastime. There were few sports cartoonists during the 1920s and 1930s; however, the cartoon became more popular as a result of wartime cartoons by Bill Mauldin and Willard Mullin. Before their time, the most famous early sports cartoonist was T. A. "Tad" Dorgan.[42] Dorgan ended his career as a sportswriter and cartoonist for the New York *Journal*. Jack Dempsey described him as the greatest authority on boxing.

It was World War II when cartoonists Mauldin and Mullin moved to the forefront of cartoon journalism. Mauldin, a two-time Pulitzer Prize winner, did not specialize in sports cartoons. His fame came from his caricatures of Willie and Joe—two G.I.s encountering the perils of infantry life during combat. Willard Mullin was more directly involved with baseball cartoons. For decades, his most famous figure was the "Brooklyn Bum," a personification of the Brooklyn Dodgers. His cartoons appeared daily in the *New York World-*

Telegram and *Sun*. The "Brooklyn Bum" caricature was often published in *The Sporting News* and in 20 Scripps-Howard papers.

A third cartoonist of note was Leo O'Mealia. He drew a six- or nine-small-frame cartoon illustrating a sequence of a ball player batting, fielding, or pitching. The sequence led up to failure by the boasting player, who was a generic, not a specific, player. O'Mealia was influenced by the work of T. A. Dorgan.[43]

Cleveland readers were fortunate to have two cartoonists who matched up with the best. Lou Darvis, a Pulitzer Prize winner for the *Cleveland Press*, was in a class with Mullin and Mauldin, and Fred Reinert had a long and illustrious career with the *Plain Dealer*. Darvis was born in Hungary and his parents moved to the United States when he was three years old. His father, a violinist, settled with his family on the west side of Cleveland. Darvis attended West Tech High School and then enrolled at John Huntington Art School. A variety of jobs followed—scraping old signs, running a mimeograph machine and announcing on radio.

In 1938 Darvis started working for the *Press*. His career was interrupted by a two-year stint in the Army. He returned to the *Press* in 1946 and spent the rest of his career there. His reputation grew in exponential leaps and bounds, and soon he was recognized as one of the finest sports cartoonists in the nation.[44] His working superior, sports editor Bob August, described Darvis as a charming professional, quite bright, and an extraordinary person. August recalled that when he suggested a topic for a cartoon, Darvis would bring in a sample within 20 minutes.[45] The special magic of Darvis' deft pen recorded the guffaws and tears, boos and cheers of all sports. For the Indians, he would depict day-by-day fortunes of a big lanky Indian, sometimes happy, often befuddled.

His reputation was enhanced by his periodic cartoons in *The Sporting News*. Occasionally, he might jab a delicate needle into a prominent sports figure. Most of the wounded kept smiling, but there were exceptions. Hank Greenberg, who became general manager of Cleveland in 1949, was a natty dresser and objected vociferously every time Darvis portrayed him in a pinstriped suit. Darvis was a winner of the Pulitzer Prize and several awards from the National Cartoonists Society, and originals of his cartoons were prized by such collectors as Casey Stengel, Roger Maris, Al Lopez, and Sid Keener, former curator of the Hall of Fame in Cooperstown.[46]

It was a rarity for any one city to retain such renowned cartoonists as Darvis and Reinert. Reinert, a native of Cleveland, grew up on the west side. In his youth, youngsters had idolized Cleveland boxers like featherweight champion Bryan Downey, and his first sketches had been of boxers.

Reinert enlisted in the U.S. Army in 1917. He saw service with the 332nd Infantry Regiment in Italy, the only American unit fighting in Italy during World War I. Though largely self-taught, Reinert attended classes at the Cleveland School of Art. He later studied portrait painting under Sander Vago, one of Cleveland's most noted artists, but he nursed a yen to draw caricatures, one the subtlest of art forms.[47]

Reinert joined the *Plain Dealer* and developed a cartoon figure called Knuckes, a fictional pitcher for the Cleveland Indians. He also drew caricatures of personalities who appeared in James E. Doyle's daily column in the *Plain Dealer*, "The Sports Trail." Some of these characters, mainly sports fans, were named Stanislaus Totaloss, Ivan Offulitch, Ku

Klux Klancy (the invisible umpire), Vera McVacuum, Rayle Byrd, Egg Shelley, Nervous Rex, and many more. Reinert's trademark appeared on the front page and sports pages of the *Plain Dealer*. It was a little Indian with rolling eyes and a hose-nose. The Indian danced after a Tribe victory and grieved with a blackened eye following a loss.[48]

Cobbledick thought his close friend to be a man of many talents: "To identify him as the man who [drew] the little Indian," commented the sports editor," is akin to remembering [Charles] Lindbergh as a fellow who used to fly mail."[49] Reinert's forte was caricature. By exaggerating the subject's strongest feature he could give the reader a laugh while producing a nationally recognizable likeness of his subject. Reinert's lines were sharp and definitive. To capture the essence of tennis immortal and very tall Bill Tilden, he made Tilden look like the Terminal Tower with black eyes and a simper.[50]

Most of Darvis's and Reinert's cartoon were topical, depicting trends and events from day to day or week to week in the major leagues with a special emphasis on the Tribe. The characters were usually talking while sitting or standing. If they were moving, they were drawn without motion lines so that the figures looked like statues.[51]

During the 1960s, as newspapers began to subscribe to wire services, syndicated and local sports cartoonists slowly disappeared from the sports pages. There is little doubt that later Cleveland cartoonists, particularly Dick Dugan of the *Plain Dealer*, still had considerable impact on fans' interest and understanding of the Tribe's fortunes.[52] (The *Cleveland News* was purchased by the *Cleveland Press* in January 1960, and within a few months, the *News* was no more.)

Daily newspapers and the weekly *The Sporting News* were the primary sources of information about the complexities of games. Photos, behind-the-scene materials, interviews—all were a part of the journalistic landscape, game by game. These news sources were available to fans in every major league city and throughout the nation. Radio reached even more fans than newspapers. The pyrotechnics of Tom Manning and Jack Graney kept Tribe listeners glued to their radios from the late 1920s until 1945. Timothy D. Taylor, et al., authors of *Music, Sound, and Technology in America* (2012), argue that radio "came to symbolize, perhaps more than any other technology, with the possible exception of the automobile, Americans' sense of themselves as modern people."[53] Listeners were bemused by sounds and signals accidentally—or on purpose—captured from seemingly ethereal origins. Jack Graney led the way as one of the first announcers to recreate game action.

From the beginning, Western Union had exclusive access to the ball parks and elsewhere, particularly to radio stations. The company sold a special service called "paragraph one." When an account of a major league game was sent by wire in Morse code, a receiving operator would type play-by-play accounts and feed them to Graney. The broadcaster was at liberty to make up pertinent information relative to given plays. If there was a telegraphic breakdown, Graney would improvise with a series of faked foul balls or even rain delays.

Graney is best remembered as a man of firsts. He was the first batter to face Babe Ruth as pitcher for the Boston Red Sox. The year was 1914. He was one of the first players to take to the field with a number on his uniform. In 1908, he was a member of the first all-star team who toured the Orient.[54] And he was the first ex-major leaguer to sit behind a microphone to broadcast big-league games.

Lacking sponsors, broadcasts of Cleveland Indians games were unavailable in 1945 and the first half of the 1946 season. Graney broadcast Tribe games from 1932 until the end of the 1953 season. After retiring from baseball, he had a brief stint broadcasting the Cleveland Barons ice hockey games. Graney died April 20, 1978, at 91.

In 1948, Graney was joined by Jimmy Dudley, who was called "siren sweet" by Curt Smith, historian of baseball broadcasters. Dudley was born in Alexandria, Virginia, in 1909 and served a hitch with the U.S. Air Force, stationed in India during World War II. He reminded Smith of Red Barber. The Virginian exuded light, rich tones. He was pleasant, seldom petulant, and was easy to listen to during the flow of the game.[55]

Dudley and Graney made a perfect team for the next six years. It is fair to say that these two announcers gave Cleveland fans the best one-two punch in the baseball broadcasting business after World War II. Dudley later commented, "Jack was my first air partner and the one who did the most to help me." He added, "85 percent of the people who listen to baseball broadcasts either know more about the game or *think* they know more about it than you do.... I never forgot what he said."[56]

The popular Dudley broadcast Indians games through the 1967 season. After a brief time with the Seattle Pilots in 1968–1969, he lost his job when the Pilots moved to Wisconsin to become the Milwaukee Brewers. There was no opportunity for him to remain with the Brewers because broadcaster Merle Harmon was entrenched in Milwaukee. Dudley retired to Tucson, and in 1997, he won the Ford Frick Award given by the Hall of Fame. He died in 1999 at the age of 90. Graney should also be honored by the Hall of Fame. He was inducted into the Cleveland Baseball Hall of Fame posthumously on August 11, 2012.[57]

The Internet and smart phones had not yet been invented during the wild and crazy tenure of Bill Veeck. Other than word of mouth, there were only three significant modes of communication between the Cleveland franchise and its fan base. First was game attendance. Fans poured into Municipal Stadium for the scheduled 77 games. After World War II, the Tribe set the pace in major league attendance records that were never broken until the 162-game schedule took effect with expansion in 1962. The Cleveland franchise held the single game record in a baseball stadium with a crowd of 86,288 in the fifth game of the 1948 World Series. (This record was broken when the transplanted Los Angeles Dodgers drew 93,103 for Roy Campanella Night at the Los Angeles Coliseum May 7, 1958. The Dodgers continued to break attendance records with three consecutive crowds of over 90,000 in the 1959 World Series against Bill Veeck's Chicago White Sox.)

Second was the press. The three Cleveland dailies printed and sold more and more papers, and circulation increased as pennant fever escalated. Fans wanted detailed information about their team's doings. Each daily employed a cadre of highly qualified, veteran sportswriters who fed their appetite. These men garnered numerous awards for their quality journalism. Sports cartoonists and humorists contributed to the appeal of the newspapers' sports pages.

Third was radio. It is difficult to ascertain the number of fans who eagerly listened to Dudley as he began the broadcasts with a familiar introduction. The voices of Graney and Dudley were heard wherever the radio signal extended as far as southern Ohio, Indiana, Michigan, western New York and Pennsylvania, and West Virginia. On a clear night, the signal might reach across the border into Canada. The flagship station was WGAR in 1947, and then broadcasts moved to WJW in 1948–1949. New station sponsorship took place in 1950, when WERE became the flagship station for the next 22 years. Select games were also aired on Cleveland stations WEWS and WXEL depending upon fan interest.[58] By 1948, a few games, including the World Series, were televised. Television was in its infancy, reception in black and white was often marginal, and there were occasional breakdowns in reception. Eventually, television smoothed out its delivery, and the number of viewers increased. This technological advancement provided another significant means of communication between the fan base and their home-town team.

In April 1947, the enigmatic Bill Veeck began his first full season as owner and "unofficial" general manager, still wondering if he had the right field manager. The 33-year-old was ready to pull any strings necessary to make the Indians pennant contenders.

An example of his determined desire to produce a winning team took place in spring training. He brought two Hall of Famers, Tris Speaker and Rogers Hornsby, to Tucson. The owner hoped these two great hitters would be able to improve the Tribe's anemic batting average. The team had compiled a mediocre team batting average of .255 in 1945, and this figure had dropped ten points in 1946 to .245.[59]

One factor adversely affected the 1947 team. Players didn't know who their teammates were from one day to the next. More than 60 players reported for spring training. Of 19 pitchers on the roster prior to March 1, only eight reported for spring training. By spring training a year later in 1948, two more of these former eight pitchers were deleted from the list, including soft-spoken and popular Mel Harder. A member of Cleveland's Baseball Hall of Fame, Harder twirled for the Indians for 20 seasons, winning 223 games. The second deportee was left-hander Bob Kuzava.

Before spring training in 1948, five pitchers were left from the 1946 staff: Don Black, Feller, Gromek, Lemon, and Eddie Klieman. Al Gettel was added before the 1947 season.[60] One notes several significant changes and additions during the 1947 season. The 1947 season started on a sour and sweet note. The Tribe and Feller lost their home opener to the White Sox, 2–0. However, Veeck smiled at the sound of turnstiles clicking as fans hurried to their seats—55,004 fans altogether, the largest Opening Day crowd in major league history to that date.

Two weeks later, the innovative Veeck put in place one of many strategies of "gamesmanship." He called it "the art of winning without really cheating."[61] The playing field in Cleveland Stadium was the largest in the major leagues, and the home team became discouraged when well-stroked balls were hit some 470 feet to center field and caught by opposing outfielders. Veeck installed a portable five-foot-high wire fence in the outfield much as he had done in Milwaukee. This fence measured 320 feet at the foul line poles and curved symmetrically to 410 feet in dead center field. Unbeknownst to other league teams, the sly one had installed five or six sets of sleeves to hold the fence in place. In the dark of night, Veeck would move the fence in or out as much as 15 feet, depending upon who was coming to town—a power-hitting team like the Yankees or a weak-hitting team like the St. Louis Browns.

Whether this ruse benefitted the Tribe is unclear. The club did increase their home run total from 79 in 1946 to 112 in 1947. Veeck searched for other "gimmicks" that might give his team an edge on the playing field. He relied on Emil Bossard, his talented and precise head groundskeeper, to implement "adjustments" on the infield. Bossard, whom Veeck referred to as Michelangelo, manicured the infield specifically to benefit the home team. The infield, for instance, was not flat but turtle-back in design. From that point, baselines can be manicured in such a way as to inhibit runners or vice-versa. For Cleveland, the most critical areas were the pitching mound and the left side of the infield. The rule at that time specified that the pitcher's mound be 15 inches above baseline level.[62] Often, teams adjusted this height to fit their own pitcher's needs. Bossard made sure that the mound was at maximum height—or a little more—if Feller was pitching, for his fastball and wicked curve benefitted from this slight adjustment. On the other hand, if Ed Lopat—a Tribe nemesis—was pitching, his curve and slow stuff might be less effective from a high mound.

Cleveland had two veterans at shortstop and third base, Boudreau and Keltner, who could no longer move with alacrity. Boudreau never played a game without wrapping his weak ankles. He always played his position by instinct. Few infielders were as adept in this respect, as he could anticipate where batters would hit the ball, so Bossard kept the grass high and well watered in the shortstop region. The same physical impediment was true for third baseman Ken Keltner. Although he was only 31, the ten-year veteran's legs were beginning to give out, so again Bossard went to work, and the third base area was soaked daily to reduce shock and strain on Keltner's legs while the grass around third base was kept at normal height. This manicuring of the infield gave these two veterans a feeling of advantage on their home field.[63]

Much to the relief of manager Boudreau, the Indians got off to a reasonably good start during the first two months of the 1947 season. No doubt he felt constant pressure to improve the performance of his team. Attendance spiraled toward another record-breaking figure as Rapid Robert set the pace for success, and on April 22 he garnered his ninth one-hitter, defeating St. Louis, 5–0. Al Zarilla's single in the seventh inning negated Feller's bid for a third no-hitter.

Ten days later on May 2, Feller repeated his one-hit antics with number ten in his career, as he whipped the heavy-hitting Red Sox, 2–0. Boston's Johnny Pesky, with an appropriate last name, stroked a single in the first inning for the only hit. In the early days of the season, Feller was pitching well. Frank Bowerman, former major league catcher who caught Christy Mathewson in the 1900s, saw him pitch that year in Yankee Stadium. A keen observer of the game, he rated Feller as "the greatest pitcher baseball has yet seen." The old timer added, "Feller had more physical equipment than I have seen in my time."[64]

However, Feller's early success was short-lived, and he fell in more ways than one. By August his record had slipped considerably below his comparable records for the preceding four years, and fans were annoyed by his performance. On Friday, June 13—not a good omen—Feller was outstanding against the Athletics. He was on fire for the first four innings, fanning nine of the first 11 batters. On his last strikeout, however, Feller caught his foot in a hole in front of the pitching mound, and this freak movement wrenched his left knee and subsequently pulled a muscle in his back.

Sportswriters Frank Gibbons and Ed McAuley later agreed that for the first four innings,

Feller had thrown harder than in other games during the season. Feller told his biographer, John Sickels, that "It was the best stuff I ever had." The *Washington Post*'s Shirley Povich, never a big fan of Feller, fired a national shot, claiming that "never before have American League hitters found Feller such a soft touch. His pitching has been strictly that of an in-and-outer."[63]

Feller returned to make his next start but for the ensuing weeks was inconsistent. His poor showing was accompanied by rumors of outside interests and personal upheaval in his family life, fans began to criticize their star pitcher, and boos permeated the air when Feller ran into trouble on the mound. In spite of his ordinary record, Feller was chosen for the All-Star Game, but asked to be released from this responsibility so his troublesome back could heal. This decision brought yet more criticism from irate fans. The final blow came on August 13, when Feller announced that he had signed to pitch in the Cuban Winter League in the fall. By now the Tribe had dropped out of the pennant race and was fighting to stay in the first division. Feller's record of 14–9 did not help the cause.

Commissioner Chandler issued an edict prohibiting any major leaguer from playing in the Cuban Winter League. Feller offered to turn his entire $18,000 winter contract over to the newly formed major league pension program, but Chandler refused to reverse his decision. Feller retaliated by making plans for his final barnstorming tour at the conclusion of the season.[66] This brouhaha led fans and the press to question whether Feller had spread himself too thin in an effort to pad his wallet. No one, not even Veeck, believed he had been overpaid—his salary was approximately $85,000. Feller, a conservative farm boy from Iowa, left little doubt that money was an important issue in his life. He riled fans throughout the years with his tendency to refuse to sign his autograph gratis.

During the disappointing 1947 season, Feller often made headlines. A much lesser known pitcher, Don Black, captured the limelight for one night that season. This was the same Don Black whom Veeck had purchased from Philadelphia on October 2, 1945. He was soon thereafter suspended by the Tribe for a drinking problem. Veeck had been aware of his pitcher's drinking problem when the 1946 season began. Black barely remained on the roster in 1946. He struggled through 18 games with a 1–2 record. The troubled pitcher was finally convinced by Veeck, in fact ordered, to join Alcoholics Anonymous. His 1946 season was finished.

Nineteen forty-seven was a much better year for Black. On July 10, in the first game of a twi-night doubleheader, he faced the Philadelphia Athletics, his former teammates. The right-hander hurled a no-hitter, beating the Athletics, 3–0. It was the Indians' ninth no-hitter and the first one recorded in the Stadium. Black completed the most successful season of his short career, winning ten and losing 12 games. He started the second-most games (28) for the Tribe and ended the year with a 3.92 E.R.A.[67]

Feller's struggles and Black's no-hitter slipped into the background with Veeck's plans to sign the first African American ballplayer in the American League. He had felt rebuffed since 1944 when he had allegedly attempted to buy the Philadelphia Phillies and place several African Americans on the roster. Veeck was determined, with his progressive philosophy, that he no longer would be thwarted in his efforts to further break the color line. (Doby was signed July 2, 1947.) Branch Rickey had broken the color barrier with his signing of

Jackie Robinson a few weeks earlier, and Veeck believed he could do the same in the American League. He did not, in this case, look upon his decision as a publicity stunt. He remembered a story his father had told him while serving as vice-president of the Cubs. William, Sr. told his son to look at the color of the money he was counting at the box office. "'Look at it, it's all green. It's all the same and you can't tell me who put it in the box office.'" I said, 'No,' that's all he had to say.... If their money is equal, they are equal."[68] Such a decision, however, was fraught with many concerns.

While on a trip to Mexico in 1946, Gordon Cobbledick had observed Ray Dandridge, a black shortstop. He reported his impressions to club officials in Cleveland. Many observers believed Dandridge was equal to any of the outstanding shortstops playing in the majors. A few weeks later Veeck met with Dandridge at his ranch in Tucson. "Veeck wanted me to be the first one [in the majors]," Dandridge commented. Dandridge was making decent money in the Mexican League. He asked Veeck about a signing bonus. Veeck declined to make an offer and Dandridge returned to Mexico. In view of his relative youth, the outstanding shortstop was afraid to jeopardize his status in Mexico.[69]

In mid–February 1947, Veeck hired Louis Jones, a black former public relations employee for the American Federation of Labor, to inform the black community in Cleveland to be ready for the arrival of an African American on the Indians' team. The inner belt of metropolitan Cleveland had been inundated since 1940 with blacks moving north for industrial jobs.

It is important to note that earlier, the inner belt of Cleveland had been largely made up of wealthy white residents who were being squeezed out by the settlement of blacks in neighboring communities. At the same time, the Cleveland Indians in many ways had often been referred to as a "white man's team."

Long-time owner Alva Bradley had never brushed shoulders with the black community. For that matter, the same held true for several of the newly settled ethnic groups who had migrated to the near east and west sides of the city. A well-meaning citizen of the "upper crust," Bradley and his family had survived the hard times of the Great Depression. His baseball franchise appreciated in value and stockholders made a modest profit.

Franklin Lewis of the *Cleveland Press* wrote that the symbolism [of the owners] was "wealth and affluence." He added, "The average fan resented for years the 'society touch' of the Tribe operation.... [Possibly] this has been because of the large laboring class in Cleveland. Maybe the nationality groups and civic clubs bristled because the team operations were from the other side of the tracks."[70]

What a difference in ownership! Veeck wanted to mingle with everyone. He was not a "suit and tie" guy. He was known to immerse himself in nearly all walks of life. He was perceived as the kind of individual who would argue baseball in a streetcar or a bar. Here was a franchise owner often seen in the stands sitting with the fans. In his later years, Veeck was often surrounded by fans in the right field bleachers of his beloved Wrigley Field.

Fortunes were made by blockbusting, despite the efforts of a forward-thinking Community Relations Board. The crowded near east side of the city became a tinderbox of racial uprisings. In poorer neighborhoods, large single family homes were subdivided and, as rental income dwindled, often neglected properties became overcrowded and ripe for racial unrest.[71]

Racial relations between 1947 and 2012 are an interesting contrast. Major league baseball was segregated until 1947. So, too, was the U.S. military until the same year. The South was blatantly segregated by state laws. The conduct of southern whites vis-à-vis blacks was an eye-opener for the author—a young, naïve soldier stationed at Ft. McClellen, Alabama, and Ft. Jackson, South Carolina, in 1946 and 1947. Overt segregation governed on busses, in schools, restaurants, hotels, theaters, restrooms, water fountains, sporting events and nearly everywhere else, including all public facilities.

Segregation in the north was more subtle but noticeable to observant citizens. Northerners had far less contact with black citizens because fewer African Americans resided north of the Mason-Dixon Line. Integration in nearly every respect was a slow process. It took 12 years from the time Jackie Robinson donned a uniform in Brooklyn in 1947, until "Pumpsie" Green played for the Boston Red Sox in 1959, for all 16 teams to be integrated. To this day, there is no doubt that racial prejudice exists in the United States, but it seems to be less evident in team sports. Indeed, team sports—notably football and basketball—are comprised of large percentages of minority players. Even politics has broken the color line at the presidential level.

Veeck sought a black player who would make a lasting contribution to the Tribe's cause. By July, Cleveland, for the most part, was out of the pennant race. The Tribe's scouts in the east told Veeck about a young prospect named Larry Doby. The second baseman was playing for the Newark Bears, owned by effervescent and astute Effa Manley. Veeck was determined to be fair in his negotiations with the well-respected Manley. The two settled on $15,000 as the purchase price. At the time of the signing, Doby was leading the International League with 14 home runs and batting .430.[72]

Many scouts questioned why Veeck did not choose Monte Irvin, playing shortstop alongside Doby. He was also an outstanding player, but the difference was age. Irvin was almost six years older than Doby. Irvin was signed by the New York Giants in 1949 and had a fine career. He was inducted into the Hall of Fame in 1973.

Much like Robinson, Doby possessed the "right" physical and emotional attributes for this momentous opportunity. Six feet, one inch tall and weighing 180 pounds, Doby was a natural athlete. The 22-year-old had been an all-state athlete in four sports in Paterson, New Jersey. In 1942, the teenager was offered a basketball scholarship by the renowned Clair Bee at Long Island University. Instead, Doby chose to enlist in the Navy, for he was likely to be drafted. He played baseball and basketball at Great Lakes Naval Station in Chicago. The young sailor was then shipped to the South Pacific, where he served as an athletic instructor with Mickey Vernon, the Washington Senators' first baseman.

This important move by Veeck to sign the first black to play in the American League was attended by blunders by Indians management. Doby was unprepared for the severity of prejudice exhibited by teammates and the public. In many ways, Doby survived greater obstacles than did Robinson. Many had thought that Doby's entry into the major leagues would be easier since Robinson had already broken the racial barrier: "Why would it have?" Doby often asked later. "What would have been [different]? I signed eleven weeks after Jackie did.... We still have problems with race today; why would it be different in 1947?"[73]

Veeck brought Doby to Chicago on July 4 after he played his last game with Newark.

The Indians owner believed it would be easier if Doby played his first major league game on the road. The press had been notified of the impending historical event. Veeck met Doby at the Congress Hotel in downtown Chicago, where he signed his contract. The room was quiet as Veeck announced that Doby was now a member of the Cleveland Indians, adding, "He'll be a great player." Doby later related, "He got up from his desk and walked over and shook my hand and said: 'Lawrence ... I'm Mr. Veeck,' and I said, 'Nice to meet you, Mr. Veeck.' He responded: 'You don't have to call me Mr. Veeck. Call me Bill.'"[74]

The Indians' business office had neglected to confirm that Doby could stay at the Hotel Del Prado, where the Indians stayed. He could not stay, "no colored allowed." The management scrambled around and found a room at the Hotel Dusable, described as "in the heart of Chicago's Negro Belt."[75]

Another mistake Veeck made was not to consult with his manager about the impending purchase of Doby. Boudreau was skeptical when he received word of the addition to the team. Where would he play the second baseman when he already had Joe Gordon? Was it another one of Veeck's publicity stunts? The team wasn't going anywhere in the pennant race. Possibly Doby would stimulate black fan attendance for the remainder of the season.

Veeck assured Boudreau that the signing of Doby was indeed a legitimate effort to improve the Tribe down the road: "He'll be all yours.... Give him a chance. He can play anywhere in the infield."[76] With Keltner and Boudreau at third and shortstop, that left only first base, a position Doby had never played. The first baseman was Eddie Robinson, a rookie from Paris, Texas, who was having a decent freshman season with considerable potential, but he was from the South. When rumors about Doby reached the Indians' players, some made threatening statements. Veeck got wind of these comments and called a rare clubhouse meeting at Comiskey Park on July 4. Many complainers were fringe players from the South. Veeck told them, "I understand that some of you ... said ... if a nigger joins the club, you're leaving. Well, you can leave right now."[77]

Before his meeting with prospective teammates, Veeck called Doby into his office for a bit of well-meant advice. Doby was young, scared, a black person breaking a major racial barrier, and no doubt felt like one climbing Mt. Everest. Yet he had to stand tall. Veeck told Doby that he must prepare for slights and insults by teammates, opposing teams, and fans and gave his new player a list of dos and don'ts: "No arguing with umpires ... no dissertations with opposing players ... no associating with white women, and above all else, act in an appropriate way as people will be watching."[78] Then Veeck told Doby something he would always remember: "We're in this together, kid." That remark cemented a lifelong trust between Doby and his new boss.[79]

Doby, unlike Jackie Robinson, had received little counseling from his manager on how to handle himself under adverse situations. One can imagine the tension this young black athlete experienced when introduced to his fellow players. On July 5 Boudreau took Doby to the Indians' clubhouse to meet skeptical teammates. It is important to note that like Veeck and management, Boudreau did not handle this history-making confab in the best possible way. When Doby was in the dressing room, Boudreau came in and shook his hand. Whitey Lewis wrote, "Most players' faces turned to the floor. Not even a single shuffle or solitary

Cleveland owner Bill Veeck signing Larry Doby to a contract at the Congress Hotel in Chicago, July 5, 1947. The first black player in the American League, Doby played ten seasons with the Tribe, hitting 253 home runs and 970 RBI. He was elected to the Hall of Fame in 1998 (courtesy William Cobbledick Collection).

spike on the floor broke the horrible, tomb-like muteness.... Then the Indians filed out of the room. Not one word was uttered."[80]

When players lined up in the dugout, Boudreau took Doby down the line to shake hands with them. Five players refused to extend their hands. Two players vehemently rejected Doby's outstretched hand, Robinson and first baseman Les Fleming.[81] (Doby, who did not know one player from another, was given this information later.) When informed of the incident, Veeck said those players would be sent far away at season's end. Les Fleming, from Texas, did not return to the Tribe in 1948. He played 24 games for Pittsburgh in 1949 and retired from the game. The second regular who did not return in 1948 was Catfish Metkovich, from California. Eddie Robinson, from Texas, played for Cleveland in 1948 and 1949, and with pitcher Joe Haynes and Eddie Klieman was traded for Mickey Vernon and Early Wynn.

Various stories have been published concerning Doby's first day on the field in Comiskey Park. A recent autobiography of first baseman Eddie Robinson gives one version of what happened. A doubleheader with the White Sox was scheduled on July 6. Between games, Boudreau came into the clubhouse and said, "'Robbie, I want to borrow your glove. I want Doby to play first base.' I told him he could borrow my glove ... but I was quitting. I couldn't believe what I was hearing."[82] Two days earlier, Boudreau had told Robinson that he was the team's first baseman and not to worry.

Robinson was so angry, he told Fleming he was going to quit if Boudreau put Doby at first base. He didn't want to be kicked around. Fleming said, "You can quit but I ain't."[83] When the second game began, Robinson stayed in the clubhouse. Fortunately for Robinson, Coach McKechnie went into the clubhouse and talked straight to the first baseman. "I understand why you quit and your teammates understand as well. But the public is not going to understand.... They're going to say you didn't want Doby to play because he's black." Robinson cooled down and returned to the bench in the sixth inning. No one made a comment but Robinson received a couple of pats on the back, likely in support of his flare-up.[84]

Doby, obviously nervous because he had not played first base before, acquitted himself well in the game. Al Zirin, sportswriter for the *Plain Dealer*, reported that Doby accepted eight putouts at first base without an error, including one double play. In the ninth inning with Cleveland ahead 5–1, Doby made a "fancy one-handed leaping catch" of a throw by Gordon in a futile attempt to prevent an infield hit by Jack Wallaesa.

Robinson later wrote that he and Doby became friends. Robinson believed Doby realized that he had threatened to quit because of his anger toward Boudreau, not because a black was coming in to replace him. He described Doby as a quiet, no-nonsense individual who could have become an excellent first baseman.[85]

Spud Goldstein, traveling secretary for the Indians, related another incident between Robinson and Doby. Boudreau had no reason to doubt Goldstein's account. Goldstein was nearby when, after Boudreau had asked Doby to work out at first base, Doby asked Robinson for his glove, but Robinson refused. Goldstein saw the exchange, and asked Robinson, "Will you loan the glove to me?" Robinson did, and Goldstein handed the glove to Doby.[86]

"There was a lot of grumbling and talk behind my back," Veeck later recalled, but he saw [the signing of Doby] as a threat to fringe players more than anything else. Veeck later estimated that club headquarters had received more than 20,000 angry letters protesting the signing. He answered many letters himself. Veeck acknowledged that he had put Doby in a difficult situation: "Not only being the first in the American League but even more difficult was the fact that he ... had never really been exposed to the virulence that racism took once he had donned an Indians' uniform."[87]

Doby's first at-bat in the major leagues was in Comiskey Park on July 6. Eighteen thousand fans witnessed this weekday game. Several spectators told Veeck that on that day, there were more colored people than they had ever seen at the Park. In true literary fashion, Terry Pluto details Doby's initial feelings:

> You are Larry Doby and your world has just ended. You struck out. You come back to the dugout, staring at your spikes. If anyone says anything to you, you don't hear it. You walk to the end of the dugout, by yourself. (Rookies, as part of the hazing process, sat at the end of the bench.) You slump down. You put your head in your hands, praying you won't cry. A moment later, you hear someone sit down beside you. You peek out between your fingers and you see Joe Gordon, *his* head in *his* hands. "I just struck out too," Gordon says.[88]

This much maligned and repeated story does not correspond with boxscore or newspaper accounts. In reality, Gordon was on third base when Doby came in as a pinch-hitter.

This camaraderie reflected in this essay is correct. The facts are a bit different. In the seventh inning, the Indians trailed the White Sox, 5–1. According to Boudreau, he called

Doby to grab a bat and pinch-hit for pitcher Bryan Stephens. There were runners on first and third and one out. Catcher Al Lopez, sitting on the bench, remarked to his teammates, "I'm glad he isn't pinch hitting for me."[89] This seems a strange racial remark by Lopez to say the least. This was the same Lopez, a member of a minority himself, who managed Doby for seven and one-half years, longer than any other manager in Doby's career. It was the same Lopez who has the best winning percentage of any Cleveland manager and was inducted into the Hall of Fame in 1977.

Doby dug in at the plate, nervous and taut, to face Earl Harrist, a right-hander from Dubash, Louisiana. The *Associated Press* described what happened next: Doby, a left-handed batter, swung from his heels and missed Harrist's first pitch—by a mile. He also went after the second pitch and connected for a scorching drive down the left field line which was foul by inches. Doby let the next two pitches go by for balls, but on the fifth toss, a little wide, he swung again and missed for a strikeout. He was loudly applauded on his way back to the bench.[90] It is interesting to note that both Boudreau and Veeck, in their autobiographies, recalled that Doby struck out on three pitches. They must have been thoroughly engrossed in the scene.

Harrist, later a deputy sheriff in Ruston, Louisiana, remembered quite well his confrontation with Doby. "We all thought he was going to be a helleva player. He was a polite boy who had been given a chance." The former pitcher added, "A lot of people try to blow up ... stuff that Larry—a black—was going to be fought against, that we were going to knock him down, and stick one in his ear.... That's your sportswriters and people trying to blow up stuff."[91]

Cleveland Jackson, a reporter for the *Call and Post*, recalled hearing Boudreau say after the game, "Well, Larry, that's over. You can relax now." It would be months, however, before Doby could feel he was really one of the boys.[92]

The next morning (July 7), the *Plain Dealer's* Gordon Cobbledick summarized what he and Boudreau thought about Doby: "He will be accepted by his teammates and the customers if he proves to be a good ballplayer and a good human being.... He will be rejected if the opposite is true." A *Plain Dealer* editorial praised Veeck's signing of Doby. "Negroes have risen to stardom in other sports. If given the opportunity, they will do so in baseball. The fans will be pulling for Doby to make good."[93] As the days and weeks passed, Cobbledick's words proved prophetic.

Editorials from other papers were less charitable. *The Sporting News*, never in favor of integration in baseball, struck a negative chord. Publisher J. G. Taylor Spink, in a lead editorial entitled, "Once Again, the Negro Question," followed with this dubious statement: "A vast percentage of ... white players in the major leagues opposed integration."[94] Fred Russell, noted sports writer for the *Nashville Banner*, charged Veeck with the cheapest kind of effort to lure more customers.

The integration of professional football and baseball, and the championship of the Cleveland Buckeyes in the Negro World Series in 1945, moved the Forest City to a leadership position relative to integration in professional sports. The movement drifted to other sports. Bill Garrett broke the color line in Big Ten basketball, playing for Indiana University from 1947 to 1950.

Halfback Jimmy Clark and Bill Willis were two of the first black players to play football at The Ohio State University after World War II. Harrison Dillard, a graduate of East Tech High School in Cleveland—Jesse Owens' alma mater—won the 100-meter dash at the 1948 Olympics in London. Four years later Dillard won the 110-meter hurdles at the Helsinki Olympic Games.

Life for these pioneering black athletes was anything but easy. They learned to endure taunts from opposing teams and opposing fans as well as from their own fans. Doby later recalled that he heard the word "nigger" directed toward him so often in center field that he thought it was his middle name.[95] When the team was on the road, Doby had no room-mate, nor was he offered the same services received by his teammates. Often he felt isolated. When Doby arrived in Cleveland for the first time, he encountered prejudice, for he could not stay at the Hotel Cleveland with his teammates. Louis Jones arranged for Doby to stay at the Majestic Hotel in downtown Cleveland, which catered to black clientele. In spite of this slight, Doby suddenly experienced a sense of well-being, particularly from the black community. A steady stream of well-wishers came to the hotel, and the newcomer felt a bit more at ease even though he couldn't eat his meals with his teammates.

The only slipup of consequence by Doby during the remainder of the season occurred on an eastern trip. Sixty-two thousand fans showed up to see Doby in the second game of the series in Yankee Stadium. On the last game of the eastern trip, as reported in the *Plain Dealer*, "The colored boy missed the Tribe train." Doby sent a telegram to manager Boudreau and departed an hour later. The young rookie was eligible for a fine. Boudreau forgave him and issued no fine.[96] The remainder of the season provided little in the way of excitement. Doby appeared in 29 games, stroking five hits in 32 at-bats for a .156 batting average. The future slugger drove in five runs. Boudreau used Doby mainly as a pinch-hitter. He played four games at second base and one each at first base and shortstop.

The season ended with two accomplishments of significance. Feller righted the ship with his fifth consecutive 20-win season. He led the league with game starts (37), innings pitched (299), and strikeouts (196). Feller compiled a respectable ERA of 2.68. The Indians' season attendance peaked again, this time with 1,521,978 fans. This number eclipsed the preceding year by 464,589.[97]

If Doby encountered social bias, Boudreau faced pressure of another kind. Was his position as manager secure? The team finished with an improved record of 80–84, a 12-game improvement over 1946, but still 17 games behind the hated, pennant-winning Yankees. In Boudreau's six-year tenure as manager, his team had finished above fourth place only once. His managerial record was 525–543.

It was no secret that Veeck thought Boudreau was one of the best players in the American League. He also believed, however, that his managership left much to be desired. He wanted a change in managers, but Boudreau was extremely popular with the fans. How could Veeck pull off a change of managers? Possibly a blockbuster trade would do the trick.

Veeck attended the New York–Brooklyn World Series and at some point, quietly called local reporters aside to ask their opinion about trading Boudreau to the St. Louis Browns. Veeck's idea was to receive the Browns' power hitting shortstop, Vern Stephens, and a couple of other players to shore up weak spots on the team. At the same time, Veeck had catcher

Al Lopez waiting in the wings to become the next manager. The reporters sat on this information for a couple of days, but unfortunately the story was leaked in a Chicago paper, and local writers decided they needn't wait any longer to report their stories. When the story broke the next day in all three Cleveland papers, the proposed deal was already dead.

Owner Bill DeWitt of the Browns had demanded that the Indians underwrite Boudreau's salary, and that demand ended a possible trade. DeWitt, who desperately needed money for an impoverished franchise, sold Stephens and pitcher Jack Kramer to the Boston Red Sox for six players and $310,000, a tidy sum in the 1940s.[98]

Franklin Lewis of the *Press* captured the reaction when fans read their papers on October 5. He wrote, "The story broke through every front door in Cleveland. As an observer said, 'it smashed and splintered and shook the community by its civic heels until all hell popped loose.'"[99] Ed McAuley of the *Cleveland News* commented, "If the [city's] Terminal Tower had fallen into Public Square, the shock would not have been as widely felt."[100] Lewis went on to ask, "Trade Boudreau! Peddle the idol of all the bobby soxers, the handsome young Frenchman? Get rid of Boudreau and take those spectacular, superhuman plays at shortstop to another city? Exile Boudreau to St. Louis?"[101]

To say that Veeck had opened a hornet's nest would be an understatement: He had totally underestimated the fan popularity of Boudreau. The *Cleveland Press* observed humorously, "It is evident that Veeck didn't know that Boudreau was immortal in Cleveland." The *News* printed a ballot, asking fans to vote on the deal—90 percent said to keep Boudreau.

This fan support for a manager was unprecedented, and Veeck knew the gods were against him on this issue, so he took his beating with a smile. In the sixth inning of the fifth game of the World Series, Veeck left Ebbets Field to return to Cleveland, where a mob at the airport greeted him as his plane landed. The first fan he talked to said, "Mr. Veeck, if you trade Boudreau my two boys will grow up to hate you."

To the great relief of fans, Veeck soon conceded that public opinion had won, and Boudreau remained in place. "This was pure Veeck," the always astute Bob August of the *Press* later wrote. "In his playful way, Veeck could make Machiavelli look like a scout leader."[102] Understanding how angry he had made the fans, Veeck spent the rest of the night going from bar to bar, apologizing and assuring one and all that Boudreau's job was safe. The absence of a trade inspired a well-known Veeckism: "The best trades are the ones you don't make."

On November 24, Veeck and Boudreau met for six and one-half hours to pound out a contract and discuss the future of the Tribe. The two-year contract called for a salary of $49,000—$25,000 as manager and $24,000 as a player. To add to Boudreau's luster, the Cleveland Baseball Writers' Association voted the Cleveland manager "Man of the Year" for 1947, an award given annually to the individual who has contributed the most to baseball in Cleveland.[103] Veeck had received the award in the previous year.

Boudreau could now prepare for Cleveland's and his own most glorious year in team history. Larry Doby purchased a Tommy Henrich book on *How to Play the Outfield* and returned to his family in Paterson, New Jersey. Except for unwarranted harassment, 1948 would also be a glorious year for young Doby.

11

The Indians' Greatest
Season Since 1920

"Every day was Mardi Gras ... and every fan was king"
—Bill Veeck, *Newsweek*, January 13, 1986

What circumstance prompted baseball's postwar journey? For author William Marshall, the 1945–1951 years were "baseball's pivotal era." He alluded to forthcoming changes in the game prompted by television, an increased number of night games, the future influx of Japanese and Hispanic players, movement of franchises, the soon-to-be introduction of new franchises, development of retrograde ball parks, increased owner-player controversies leading to free agency, and the diminution of minor league teams.[1]

Historian G. Edward White believed baseball was beginning to lose some of its glamour as "America's pastime." During the first 50 years of the modern game, franchises and owners survived the advent of the electric light, radio, television, and the airplane. The game received a boost shortly after the start of World War II, when President Roosevelt allowed play to continue with a full schedule on the premise that the game was good for American morale.

After the 1950s, however, the major leagues experienced significant changes on two fronts: the demographics of team ownership affected the entire revenue base of new and old franchises; and the handling of player contracts were radically altered by the formation of a players' union and gradual absolution of the reserve clause. Volumes have been written describing the dramatic effect of these changes during the second half of the twentieth century.[2]

In the late 1960s, looking back to what Marshall had recognized as a pivotal era, Ted Williams stated, "I don't think baseball has [ever] been played better than from 1946 to 1950."[3] Players contended that teams of that era could more easily maintain their concentration over the long season—154 games. Usually the schedules called for doubleheaders on Sundays and a day of rest on Mondays. Train travel provided players more time to relax, and the end of the Great Depression and World War II provided fans the opportunity to study the intricacies of the game more seriously and to support their favorite teams.

The 1948 American League pennant race was one of the most exciting of all time. Fire sales by the Browns, White Sox, and Senators sent reputable talent to primary contenders—the Red Sox, the Indians, and as always, the Yankees. As a result, the drive to the finish was a real "horse race." For the first time in American League history, a one-game playoff was needed to determine a league champion.

Nineteen forty-eight was a year unlike any before or since in Cleveland sports history. The Cleveland Browns went 15–0 to capture their third consecutive All-American Football Conference championship, and the Cleveland Barons won the American Hockey League's Calder Cup. But it was the Tribe who kept their fans, black and white, in an environment of ecstasy and agony. Twenty-eight years had elapsed—a generation—since manager Tris Speaker guided the Tribe to their first World Championship. The promotional genius of Bill Veeck, the intrepid owner of the Cleveland franchise, kept the multitude of fans on the edge of their seats throughout this hectic and unbelievable roller-coaster season.

Many baseball writers call 1948 the "Miracle on Lake Erie" because the season possessed a fairy tale-like quality. Veeck was determined to realize his 1946 prediction that the Tribe would play in a World Series within three years. For six months, statewide Indians followers—particularly Clevelanders—alternately experienced hope or despair as their team battled day-in and day-out all the way to October.

Veeck explained the Indians' success during that season:

> I built an exciting ball club, several of my players had outstanding years, the city was starved for a pennant winning team, and I am one of the few owners who knows how to cultivate and entertain the guests—not bad for a team that operates in one of the smallest markets and that in 1946 was still so penurious that it demanded the return of all foul balls hit into the stands.[4]

The *Plain Dealer* and *Press* portrayed the Cleveland franchise as a civic asset. Newspaper advertisements by the Indians and several local corporations advanced the idea that this team belonged to every supporter. Articles and editorials alike reminded readers that Cleveland had grown into a large, thriving city which now had to present itself in a manner befitting its new stature. Keeping the city clean and treating visitors like welcomed guests were priorities leading up to Opening Day. Editorial cartoons introduced characters—"Joe Cleveland" and another cartoon of a family covering three generations of locals—showing how other interests and issues, both local and national, took a back seat to the Tribe's drama.

Sports editor Ed Bang of the *Cleveland News* reminded readers that the Indians promoted civic pride and commercial success. His theme was the strength of communal beliefs culminating in the final benefit: spiritual uplift. Bang exulted, "I am happy to say ... THIS IS CLEVELAND ... the city of which every last citizen should be justly proud, just as I am proud of the citizens in general for there is none to match them anywhere."[5] The Cleveland *Call and Post* also reminded readers of the pride with which they should embrace the Indians. During the 1948 season, this weekly newspaper shuffled its focus of baseball coverage among the Cleveland Buckeyes, Jackie Robinson and the Brooklyn Dodgers, and the Indians' Larry Doby and Satchel Paige. (The Cleveland Buckeyes disbanded after the 1950 season.) The three white dailies praised the civic excellence of the Indians' performance. The *Call and Post* more effectively conveyed the conviction that "They're Really Our Indians," emphasizing that the Tribe was no longer just another team to the black community: "Instead the Tribe was a symbol of all that is decent ... clean ... fair and democratic in American life."[6] Bill Veeck and the franchise were praised for leading the fight against Jim Crow by scoffing at ideas of race, color, and creed, and Doby and Paige exemplified the successes that could ensue when America took off its color-conscious glasses.

The Tribe embarked on a second spring training season in Tucson, and optimism prevailed among fans and the team as players and writers enjoyed Arizona's beautiful clear sky, infrequent spring rain, and humidity lower than that of Florida. Players and local writers knew their team had the potential to be good even though holes in the lineup needed to be resolved; shortcomings were most noticeable in the outfield and pitching. Chief competitors appeared to be the A's, Red Sox, and Yankees. Help would come in the most unexpected manner. Probably not enough has been written about Veeck's efforts to keep his team near the top in the pennant race.

Veeck knew his team was weak in relief pitching, but first he flew to Orlando, Florida, to try to persuade President Clark Griffith of the Washington Senators to trade or sell pitcher Early Wynn, but without success. He recalled, "I had an appointment to have breakfast with Cobbledick at St. Petersburg the next morning. So I flew to St. Petersburg, had breakfast with Cobby and told him, 'Come on, let's go.' Cobby asked, 'Where are we going?' 'I've got to see Mr. Mack [A's manager] in Orlando. I've got to talk him out of a pitcher.' 'I thought you just came from Orlando,' the puzzled Cobby replied. 'I did, I couldn't break a breakfast appointment with you, could I?' Cobby and I grabbed a cab to drive us the 120 miles back to Orlando."[7]

Veeck respected the Cleveland sportswriters, particularly Cobbledick. During a spring training trip in 1947, a group of six was flying back to Cleveland with a stop in Charlotte, North Carolina, where Veeck recalled that two young ladies had been bumped from their plane. By 8:00 p.m., Cobbledick had written his column and asked Veeck, "'What've we got that's so important?' So we gave the young ladies our tickets and [Veeck] called Eddie Rickenbacker to get us two tickets for the next morning."[8]

The pitcher Veeck had shown interest in was Russ Christopher. Christopher had a hole in his heart, an irreparable condition at the time. He was a "blue baby" grown up. Although Christopher was in bed with pneumonia, Veeck offered Mack $25,000 for the right-hander; but Mack, always the gentleman, said he couldn't make such a deal with a player likely to die soon. Veeck received permission to talk to Christopher. Understanding the situation, Veeck was prepared to see him—gaunt and hollow, with a sickly bluish cast around the eyes. Veeck asked him if he thought he could pitch, and Christopher said he didn't know: "I'm going to ... buy your contract," Veeck told him, "I'll take a gamble on you." Christopher responded in a weak voice, "I think you're crazy but you have my word on one thing. I'll do the best I can for you."[9] That he did, saving game after game (a total of 17) for the 1948 Tribe with his swooping, almost underhanded motion. After this, his last season, he spent his remaining years in San Diego. Russ Christopher died on December 4, 1954, in Richmond, California, at 37. He finished his pitching career with a 54–64 record.

In Tucson, the main story was Larry Doby's first spring training experience. Naturally, the soft-spoken, well-mannered Doby was anxious to succeed. He had come to Tucson in top physical condition; unlike most players on his team, he did not smoke or drink alcohol or coffee. Veeck hired Tris Speaker, one of the greatest defensive outfielders of all time, to work with Doby on his outfield skills: "No man knew more [about fielding in the outfield],"

Veeck later reminisced.[10] To be on the safe side with his outfield, Veeck purchased Thurman Tucker from the White Sox and Walt Judnich, a first baseman-outfielder, from the St. Louis Browns, and traded pitcher Red Embree to the Yankees for outfielder Allie Clark.

Indians traveling secretary Spud Goldstein scouted Tucson for housing for Doby. Luckily, he ran into Chester Willis, a black foreman who supplied the Santa Rita Hotel with clean sheets and towels. After consulting with his wife, Lucille, Willis offered Doby a room in their home. The couple had three small children, giving Doby a feeling of a family atmosphere.[11] Later in his career, Doby reminisced that he had "missed not having another player to ... talk to about the day's game ... and start me thinking about the next game."[12]

Doby was the subject of a spring training column written by Cobbledick:

> Larry Doby has come a long way since that afternoon last July [1947] ... at Comiskey Park. With the tension gone, he has earned new respect ... namely, that he is a richly gifted young athlete with a better than average chance to become a top flight big league star.[13]

He had six weeks under the Arizona sun to learn a new position, and he continued to make steady improvement. The record provides mixed signals about Boudreau's relationship with Doby. As manager, Boudreau could not show favoritism. Indeed, he seemed somewhat aloof or indifferent in his handling of the newcomer and wavered on whether to send him to a Triple-A club for more seasoning. Terry Pluto wrote in *A Baseball Memoir* that, "This is a manager whose job is on the line and he is not about to take a chance on you [Doby]."[14]

For his part, Veeck faced the wrath of fans for his hiring of Doby. He had long displayed his support of the civil rights movement and continued to do so until his dying day. Later, he acknowledged that he had indeed put a young black player in a difficult situation: "Not only being the first in the American League but even more difficult ... that he had never really been exposed to the virulence that racism took once he donned an Indians' uniform."[15] Sixty-five years later, African American Wyonella Smith, wife of journalist Wendell Smith, commented, "I [never] felt Bill ... got the credit [for] Larry Doby."[16] Writing for the *Cleveland Press*, Lewis described Doby's early days on the field: He was a "six-hour ball player and off the field he was an 18-hour Jim Crow personality."[17] Living in segregated hotels as the Indians barnstormed northward toward Cleveland, Doby described himself as "lonely."

Specific examples of hateful behavior were despicable. In Texarkana on the Texas-Arkansas border, Doby dressed for a game in a private home, and in trying to get to the ballpark, found out that he could ride only in Jim Crow cabs, both of which were in use, so he walked to the ballpark in his uniform. When he reached the ballpark, the gatekeeper would not admit him. At length, after Doby waited in humiliation, Boudreau rescued him from a white crowd which had gathered there. The year was 1948. More humiliating, Doby had to be taken out of the game when a barrage of bottles and other objects was heaved at him in center field. Boudreau had no choice.[18] The now angry Doby had not experienced such behavior as exhibited in the Deep South.

There were verbal slams. Pitcher Lou Brissie of the Philadelphia Athletics told biographer Ira Berkow what he had heard from his own dugout. Teammates had shouted: "'Porter, carry my bags,' or 'shoeshine boy, shine my shoes,' ... and the N-word." Severely wounded and left for dead in Italy during World War II, Brissie pitched with a large metal brace on his leg and identified with Doby: "He was kind of an underdog, like me," Brissie told Berkow.[19]

Twelve years later (1960), the White Citizens' Council took out a full page advertisement in a New Orleans newspaper urging a boycott of the weekend exhibition series between Cleveland and the Boston Red Sox. Locals and the White Citizens' Council took the viewpoint that the blacks' presence on the ball field might affront the town's right-thinking Christian Americans.[20] By this time, the Indians had three black players on a squad of about 30. Pumpsie Green had been signed by the Red Sox in 1959, making them the last major league team to field an African American. It had taken 12 years for integration of the major leagues since Jackie Robinson first stepped to the plate for the Brooklyn Dodgers in April 1947.

Reporters remembered Doby's first appearance at an exhibition game after the team left Tucson. It was 1948 in Houston, Texas, and the early hostility was frightening in its intensity. In the top half of the first inning, Doby made a diving, somersaulting catch to rob a Giants hitter of an extra-base hit. In the bottom half of the inning, Doby hit one that Jack Graney used to call a "country mile" over the fence in right center field. From then on, the young player was the darling of the crowd, who cheered his every move through the rest of the game. When the game was over, fans stood in line to solicit his autograph, proving perhaps that some people were better and smarter than members of the White Citizens' Council.[21]

As Opening Day approached, Doby shared his thoughts about spring training with Franklin Lewis: "It's been a rough spring," the rookie remarked. "Oh, maybe rough isn't the right word. But it's been lonely, believe me. I've been lonesome, though I wasn't surprised. I expected to be."[22] After snaring a fly ball in the outfield, Doby came back to Lewis and added, "Whatever has happened has been worth everything to me." He went on, "if I can stick with this..." His voice trailed off.[23]

By this time, Veeck had made a management move that would affect the careers of both Boudreau and Doby. During the 1947 World Series in New York, Veeck had befriended Hank Greenberg, who had retired from the Pittsburgh Pirates. Impressed with the future Hall of Famer, Veeck persuaded him to take a position as vice-president of the Tribe.

The next spring at the close of spring training, Doby worried that the club would send him to the minor leagues and appealed to the new vice-president: "Mr. Greenberg, I know I can hit major league pitching." "What makes you think so?" queried Greenberg. "Because I've hit better pitching," he responded. "Where?" demanded Greenberg. "In the Negro National League," shot back Doby. "You mean occasionally?" questioned Greenberg. "No, every day. The pitching is better in the Negro National League," answered Doby.[24]

In his autobiography, however, Greenberg wrote disparagingly of Doby's adjustments to major league baseball: "Larry was obsessed with the idea that he wasn't getting the publicity that Jackie Robinson was getting. I tried to explain to him that Jackie was with the Dodgers and he was with Cleveland and it was like night and day. Playing in Cleveland, Larry could never hope to get the same degree of publicity Jackie received in New York. Larry was ... bitter about it throughout his career."[25] Greenberg added,

> Larry Doby could be a grouchy person and was not popular with the team, the fans, or the media. Unlike ... Robinson, who seemed to take pride in his role as a pioneer in baseball and was extremely popular among the other black players who joined the Dodgers in the late for-

ties and fifties, Doby was as belligerent toward his black teammates as he was with everyone else.... I always thought Larry resented the other black players. It was as though Larry felt he was the first black player in the league so he deserved special recognition.[26]

Maury Wills of the Los Angeles Dodgers expressed a similar insight. He believed Doby carried a huge burden doing the same things as Robinson was doing, blazing the same path, but nobody seemed to know. Ironically, Greenberg himself displayed several of the same traits that he saw in Doby.

As per Greenberg's suggestion and Boudreau's approval, Doby was retained on the roster, and eventually showed Veeck that he had made the right choice in recruiting him. The center fielder went on to play ten seasons with the Tribe. His major league record included five seasons of 100 or more RBI, 253 home runs, and six appearances in an All-Star Game. Veeck contended that the sensitive Doby had never realized his full baseball potential because of the emotional turmoil he harbored inside: "If Larry had come up just a little later, he might very well have become one of the greatest players of all time."[27]

The Greenberg-Boudreau relationship was another story. When the team returned to Cleveland for the beginning of the 1948 season, Greenberg took over the role Boudreau had given up the previous season as Veeck's post-game companion. Boudreau recalled, "I was glad because I knew Veeck loved to go out after games and talk, but it ... demanded too much of my time because I was still playing."[28] However, the developing relationship between Veeck and Greenberg did not bode well for Boudreau. Often discussing Boudreau's managerial strategies and decisions, the two kept scorecards during games, and would often call Boudreau and ask him to explain his reasons for certain strategies. This continual interchange bothered Boudreau and led to a rift with Greenberg.

After Veeck returned to Cleveland, he continued to fine-tune his team in preparation for the opening game. First, he dealt with Ken Keltner, the versatile third baseman who was known for his extra-curricular activities after games. After a poor season in 1946, Veeck had promised Keltner a $5,000 bonus if, in Veeck's view, he had a good year, but for the second straight year, the popular third baseman had a less than satisfactory season in 1947, with a .257 batting average and only 11 home runs. For a second time, Veeck summoned Keltner to give him another pep talk and $5,000 bonus offer. Keltner walked away with a sober look and a determination to be ready for the 1948 season. He spent all winter getting in shape and led the team early in the season with a dozen home runs by mid–May.[29]

The 1948 pennant race combined unprecedented fan interest, great individual performances, and dramatic changes in several American League clubs. With seven games to go, three teams tied for the lead, and later, with two games to go, only one game separated them. Twenty years later, Harold Kaese of *The Boston Globe* called 1948 "the season of seasons." Even those who lived through it often forget exactly how incredible it turned out to be."[30] No doubt the individual who found himself most on the spot as Opening Day arrived was manager Boudreau. He had come to camp with a noticeable pot belly and two aching ankles, but none of these conditions would add to his slowness. Such issues did not matter to the highly competitive Frenchman. He was determined to take the material given him by his boss and to develop a winning team. Boudreau was determined to remain the fans' idol.

Cleveland opened the season at home with the St. Louis Browns before a record-breaking

crowd of 73,163 fans. Bob Feller was the starting pitcher a sixth time for the Indians, shutting
out the Browns, 4–0, on just two hits. For the first time, a black would be in the Indians'
Opening Day lineup, as Doby took his place in right field. He would go on to play in 121
of the 154 scheduled games, with solid results. The Tribe broke out of the gate with six
straight victories. By May 10, they were in first place, tied with the surprising Philadelphia
Athletics. This fast start prompted Boudreau to claim that in his seven-year managerial
tenure, "This is the best club I've had."[31]

A good omen of the Tribe's early success proved to be the contribution of second baseman Joe Gordon. Veeck appreciated Gordon's competitive spirit, particularly against the
hated Yankees. In his first game in Yankee Stadium in 1947, he walked twice, singled twice,
and hit a home run—virtually beating the Bronx Bombers on his own. Referring to Larry
MacPhail, the Yankees' general manager, Veeck remarked after the game, "I hope Old Liver-
lips was watching that one." Arthur Daley of the *New York Times* later recalled: "[Veeck's]
eyes twinkled but there was no mistaking the venom which dripped from his words."[32]

On May 5, Veeck endured his third amputation, with another critical inch removed
below the knee, and was in and out of the hospital for the next few weeks. However, he
worked continually to keep his name before the public and appointed Abe Saperstein of
Harlem Globetrotters fame to devise and implement a nationwide scouting plan to find
more African American baseball players for the Cleveland farm system. A few days after
Veeck's operation, Wendell Smith of the Pittsburgh *Courier* spotted him at a meeting of the
National Conference of Christians and Jews. Smith noted that when he left the luncheon,
Veeck stowed his crutches in the back seat of his automobile and headed to Ashtabula to
deliver an address on brotherhood and diversity, using the 1948 Indians as his prime example.[33]

The Indians' potential for winning a pennant took a sharp turn for the better during
Veeck's recuperation. In early May, Boudreau realized that he needed more pitching help,
particularly left-handers. Unexpectedly, Feller was having an inconsistent season—pitching
well one time and poorly in the next outing. On the other hand, Bob Lemon was becoming
a frontline pitcher, but on May 8 Boudreau decided to gamble with knuckleballer Gene
Bearden, who had logged only one-third of an inning in the majors. He started against the
Washington Senators, whose record against left-handers was poor. This decision proved to
be shrewd for Bearden and the Tribe: The left-hander was sensational with his dancing
knuckleball, pitching a three-hitter and a shutout until the ninth inning, and the Indians
won, 6–1. In many ways, this day was a turning point in the season.

After the game, Bearden made known publicly for the first time that he had been
severely wounded in the war. He had been a machinist's mate on the cruiser USS *Helena*,
one of the few ships in Pearl Harbor that had survived the December 7 attack. On July 6,
1943, the ship was part of an American task force battling the Japanese in the South Pacific
near the Solomon Islands. Bearden was in the engine room when the first torpedo hit. The
damage was severe, and an order was given to abandon ship. He scrambled up the ladder
leading out of the engine room when suddenly a second torpedo hit, the ladder crumpled,
and he was hurled to the deck. His knee was twisted and crushed and his head was split
open by flying shards of metal as he lay unconscious in the pit of a sinking vessel: "Someone

pulled me out. I don't know how he did it," he related. The ship went down in 17 minutes. The pitcher added, "All I know is that I came to in the water sometime later."[34]

Bearden was finally rescued by a destroyer and shipped to the States. He was in a U.S. Naval Hospital for the better part of the next two years, and was told that he would never play baseball again. A plate was inserted into his skull and a hinge in his damaged knee. He had kept all of this to himself until after his first game "because [the Indians] might get the idea that I'm not strong enough to pitch."[35] After all Bearden had been through during the war, he would prove to be the mainstay of the Tribe's pitching staff in 1948.

As the season moved into June, the Indians held onto first place, followed closely by the Philadelphia Athletics and, of course, the Yankees. The fourth eventual challenger—the Boston Red Sox—languished in seventh place, seven to ten games behind the leaders. Veeck, always on the lookout for players to help the team, tweaked the roster. First, he traded outfielder Pat Seerey and pitcher Al Gettel to the Chicago White Sox for outfielder Bob Kennedy. Seerey, a home run threat, had led the league in strikeouts for three straight years and was an average outfielder at best.

His most important acquisition was "Sad" Sam Zoldak from the St. Louis Browns, who were having a fire sale of their players. The Indians, with newcomer Bearden as their only left-handed starter, needed better balance in the pitching rotation. Two hours before the trading deadline (June 15), Veeck asked Browns owner Bill DeWitt, "What will you take for Zoldak?" "$100,000," he replied. "It's a deal," Veeck said.[36] Veeck knew the left-hander wasn't worth $100,000 or even $50,000 to a team fighting for third place, not even $20,000 to a team in the second division. At that moment, however, Veeck knew that with the team he had, Zoldak was worth the price. In spite of Zoldak's five year record of 23–27, Veeck knew he had purchased the best left-hander available, and indeed, Zoldak proved to be the tonic to help the Tribe over several bumps during the rest of the season.

Veeck desired not only to win but also to take full advantage of a stadium that held more than 80,000 fans. It rankled him that Larry MacPhail and the Yankees had established a season attendance record of 2,265,000 the year before. This record had broken Veeck's father's record-breaking attendance held by the Chicago Cubs in 1920, and in 1948, he aspired to break the Yankees' attendance record.

First, he expanded his overhead with an enormous increase in the number of employees: 179 ticket takers, 187 ushers, 122 special policemen, and 117 scorecard boys. Full-time employees included 20 office workers and executives, five dining room staff, 28 scouts, 58 players and a grounds crew of 56. These figures did not include concessions or farm system personnel.[37]

Veeck traveled throughout Ohio promoting the Tribe. The public relations office mailed out 35,000 pieces of literature per month about the team, distributed 7,000 window posters, and posted 350 street cards on telephone poles around the city. Banks, stores, and restaurants were furnished with picture displays of the Indians, and 350,000 schedules were mailed out. Assorted reading materials about the team were available in the 2,500 newsstands throughout the city.[38]

Large contingents of fans came from out of town on hundreds of buses and special trains from as far away as Buffalo, Rochester, Niagara Falls, Erie, Pittsburgh, and Detroit, as well as from cities and towns within Ohio. And, of course, there were always the Veeck "give-away specials" as gate attractions. One innovation was the installation of a nursery in Tower D of the stadium.

Veeck had his mind set on breaking every baseball attendance record possible during the 1948 season, and he would do so. His first attempt occurred on May 23, a scheduled doubleheader with the Yankees, but the weatherman did not cooperate. A continuous drizzle held the crowd to 78,431, not enough to break MacPhail's record set at Yankee Stadium on May 30, 1938 (81,841).

The magical day came on Sunday, June 20 (Father's Day); the schedule called for a dou-bleheader with the Philadelphia Athletics, a formidable team that hung close behind the Tribe. In the second game, Veeck took the loudspeaker and announced to a cheering crowd that they were part of the largest crowd to ever see a major league game. The official turnout was 82,781. Amazingly, only 15,000 fans had shown up for the Saturday game before this record-breaking crowd. The local team on the field made the sea of humanity even happier, sweeping the doubleheader. The two Bobs—Feller and Lemon—were the winning pitchers, and the Tribe led the American League by 3½ games. That lead would not last long.

One of several record-breaking crowds at Cleveland Municipal Stadium during the torrid 1948 pennant race. This throng of 82,781 overflowed beyond the outfield fence.

Ed McAuley of the *Cleveland News* described what it was like for a fan trying to get to this doubleheader, particularly at a time when interstate highway systems were but a dream:

> Traffic arteries for 100 miles in all beside the bleachers directions were clogged with private cars headed for Cleveland. As early as noon, the bridge leading to the Stadium was thick with fans. And at 1:00 the last seat in the park was occupied and the public address horns around the Stadium started blaring "Standing Room Only." That didn't discourage the customers. They overflowed the stands and stood, perhaps 5,000 of them, on the grass behind Veeck's fence-within-a-fence. Some of them found vantage points on the concrete runway and stood there for ... five hours—about 450 feet from home plate.[39]

None of the four contending teams could solidify a hold on first place. Boston made a charge near the end of the season to stay in the hunt. The cautious Boudreau discontinued his "no comment" position on his team's chances. In mid–June, he told a Philadelphia writer, "This might be the year," as the season approached the halfway mark.[40] The Indians remained on top throughout June. Lemon finished off the month with a no-hitter on June 30 against the pesky Tigers. It was the first time Detroit had been held hitless in twenty-two years.

The often underrated Tribe catcher Jim Hegan recalled the drama of the ninth inning in that game. With Tigers second baseman Eddie Mayo at bat, Lemon threw a pitch six feet wide of the plate. Hegan took a new ball from umpire Cal Hubbard and walked slowly to the pitcher's mound. "What did you say to Lemon?" the catcher was later asked. "Bob was as white as a sheet. 'Let's get this guy out of there,' [Hegan] said." Lemon replied, 'Okay.' He then fired a swinging third strike past Mayo, and the future Hall of Famer George Kell grounded out to Lemon for the third out."[41]

Two major events monopolized the Tribe wigwam in July, both involving pitchers, one a veteran and one a newcomer. The first involved Rapid Robert Feller, whose season-long unpredictable performances had bewildered teammates and fans. In one game, he would be unhittable, and in the next, batters treated him like a batting practice pitcher. One of Lou Darvas' famous cartoons showed fans giving advice: "Hm-m-m he needs protection," a local gangster commented; another complained, "he ain't keeping his feet flat on the ground," or "maybe he ought to dust off a few," or "he needs to eat more steaks," and so on. Feller's wife, Virginia, came to his defense. She intimated that due to her slow recovery after the birth of their second child, Feller felt obligated to be with her and the children more frequently, and these family issues had added to the pitcher's stress. As is often true with star athletes, fans were unmerciful on his bad days.

The Cleveland press was a bit more tolerant. Cobbledick recalled having asked a fan his opinion of Feller after he had pitched 11 scoreless innings against the Washington Senators and had been taken out of the game which the Indians eventually won in the 15th inning. The fan replied, "Yeah, but he didn't win." Such comments led Feller to remark, "According to the fans, I've been washed up so many times, I must be the cleanest player on the team."[42]

This issue came to a head when Feller was picked for the All-Star Game. Feller knew he didn't deserve to be picked (his record was 9–10). The rumor flew that Boudreau and Veeck had not wanted him to pitch—they wanted instead to save him for the second half of the pennant race. Feller later claimed that Veeck had tried to convince him to fake an injury: "Wrap your finger in a bandage," Veeck suggested, "And tell the press you cut yourself on a razor blade or got hit with a buzz saw."[43]

The following morning, the Indians announced that Feller would be unavailable for the All-Star Game, though the reason was unclear. This statement created a firestorm, directing more criticism toward Feller. American League manager Bucky Harris was furious that Feller had been sidelined. Veeck reacted by suggesting that Harris had picked both Lemon and Feller in order to sabotage the Tribe for the second half of the season. Commissioner Chandler issued a terse statement: "In the future, all players selected for the All-Star game will be on the scene in uniform if at all possible."[44]

J. G. Taylor Spink of *The Sporting News* added fuel to the fire, taking Feller to task for greed: "What he has done in the latest two All-Star games is shabby recompense for the vast benefits the game has bestowed on him."[45] Unfortunately, these negative reactions embellished a wide-spread legend of Feller's self-centered and greedy behavior. The truth of this specific incident came to light in 2002, when Feller confessed that he had been responsible for skipping the All-Star Game and that Veeck agreed to cover for him: "It was my idea. I had a lousy year and I didn't deserve to go," he told biographer John Sickels.[46]

Feller's first start after the All-Star Game was a disaster. Booed and taunted mercilessly at Philadelphia—one banner read "Feller the Quitter"—the beleaguered ex-military veteran was knocked out in the first inning. Fortunately for the Tribe and Feller, he would turn jeers to cheers, winning ten of his next 13 decisions before taking the mound for his final game of the season. As Feller's troubles receded into the background, Veeck decided he needed more pitching help. While in the Detroit Tigers press box for a game, he met with Abe Saperstein, who suggested to Veeck the possibility of signing Satchel Paige. Veeck had earlier inquired of Feller if he thought Paige could be helpful. A frequent competitor against Paige on their barnstorming tours, Feller gave Veeck a favorable recommendation, noting only that Paige had lost some speed on his fastball.

Veeck needed no more encouragement and brought Paige to Cleveland for a tryout with Boudreau and Saperstein in attendance. Six feet, three and one-half inches tall and 180 pounds, Paige presented a languid, self-possessed bearing in Veeck's office. On the field, the easy-going Paige slowly jogged about 75 yards and came back to Boudreau. "Mr. Lou," which is what he always called the manager, "I'm ready, I pitch with my arms, not my legs."[47] After throwing to Boudreau a few minutes, he came back to him with a folded-up handkerchief, and told him to put it on the plate, inside, outside, middle, wherever. Paige threw ten pitches— fastballs and sliders—all with something on them. Nine of the pitches came right across the handkerchief. Boudreau moved the handkerchief to the other side, and again seven or eight pitches came across the cloth.

Veeck asked Boudreau to bat against Paige. Boudreau did so and was impressed, hitting two balls for Veeck; one was hit fairly well and might with luck have been scored a base hit, and the other was a ground ball which kind of trickled over the infield. Greenberg was going to hit but decided not to, telling Veeck not to let him leave without a signature on a contract. The men retreated to the dugout where Paige, on his 42nd birthday—no one knew his age for certain—became the second black player to sign with the Tribe. His salary was undisclosed, but with Veeck, chances are that the amount was fair.

Paige was a character, to say the least. He claimed that he had once pitched 29 consecutive days and that he had been able to do so because he rubbed his arm with a special snake-oil concoction that he obtained from a Sioux Indian. Batboy Billy Sullivan remembered that when Paige joined the team, he was accepted immediately. The players knew how superior he was and that he could help them win. Sullivan remarked, "More than once Boudreau sent me out to try and find Satch. Sometimes he forgot there was a game." He added, "I never saw a player spend as much time in a whirlpool as Satch. Kept the water way over 115 degrees. Nobody else could stand it. Said it kept his body young and his arm loose. Who could disagree?"[48]

Paige's interesting set of rules for living are well-known and as popular as Yogisms:

> Avoid fried meats which angry-up the blood; if you [*sic*] stomach disputes you, lie down and pacify with cool thoughts; keep the juices flowing by jangling around gently as you move; go very light on the vices, such as carrying on in society (because) the social ramble aint restful; avoid running at all times; and don't look back, something might be gaining on you.[49]

To say that the press reacted negatively to the signing of Paige would be putting it mildly. Billy Evans, general manager of the Detroit Tigers, called Veeck a "pop-off" and a publicity sensationalist, and the signing of Paige was "outright exploitation and an affront to major league baseball." Shirley Povich of the Washington *Post* struck back: "[Veeck's] making them all rich with big crowds the Indians are drawing everywhere."[50]

The loudest blast came from J. G. Taylor Spink of *The Sporting News*, who lambasted Veeck for signing the "old man." To sign a hurler of Paige's age, he wrote, demeaned the standards of baseball in the major leagues. He suggested that American League president William Harridge void Paige's contract. For obvious reasons he did not do so. "If Paige were white," Spink went on, "he would not have drawn a second thought from Veeck."[51] Veeck responded with a zinger: "If Satch were white, he would have been in the majors twenty-five years earlier."[52] Spink's long-time opposition to blacks playing in the major leagues had not diminished. He believed they should continue playing in their own Negro Leagues. The age factor was not an issue as there have been several pitchers who performed in the majors at the age of 42 and beyond.

Later, Veeck had the last word with Spink. Whenever there was a hint that Paige might pitch, the ballparks were nearly always sold out. At a home game on August 20, before 78,382 fans—the largest crowd yet to witness a night game—Paige shut out the White Sox for a second time. The sly one—hesitation-pitch and all—ran his scoreless string to 26 innings for his fifth victory in six weeks. Veeck could not resist sending *The Sporting News* a telegram: "Paige pitching no runs, three hits. He definitely is in line for *The Sporting News* Rookie of the Year award. Regards, Bill Veeck."[53] Images of Veeck and Paige together appeared in newspapers and magazines across the country, and they seemed totally at ease with one another. Paige called Veeck "Burrhead," and Veeck called Paige "Leroy," just as he had insisted on calling Doby "Laurence."

The easy-going Doby was the roommate of the sometimes delinquent Paige. The young outfielder had come into his own as a major leaguer. His speed, excellent fielding, and power potential were rewarded, and he played in 121 games in 1948. In rare exceptions, his fielding efforts betrayed him. In one mid-season day game, a fly ball is said to have bounced off his

Leroy "Satchel" Paige, left, joined Larry Doby and the Indians on July 7, 1948, and won six of seven decisions to help Cleveland take home their first pennant in 28 years (author's collection).

head, but there are varying reports of what really happened. The sun is vicious at certain times in the late afternoon in the Stadium, and Doby was unaccustomed to wearing sunglasses and on occasion failed to flip them down. In this case, the ball hit his cap visor—some say it hit the top of his head—and to the fans it looked like a terrible play. Doby redeemed himself in the next inning with a sparkling catch.

Often the shortstop or second baseman of the opposing team would tag Doby hard when he slid into second base. Then the player would follow up by spitting in his face and bellowing, "Take that, nigger."[54] Years later Veeck recalled that "Larry had not been bruised as a human being. He didn't have his nose rubbed in it [racism]. It hit him later in life and at a time when he thought he had it licked. It hit him hard.... He was not a man to shake off those slights and insults easily.... All the inner turmoil was a drain on him."[55]

In late July and through August, Doby, in spite of occasionally playing from one extreme to the other, came to be accepted by teammates and became an integral part of a determined team. On one occasion, voices came drifting out of the locker room. With Doby as lead, Jim Hegan as tenor, Eddie Robinson as baritone, and Paige as bass, the most unusual

Player-Manager Lou Boudreau congratulates Larry Doby after hitting a home run in Cleveland Municipal Stadium, summer of 1948 (author's collection).

quartet sang "Down Among the Sheltering Pine," "Sweet Sue," and "Old Black Joe" in an expression of team unity that no one could have imagined a year before.

Playing the Yankees at home, the "black dart" made a catch that made him famous. He leaped high above the right center field fence to thwart George McQuinn's bid for a home run. Later in the same game, he ran almost 60 yards to deprive Joe DiMaggio of a triple, described by a reporter as "one of the most sensational sprints seen in this town since Tris Speaker roamed the pasture."[56] A few days later Doby crushed the White Sox in both games of a doubleheader. In the first game, he staked Feller to all the runs he needed, doubling with the bases loaded to score three runs. Doby singled to produce the only run Lemon required in a shutout victory in the second game.

Ignoring advice given by Veeck, Doby almost self-destructed in a rage of temper in St. Louis. Furious at a heckler who had insulted him with racial epithets, Doby grabbed a bat and started to climb the low fence behind the Indians dugout. In the uproar that followed, reporters weren't sure who among the following—Paige, McKechnie, Thurman Tucker or Hal Peck—restrained him.[57] Doby's feelings, however, did not derail his game. In late August, he launched a 21-game hitting streak, raising his batting average to a respectable .288 and playing center field with more confidence day by day.

When baseball fans read the newspaper on the morning of August 4, they were amazed to find four teams tied for first place in the American League, the Tribe among them. Cleveland now had to contend not only with the A's and Yankees, but also with the onrush of the Red Sox led by Ted Williams, Bobby Doerr, Johnny Pesky, Dom DiMaggio, and Vern Stephens. The latter, acquired from the Browns in a fire sale before the 1948 season began, compiled 137 RBI by season's end.

Without doubt, the most memorable weekend of the season, and for many seasons, took place in early August when the Tribe faced the despised Yankees. On Friday, August 6, Bob Feller opened the series before 71,268 fans and showed signs of pulling out of his slump. To date, he had won only ten games and had not pitched a complete game since July 11. He was opposed by Eddie Lopat, one of two nemeses the Indians faced in this series. The Indians went ahead, partially as the result of a two-run single by Feller, a notoriously poor hitter. Future television star Johnny Berardino bobbled a double-play ball in the eighth inning, but the Indians hung on for a 9–7 victory.

On Saturday, August 7, the Indians faced another nemesis, Vic Raschi. The right-hander had a league-leading record of 13–4. He was one of the Yankees' triumvirate of pitchers—Lopat, Raschi, and former Indian Allie Reynolds—who were mainstays of the Yankees pitching staff for several years. And he proved it again before 66,000 fans as he shut out the Indians, 5–0, on four hits.

Sunday's doubleheader was a special day that Indians fans of that era will never forget. It must be remembered that Boudreau had not played in Saturday's game. In spite of injuries, the player-manager had come through one close situation after another, but he was out of commission for this series, on the bench unable to play, nursing ankle, knee, and shoulder injuries incurred three days earlier in a collision at second base. With 73,484 fans in the stands, Boudreau sat in the dugout with his left foot soaking in a bucket of ice water, his back and thumb taped up and a brace on his knee.

Boudreau selected left-hander Sam Zoldak to pitch in the first game. The Tribe trailed, 6–1, in the bottom of the seventh inning. Left-hander Spec Shea was in control for the Yankees. In that inning Keltner walked, and Johnny Berardino cracked a two-run homer. (He hit only 36 home runs in his 11-season career.) Eddie Robinson followed with another home run, and now the score was 6–4. Jim Hegan kept the rally alive with a single. Yankees manager Bucky Harris brought in the team's ace left-handed reliever, Joe Page but Allie Clark walked and Dale Mitchell singled to load the bases.

Boudreau faced a dilemma. Left-hander Thurman Tucker was the next batter and had gone 0-for-7 in his last two games. Boudreau looked at trainer Lefty Weisman and asked if he—Boudreau—should pinch-hit. Weisman shook his head, emphasizing that if he reinjured himself, he might miss a lot more games. Boudreau believed it might be the team's last shot, and as immodest as it seems, he knew he had the best shot at getting a hit, with only Joe Tipton and Bob Kennedy left on the bench.

While Page warmed up, Boudreau put on his sock and shoe and went to the bat rack. Coach Bill McKechnie nodded his head and smiled. This was baseball drama at its best, and the fans knew it, as did the loyalists at home who were listening to broadcasters Jimmy Dudley and Jack Graney describe the action. Boudreau later described the game-changing action:

> When I stepped out of the dugout ... field announcer Jack Cresson intoned, "Attention please, batting for Tucker, no. 5, Lou Boudreau," and the fans went crazy. Their cheers were deafening and sent a chill up my spine. I forgot how badly my ankle hurt or that my back was stiff or that my thumb was so sore.[58]

Page's first pitch was a ball. Boudreau fouled off the second pitch, and the third pitch was inside for ball two. Page could not afford to walk Boudreau with the bases loaded. The fourth pitch was a called strike. Boudreau let umpire Art Passarella know that he didn't like the call: "I figured Page would come in with another fast ball. He did." Boudreau hit a solid line drive over second base into right center field, scoring two runs and tying the game. As Boudreau later joked, "I doubled and stopped at first" because that was as far as he could run. The ovation Boudreau received as he limped off the field for a pinch-runner was even greater than when the manager had been announced as a pinch-hitter. As he recalled, "I didn't have time to think how important it was or what a great move it was, I was just trying to win the game."[59] And win the game the Tribe did by a score of 8–6 when Robinson later hit a second home run. Later, Gordon Cobbledick told Boudreau that Veeck exclaimed in the press box, "Even if Boudreau doesn't get a hit, this is the most courageous thing I've ever seen in baseball."[60]

The second game of the doubleheader seemed anticlimactic but not in this tight race. Steve Gromek, eight-year pitching veteran with the Indians, came into his own at a critical time. With Eddie Robinson hitting his third home run of the day, Gromek held the Yankees off, 2–1, for the doubleheader sweep. Gromek would compile a 9–3 record for the season. The next day the headline on page one of the *Cleveland Press* announced, "Now It Looks Like a Pennant." However, 56 games or more than one-third of the season remained. On the plus side, the Indians were spurred on by their manager, whose determination to show Veeck and Greenberg he could win was intense.

In mid–August, the Tribe made a run of eight straight victories which included four straight shutouts. Eventually, the pitching staff broke the American League record with 47 consecutive scoreless innings. Satchel Paige pitched the last game of this winning streak, defeating the White Sox, 1–0, with a three-hitter. Paige had drawn a total of 201,829 fans for the three games he started.

As the Tribe moved toward the end of the season, however, the roof began to fall in. In the 18 games through Labor Day, the Indians won eight and lost ten. Throughout the season until Labor Day, the club had difficulty in winning one-run games, with a record of 9–17. Fans in Cleveland awoke the day after Labor Day (September 7) to find the Indians 4½ games out of first place and five games in the loss column. The team trailed first-place Boston by the largest margin all season. Their situation was dire. Cobbledick wrote that Cleveland would have to go 17–6 to have a chance to win the pennant. Veeck was quoted in the *Press:* "There's not much chance left now.... It will take a miracle for us to win."[61] However improbable, a miracle began to take shape. Feller regained the form that had made him the American League's premier pitcher. Lemon and Bearden had been the glue that held the ship together to this point. Bearden, who was 6–3 in late June, went on to win 13 and lose only 4. By September 20, with Feller and Bearden leading the way, the Tribe climbed to second place, one-half game behind Boston.

Only one major glitch spoiled this exciting run by the Tribe. On September 13, Don Black, the recovered alcoholic and spot pitcher, started against the St. Louis Browns. Black pitched two strong innings. At bat in the bottom of the second, he swung viciously at left-hander Bill Kennedy's pitch and fouled it into the stands. He staggered away from the plate, turned in a small circle, and with an odd look on his face asked umpire Bill Summers, "My God, Bill, what happened?"[62] He then sagged and crumpled to a kneeling position. Summers bent over and asked, "What's wrong, Don?" "It started on the last pitch to [Eddie] Pellagrini," he responded. The St. Louis shortstop had taken a snapping curve ball from Black for the third strike the inning before. According to Lewis of the *Press*, "The physical effort expended on that pitch plus the full-bodied swing a few minutes later, snapped an aneurysm."[63]

A short time later, Black lapsed into a coma and was rushed to the hospital. He had suffered a cerebral hemorrhage, and his condition was deemed critical and would be for days. His immediate chance for survival was posted at 50–50. Of less significance, the Indians lost the game to the lowly Browns and fell 1½ games behind the league-leading Red Sox. The next day, Harry Jones of the Cleveland *Plain Dealer* stated that "the team's prospects were dimmed to a mere flicker."[64] Black recovered but never pitched again. He died on April 21, 1959, at age 42 in Cuyahoga Falls, near Cleveland.

Soon after Black's hospitalization, Veeck, the player's friend, announced that he would hold a Don Black Night on September 22 and the Indians' share of the gate would go to Black. Red Sox owner Tom Yawkey kindly volunteered to give his share of the gate as well to the fund, but Veeck turned down the gesture, saying it was a "Cleveland affair." The decision to play the game at night—the game had originally been scheduled for daytime—rankled Red Sox manager Joe McCarthy because he knew that Feller would be more effective under the lights, and Feller was just that. He held the Red Sox hitless for five innings as a mammoth crowd of 76,772 cheered the Indians to a 5–2 victory. When the smoke cleared, Veeck was happy to announce that the franchise had provided Don Black with a $40,000 get-well purse—equal to approximately $500,000 today. Greenberg later commented,

> The only owner I ever knew who gave a damn about his players was Bill Veeck. Bill genuinely cared about them and he always worried about them individually. It was almost like hero worship for Bill. The ballplayers were first in his book and he would do anything to help their families, or ease the way if they got into trouble.[65]

Joe Earley, 34-year-old World War II veteran from Lakewood, Ohio, was a security guard at a local Chevrolet plant who had written a facetious letter to the *Cleveland Press*, complaining that there were too many "special" days or nights honoring ballplayers, past and present, and even club owners. How about a night for good old Joe Earley? It didn't take long for Veeck to seize the public relations possibilities of Earley's idea. Warren Brown of the Chicago *Herald Tribune* regarded Veeck's ploy in the midst of a torrid pennant race as the "master psychological stroke of the entire season." On September 28, 60,405 fans poured into Municipal Stadium for "good old Joe Earley night." Veeck also called the event Princess Aloha Orchid night, and chartered an air-conditioned plane to fly in 20,000 Princess Aloha orchids from the Hawaiian Islands, along with a florist and a young Hawaiian woman, who dressed in a grass skirt to help pass out the precious flowers.

After most of the throng was seated, Veeck entered the field and grabbed a microphone. The puzzled White Sox looked on from their dugout as Veeck, in his element, picked fans at random and presented them with such "useful" gifts as 50-pound blocks of ice, live turkeys, guinea pigs, white rabbits, and bushel baskets of apples, peaches, and tomatoes. One man was presented with three stepladders and another with a sow and her piglets. Then came the main event: Joe Earley, looking like a leading man of his era, was escorted to the diamond with his wife, and the ultimate tribute to an average fan was about to begin. Author Paul Dickson captured the hilarity which followed:

> Veeck announced that the Indians were rewarding Earley with a brand new home, built in "early American architecture." A flatbed truck rolled in from the outfield carrying a dilapidated outhouse. The crowd roared. Then Earley was told that he was being presented with a car, and with that a rickety Model T Ford rolled out onto the diamond. It was a tricked-up circus car filled with young female models who piled out on command. The bumpers fell off when the horn was honked. More gifts followed, some of them whimsical, including livestock, a case of Wheaties, and some of them generous—a truck filled with appliances donated by business owners, and most delightful for Mr. Earley, a brand new 1949 yellow Ford convertible. Veeck personally gave the Earleys luggage, books, clothes, and a cocker spaniel. Joe, with a wide grin on his face, also received a gold lifetime pass entitling him to entry to any American League ballpark.[66]

The "average fan" had had his day, and the effect was one that many fans would never forget. Noted sports columnist Terry Pluto wrote in *Our Tribe: A Baseball Memoir*, "my father was one of the fans at the Stadium.... He didn't receive a gift but he understood what it was like to be Joe Earley. In 1948, Bill Veeck and the Indians made him feel special."

With a rare losing record of 9–12 as late as July 23, and then 12–14 on August 22, Feller won seven straight games for a respectable 19–14 record. Excluding his war service and the abbreviated season in 1945, this was the first year since 1938 that he had not won 20 or more games. From Labor Day to end of the regular season, the Tribe won 19 of 24 games. The final weekend of the season began on October 1. The Tribe was 1½ games ahead with two fewer losses than both the Yankees and Red Sox, who were scheduled to play each other twice in Boston.

They were perched in first place with Lemon, Bearden, and Feller scheduled to pitch against the always dangerous Bengals from Detroit. However, the best-laid plans do not always come to fruition. In the first game of the three-game series, while the Yankees and Red Sox were idle, Lemon, who had pitched more innings (285⅓) than any twirler in the American League and held a 3–2 lead going into the ninth inning, was exhausted. An uncommon error by Lemon led to a three-run rally by the Tigers, and Cleveland went down, 5–3. Meanwhile, Boston had defeated the New Yorkers 5–1 to close the gap. All was not lost, however; rather the loss was like a burr in their saddle. Reportedly, the Indians stormed into the clubhouse where they apparently indulged in a brief orgy of mutual recrimination. A crowd of only 15,989 went home in an unsettled frame of mind. Would the Tribe make it after 28 years?

Saturday was another day. With a Red Sox defeat and Indians victory, the pennant would belong to Cleveland after 28 long years. Only half of this projection came to fruition. Fifty-six thousand fans came to Municipal Stadium on a dark, cold, and windy fall day, hoping for the best. The Tribe received an unexpected break when Tigers manager Steve O'Neill was forced to replace pitcher Fred Hutchinson from the lineup with rookie right-hander Lou Kretlow. Hutchinson, a mainstay on the Tigers' pitching staff, came down with the flu and had a 102-degree fever. O'Neill called both managers Joe McCarthy (Boston) and Bucky Harris (NY) before the game to apologize for the switch.

For Cleveland, the result was little in doubt after the team scored five runs in the fourth inning. Bearden pitched his sixth shutout for the season, winning 8–0, and the workhorse was pitching his third game in eight days, this time on three days' rest. Meanwhile in Boston, the Red Sox kept the pressure on the Tribe by eliminating the World Champion New Yorkers, 5–1. It was not the Bronx Bombers' year, although New York writers eventually judged the 1948 Yankees team stronger than the 1947 and the 1949 World Champion squads.

Now the season came down to the final day, with the Indians holding a one-game advantage. Cobbledick reviewed the season during which any one game could have been won or lost to alter the final scenario: "win or lose there's one thing you can't take away from them. They've given it the best they had, right down to the wire and they've given us the most exciting baseball season in history."[67]

The Yankees–Red Sox game had begun an hour earlier, and Tribe fans saw the score on the Stadium scoreboard throughout the afternoon. The news was not good—the Red Sox were leading and were about to sweep the Yankees. The weather in Cleveland was cool but sunny. A crowd of 74,181 helped set a major league season attendance record of 2,620,627, a record that lasted for more than 30 years.

Several behind-the-scenes issues developed before the Tigers–Indians game even began. On the Tigers' side, pitcher Hal Newhouser was furious that he had to pitch the season-ending game. The future Hall of Famer had won his 20th game on just two days' rest against the Browns on the previous Wednesday, and like many players out of the race, wanted to go home. This was the same individual who had won the MVP Award in the American League in 1944 and again in 1945 while pitching the Tigers to a World Championship.

On the other side of the field, Bob Feller was warming up. The stakes were high for the "Rapid One," as a victory meant the pennant; for him personally, it meant that and he would become a 20-game winner for the sixth full season in a row. He expected to pitch in his first World Series game. Feller had a 7–1 lifetime record against Newhouser and was shooting for his eighth straight victory. While warming up, however, Feller knew he would need some good fortune, as his good stuff was not there, and his premonition was correct.

In the third inning, Feller was knocked out of the box when the Tigers scored four runs, and for all practical purposes the game was over. The enormous crowd of 74,181 sat silent and horrified. Sitting in the dugout, reserve outfielder Bob Kennedy quietly remarked, "You could have heard a pin drop on the grass." Totally in command, however, Newhouser pitched as though he were going to the World Series. Larry Doby commented, "Newhouser was unhittable."[68] By the end of the eighth inning, the smooth-throwing left-hander had faced only 27 batters, three over the minimum. The final score was 7–1, and Boudreau mulled over who would pitch the playoff game in Boston.

The huge crowd began filing out in large numbers in the seventh inning. Veeck paced back and forth in the press box and eventually retreated into a stony, uncharacteristic silence. As one paper put it, "The gay victory polka slowed down to a dirge."[69]

When the game finally ended, the disappointed Indians trudged into the clubhouse. In a coin-tossing ceremony on September 24 held by American League president William Harridge, the flip had given the Red Sox home field advantage if Cleveland and Boston tied. Boudreau closed the door, met briefly with his coaches and then with the players, and said, "What the hell, we were planning to go to Boston [to play the Braves in the World Series] anyway."[70] At season's end, all pitching staffs of the contenders were worn down, and the Tribe was no exception. After due consultation, Boudreau informed the team that he believed that Bearden was best equipped to start—the knuckleball does not tax the arm to the extent of other pitches. The team sat silent, and Boudreau added, "We're all in this thing together.... [I]t's your money as well as mine and if you have any ideas of your own, speak up."[71]

Only Johnny Berardino questioned the wisdom of starting a left-hander in Fenway Park, where the left-field wall is a friendly target for right-handed batters. Boudreau had reviewed the performances of Indians pitchers against the Red Sox for the season, and Bearden had the best record. Discussion followed, and finally Gordon spoke up: "Lou, we went along with your choice for 154 games and finished in a tie. There's not a man in this room who [several] weeks ago, wouldn't have settled for a tie. I'm sure we can go along with you for another game." Berardino chipped in, "I'll go along with that, too."[72] And the issue was settled.

The players and Boudreau agreed to withhold the announcement of the decision to pitch Bearden, partly in order to keep the Red Sox on edge and partly to protect Bearden from reporters' questions. For several weeks, Boudreau had not allowed reporters into the locker room after games. Bearden responded to Boudreau's choice: "I wasn't surprised. I got along real well with Boudreau. He knew what he was doing; he told you the way it was going to be and that was it."[73]

Privately, however, the team was worried. Without a chance to go home to their families, the team had to dress and go directly to the nearby railway station to catch a nine o'clock

special train to Boston. No club had ever felt confident playing in Fenway Park. Several players—including Ken Keltner—doubted that Bearden would last very long. The Indians had
won four of their first five games at Fenway Park and then lost five of six during the season.
Despite Boudreau's brave front, he, too, had lost some of his confidence. As he left the park
for the train station, a *Plain Dealer* photographer snapped a picture of him in his suit and
overcoat, his head down, his shoulders hunched, his eyes cast downward, the picture of
dejection.

The next morning, the team arrived in Boston no doubt tired and disgruntled. Bearden
remembered the trip: "We had a little crap game in the Pullman—me, Satchel Paige, Keltner,
Allie Clark. It was just nickel and dime stuff—didn't last long. I went to bed around ten or
ten-thirty. I slept."[74] A small army of sportswriters accompanied the team, including Cliff
Keane of *The Boston Globe*, who covered the Red Sox. He had come to Cleveland to cover
the Tribe's last game. Keane noticed Bob Lemon and Ken Keltner—the most notorious party
animals on the Tribe roster—having a few drinks and deduced that Lemon would not pitch
in the playoff game. He made a mental note to observe how well Keltner performed. Marsh
Samuel, publicity director for the Tribe, recalled that if Keltner had been drinking water,
he would have been worried.[75]

For the Red Sox as well, it was difficult to decide who would pitch against a strong
Indians lineup. Jack Kramer, with an 18–5 record, looked promising, but he had recently
pitched. The other possibilities were Mel Parnell, Ellis Kinder, and Denny Galehouse. Man-
ager Joe McCarthy had been criticized over the years for his pitching assignments. Galehouse,
a right-hander from Doylestown, Ohio, had begun his 13-year career with Cleveland in 1933.
McCarthy recalled that Galehouse, basically a .500 pitcher, had pitched well against the
Indians the last time they had faced each other, and he was well rested. McCarthy chose
Galehouse, the hot and cold pitcher with an 8–7 record.

The Indians arrived at Fenway Park, Bearden carrying his pet poodle and smoking a
cigar. Boudreau stirred up a hornet's nest when he made a couple of "hunch" changes in his
lineup. To take advantage of the short left field wall, he inserted right-handed-hitting Allie
Clark at first base in place of a disappointed and disgruntled Eddie Robinson, who was
physically hurt. Clark, a good hitter, had never played first base in the major leagues and did
not even have a first basemen's glove. To say he was nervous was an understatement. In addition, the manager put right-handed hitter Bob Kennedy in right field to replace Walt Judnich,
who had played there most of the second half of the season. His decisions caused conster-
nation in Veeck and Greenberg, who questioned in particular the choices of Bearden and
Clark. In Greenberg's book, *The Story of My Life*, he said about Boudreau's lineup moves,
"You can imagine Bill Veeck's shock. I had to agree with him. It was a daring move. It took
a lot of guts."[76]

Both managers were slow to let the opposing team, or the press, know who the starting
pitchers would be. The Red Sox did not know that Bearden was starting until he began to
warm up. Boudreau was suspicious of McCarthy's intentions. His lineup of six right-handed
batters had been designed to face left-hander Mel Parnell. The Indians saw Denny Galehouse
warming up. "Go under the stands," Boudreau told traveling secretary Spud Goldstein. "See
if Parnell's warming up somewhere." Goldstein searched, but none of the other Red Sox

pitchers were warming up under the stands.[77] Galehouse, whose success would depend upon his control, was the starting pitcher.

The biggest game in American League history and the league's first playoff game began at 1:30 p.m. with 33,957 fans on hand—what a contrast to the mammoth crowds who had regularly attended Cleveland's games that summer. Both teams were hungry. The Red Sox had won only one pennant (1946) since 1918; the Tribe had garnered its only league championship in 1920.

The wind was blowing toward left field and Veeck and Greenberg would no longer need to fret over Boudreau's strategy, for in fact, Galehouse's control was not sharp. In the first inning, Boudreau drove a curve ball that hung into the favorable 20-mile-an-hour wind toward left field. Williams took a few steps and watched the ball drop into the net for a home run, and Boudreau put the team on his shoulders the rest of the way. The tightness was gone; the looseness that characterized the team most of the season was back.

The Red Sox retaliated with a run in the last of the first inning as Bearden struggled with his control. In the second inning Bearden allowed a single and walk, but a double play saved the inning. Boudreau began to second-guess his decision to start Bearden, as did several teammates. They need not have worried, however, for Bearden settled down, checking the Red Sox for the next three innings. With men on first and second in the top of the fourth inning, a sober Keltner came to bat. Strategy called for a sacrifice, but Boudreau remembered that Casey Stengel had once advised him to "always let hitters hit." That Keltner did, slamming a three-run homer over the Green Monster.[78] Bedlam broke loose in the dugout and in Cleveland. Doby followed with a double off right-hander Ellis Kinder, who replaced Galehouse. A sacrifice bunt and infield out scored the Tribe's fifth run.

Boudreau continued the onslaught in the fifth inning with his 18th home run, making the score 6–1. Bearden was touched up with a two-run homer by Bobby Doerr in the sixth inning. It was one of only two hits Bearden allowed in the first seven innings of the game. By now, Eddie Robinson had replaced Allie Clark at first base.

When Boudreau came to bat in the ninth inning, he remembered, "The fans gave me a standing ovation, even though most of them were for the Red Sox. It provided me with a memory I'll forever cherish…. Then I singled again, going 4 for 4."[79]

The Indians added runs in the eighth and ninth inning, making the score 8–3. Bearden disposed of the Red Sox in the bottom of the ninth inning. The game was over. The Indians had won the American League pennant, and now they were ready to play another Boston team—the Braves—for the elusive World Championship.

After the final out, the Indians lifted Bearden onto their shoulders and carried him to the dugout. Bearden was the most surprised person in the park because he thought it was only the eighth inning. Winning his fourth complete game in ten days, Bearden had actually lost track of the inning.[80] Boudreau ran to a box behind third base and hugged his wife, Della. The victory gave Bearden 20 wins in his rookie year and the league ERA title (2.43). If there had been a Cy Young Award in 1948, Bearden would have been a shoo-in for the trophy.

While the dugout celebrated, Veeck jumped over a railing and hobbled across the field to congratulate his team and Boudreau. With tears in his eyes, Veeck threw his arms around

Boudreau and said, "Thanks. Just thanks." Bearden spotted Veeck, held up a bottle of soda pop and toasted the owner, pouring its contents over his head. Later, Veeck paid Boudreau the supreme compliment: "We didn't win the pennant in 1948 ... we won it on November 25, 1947, the day I rehired Lou Boudreau."[81] It was after the Indians had won it all that Veeck coined the expression: "Sometimes the best trades are those you don't make."[82]

In a column the next morning in the New York *Herald Tribune*, Red Smith referred to Boudreau's long-standing problems with Veeck and the early doubts about his leadership: "The playoff," he wrote, "was Boudreau's chance to prove himself as a manager. He started managing in the first inning when he homered.... It made him the greatest manager in the world."[83]

The partying continued in the dugout into the night. As the party wound down, Boudreau called the team together, "All rules off tonight ... party at the hotel." Then he shouted, "Practice at Braves Field tomorrow."[84]

Old Bill McKechnie, who had watched Boudreau throughout the season more closely than anyone, put his arms around him: "You did it, Lou," he said quietly. "You did it." As McKechnie walked around the room smiling and shaking hands with one and all, a writer remarked, "You look as happy as if this was a new experience for you." "It never gets old, son," said McKechnie, who had won his first pennant in Pittsburgh in 1925.[85] In a 25-year career as a manager, he had added three pennants to his portfolio: the St. Louis Cardinals in 1928 and the Indians' downstate rival Cincinnati Reds in 1939 and 1940.

McKechnie returned to Boudreau. The Deacon, like other Indians coaches, was already looking ahead to Wednesday's opener of the World Series. "Let's get out of here," McKecknie said to Boudreau, "Let's go over and take a look at that other ballpark."[86] The Indians and Braves were eager to "go at it" after a long hiatus from the World Series scene.

12

A Second World Championship
and the End of the Veeck Era

In many ways the dramatic finish to a nail-biting season left fans and the press wondering if the World Series would be anticlimactic. The other Boston team, the Braves, also was hungry to claim a world championship, not having won a World Series since the amazing comeback of 1914. Led that season by manager George Stallings, Boston was in last place on July 15 with a 33–43 record but leap-frogged over three teams, and in September swept aside John McGraw's New York Giants to win the pennant by 10½ games. "When you're hot, you're hot!"[1] And the Braves proved so, sweeping the World Series over Connie Mack's favored A's in four games.

Six years later, during his first full season as manager, Tris Speaker led the Tribe to their first pennant in a tight race against the Chicago White Sox and New York Yankees. On September 25, 1920, the Chicago team was decimated when six key players and a reserve player suspected of throwing the 1919 World Series were suspended. The Indians trumped the Yankees by appearing in a World Series one year before the Yankees' first World Series in 1921. The Indians' opponent was the Brooklyn Robins, managed by venerable Uncle Wilbert "Robbie" Robinson. The next-to-final nine-game World Series lasted only seven games, Cleveland winning their first World Championship five games to two. Now they were in position to win their second.

After a riotous Monday night celebration at the Kenmore Hotel, Boudreau questioned whether his team would be ready for the Series. Billy Sullivan, the Indians' 15-year-old bat boy, recalled that during the celebration, "I had a soft drink with Russ Christopher (a tall, skeleton-like pitcher) who wasn't allowed to drink anything alcoholic."[2] On Tuesday morning, a day of practice, Billy had breakfast with Gene Bearden. He recalled, "[Bearden] had a couple of scotches. Boudreau told me to tell the players that their wives were coming in on the one o'clock train as guests of Bill Veeck for the World Series." The players sobered up fast when they got this news.[3] When the players showed up at Braves Field, Boudreau looked at them and exclaimed, "What a sorry looking bunch of hung-over guys!" He said this with understanding and later noted, "They'd earned the right to enjoy what they'd accomplished, and were entitled to relish the spotlight directed their way."[4] The team did little more than suit up and exercise a bit—no running and no hitting. Trainer Lefty Weisman passed out numbers for players to line up for their turn to ease into the whirlpool and soak away the champagne still in their bodies.

Bill Veeck, accidentally or intentionally and with a stroke of genius, may have helped his team's cause before the first pitch was thrown. Johnny Sain, Boston's pitcher, said, "Hardly anybody realized the importance of it at the time."[5] Veeck had asked Boston owner Lou Perini if he would agree to do away with travel days. That would mean playing seven straight days (October 6–12). Sain wondered, "I don't know why [Perini] agreed, unless it was to save money. It bothered me but there was nothing we could do about it." At this time, the players had no union through which these decisions could be challenged.[6] By playing in Cleveland without a day off between the second and third games, the Braves' hotel expenses were reduced, as were expenses between the fifth and sixth games.

More importantly, had the Series stretched over nine days instead of seven and gone seven games, as Sain pointed out, "I could have started four of them because I [had] worked with two days' rest many times that year."[7] Sain won 25 games and lost 14 with an ERA of 2.60. The workhorse started 39 games, going all the way in 28, as well as pitching in relief in three games. Warren Spahn, Sain's sidekick, started 35 games, finishing 16. His record of 15–12 was modest for Spahn, who was just beginning his spectacular pitching career that included 363 victories and 13 20-win seasons—one more than Walter Johnson. The Braves had little additional pitching help. Thus the birth of one of the most popular ditties in baseball lore: "Spahn and Sain and pray for two days of rain." The elimination of the two so-called "travel days" deprived Sain of a third pitching assignment. He concluded, "I don't know if that was Veeck's intention, but it [likely] worked in the Indians' favor."[8] Veeck surmised that he had spent lots of money on special nights at the Stadium, paying for gifts of all kinds, for team parties and helping out members of his team, and thus he needed to watch his finances.

Boudreau chose 30-year-old Bob Feller to open the Series. In spite of Feller's somewhat mediocre season, he had come through at the right times, and he had waited ten years for this opportunity. His opponent was, as expected, the soft-spoken Arkansan, Johnny Sain. "Power will win for the Indians," ran almost every World Series prediction. Yet according to Franklin Lewis of the *Press*, "seldom has there been a World Series with less power revealed or with less animation by the players. The Indians were tired at the outset."[9]

The tone of the Series was established in the first game. The contest turned out to be a classic pitchers' duel, witnessed by what reporter Frank Gibbons described as 40,135 "uncultured Bostonians," and featuring one of the most controversial calls in World Series history. The game was scoreless going into the eighth inning; Feller had allowed only one hit and Sain had given up just four hits. Sain remembered that "I had a very good curveball that day." Boudreau concurred. When the manager struck out for only the tenth time that year, he later commented, "The curve ball he struck me out with was one of the fastest breaking hooks I have ever seen."[10]

Although he struck out only two batters in eight innings, Feller was throwing his customary heat. He made one critical mistake: He walked catcher Bill Salkeld on a three-and-two pitch to lead off the eighth inning. Phil Masi, the Braves' other catcher, ran for Salkeld and was bunted to second by Mike McCormick. Boudreau told Feller to intentionally walk

Eddie Stanky, the next batter, in order to set up a double play. Feller tried to talk his manager out of this decision, and as Boudreau later second-guessed himself, he admitted it was a mistake. He remembered that Branch Rickey once commented, "Stanky can't hit, can't run, can't throw, and he can't field—all he can do is beat you."[11] Indirectly, that is what happened.

With men on first and second, Tommy Holmes, one of the National League's best hitters with a .325 average, was the second batter scheduled to the plate. It was time for the famous Boudreau-Feller pick-off play which Boudreau had devised for just such a situation. The strategy was to hold men close to second base so that a single would not score the runner, and if the runner was picked off, so much the better.

Boudreau explained how the play had developed: "I was playing right behind ... Masi and I gave the pick-off sign which was the glove over my left knee."[12] Feller saw the signal, looked back toward the hitter, counted a-thousand-one, a-thousand-two, then wheeled and fired to second base. As soon as Feller turned his head to the hitter and Boudreau saw the back of his head, he broke for second base. Theoretically, the break gave him a one-step lead ahead of the runner.

When Boudreau flashed the signal, Feller whirled and fired the ball to his shortstop cutting toward second base. Masi had taken a generous lead and dove back to the bag. Boudreau insisted, "Feller's throw beat Masi." He added, "The throw was a little high. I tagged Masi as he dove back to the bag, from his elbow up to his shoulder.... [T]he tag was not made at the base because of the throw from Feller being up high."[13]

However, looking at the base for the tag, Bill Stewart, a National League umpire, flattened his palms and ruled "Safe." Boudreau charged Stewart, vehemently yelling and objecting to the call, but Stewart did not change his call. After Sain made the second out, Holmes, on a count of one-and-one, smashed a line drive to left field, scoring Masi with the only run of the game. Sain retired the Indians in the ninth inning, in spite of a two-base error by third baseman Bob Elliott on a ground ball by Keltner.

Sain was magnificent in victory in a game that had taken only one hour 42 minutes. There is no assurance that the Indians would have won the game even if the umpire had made the correct call. Later, besieged by reporters, Stewart held his ground regarding his call. He umpired in the National League for 21 years and died in 1964. Later at an old-timers' game, Masi insisted to Boudreau that Stewart had made the right call, but after Stewart died, Masi admitted to Boudreau that Stewart had, indeed, missed the call.

The loss was a bitter pill for the Tribe and Feller. A World Series victory had eluded him in his long and illustrious career. He was charitable, however, saying that Stewart's ruling hadn't cost him the game: "It beat me out of a tie. I lost because I walked the first batter."[14] The right-hander would have his last chance to win a Series game a few days later.

One highlight of this Series was strong pitching. The 1–0 game was the first in 25 years of World Series play, since Art Nehf of the New York Giants defeated the New York Yankees in October 1923. Feller joined Morton Cooper of the St. Louis Cardinals as the only two to pitch a two-hitter in a World Series game and lose. Cooper was beaten in 1944 when George McQuinn of the St. Louis Browns clubbed a home run to give, of all people, Denny Galehouse a 2–0 victory.

Thursday, October 7, would be a better day for the Tribe and Boudreau's strategy to use a pickoff play, but not a particularly better day for Satchel Paige. For whatever reason, Paige could not persuade the attendant at the players' gate to let him through. When he was just about ready to give up and return to his hotel to listen to the game, another player came by to vouch for his identity. "Can you imagine that? That fellow musta thought I was Jackie Robinson, for he said I was too young to be Satchel Paige."[15] Boudreau chose Bob Lemon as his starter in the second game. The pitcher with the great sinker-slider had just completed the first of seven seasons in which he would win 20 or more games, surpassing Feller by one and Early Wynn by two.

A nervous Lemon ran into trouble in the first inning. After one out, Gordon muffed a ground ball by rookie shortstop Alvin Dark. Earl Torgeson and Bob Elliott followed with singles, scoring Dark and leaving runners on first and second. With Marv Rickert at the plate and Torgeson carelessly leading too far off second base, Boudreau gave Lemon the same pick-off signal he had given Feller 24 hours earlier. Lemon counted one-thousand-one, one-thousand-two, then wheeled and fired to second base. His throw was on the mark and in plenty of time for Boudreau to tag the befuddled Torgeson diving back to the base. This time an American League umpire, Bill Grieve, called the runner out. Lemon struck out Rickert and ended the Braves' scoring for the day.

After being held scoreless for consecutive innings, the Tribe turned the ship around in the fourth inning: The Indians scored two runs on Boudreau's double and singles by Gordon and Doby. The knockout blow came in the fifth inning when Dale Mitchell led off with a single, was bunted to second, and scored on Boudreau's second hit, knocking out Spahn.

A final run scored in the ninth inning when Jim Hegan reached first on an error by Dark, took second on Lemon's infield out, third on another grounder by Mitchell, and scored on Bob Kennedy's single. Meanwhile, Lemon settled down and cruised to a complete game in two hours and 14 minutes.

The 1948 World Series was the first to be televised—in black and white. This innovation had little negative effect on local attendance at Series games since only three percent of the country's population possessed televisions.

The teams returned to Cleveland for the next three games. The Tribe did not plan to return to Beantown. Boudreau chose Bearden for this next pitching assignment against Vern Bickford. This game featured the third straight pitching duel in the Series. Bearden came through in grand fashion before 70,306 fans witnessing their first World Series game in Cleveland in 28 years. The surprise was that the Stadium was not filled to capacity. The reason, according to Cleveland officials, was a "ticket snafu." It would not happen again. A chorus of boos spilled out of the Stadium when Bill Stewart, villain of the first game, was announced as the home plate umpire.

Bearden's marvelous control of his "dancing" knuckleball was superlative. He did not issue a walk, fanned four, and kept most of the Braves hitting into the dirt. He was masterful not only on the mound but also with the bat, stroking two of the Indians' five hits. In the third inning, he doubled and scored on an error by Dark, trying to complete a double play. The Indians added an insurance run in the fourth inning when Keltner walked, advanced to second on a single by Eddie Robinson, and raced home on a single by Jim Hegan. The final score was 2–0 in a game played in a brief one hour, 36 minutes.

Boudreau, now holding a 2–1 lead in the Series and feeling more confident, decided to gamble by pitching right-hander Steve Gromek and allowing Feller to have an extra day of rest. Gromek, a side-arm pitcher, faced none other than Johnny Sain.

A record crowd of 81,897 fans crowded into the Stadium—a number that seems unbelievable today—bonkers over their hometown team. Even so-called "hardened" professionals respond to the cheers of a crowd. Boudreau set the pace with a double in the first inning after Dale Mitchell led off with a single. The manager tried to stretch his double into a triple. On a close play, he was called out by—guess who—Bill Stewart.

In the third inning, Larry Doby added a second run with a 410-foot home run over the right-center field fence. From that point on, gutsy Sain allowed only one hit over the remaining five innings. Meanwhile, Gromek, the darling of fans that day, was pitching as if there were no tomorrow. He held Boston scoreless until the seventh inning, when Marv Rickert, left fielder and replacement for injured Jeff Heath,[16] hit a home run into the lower right field stands. One Braves player was heard to mutter that it "served the son-of-bitch right." Heath continued to be a "cancer" in the dugout. Hegan was his usual sterling self behind the plate. Gromek, now in his eighth season with the Tribe, finished strong with a seven-hitter to win, 2–1. It marked the fourth straight complete game pitched by Indian twirlers. The relief pitchers had fallen asleep in the bullpen.

To many the highlight of this game occurred after the last out. The public did not see it until the newspapers hit the streets the next day. As the Indians filed into the clubhouse, Steve Gromek ran over and gave Larry Doby a man-sized hug. An alert photographer caught the picture, which became a "must" in papers throughout the country the next day, for in 1948, published photos of a white man hugging a Negro were rare.[17]

With the Clevelanders leading the Series three games to one, the fifth game was set up to be a day of ecstasy; instead, it turned out to be one of agony, and for Cleveland's greatest pitcher of all time, it was a day of deep disappointment. Bob Feller faced what would be his last opportunity to win a World Series game. Before the largest crowd in baseball history to date (86,288), a desperate Boston unloosed their silent bats to turn a pitchers' series into a pitcher's nightmare. Feller was the primary victim.

The Braves prevailed, 11–5,

Larry Doby and pitcher Steve Gromek embrace after Gromek won the fourth game of the 1948 World Series over Boston, 2–1. Doby, commenting about the occasion, said, "I will always cherish it because it showed that emotions can be put into a form that's something other than skin color" (author's collection).

clubbing three home runs off Feller, including two by Bob Elliott, their leading home run threat. The right-hander was driven from the mound in the seventh inning after allowing seven runs on eight hits. Feller offered no excuses: "All I can say is that I just didn't have it."[18] Feller was crushed, and as he walked off the mound, the hooting and jeering were deafening. The relief pitching was not much better, as four relievers tried to stem the tide. One reliever, Russ Christopher, could not stop the ferocious Braves. It would be his last appearance on the mound. For the disheartened fans, the appearance of Satchel Paige was encouraging, and he received a great hand from the huge crowd. He was the first black pitcher to take the mound in a World Series game. Paige retired both men he faced although he committed a harmless balk.[19] The loss meant that the Series winner would be determined in Boston.

The press was, in general, supportive of Feller. A brouhaha erupted the next day (October 11) when Gordon Cobbledick lambasted Boudreau for having left Feller in the game too long. The columnist reasoned,

> It was obvious as early as the third inning that unless he suddenly found his missing fastball
> ... Feller would be beaten. Boudreau was tempting fate when he allowed him to stay in the
> game.... The Braves might have beaten any pitcher whom Boudreau could have used in relief
> ... but Boudreau owed it to the game and to the record to make them beat the best he had.[20]

Dismayed, Boudreau went to see Cobbledick: "'Gordon,' I said, 'that's the first time you wrote a column without understanding the situation.' It was the only time I had anything against Gordon." Cobbledick apologized and said that perhaps he had used the wrong words.[21] To his credit, Feller always took the blame for the loss. As it happened, Cobbledick's analysis was essentially correct, for there was no reason, other than sentiment, why Boudreau stayed with an ineffective Feller for so long—not when he had a well-rested bullpen.

There was always the next day and the next day after if necessary for the Tribe. A *Time* magazine reporter cornered Boudreau in the Cleveland dressing room and asked who would pitch tomorrow: "It'll be Bob Lemon," responded Boudreau. When asked about Tuesday, Boudreau snapped, "There'll be no game Tuesday."[22] The confident manager was correct: Boudreau would have Bearden in the bullpen. The Braves gambled that there would be a seventh game, so Southworth held back ace Johnny Sain and started Bill Voiselle.

The sixth and final game was the best of the entire Series. Lemon, seeking his second Series win, outpitched Voiselle for seven innings as 40,103 loyal New Englanders groaned. In the first inning, the Tribe broke into the lead on doubles by Mitchell and Boudreau. The Braves came back with an equalizer in the fourth on Elliott's single, a walk and Mike McCormick's single. Gordon regained the lead for the Tribe in the sixth inning with a mighty drive over the left field fence. A walk, Robinson's single, and an infield out produced a second run. In the eighth inning, after Warren Spahn replaced Voiselle, the Indians increased their lead to 4–1 on successive singles by Keltner, Tucker, and Robinson.

But the Braves would not give up. Lemon began to tire in the home eighth. Holmes singled and Torgeson advanced him to third with a solid double to right field. Lemon—unnerved—walked Elliott, filling the bases. Boudreau came to the mound and signaled Bearden to replace Lemon. But this was not the invincible Bearden of earlier Boston conquests. Outfielder Clint Conatser, batting for Rickert, lined out to Tucker in center field, Holmes scoring and Torgenson taking third. Catcher Phil Masi, batting for Salkeld, stroked a double to left field, scoring Torgenson and sending Elliott to third base. The score was now 4–3.

The Indians were in deep trouble. Should Boudreau replace Bearden? He decided to stick with the knuckleballer. "How could I not go along with him after all he had done in the previous sixteen days?" he reasoned.[23] Bearden's tally included starting—and winning— five games, including one that clinched a tie for the pennant, one that won the playoff game, and the third game of the World Series.

Bearden induced Mike McCormick to slap a ball back to the mound, and Bearden threw him out for the third out. Bearden later reflected that he had had "no choice but to stop the ball or get killed." He added, "If it had hit me or gone past me, the runners on second and third would have scored."[24]

Bearden started the ninth inning on shaky footing by walking Eddie Stanky. Then "Ole Reliable" came through—in this case, catcher Jim Hegan. Sibby Sisti, attempting to lay down a sacrifice bunt, popped up, and Hegan raced out in front of the plate, snared the ball, and fired it to first base as Connie Ryan, running for Stanky, broke for second. The result was a double play. Holmes lofted a fly to Kennedy in right field. The Cleveland Indians were World Champions for the first time in 28 years!

Frank Gibbons of the *Press* caught a bit of the ambience: "The Braves hurried down their runway. From the Indians bullpen far in the right field corner came a slow parade of the ... bullpen corps ... last were Russ Christopher and Satchel Paige—those gents don't ever hurry."[25]

Amidst the subdued locker room celebration, syndicated columnist Oscar Fraley noticed that Bob Feller was almost a forgotten man. He knew that he had done little to help the team to their championship. This was the same man who had excelled, surpassing his teammates with his performance for the Tribe during the past ten or so years. As Feller sat on the locker bench, Larry Doby, one of the stars of the Series, walked over to Feller and with his piano key smile, stuck out his big brown hand. Feller's eyes lighted at the friendly gesture, as they warmly clasped hands.[26]

Cleveland fans saw the final Series game on television, but technical difficulties prevented transmission to other Midwestern cities. A converted B-29 bomber flying at a 25,000 feet altitude over Pittsburgh for the duration of the game picked up the telecast on a relay from Baltimore. Video sets within range of the bomber also were able to receive the picture. The team quickly boarded their special train for their overnight trip back to a city of delirious fans. The trip would be a night of celebration that no one on board would soon forget. For many, the biggest thrill occurred soon after the train pulled out of South Station. Bill Veeck walked into the dining car, and all the players stood and applauded. Seldom has a major league franchise seen such rapport between an owner and its players.

Later, in the dining car, future Hall of Famer Joe Gordon stood up and asked for quiet, raised his glass, and fixed his eyes on Boudreau: "To the greatest leatherman I ever saw, to the damnedest clutch hitter that ever lived, to a doggone good manager, Lou."[27] Non-drinker Jim Hegan toasted the victory with milk, and Doby had a good stiff shot of iced tea; then both retreated to the lounge car, a venue much quieter than the noisy dining room, to discuss how Doby would use his Series check to furnish his new home in Paterson, New Jersey. In the far corner of the dining car, a young, grinning owner of the team lifted his own glass, and there was a glaze of tears over his eyes. Bill Veeck, 34, had hit the jackpot early in his life.

All that remained was the celebration with fans in an already boisterous Cleveland. Veeck rented a club car to be added to the New York Central passenger train. For the celebration at home, "Veeck had arranged for the team to arrive … at 8:45 a.m." Baseball announcer Jimmy Dudley remembered, "The team arrived at the Terminal Tower at 9 a.m. and … went up the stairs into a lineup of cars and the parade started right in the middle of the morning rush and thousands of people were stopped in their tracks." "How many people would think of that?" Dudley added, "The genius of the man."[28]

Euclid Avenue was strewn with roses and confetti and lined with more than 200,000 fans. Jack Ledden of *The Sporting News* described the scene:

> Flags flew … banners were waved frantically while whistles and horns tooted. School children carried signs saying "We knocked the Beans out of Boston." Thousands of balloons floated down from buildings. A few spectators thrust packages containing gifts into the car bearing Louis and Mrs. Boudreau and President Veeck. Ticker tape fluttered out of windows in Public Square and all along the avenue…. Stenographers, bellhops, policemen, bus drivers, and executives jockeyed for positions near the [front] of the line … so they could wave to the victorious players. Public Square was a mass of humanity … jammed into a six block area. Street cars and buses were stalled and boys and girls climbed atop them to get a better view…. As the parade moved toward University Circle two miles away, the biggest cheer in Cleveland history shattered the air. It ignited like a fuse and continued its din until the line of cars disbanded near Western Reserve University.[29]

Never in the city's history had a returning hero or band of heroes home from war or otherwise received such a welcome. Hal Lebovitz described the 1948 season as "the Indians' greatest—most thrilling, exciting, wondrous, glorious, take your choice—season in the history of the franchise." Veeck added, "I never knew the real Cleveland until today. This is impossible to believe."[30] Banquets and more accolades would be forthcoming in the fall and winter months.

Veeck lived alone in an apartment only a few blocks from where the parade ended:

> I sat in an empty apartment … sunlight all around me…. I thought of my son who was less than proud of me…. I thought of my wrecked marriage and my lost family…. I thought of Harry Grabiner in a deep coma, waiting for death. I had … everything I'd hoped for when I came to Cleveland. Everything and more. I had never been more lonely in my life.[31]

Later Bill Veeck talked about what it was like during his three-and-a-half years as owner of the Indians, "…you weren't in Cleveland … when the Indians pushed the world news from the front pages. You weren't in Cleveland … when the Indians brought the people of the city so close together that it was as though everybody was living in everybody else's parlor. You weren't in Cleveland in those days of cheer" and triumph when every day was Mardi Gras and every fan a king.[32]

Veeck recovered from his miseries while the city and team continued days of celebration. Records were broken and awards announced by the press. Behind the scenes, Veeck was asked whether he might be interested in selling his franchise: "Anything is for sale," generalized Veeck, and he added wryly, "For a price, of course. And we've had offers."[33]

In the meantime, each player received one of 34 shares worth $6,772 each, the largest share in the history of World Series play, eclipsing the Tigers' share of $6,544 in the 1935 World Series. This Series broke all records for single game attendance and total attendance with 358,362 fans for the six-game classic.

Terry Pluto likely best described the performance of the Indians, commenting, "The Indians were not a great team. They were a good team with several players who had great years."[34] For example, who would have predicted that Gene Bearden would win 20 games with a league-leading ERA of 2.43? He won only 25 games during the remainder of his seven-season career. In contrast, Bob Lemon recorded his first of seven 20-win seasons. The future Hall of Famer would retire as one of Cleveland's greatest pitchers. Certainly, Veeck helped the pitching staff with his *coup de grâce* by signing Paige in mid-season, providing the Tribe with six vital victories down the home stretch. Veeck's "manipulation" of the outfield fence was also a strong adjunct to the team's success.

Lou Boudreau led a trio of infielders who had career-best seasons. His performance was easily the best of his 15-year career. His batting average of .353 has been topped by only six other shortstops.[35] He stroked 199 hits, 34 doubles, and 18 home runs, and drove in 116 runs. The tenacious batsman struck out only nine times in 560 times at bat. The player-manager won the American League's Most Valuable Player Award, easily outdistancing Joe DiMaggio and Ted Williams, and was later chosen as Cleveland's "Man of the Year" by the Cleveland press. The only other Cleveland player to win the Most Valuable Player Award—under different voting requirements—had been first baseman George Burns in 1926.

Third baseman Ken Keltner and second baseman Joe Gordon, with Boudreau, furnished the major power for the team. Keltner stroked 31 home runs and drove in 119 RBI and Gordon led the team with 124 RBI and a team-leading 32 home runs. The three infielders accounted for 43 percent of the team's 802 RBI.

Eddie Robinson offered strong support at first base. Adept as a defensive player, he hit 16 home runs and garnered 83 RBI. Jim Hegan, a master at handling pitchers, was one of the greatest defensive catchers of all time, providing the team with a career-best offensive season, hitting 14 home runs and delivering 61 RBI in 121 games. The outfield was strengthened by break-out seasons for Dale Mitchell (.336 average) and Larry Doby—14 home runs and 66 RBI in his first full season.

One individual who provided the mix for success did not score a run or pitch an inning. That person was Bill Veeck, adept in making successful trades and acquiring players, who helped the team beyond expectation. While the Gordon-Reynolds trade may be considered a tossup as to who gained the most, Gordon was the right person for the Tribe at this juncture. Russ Christopher was a godsend for the relief staff. The purchase of Sam Zoldak from the Browns for $100,000 meant that each of his nine victories cost $11,000. This figure may have seemed exorbitant in 1948. However, from Veeck's standpoint, Zoldak's contribution was well worth the investment, as an owner trying to win the franchise's first championship in 28 years.

After the city-wide celebration subsided, Veeck's well-known generosity with his players continued. One beneficiary was Steve Gromek, unsung hero of the Series. Gromek, often referred to as a wartime pitcher only, had won 19 and lost nine in 1945 before veterans returned to the playing field. In 1947, the right-hander hurt his knee and did not contribute much that year, compiling a 3–5 record. When the 1948 season began, Veeck cut his salary by $2,500, promising that he would make it up to him if he had a good year. As the season moved into September, Gromek worked his way up to be a fourth starter along with Sam Zoldak (the two combined to win 18 games). When the Indians needed a stopper, he won a crucial game on September 19 against the Athletics. Gromek ended the season with a 9–3 record in addition to a big victory in the fourth game of the World Series.

Later in the fall, Veeck called Gromek into his office and gave him a bonus. Gromek later revealed the amount was $5,000. Veeck also gave batboy Billy Sullivan an extra $1,000 to add to his World Series share of $1,693 plus player tips, sending him home with approximately $3,000. Two weeks after Don Black left the hospital, Veeck presented him with a full-share World Series check. His record was only 2–2, but the owner knew that Black was worth everything he paid him and more.

In late October, Veeck mourned the loss of Harry Grabiner, his closest friend and the "smartest man I ever met in baseball." Grabiner had spent years as executive with Charles Comiskey and the Chicago White Sox. Cobbledick captured what Grabiner had meant to Veeck:

> He was a balance wheel for Veeck. The Indians' young president recognized that he himself was impetuous. Veeck … emphasized the vital role played by Grabiner in the business of the Cleveland club and Veeck told an interviewer that you spell his name as follows: "I-N-T-E-G-R-I-T-Y."[36]

In the aftermath of the 1948 season, there were shakeups in the Red Sox, Yankees, and White Sox organizations. The most shocking move was the sacking of Bucky Harris by the Yankees. He had led the Yankees to a World Championship in 1947 and a near pennant in 1948. His replacement was the inimitable Casey Stengel, whom Veeck had wanted to hire as a replacement for Boudreau in 1947. Stengel proved to be a thorn in the Indians' side for many years. From 1949 through 1960, Stengel's Yankees won nine pennants, finished second to Cleveland in 1954 and finished third in 1960. The Tribe's six second-place finishes during this period went for naught.

Veeck's third and final year as owner of the Cleveland franchise developed into the most disappointing season of his tenure. After the first of the year, Veeck spent several weeks in New York City, reveling in his good fortune. In many ways, he was king of the hill. He wined and dined with such notables as Elsa Maxwell, Greenberg's wife Carol Gimbel, artist Salvador Dali, English comedienne Beatrice Lillie and noted columnists Earl Wilson, Leonard Lyons, and Walter Winchell.

On one occasion, Della and Lou Boudreau went to New York to dine and visit with Veeck. A few days later, Bob Feller visited to discuss his 1949 contract. By his own standards, Feller had had a subpar year. "If I had your talent," Veeck confided, "I'd get $125,000."[37] The contract discussion was interrupted by a sobering phone call for Veeck. Eleanor Veeck, his wife and the mother of his three children, had filed for divorce earlier in the day in Tucson. Papers had been served and accepted by his lawyers. The papers claimed desertion by Veeck, and Eleanor requested custody of the three children, in addition to alimony and child support.

Eleanor's lawyer issued a terse statement: "They're both fine people but [Eleanor] likes life on the range." Neighbors called her a "quiet homebody." Years later, their daughter Ellen, avoiding discussion about the divorce, said simply, "I think they were mismatched."[38] Veeck had known the anvil would fall soon, and the news put a damper on his celebration.

After catching his bearings, Veeck returned to meet with Feller. The two agreed on a base pay of $72,000 for his 1949 contract, a decrease of $10,000. He would remain the third-highest paid player in the game after Ted Williams ($85,000), and Joe DiMaggio ($100,000).

A few days later, Veeck continued to make headlines when he flew to San Juan to sign 29-year-old Artie Wilson, a black, to a minor league contract. Wilson had been recruited by Veeck's friend and promoter, Abe Saperstein. Upon word of the signing, New York Yankees general manager George Weiss claimed that he had been close to signing Wilson and that Veeck had engaged in "unethical behavior." A verbal duel ensued, and Veeck threatened to sue over the use of the word "unethical."[39] Commissioner Chandler did not void the contract, and Wilson never played an inning with either the Indians or Yankees. Wilson's only major league experience was 19 games with the New York Giants in 1951.

Journalists and baseball authors often questioned Veeck's authenticity in pursuing black players. Was it a publicity stunt, or was he sincere in his efforts to integrate the game? According to his biographer Paul Dickson, Veeck had first thought of bringing blacks into the major leagues while recuperating in a naval hospital. In a bed next to him was a Negro with whom he had spent hours talking about minority rights, and he concluded that in baseball, as in other sports, a player should be evaluated on ability and nothing else.

Veeck demonstrated his liberal social values by joining the National Association for the Advancement of Colored People soon after arriving in Cleveland. He appeared on a recruiting poster with Paige and Doby, gave talks to school and community organizations, and made sure to integrate every level of his staff operation from ushers, food vendors and grounds crew to the front office. In May 1949, he hired local track and field luminary Harrison Dillard, Olympic sprint champion and world record holder, to work in the Indians' public relations department.

New York's *Amsterdam News* coined him "The Abe Lincoln of Baseball," a designation supported by the observable fact that the Indians led the major leagues with 14 black players scattered throughout the organization. *The Sporting News*, with pictures of Lincoln and Veeck side-by-side, printed a caption, "Lincoln ... freed the Negroes. Bill Veeck ... gives 'em baseball jobs."[40]

The wily Veeck made what Russ Schneider called the third-best trade in Tribe history on December 14, 1948.[41] For months, he had had his eye on Early Wynn and Mickey Vernon of the Washington Senators, but owner Clark Griffith detested Veeck and would not make a trade with him. So Veeck took a hostage. He discovered that journeyman pitcher Joe Haynes of the White Sox was married to Griffith's daughter. Haynes was also about to undergo arm surgery, which made his trade value minimal. Veeck offered Indians reserve catcher Joe Tipton, a bit of a clubhouse rebel, in an even-up trade to the astounded Chisox, who gladly unloaded Haynes. Twenty-two days later, Veeck, knowing Griffith desperately wanted to acquire his son-in-law, packaged Haynes with Eddie Robinson and Ed Klieman for Early Wynn and Mickey Vernon. Wynn was the prize. He won 163 games for the Indians in nine seasons, four of them with 20 or more wins. Vernon spent one year plus a few games in 1950 with Cleveland before returning to Washington.

Conversely, Haynes was 10–21 from 1949 to 1952 and was finished as a major league pitcher. Klieman pitched two games for Washington, then was traded to the White Sox, where he won two games. Robinson had a respectable year, batting .294, and was traded the next year to the White Sox. The Indians also picked up catcher Mike Tresh and pitcher Frank Papish from the White Sox. Both were used sparingly, it being Tresh's last year in the major leagues, and Papish won one game—his last one.

Over the objections of now vice-president Hank Greenberg, Veeck renewed Boudreau's contract, making it a two-year deal. Greenberg had little regard for Boudreau's managerial ability. "I didn't think he was anything but a hunch [manager]," he often remarked.[42] The Indians departed on March 5, 1949, for their third sojourn to Tucson to begin spring training. Hopes were high, with a blend of veterans and a group of newcomers who would eventually become team pillars for future manager Al Lopez. The racially diverse group included the "old man," 35-year-old, African American first baseman Luke Easter, second baseman Bobby Avila from Mexico, third baseman Al Rosen of Jewish heritage, shortstop Ray Boone, and outfielder Minnie Minoso from Havana, Cuba.

For the second year in a row, the Santa Rita Hotel refused to honor reservations for Negro players, despite having promised Veeck that in 1949 its policy would change. Indeed, Veeck had moved his camp from Florida to avoid such a situation. However, he was optimistic that in time change would take place, citing the Biltmore Hotel in Los Angeles, which changed their policy in 1949 to allow Doby, Paige, and others to stay there.

Once again, the black players stayed with the Willis family. From 1949 through 1951, this black family had as many as five players at a time residing at their modest five-room home on the west side of Tucson. Accommodations were not lavish. Luke Easter, 6'4" and weighing 220 pounds, had to shower at the ballpark facility because he couldn't fit in the family's small bathtub. Breakfast was at 7 a.m., with fruit juice, dry cereal, eggs, ham, rice and grits served by their hosts. The players left for Hi Corbett Field at 8:30 a.m. In the evening, a typical meal might be macaroni and cheese or a roast with string beans and peas. Special items included carrots for Doby, black-eyed peas for Easter, and chicken and candied yams for Wilson. Lemon pie was a favorite dessert. Paige's nervous stomach posed a special problem in food preparation; he survived on a special diet of soup and oatmeal. Hot water helped soothe his stomach. Paige blamed his problems on bad food and water ingested during his trips to South America.

The Willis family was so honored to have Paige as a guest that they slept on the back porch and gave Satchel their bedroom. The first morning, Paige bolted out of his bedroom, gave Lucille a big hug, and said he had never slept better. Lucille laughed, saying, "Satchel was so full of bull you never knew if what he was telling you was true."[43] The Willises missed the players in the early 1950s when Tucson hotels finally opened to African Americans.

Sam Lacy, reporter for the Baltimore *Afro-American*, wrote about these players at their training camp, calling them "The Tan Tribesmen." He noted the irony of black players dressing with white players in the locker room but becoming "colored" upon leaving the locker room.

The team arrived in St. Louis for their April 19 opener against the St. Louis Browns.

Seldom did the Cleveland franchise and their fans experience a more dysfunctional and topsy-turvy season. It began badly in the first game when the usual Opening Day pitcher, Bob Feller, suffered a pulled shoulder muscle injury and had to leave the game after two innings, trailing 1–0. Feller was shelved for the rest of April. The Browns went on to win 5–1 behind baby-faced Ned Garver, a potential star for a struggling franchise.

The Tribe won the next two games behind the pitching of Bob Lemon and Steve Gromek, and returned to Cleveland for their first home game as World Champions. Their opponent was the Detroit Tigers, under new manager Red Rolfe, a former stalwart third baseman for the Yankees. A large crowd of 63,725 fans greeted the Tribe, who responded by winning a thriller in extra innings, 4–3. But another glitch developed in the Tribe's efforts to repeat their winning ways. Gene Bearden went the route, winning the game, but gave a preview of wildness that was to plague him in 1949 and lead to an early retirement. The rangy knuckleballer issued five walks and uncorked three wild pitches in a game that took a little over two hours to play.

The proverbial merry month of May turned out to be anything but merry. The team started the month by winning three of four games but in the next three weeks went into the tank. In 19 days, they lost 13 of 16 games, dropping into seventh place—8½ games out of first place. Injuries slowed Feller and Lemon, who suffered a torn rib cartilage. Lemon did not win one game in May. Veeck was so disturbed that with a Veeck-like flair, he declared a second Opening Day on May 27 with typical Opening Day ceremonies. The opponent was the White Sox, and before 33,000 fans, the Tribe and castoff Al Benton coasted to a 4–0 victory. The team regrouped with impressive victories by Wynn, Paige, Bearden, and a budding star, right-hander Mike "Big Bear" Garcia.

Three off-field sidelights detracted from Cleveland's efforts to repeat as a pennant winner. At the end of May, Clevelander Charley Lupica promoted a Veeck-like publicity stunt. On May 30, Lupica, a confectioner, and a few friends stopped for a drink on their way home from work. He heard nasty remarks about his beloved Indians from patrons at a nearby table—as one might guess, they were Yankees fans. Lupica exchanged words with the offenders, who urged him and his friends to move to New York. The Yankees group continued. "If you like the Indians so much, why don't you sit on a flagpole until they get into first place?"[44]

Lupica, noted for his publicity stunts and special promotions, accepted the challenge. He erected a 60-foot pole in his neighborhood with a platform on top containing a four-by-six-foot, enclosed dwelling. He vowed not to come down until the Tribe was back on top of the standings or eliminated from the pennant race. This stunt commanded attention throughout the country. Atop his pole, he had lights, a telephone, a portable radio, a television, and a public address system—mostly donated by admirers.

The second distraction was Veeck himself. In his third anniversary as president of the Cleveland franchise, he was less than enthusiastic about the team. No doubt the impending divorce was a major factor, and the loss of Harry Grabiner added to his plight. According to Greenberg, "[Veeck] lost enthusiasm for the game, and ... wasn't able to instill the same spirit and determination into the entire organization as he had previously. He didn't show up at the ballpark as often ... put in as many hours ... didn't have the same attitude that he had ... in 1948. It ... reflected in the way the team played."[45]

The third off-field development, again with Veeck the key figure, was the unfortunate production of a movie featuring the Indians. After the exciting 1948 season, the team had been a hot news item. Veeck was approached by Republic Pictures, or vice versa, to make a movie entitled *The Kid from Cleveland*, a quintessential children's baseball movie with moralistic overtones, featuring real-life baseball heroes. The plot concerned a youth named Johnny Barrows—played by 15-year-old Rusty Tamblyn—who is rescued from delinquency when he is made batboy for the Cleveland Indians. Barrows is saved from a life of crime by sportscaster Mike Jackson—played by established movie star George Brent—who tries to straighten the teenager out by getting him the job as batboy. The "godfathers" of the movie were team members. Several players had speaking parts, particularly utility infielder Johnny Berardino— later an idol of several television soap operas. Veeck played himself, and Boudreau and Greenberg made appearances in the film to converse with Johnny and Mike.

Cleveland Press film editor Omar Ranney commented on the players' roles, suggesting, "Boudreau is no thespian. Given dialogue to speak, he has the authority of a wooden Indian, with a mechanical voice."[46] (Unfortunately for Chicago baseball fans, Boudreau's nonmelodic voice would later permeate the airways of WGN in Chicago for 30 years as color man for the Chicago Cubs.)

The filming began early in the season at League Park around nine o'clock in the morning. There was a break for lunch, and then the players showered, dressed in street clothes and reported to the Stadium a couple of hours before game time. The routine was much like being on the road every day until about the first of June. It was not only tiring but also distracting and had a negative effect on the team.

In Boudreau's opinion, "Veeck never admitted it; I've got to believe he was sorry [that] he let us go ahead with [the film], but by then it was too late to back out."[47] The film opened on September 2, 1949. It was not a good movie. Likely the most favorable review was written by Bosley Crowther, *New York Times* film critic: "The only mild salvation of this sentimental fable ... is a reasonably decent conclusion and a general intention to do some good." He continued, "Whether this purpose will be realized by the picture is questionable."[48] Boudreau and Veeck appraised the film less charitably: "I would like to buy every print ... and burn it.... [T]hat picture was a dog," said Boudreau. Veeck was more vitriolic: "I have one unwritten law at home that I adhere to: I never allow my kids to mention or see that abortion."[49]

Back on the playing field, on June 6, 1949, Veeck took unusual action with his struggling team. Frustrated with the team's lackluster season, he demanded that Boudreau bench third baseman Keltner, move himself to third, and insert young Ray Boone at shortstop. Keltner was having a dreadful season—his last one with the Tribe. The team continued to struggle for the next few weeks, unable to make a real charge for the pennant. Keltner, Boudreau and Gordon were experiencing sub-par years. Most of the power was generated by Larry Doby, who led the team with 85 RBI and 24 home runs, Dale Mitchell (.317 batting average), and first baseman Mickey Vernon with 83 RBI and 18 home runs. Soon thereafter, new faces that became the nucleus of the team were third baseman Al Rosen, Boone, second baseman Bobby Avila, and first baseman Luke Easter.

The pitching staff also faltered. Bearden ended the season winning 13 fewer games (eight) than in 1948. Early Wynn suffered from a sore arm part of the season, and Feller

"The Kid from Cleveland," a Class C movie promoted by Bill Veeck and starring George Brent. The film was a bust, and the making of it distracted and inhibited the Tribe from following up their 1948 championship. From left to right: Bill Veeck, Gordon Cobbledick of the Cleveland *Plain Dealer*, actor George Brent; Frank Gibbons of the *Cleveland Press*, and Franklin "Whitey" Lewis of the *Cleveland Press* (author's collection).

headed into the twilight of his career with a 15–14 season. The pitching staff was anchored by the steady work of Bob Lemon with his second straight 20-win season and by the surprising Garcia, who completed his first full season with the Tribe, becoming one of "The Big Four."

After a 21–9 record in July, the Tribe was poised for a last-ditch run toward a pennant. It was not to be. In early August, the Indians moved to within 2½ games of the Yankees, the closest that the team had been to first place all season. For all practical purposes, the *coup de grâce* came in mid–August in the last series of a 14-game road trip. In a four-game series against Connie Mack's Philadelphia A's, the Tribe lost three games. After the season ended, Ed McAuley of the *Cleveland News* cited this series as a turning point that had severely damaged the Indians' run for a second consecutive pennant.

Meanwhile, rumors continued to swirl about the baseball world that Veeck was actively pursuing a buyer for the Cleveland franchise. Dan Thornton , a wealthy Colorado cattleman, was rumored to be interested in the Indians, but this rumor was denied by Veeck. The same was true of a report that Hank Greenberg was going to purchase the team, which was denied by the former Tigers slugger. However, rumors continued until November.

Remember Charley Lupica, the pole sitter? After 117 days—a national pole-sitting record—Lupica gave up on September 25, 1949. While he remained in his flagpole home, his wife gave birth to their fourth child. Veeck had Lupica's flagpole home—with Lupica inside—placed on a hydraulic lift and driven across town to Municipal Stadium, where it was positioned at home plate. Charley climbed down from his perch with tears in his eyes and kissed his wife and four children. Although wobbly, he was able to navigate without the aid of three nurses and an ambulance provided by Veeck. Thirty-four thousand fans watched as Veeck rewarded Lupica's loyalty with gifts for the children, a souvenir 50-foot flagpole, bathtub, range, puppies, and a new Pontiac sedan. The Indians rewarded loyal fans and the Lupica family with a victory over Detroit.

Two days earlier, Veeck, never at a loss to create an outlandish promotion, came up with a bizarre season finale. The Tribe was now officially eliminated from the pennant race. He staged a mock burial of the 1948 American League Championship pennant prior to a night game against Detroit. The flag was tenderly laid on a horse-driven hearse, which had unexpectedly appeared on the field. Dressed in black with a top hat, Veeck climbed into the

On September 23, 1949, Indians owner Bill Veeck held a pregame burial of the 1948 pennant. Wearing a top hat, Veeck led a horse-drawn hearse and funeral procession to a grave behind center field. Manager Lou Boudreau and various players were pallbearers. The tombstone read "1948 Champs," Rudi Schaffer, the team's business manager, read the last rites from the "Bible of Baseball," *The Sporting News* (courtesy Dorn Cobbledick Collection).

driver's seat and dolefully began a funeral procession, dabbing his eyes frequently with an oversized handkerchief. He drove the horse-pulled hearse around the field, and Boudreau, his coaches and beat writers who covered the 1948 season followed.

The cortege moved to a spot just beyond the center field fence where a real casket under a cardboard tombstone bearing the inscription "1948 Champs" was lowered to the ground. As taps played, Boudreau and his coaches shoveled dirt into the shallow grave and final resting place for the flag. Traveling Secretary Rudi Schaffer read passages from *The Sporting News*—the "Bible of Baseball." Veeck topped off the stunt by wiping away imaginary tears as he rode around the field. The fans responded to this elaborate spectacle with loud cheers and applause. Fittingly, the Tribe gave the loyal followers something else to mourn, a loss to pitcher Virgil "Fire" Trucks and the Tigers, 5–0.

Cleveland finished with a rush, winning their last seven games, but it was too little, too late. The late-season heroics took a bit of the sting out of an otherwise disappointing season. This victory string carried the Tribe past Detroit into third place with a record of 89–65—eight games behind New York. The Yankees resumed their winning ways and took the pennant in dramatic fashion by defeating Boston, 5–3, on the last day of the season. The Bronx Bombers went on to defeat the Brooklyn Dodgers in five games.

As in any situation when a team does not do as well as expected, there are valid reasons and possibly even a few excuses. Certainly injuries and an aging team contributed to a poor season. Every team encounters these problems. Outside distractions, particularly the film production, did not help in the big picture. Bill Veeck was not the same energetic high flier of 1948. He was less than enthusiastic about Boudreau's management, his behavior was more volatile, and he occasionally interfered with on-field decisions. His nervous pacing in the press box during close games and acid remarks by Greenberg must have unnerved Boudreau and his players, and Veeck continued to wrestle with the fallout from his impending divorce.

Ed McAuley of the *Cleveland Press* suggested that "Boudreau's desperate juggling of his lineup gave the team a feeling of confusion and desperation."[50] Boudreau's inspirational leadership and clutch performances, so telling a force in the previous year, were missing, and he had a very unproductive year. The manager was tired, and no one in the lineup stepped up to rescue the Indians during his troubles. Combined with his personal poor efforts on the field and carping from management, the team did not live up to expectations.

There were bright spots, however. Most seasons, an 89–65 record would be quite acceptable. Attendance dropped to 2,233,000, a decrease of 400,000 fans from the previous season. Yet it was the second-best season attendance ever for the Tribe until 1995, when 2,842,000 filed into new Jacobs Field. On the pitching front, Bob Lemon excelled with 22 wins, an ERA of 2.99, and 279⅔ innings pitched. Mike Garcia came into his own with a record of 14–5 and an ERA of 2.36. His season was an omen for future outstanding seasons with the Tribe. Al Benton complemented his spectacular 2.12 ERA with ten saves, second only to Yankees fireman Joe Page according to calculations made for the Retrosheet.org website created a half-century later.

The triumvirate of Dale Mitchell, Larry Doby, and Mickey Vernon provided most of the offensive power. In the twilight of their careers, Joe Gordon and Ken Keltner saw their offensive efforts wane, although Gordon hit 20 home runs and drove in 85. Venerable Connie

Mack of the Athletics likely said it best: "There's something wrong with that ball club.... Any time such good hitters ... get in a slump and stay there all season, something is wrong."[51] Nineteen-fifty would be a new season with fresh hopes.

An unexpected bombshell struck Cleveland fans and the team in November 1949. Veeck had been receiving serious offers to buy the club, and these offers became more important to him for a reason beyond just unloading the franchise. A month earlier, Veeck had met Mary Frances Ackerman, a 28-year-old former drama student who was now a press agent for the Ice Capades, then performing in Cleveland. For Veeck, it was love at first sight. Two weeks later, he asked her to marry him when his divorce was finalized. Veeck's divorce took place soon thereafter.

The nuptials would not take place as soon as Veeck had desired, for there was an obstacle. Mary Frances was a devout Catholic and Veeck a divorced man, so her conditions for marriage demanded that he immediately begin taking appropriate Catholic instruction. In addition, she insisted they stay apart for a period of six months following his formal divorce. These demands slowed Veeck, but he came up with a plan. He contacted long-time baseball executive and devout Catholic Buzzie Bavasi for urgent assistance. "Buzzie," Veeck propositioned, "I know that you are a good Catholic, and I need a favor. I have asked Mary Frances to marry me. She agreed, provided I take six weeks of instruction in the Catholic Church. I agreed, but there is no way I can do it. Being a good Catholic, I am sure you know the Pope. Please call the Pope on my behalf and ask him if I could be excused from doing this six weeks bit."[52] Years later, Bavasi affirmed that Veeck believed this request could be granted by the Pope.

His reluctance notwithstanding, Veeck yielded to Mary's request with considerable skepticism. "He had the toughest mind I've ever encountered," recalled the Rev. George Halpin. "He was a great student of comparative religions. He never asked an ordinary question."[53] Veeck was baptized in the fall and became a member of the Catholic Church.

This unexpected turn of events meant Veeck, now acting like the person friends knew him to be, had to go into action. He had serious financial obligations from his first marriage, and soon he would likely assume the responsibility of a family again.

The team was solid, fan interest was high, and in many ways it was the right time for Veeck to sell. On November 15, 1949, Gordon Cobbledick reported in a *Plain Dealer* column that a group had unsuccessfully attempted to buy the club with the stipulation that the new owners would dispose of the Indians' African American personnel as quickly as it was convenient to do so. The *Call and Post* contacted Cobbledick for verification of this news release and pledged not to reveal the names of the men who made the statement. It made little difference because Veeck refused to sell to this group, and by the time this article ran in the *Call and Post*, new owners assured the newspaper that there would be no change in policy concerning Negro players.

On November 21, 1949, Veeck sold the Indians for $2.2 million to a group of local businessmen led by Ellis W. Ryan, a 45-year-old insurance executive. Veeck left his office with a personal gain of approximately $500,000. After paying 25 percent capital gains tax, alimony, and child support expenses, he retained approximately $375,000 to begin a new life with Mary Frances.

As expected, the city and fans reacted in several ways to the news that Veeck was leaving. *Time* magazine noted upon his departure that Veeck "had turned the crank that gave [Cleveland] its dizziest merry-go-round ride in years."[54] The stunts, entertainment, and most of all, the aura of victory that Veeck provided in Cleveland were significant contributions to the city's well-being. It was a far happier city than what he had found in 1946.

Cleveland had relished the enjoyment that comes from a winner. The Indians and their colorful front-office boss had given the city something to cheer about and the opportunity to bask once again in favorable national light. It is fair to say that the city and loyal Indians fans had never experienced such an exciting and tumultuous three years in the history of the team.

However, Veeck's sale of the team—for personal reasons—drew the ire of many fans who believed that he had deserted the city. Cobbledick attempted to allay this anger by pointing out that Veeck owned the team and had sold the franchise for his own reasons. Was that not his business? Cobbledick went on to respond to the sudden discovery of flaws in Veeck's character. He reasoned,

> His character is ... what it was in June, 1946 when he took over the operation of a sixth place club, and in October, 1948 when he was acclaimed builder of a champion. He is enthusiastic, imaginative, and energetic.... If he is not all things admirable, he approaches that ideal as closely as most of us ever do.... He woke this town up as nobody ever did before.[55]

Arthur Daley of the *New York Times* added an interesting sequel: "If we are to believe the history books, there once was a fellow named Alexander. He used to wander about in search of new worlds to conquer. Bill Veeck was not a lineal descendant of Alexander the Great but he has the same conqueror's zeal."[56]

One group not sorry to see Veeck leave Cleveland was his fellow American League owners. Cobbledick wrote, "Before Veeck joined their ranks, they had been in a comfortable rut," and added, "They never knew which way he was going to jump next and although his fantastically successful club operation has enriched them all, they wish on the whole, that he would go to Milwaukee so that they could resume their naps."[57]

After a brief respite, Veeck rejoined the ownership fraternity, first with the woeful St. Louis Browns and twice with the Chicago White Sox. Baseball owners and fans had not heard the last of William Veeck, Jr.

Mike Veeck, his son, may have defined his father best:

> Dad was ahead of his time when it came to managing people and running a business. He sought input from everyone, answered his own phones.... He took the doors off of offices ... to foster an open-door policy. Dad was among the last men to own a professional sports franchise not having made a fortune in another business. The creative financing he put together to purchase teams was legendary.[58]

When Veeck died in 1986, the family had him cremated so that he wouldn't constantly be rolling over in his grave. They believed that with the way contemporary baseball operated, he would never get any rest. The last line on Veeck's plaque in the Hall of Fame reads, "Veeck was a champion of the little guy," a wonderful legacy for one of baseball's great icons.

With the departure of Veeck, the baseball scene in Cleveland took on a different look. The team's new owners, led by Ryan, appointed Hank Greenberg, a significant stockholder, vice president and general manager. This changing of the guard was of considerable concern to manager Boudreau, who had one more year on his contract. Ryan was quoted as saying, "I understand Boudreau has another year to go on his contract."[59] Period! Boudreau knew he was under the gun now that Greenberg was in control.

From the time Greenberg joined Veeck in late 1947, Boudreau felt that Greenberg did not appreciate his managerial ability. Boudreau had great admiration for Greenberg as a player but did not consider him a close friend. He also knew Greenberg had great respect for veteran catcher Al Lopez, who was on the Indians' roster in 1947. Veeck and Greenberg helped Lopez obtain a managing position with the Triple-A Indianapolis Indians of the America Association, a Pittsburgh Pirates farm team. Lopez's team won 100 games and the pennant in 1948 and finished second with a 93–61 record in 1949. The future Hall of Famer was waiting in the wings for a major league manager's position.

Boudreau felt the pressure, but was motivated by the challenges the 1950 season offered. He encountered a number of coaching changes, losing Bill McKechnie to retirement—temporarily—and Steve O'Neill, also to retirement (he then changed his mind to manage the Boston Red Sox.) Boudreau picked up good friends Oscar Melillo and Muddy Ruel, kept Mel Harder, and added Al Simmons.

Boudreau believed he would have a competitive team with a pitching staff which featured the "Big Four": Feller, Lemon, Wynn and newcomer Mike Garcia. Unfortunately, the pitching rotation did not reach the team's winning expectations. Feller had another subpar year, winning 10 and losing 11. Garcia finished with an 11–11 record, and Wynn suffered an early injury before compiling an 18–11 record.

Greenberg wasted little time in making personnel changes. The most hurtful to Boudreau was the release of Ken Keltner, who had spent most of his tenure with Boudreau and had had an outstanding career. There was little doubt that the third baseman was over the hill after hitting .237 the previous season. Greenberg knew that Al Rosen was ready to fill Keltner's position. Fans rode Greenberg for bringing up a young rookie Jewish player to replace a "nice" Catholic veteran.

It is likely that had Veeck remained the owner, he would have tolerated Satchel Paige for his drawing power at the gate. However, Paige became a liability to the team after Veeck departed. Greenberg thought differently about keeping Paige, for a valid reason. He released Paige for his "complete disrespect for training and for train time and game time."[60] Greenberg liked Paige, thought he was a good man, but believed his behavior on the team had deteriorated to the point that there was one set of rules for Paige and another for the rest of the team. For example, Paige was late for practices and would occasionally show up just in time for the start of the game. The players liked Paige, but taciturn Greenberg could not tolerate such behavior. Years later, Greenberg explained that dumping Paige might have been shortsighted. He implied that management may not have realized and appreciated that Paige was an unusual and outstanding performer who had pitched too many years in the Negro Leagues to be considered a rookie.

The *Call and Post* was pleased that Paige was not returning, headlining a story, "Paige release may [give] Minoso better chance."[61] Orestes "Minnie" Minoso was a promising young Cuban player who had narrowly missed making the 1949 team. Though not African American, Minoso was often grouped with black players. He had great potential, but in 1951, in one of the Tribe's poorer trades, he was shipped to Chicago after playing only 17 games for Cleveland. The speedster compiled an illustrious 17-season career, returning to Cleveland in 1957–1958 and batting .302 in each season.

At first, Rosen was unpopular and fans let him know it. Greenberg told Rosen to "not ... pay any attention to the bigots, just play to his ability and ignore the bums."[62] Rosen had a terrible temper and often wanted to go into the stands and beat up fans when they taunted him about being Jewish. As the season progressed, however, he controlled his temper reasonably well and ultimately won the fans over with his bat.

Greenberg left little doubt among Tribe players that he planned to be a hardheaded general manager, particularly with respect to salary negotiations. Bearden had little respect for the new general manager, and the two clashed early on. "I didn't like Greenberg worth a damn," he later said, "because of the way he treated everybody." Prior to his eventual release by the Tribe that season, Bearden told Greenberg he "ought to learn how to treat people. That was it ... a clash of personalities, between him and me."[63]

Greenberg continued to revamp the Indians, piece by piece. He knew that Joe Gordon was nearly finished with his career. Boudreau inserted the next Indians second baseman, Bobby Avila from Veracruz, Mexico, into the lineup. Avila became a solid second baseman for the Tribe the following eight years. Gordon, a true professional, retired and was elected to the Hall of Fame posthumously in 2009.

Luke Easter replaced Paige on the Cleveland roster and became the Indians' regular first baseman in 1950. An old rookie at the age of 35, he was the target of abuse by fans when he arrived on the scene in 1949. Luscious Luke, six foot, five inches and weighing 240 pounds, changed the fickle fans' attitude in 1950. A genuinely nice guy, he soon became a fan favorite. According to Boudreau, on June 23, 1950, Easter hit one of the longest home runs ever at Municipal Stadium. The ball flew 477 feet into the upper deck of the right field stands. He gave the franchise three great seasons before reaching his 40th birthday, recording 86 home runs and 307 RBIs.

In a continual effort to strengthen the team, Greenberg made one of his worst trades. One day before the trading deadline (June 15, 1950), he shipped Mickey Vernon back to Washington in exchange for relief pitcher Dick Weik. Weik won one game and lost three in his short stay, whereas Vernon played nine more years, claiming the American League batting championship in 1953, depriving Al Rosen of the Triple Crown.

Boudreau felt good about the player changes that had been made when the 1950 season began. The team started slowly but climbed into third place by mid–June. The competition was strong as always, with the Detroit Tigers joining the Red Sox and Yankees in the race for the pennant. Cleveland stayed in third place until the end of August. Then late in September the Red Sox overtook the Tribe, who finished in fourth place only six games out of first place.

The Tribe finished with a 92–62 record, nominally considered a successful season. Boudreau commented: "We did it with a young team that would be a contender for the next several years."[64] But after the Clevelanders dropped into fourth place and lost four straight games to the lowly St. Louis Browns in early September, Greenberg saw things differently.

He publicly criticized the manager and the team, saying, "We may lose the flag in 1951, but not with this team."[65]

Several players excelled. In his first season with the Tribe, Al Rosen led the league in home runs (37) and drove in 116 runs. Luke Easter had been called the "Negro Babe Ruth" in 1949 when he hit 25 home runs in 80 games in the Pacific Coast League. He resumed his assault in 1950 with 28 homers and 107 RBI. Doby continued his steady play, hitting 25 round-trippers and driving in 102 runs. Bob Lemon posted a Cy Young–like season, leading the league in wins (23), strikeouts (170), and innings pitched (288). Wynn added 18 wins, followed by Feller with 16. Most disappointing, however, was the drop in attendance, 500,000 fewer than in 1949, culminating in a decline of approximately 900,000 in the two seasons since the record-breaking 1948 season.

During the season, the relationship between the manager and Greenberg became strained. Every morning, Greenberg would meet with Boudreau to go through an exhaustive replay of the previous day's game. After the 1950 season ended, Boudreau went back to his home in Harvey without a decision concerning his managerial future.

Greenberg indicated that he wanted to re-sign him at the same contract he had for the 1949 and 1950 seasons ($62,000). The media thought Boudreau would be back. Owner Ellis Ryan and Greenberg ducked questions about Boudreau's status. Harry Jones of the *Plain Dealer* reported that the salary issue was "the only cause of delay" in re-signing Boudreau.[66]

On November 7, Cobbledick wrote in the *Plain Dealer*, a fan asked Greenberg if he would go ahead and complete a [player] deal without consulting the Indians' 1951 manager. "Oh, no," Greenberg replied, "I certainly won't complete any trades until I've talked them over with Lou."[67] Cobbledick concluded that this remark meant that Boudreau would be at the old stand next spring.

A formal notice came three day later. On the morning of November 10, Greenberg called a press conference: "Gentlemen, here's your next manager of the Indians," and Al Lopez walked through the door. Greenberg went on to report, "We knew we had a man as manager who was probably the most popular player in the history of the Cleveland Baseball Club.... [F]or a month we have been working diligently to get Lou a manager's job.... [W]e learned of one club that was interested and I think he will have a job in the major leagues."[68]

Meanwhile Boudreau received a call from owner Ellis Ryan that Cleveland management was going to make a change. Boudreau was surprised and disappointed since he had always wanted to end his career as a bench manager for the Tribe. It was hard for him to think that he would no longer be a member of the only team he had played for, the Cleveland Indians. He asked Ryan, "Haven't you even considered me as a player?" Ryan responded, "We hadn't thought of that. Let me talk it over with Hank, will you? I'll call you right back."[69]

After talking it over with Della, Boudreau called Ryan to say he had changed his mind. He realized that he didn't want to play under another Cleveland manager and would be better off with another team.[70] Boudreau requested and received his unconditional release.

Under other circumstances, Ryan might well have refused to give Boudreau his release. Boudreau's services as a ballplayer still had value; under baseball law at that time, his services were reserved to the Cleveland club and could be disposed of only by a trade or outright sale. From the standpoint of good public relations, however, and in view of the manner in which the Indians had dismissed Boudreau after his long years of service, conditions made it virtually impossible for the ownership to treat him in any other way.

After nine years as manager for Cleveland, Boudreau signed with the Boston Red Sox for the 1951 season, batting .267 and driving in 47 runs in 82 games. In 1952, he returned to managing with the Red Sox for three years, the Kansas City A's for three years, and the Chicago Cubs for one year. Boudreau managed 16 years, and his composite record was 1162 victories and 1,224 losses for a .487 percentage.[71]

From an ownership standpoint, Boudreau's 16 years as a major league manager are marginal in evaluating success and failure. Since 1900, of 30 managers who managed 17 or more years, only five completed their managerial tenure with a winning percentage lower than Boudreau's.[72] His nine-year managerial record with the Indians was a respectable 728–649 for a winning percentage of .529. Unfortunately, Boudreau finished above fourth place only three times. These figures do not denigrate his triumph in the great world championship of 1948—one of only two in the 114-year history of the Cleveland franchise.

Conversely, fans and the press saw Boudreau display his on-field magic and team leadership season after season during the glory years. Many Indians fans may argue, and rightly so, that Omar Vizquel was a better fielder than Boudreau. The difference was, as Terry Pluto wrote, "Vizquel could never be a player-manager in the 1990s. The game is too complex, the egos too much for one man to handle." Or as Pluto's father said, "There probably will never be another Lou Boudreau."[73] The Boudreau-Veeck era faded into the twilight and fans awaited the Greenberg-Lopez era about to unfold behind the scenes.

13

An Indians Summer, Then
Forty Years of Winter

"I wanted to be defined. I wanted people to know I was a Jew.
My Jewish pride increased as time went on"—Al Rosen,
from Larry Ruthman's *American Jews and America's Game*

More than 60 years later, one might speculate why Lou Boudreau was fired after the 1950 season, in which the Indians had compiled a 92–62 record. There were two reasons: The Indians had finished in fourth rather than second place, and general manager Hank Greenberg had wanted a new manager. Excluding the years covered in this final chapter (1951–1955), not one Tribe team in the next 40 years matched Boudreau's 1950 record. Lou Boudreau, the longest serving manager in Tribe history, was gone. The Cleveland franchise was now owned by the "Big Seven," a group of powerful businessmen, longtime residents of greater Cleveland, with political connections but little acumen about the management of a baseball franchise. Not one was a Bill Veeck.

Nate Dolan, manager of the Cleveland Arena, was the brains behind the purchase of the team from Veeck.[1] The new owners selected 45-year-old Ellis Ryan, who had inherited his father's long-established insurance company, to serve as president of the club. A well-dressed individual, Ryan was a far cry from the sport-shirt, no-tie, exuberant William Veeck. Seemingly, the owners had made a wise choice in selecting future Hall of Famer Hank Greenberg as general manager, for he had served a two-year apprenticeship under Veeck. Waiting in the wings to become manager was Al Lopez, a longtime catcher in the major leagues and a successful manager of the Indianapolis Indians. His forte was working with a pitching staff, of which Cleveland had one of the best.

When Greenberg returned from the service in 1945 after having served twice in World War II, he became disillusioned with major league baseball. He had alienated himself from Tigers owner Walter O. Briggs, the press, a segment of fans, and *The Sporting News*. And there was a steady current of anti–Semitism.[2] After leading the American League in home runs (44) and RBI (127) in 1946, Greenberg was unceremoniously released to the Pittsburgh Pirates for the standard $10,000 waiver price.

When Greenberg joined Pittsburgh, competitively inferior to Detroit, he played first base, though not well. On one occasion, when Jim Bagby, Jr., a former Tribe pitcher, was pitching, Rip Sewell of the Pirates reported, "When the batter hit the ball, it was an easy play. Bagby ran over to cover first and the ball went through Greenberg's legs. So Bagby right there said, 'Hey, you big Jew son-of-a bitch, you make enough money to catch that kind of ball.' Greenberg responded, 'I'm going to kill you after this game is over.' Bagby was taken out of the game, and he went into the locker room.... He put on his tennis shoes." The Pirates had just built a new men's room in the clubhouse and it had a tile floor. When the game ended, Greenberg stormed into the men's room, where Bagby was waiting for him. Greenberg recounted, "I forgot to take my spikes off, so when I went to swing ... my feet flew out from under me and just at that time [Bagby] punched me in the eye, and I came out of it with a black eye. The players separated us and that was the end of that, so I guess I lost that one."[3]

Late in 1947, Greenberg joined Veeck in a congenial matchup of opposites working together. In 1948, Veeck gave him additional duties as farm director, and in 1950, the new ownership appointed Greenberg general manager. Now he was ready to test what he had learned under Veeck. While on the "hot seat," Greenberg had been, in contrast to Veeck, serious and abrasive. Some had called him arrogant. A Jewish person in baseball, not unlike a black person, was subject to verbal abuse and ridicule. Greenberg knew what he faced. "I started off my role as general manager with more or less two strikes against me, so it was fortunate that we had a pretty good team." He had to work with new management who had no experience in baseball and who, after watching their new team for two or three weeks, thought they knew all about the game and tended to second-guess the manager and the players.[4]

Not long after Greenberg had, for all practical purposes, contrived to remove Boudreau, one of the most popular players in Cleveland history, from his managership, he was confronted with another tough decision. Popular third baseman Ken Keltner was slowing to the point that Greenberg had ordered Boudreau to cut him at the termination of spring training in 1950, a move highly unpopular with Cleveland fans.[5] To add insult to injury, Keltner's replacement was 26-year-old Al Rosen, who was Jewish. Now Cleveland had two prominent Jews holding important positions with the franchise. The working class and conservatives in Cleveland did not appreciate a Jew replacing a Catholic at the hot corner.

The *Akron Beacon Journal*'s noted reporter Jim Schlemmer cast slurs on Greenberg's being Jewish. On Opening Day in 1950, when the public address announcer stated that Rosen would play third base, many of the 65,744 Cleveland faithful shouted, "We want Keltner!" It was for naught. The fans targeted Rosen with their unhappiness but saved their derision for the general manager.[6] "The newspapers started picking on me," Greenberg later wrote. "Every time the writers had a chance to jab me or the club in the press, they did so."[7]

Rosen, like Greenberg, was destined to be controversial but soon made fans forget Keltner. Rosen was born in Spartanburg, South Carolina, and grew up in Miami, where he boxed, played football, and pitched for a softball team. His passion, however, was baseball, and the Red Sox offered him a tryout and sent him to a farm team in Virginia. Manager Elmer Yoter, a one-time Chicago Cubs infielder, who was unimpressed with the 18-year-old, told him to "get a lunch pail and go on home."[8] But a local YMCA director took pity on him and told Rosen that a friend of his in Thomasville, North Carolina, needed a third baseman. Rosen took the five-hour bus ride to Thomasville and signed a contract for $90 a month. His first time at bat, he singled, and it was soon recognized that Rosen had major league potential.[9] At the end of the season, Rosen enlisted in the Navy, earning the rank of lieutenant. When he was discharged in 1946, Rosen—now property of the Tribe—advanced through the Cleveland farm system. He had cups of coffee with Cleveland in 1947 and 1948, playing seven games with the parent club the first year and five games a year later.

Rosen was confident, observant and quick tempered. He was not reluctant to go into the stands and attack somebody who had taunted him about being a Jew. The budding star had put up with the sting of anti–Semitic barbs during his time in the minors. Realizing that Greenberg had endured worse and had survived, he planned to do the same. Greenberg was everything he aspired to be, so he listened intently when the general manager told him to ignore the bigots and play to the best of his ability.[10]

Although Greenberg was chastised for having released Boudreau as manager, he regained credibility with the hiring of Al "El Señor" Lopez as Cleveland's new manager. Both Veeck and Greenberg had wanted Lopez to manage the Indians in 1948 had the Boudreau–Vern Stephens trade been consummated. Even Greenberg's harshest critics conceded that Lopez was a good choice.[11]

As a teenager in Tampa, Lopez earned five dollars a week catching for Walter Johnson of the Washington Senators during spring training. He enjoyed 19 years in the major leagues, then went on to manage for three years with the Indianapolis Indians, then a Pittsburgh Pirates farm team, finishing first once and second twice. Lopez, due to his catching experience, was the perfect fit to work with Cleveland's pitching staff.[12]

Lopez was quiet and professional. "He never said much, but he knew every damned thing that was going on," outfielder Al Smith later remarked. "He rarely called clubhouse meetings because he thought they were a waste of time." Because he was plagued with an excessive number of injuries during his six-year tenure as manager of the Tribe, he reminded players, "Look, if I put your name in the lineup, I expect 100 percent effort. If you can't give that to me, all you have to do is tell me that you're not able to play that day."[13]

Lopez was what one might call a "laid back" type of manager. He had known many of the older players when he had been player-coach with the Indians in 1947. The new manager knew he could not "buddy-buddy" with these players. "I wasn't tough, but I think everyone respected me." He set a curfew and told his players that if they could not make it back in time, to call him or one of the coaches.[14] David Hoskins, a minor league outfielder, transferred to the mound. Lopez said he fined Hoskins, "one of the nicest guys you'd want to meet, $200 for missing a train. I gave it back to him when the season ended because he never screwed up again."[15]

The truth of the matter, for all his success managing the Indians, was that Lopez disliked managing: "Hell no," he snapped when a reporter asked him if managing was fun.[16] He suffered from chronic insomnia and after night games often read Westerns or detective stories until he dozed off at 4:00 in the morning. The tense Yankees-Indians pennant races were miserable on his stomach, and doctors warned him to avoid raw foods and ice cream at night. Lopez took defeat hard. "There's only one thing worse than losing a game," said Bob Lemon, "and that's watching Al sit ... in the dugout and stare at his toes after you've lost one."[17]

Lopez's outstanding playing and managing record led to his election to the Hall of Fame in 1977.

Under the direction of strong-minded Greenberg, the Indians presented a different face in 1951 from the dramatic team of 1948. This team relied on more offensive power and a well-established pitching staff. The "Big Four" featured Bob Feller, Bob Lemon, Early Wynn—all in the Hall of Fame—and a developing Mike "Big Bear" Garcia. The club started out fast and played well for the first two weeks. On April 30, Greenberg made one of his few unfortunate trades, shipping Orestes "Minnie" Minoso, the key figure in this three-team trade, to the White Sox along with pitcher Sam Zoldak, and sending catcher Ray Murray to the Athletics. Greenberg received pitcher Lou Brissie and outfielder Paul Lehner from the Athletics, and the Athletics received Gus Zernial and Dave Philley from Chicago.

Before the trade of Minoso, Cleveland had four black players. Reporters wondered whether Cleveland had settled on a quota of black players, hence the need to reduce the number to three. To that date, no major league team had had four blacks on their team at one time. Lopez later denied the existence of a quota on the Cleveland team. According to Joseph Moore, Larry Doby's biographer, Doby and others had become convinced that either Minoso or Harry "Suitcase" Simpson, another black, would be traded or released. "We heard," Doby said, "that Greenberg had made a choice.... He kept Simpson because he was a long ball hitter, which fit into Greenberg's pattern of thinking."[18]

After the deal was completed, Greenberg mystified everyone and proved prophetic when he predicted that Minoso would become "one of the really good players of our time."[19] Minoso went on to hit .326 in 1951, better than any player on the Indians. He led the league in triples (14) and stolen bases (31). Simpson, who remained with Cleveland, batted only .229 and recorded 24 RBI.

In early May, Cleveland slumped and dropped to sixth place before fighting back to regain the league lead on August 12. In July, fans were treated to Bob Feller's third and last no-hitter, a 2–1 victory over Detroit. Eleven days later on July 12, 39,195 fans visited Municipal Stadium to see if Feller could duplicate his feat. They saw a no-hitter, but it was Yankees pitcher Allie Reynolds, not Feller, who twirled a no-hitter, winning 1–0.[20]

During August, the Tribe won 13 straight games—a club record. On August 23, the Indians, with a 78–43 record and three-game lead over Casey Stengel and the Yankees, looked to have a fighting chance for another pennant. However, looks can be deceiving with respect to the Bronx Bombers. On September 15, Cleveland led the New Yorkers by one game, but the season suddenly turned around—in the wrong direction. On September 16, the opener of a two-game series, Allie Reynolds, former Indians teammate, bested Bob Feller and the Tribe, 5–1. The following day, Eddie Lopat, the Indians' nemesis, did it again, beating Bob Lemon, 2–1. The Indians dropped eight of their last 11 games, while New York won nine of 12, and the Yankees captured their third straight pennant and 18th in 31 years.

No one was more disappointed than Lopez and Greenberg, who believed the Indians should have won the pennant. It was easy to ascertain the cause of the failure: anemic hitting. The collective batting average for the team was .256, second lowest in the league. Al Rosen did not measure up to his outstanding performance in 1950. Luke Easter suffered from aching knees and an overflow of advice from well-meaning teammates. His stats were fine for only 128 games, with 27 homeruns and 103 RBI. Larry Doby also failed to match his 1950 performance.

There were mutterings that Doby had cost the Indians with his poor showing in the final weeks of play. In fact, it was no secret that Doby had suffered many of the injustices endured by the black pioneers in the major leagues. For one thing, several Cleveland writers expected more of him than might have been possible. Secondly, sports writers often wrote to shock their readers, or displayed bias or exaggerated because it was their duty or style.

For example, Franklin Lewis wrote in October 1951 about Doby's end-of-season slump. "He heard trade rumors. Already wearing the shield of the Negro on his nameplate, he [then] withdrew further into his mental dungeon." He added, "Larry Doby, impassionable as to his color, was a thousand-fold pierced by the awful thought that his co-workers might not accept him ever, competitively. He has been hurt physically. Now he was wounded in his mind."[21]

Gordon Cobbledick of the *Plain Dealer* added fuel to the criticism of Doby when he wrote to the nationwide readership of *Sport* magazine about Doby's statistics in 1951: "For a guy named Joe ... would have been a fair enough performance. For a candidate for immortality, [the statistics] leave much to be desired." Cobbledick added, "A succession of crippling injuries ... explained Doby's decline in part. Behind ... his physical troubles, increasing evidence of mental and emotional confusion, Larry's a mixed up guy—a badly mixed-up guy."[22]

These were strong words but not uncommon among sports writers competing for readership in a metropolitan setting. Joseph Moore wrote that some of Cobbledick's judgments were correct. Doby was not a gregarious individual. He did not drink or play cards, two of the major pastimes of his teammates. He preferred the company of Helyn, his wife, his two-year old daughter, and friends not associated with baseball.

But Doby rejected Cobbledick's description of him as a loner. "I think the word 'loner' is an unfair word to describe anybody. I needed my privacy to deal with some of the insults that were directed to me because of my race." He added, "That's how I handled the insults, in private. If I had stayed in the clubhouse and spoken about my feelings, I think the writer would have called me 'militant.' I feel that they had me in a no-win situation."[23]

Regardless of the brash reaction of local sports writers, certainly Doby faced many challenges, much like Jackie Robinson. He was more of an introvert than Robinson or Easter, though he mellowed as the years went by. Russ Schneider, who covered the Indians for many years, had Doby and his family to his home several times. He found him to be a most congenial and personable individual.[24]

The first three black players to succeed in the major leagues were Robinson, Doby, and Paige (and Campanella soon thereafter). Cobbledick, who occasionally received letters addressed "Nigger Lover," later wrote:

> Each of them met the inevitable problems in a manner determined by his background and temperament. Discrimination, or the bare suspicion, angered Robinson. It wounded Doby. To the philosophical Paige, it was one of the inescapable facts of life and he accepted it with a shrug.[25]

Cleveland's pitching was the best in the league, led by the first triumvirate of 20-game winners in the American league—Bob Feller, Early Wynn, and Mike Garcia—since the Philadelphia Athletics in 1931. Rube Walberg, Lefty Grove and George Earnshaw won 72 games, led by Grove's 31–4 record. These three Tribe pitchers combined for 62 victories. Lemon, for the first of only two times in his productive career, failed to win 20 games. Feller, the American League's leader in victories (22), was named the American League "Pitcher of the Year" by *The Sporting News*. He finished fifth—one position below deposed Minnie Minoso—for the Most Valuable Player Award, won by Yogi Berra of the Yankees.

Despite the Indians' tumble at the end of the season, the team continued to hold steady at the gate, drawing 1,704,000 fans—only 23,000 fewer than in 1950. The 1951 season would be the last attendance over 1.5 million fans until 1993, the beginning of the Jacobs Field-Hart-Hargrove era.

At the conclusion of the 1951 season, President Ellis Ryan, pleased with Greenberg's leadership, gave him a two-year contract. Gordon Cobbledick supported Greenberg's retention, in spite of negative reactions of the press and fans. In 1951, the Indians had finished in second place with nearly the same personnel that had finished in fourth in 1950. Cobbledick gave his opinion:

> If I have assessed accurately the temper of the public, this opinion won't win any popularity prize but I believe ... Greenberg has done exactly what Ryan said he has done—an excellent job. No swivel-chaired stuffed shirt, High Henry works harder at his job than any other man in baseball except the one who invented hard work, Bill Veeck. It'll pay off. Just wait and see.[26]

Cobbledick's words were prophetic. Certainly, until the Hart-Hargrove era, no Tribe manager compiled a better record than the "Señor." Pundits have often called the early 1950s the "Golden Era" of Cleveland baseball.

From his tutoring with Veeck, Greenberg realized that for Cleveland to remain near the top of the standings, management must aggressively search out black players with the potential to play in the major leagues. Greenberg added outfielder Al Smith, pitcher Dave Hoskins, and Minnie Minoso, a 23-year-old Cuban.

By 1950, the Brooklyn Dodgers and New York Giants, along with Cleveland, had successfully integrated their teams. According to historian Jules Tygiel, "The Dodgers and Indians [led all teams] in selecting Negro talent in a non-competitive market."[27] During Greenberg's reign, Cleveland continued to sign black players. A prized recruit was mammoth Luscious Luke Easter, six foot four and one-half inches tall and 240 pounds. Veeck kept track of Easter when he played semi-pro in Puerto Rico after World War II. From 1946 to 1948, the prodigious slugger hit home runs for the St. Louis Giants, Cincinnati Crescents, and Homestead Grays. Easter was tagged as the "Black Babe Ruth."

His reputation secured his purchase by the Indians from the Grays for $8,000 and in 80 games in 1949 with the Triple-A San Diego Padres, he batted .363 with 25 home runs and 92 RBI. Easter was promoted to Cleveland in late August and appeared in 21 games for the remainder of the season. He failed to hit any home runs.[28]

As the 1949 season ended, an increasingly troublesome issue triggered headlines. A dispute broke out in print between the sports editors of two African American newspapers. Wendell Smith of the Pittsburgh *Courier* wrote a column entitled: "What's Happening in Cleveland?" The noted editor stated that not only had city officials tried to double Veeck's rent of Municipal Stadium and provided insufficient police protection for the team's

big crowds, but the so-called "politicians in the city led a campaign against Veeck for employ-
ing too many black ballplayers." Through devious means, influential individuals organized
a gang of hoodlums to harass Larry Doby, Satchel Paige, and Luke Easter. Smith decried
that Cleveland did not deserve a man of Veeck's integrity, and accused the people of Cleveland of being a "sheepish, shiftless, and ungrateful lot."[29]

John Fuster of the Cleveland *Call and Post* responded with an expletive response. He
stated that Smith's column had not appeared in the Cleveland edition of the *Courier* because
local readers would know that the article's claims were false. "As one of those more than one
million Clevelanders whom Mr. Smith has glibly called 'lazy and placid' one of those more
than 2,000,000 Clevelanders who last year paid their way into the Cleveland Stadium to
cheer ... the Indians on to the 1948 World's Championship, I resent Mr. Smith's uncalled
for, vicious, and locally untrue statements."

Fuster noted that when Larry Doby made a magnificent catch against the Chicago
White Sox, he received the greatest ovation Fuster had ever heard at the stadium; that all
the Indians players, white or black, were booed at one time or another, with the single exception of Satchel Paige. And as far as Smith's home team was concerned, the Pittsburgh Pirates
had yet to sign a black player.

According to Paul Dickson, author of *Bill Veeck, Baseball's Greatest Maverick*, this
exchange between two black editors was puzzling, shedding more heat than light on the
racial issue in Cleveland. He quotes Stephanie M. Liscio, author of *Integrating Cleveland
Baseball: Media Activism, the Integration of the Indians and the Demise of the Negro League
Buckeyes*, who concluded that the truth may lie somewhere in the middle. Liscio concluded
that the *Call and Post* was extremely reserved in its coverage of racial matters and tended
to shy away from anything that worked against racial harmony. She added that the *Courier*
was much more of a warts-and-all paper. That said, Liscio suggested that there were probably
no organized gangs of hoodlums enticed by politicians but there were fans who were particularly rough on black players, especially Luke Easter.

In 1952, the Cleveland pitchers once again dominated the American League, but, alas,
whatever they accomplished was not enough. For the fourth straight year, the Yankees prevailed in one of the American League's closest and most exciting pennant races. The Tribe
started in grand fashion, winning their first seven games. Two nights later, Feller and the St.
Louis Brown's Bob Cain tangled in an epic pitching duel, a double one-hitter—the 11th and
next to last one for Feller. The contest was the lowest-hit game in the 52-year history of the
American League. Cain won the game, 1–0; however, Luke Easter's single in the fifth inning
spoiled his no-hitter.

The Clevelanders moved into first place in May and held that position for three weeks.
From that point, the American League pennant race was a roller-coaster ride until the end
of the season. At the All-Star break, only 6½ games separated the top five teams, and by the
final week in August, four teams—New York, Chicago, Cleveland, and Boston—remained
in the race, with the Senators dropping out.

On July 22, the Yankees swept a doubleheader at Municipal Stadium, besting Feller
and Steve Gromek, 7–3 and 8–1. The Tribe fought back to beat the New Yorkers the next
two days, 7–3 and 4–2, behind the pitching of Bob Lemon and Mike Garcia. On August

22 their Tribe's hopes rose as they overtook New York by a margin of .001 when Garcia, with the help of Lemon, beat the Yankees 6–4. After Early Wynn lost, 1–0, to Vic Raschi the next day, despite the Tribe going 24–9 for the rest of the season, the best they could do was climb into a tie with the Yankees on September 11—but only for a day. Cleveland lost to Boston and then met the Yankees for the last time.

Throughout the history of great games between New York and Cleveland during the early 1950s, three Yankees pitchers were poison to the Tribe, namely Allie Reynolds, Vic Raschi, and in particular Eddie Lopat. As expected, Lopat faced the Indians on September 14. The "Indian killer," as Lopat was called, outpitched Mike Garcia and the Indians to win, 7–1. The Yankees were now two games ahead of the Tribe and they held that lead until the end of the season. The game attracted 73,608 fans to Municipal Stadium, the largest major league crowd of the season. Lopat's victory raised his nine-year record against Cleveland to 35–9.[30]

The Indians' erratic defense hampered their pennant efforts. Attendance continued to drop, with 1,444,000 fans attending during the 1952 season, a decrease of 260,000 from the year before. Again, Cleveland had the 20-game winners: Early Wynn (23), Bob Lemon (22), and Mike Garcia (22). Feller did not join the threesome, however, posting the worst record of his career, 9–13, and there were whispers that Feller was nearly ready to call it quits.

Another disappointment in the early season was Luke Easter. His batting average dropped to .208, and on June 30, he was sent to Triple-A Indianapolis. After two weeks, he was recalled and hit .319, with 20 home runs and 64 RBI for the rest of the season. On the positive side, Larry Doby led the American League with 32 home runs, followed by Easter with 31. Al Rosen rebounded from an off year to lead the American League in RBI (105), followed by Doby (104).

During the winter of 1952-1953, unrest permeated the wigwam. Two straight second-place finishes, particularly to the hated Yankees, left fans, stockholders, and the front office chagrined, and Greenberg and President Ellis Ryan absorbed the brunt of this displeasure—Greenberg suffering poor relations with the press as well. Bob August of the *Cleveland Press* suggested that animosity toward Greenberg, particularly from Franklin Lewis and Gordon Cobbledick, had emanated from two issues. First, Greenberg seemed to be arrogant, and second, he dismissed out of hand almost all criticism from journalists.

After all, Greenberg had been a great home-run hitter, had almost broken Babe Ruth's single season record, and would be elected into the Hall of Fame in 1956. But his attitude of "what do those guys know about the game?" was not uncommon among former major leaguers who had advanced into management. August had reason to believe that Greenberg's wife Carol, a member of the Gimbel family, had been less than cordial to several reporters, including Lewis and Cobbledick, at several social events.[31]

The press excoriated Greenberg for his mistakes and prickly manner. Whitey Lewis, the *Cleveland Press* sports editor, was especially hard on Greenberg, relentlessly second-guessing and criticizing him, and at some point, Greenberg questioned whether Lewis had ambitions for his job, an unlikely possibility. Of course, no one can accurately ascertain how many in the press disdained Greenberg because he was Jewish. He was not, in fact, treated very well by even his fellow franchise owners. Greenberg lashed back, lambasting Lewis for irresponsible stories about the Tribe. But the damage had been done by Lewis and other members of the press, and their constant criticism was beginning to turn fans against him.[32] To add to Greenberg's troubles, in a scenario not unlike that of Veeck's own failed marriage, his wife was threatening to file for divorce.

In addition, there was conflict between Ellis Ryan and his associates in the board room. By 1952, Ryan had become more involved in the day-to-day operations of the franchise and several times had indicated his intention to remove Greenberg from his responsibilities. His involvement divided the board of directors and divided Greenberg's supporters from his.

One newspaper account quoted a director as having said anonymously, "The big thing wrong with Ellis [Ryan] is that he can't make up his mind as to what he wants to do."[33] A meeting of the stockholders in December 1952, brought the rift into the open. Ryan was unable to muster a majority of the 3,000 voting shares, resigned his position, and sold his 551 shares to the opposition group. He had purchased the shares at $100 per share: three years later, he sold them for $600 per share, the transaction netting over $250,000.[34]

Myron H. "Mike" Wilson was elected the next president, although he owned only 100 shares—approximately three percent of the total. Still, he was the key figure in Greenberg's retention as general manager, and when the fight for control of the franchise developed, he had considerable influence over other board members, casting the deciding vote that had led to Ryan's resignation. Restructuring of the ownership meant Greenberg had received a vote of confidence and authority over player personnel.

Another controversy developed in Greenberg's contract negotiations with Rosen and Doby. In 1950, 16 percent of Cleveland's population of 915,000 was black, somewhat above the national average.[35] The white majority did not want to see blacks taking jobs from whites, either in the factories or on the ball field. Not to be deterred, Greenberg continued the practice, initiated by Veeck, of signing capable black players. At a time when other teams resisted integration or signed only a token black or two, Greenberg had no quota. Fans blamed that policy for Cleveland's failure to topple the Yankees. "We have five of them," the fans said. "That's three too many." Fans wrote letters of protest, but Greenberg noted, "The only time fans complain is when the Negroes aren't delivering."[36] On a road trip with the team in late 1955, Greenberg discovered that the Lord Baltimore Hotel in Baltimore would not allow Cleveland's five black players to stay there. The same was true in St. Louis and Washington. And so, in 1956, the general manager instructed traveling secretary Spud Goldstein to find only hotels that accommodated the entire team—with no exceptions. Greenberg blazed the trail, and according to Stephen Norwood and Harold Brackman, "His determination in the front office to promote desegregation was undoubtedly influenced by the anti–Semitism he experienced in baseball."[37]

For all of Greenberg's compassion and open-mindedness in race relations, however, he did not soften his negotiations with his players—white, brown, or black. In 1952, after Doby had slumped to .295 from .326 the year before and his RBI total had dropped from 102 to 69, Greenberg sent him a contract for $19,000, representing a $6,000 pay cut. Doby thought it was a joke, but Greenberg said he was serious. Doby finally signed, and in 1952 led the league in homers (32) and drove in 104 runs. Doby asked for a restoration of his raise, but Greenberg balked, saying that his batting average had dropped 19 points to .276.[38]

The press criticized Greenberg for his hard-headedness in this instance. The African American press noted, "After Hank got all he could get when he played for Detroit and Pittsburgh, he agreed to pay Bob Feller, a nine game winner in 1952, $40,000, he should have jumped at the chance of getting Doby for $25,000." Doc Young wrote in *Jet* magazine, "Even Al Capone would have drooled over that deal."[39]

Greenberg admired Doby's talent but did not like him, finding the star center fielder "belligerent" and "grouchy."[40] There is an element of truth to this judgment, for Doby continued to grouse that he had not received acknowledgment comparable to that of Jackie Robinson for having been the first black player in the American League. Perhaps unsurprisingly, Greenberg traded Doby to the White Sox after the 1955 season. Although Doby was then in the twilight of his career, Greenberg received little in return—outfielder Jim Busby and an over-the-hill Chico Carrasquel. This trade did not set well with the Indians fans.

Although the press dwelled on his mistakes, to Greenberg's credit he had traded judiciously and had made several trades and acquisitions which definitely strengthened the team. In August 1952, he purchased outfielder Wally Westlake from the Cincinnati Reds. Earlier on June 15, he had made a major trade, giving up Steve Gromek and Ray Boone and receiving pitcher Art Houtteman, who became a vital addition to the Tribe's staff.

The 1953 pennant race was another despairing year. Russ Schneider of the *Plain Dealer* wrote, "Those Indians came close again, but this experience only served to heighten their frustration." Another reporter noted, "A measure of apathy had set in as the season began."[41] The frustration of the fans was evident, with a drastic decline in attendance of nearly 400,000. It was not that performance was slipping; rather, it was the fault of Casey Stengel, whose Yankees continued to harass the Tribe by becoming the first major league team to win five consecutive pennants.

During that season, the Yankees occupied first place 158 of 167 days. The Indians started out with a 13–6 record and in early May were in first place. The Yankees left no doubt of their superiority after an 18-game-winning streak starting in late May, the last four in Cleveland. The winning streak included a doubleheader victory in Municipal Stadium witnessed by nearly 75,000 fans. But days of mammoth crowds for baseball games in Municipal Stadium were about to end.

A race developed briefly in late June, when the Yankees went into a tailspin, losing nine straight games, including a three-game sweep with Mike Garcia, Early Wynn and Bob Lemon on the mound. In late July, Garcia, Wynn, and Lemon defeated the Yankees again to reignite a flicker of hope, but by August 19, the Tribe was 15 games behind the Yankees. Lo and behold, for the second time that season, on August 27–29, Garcia, Wynn, and Lemon swept the Yankees, and the Tribe went on to win 20 of 23 decisions—but too late. Cleveland held off Chicago to finish in second place for the third straight year, winning one game less than in 1952.

The Tribe's downfall was its record on the road. Their home record was a laudable 53–24, but away from the Stadium, their record was only 39–38. A serious injury to Luke Easter did not help the cause. He was hit by a pitch from Lou Kretlow of the White Sox in the fourth game of the season, fracturing his left foot. He was out of the lineup until June 22 and played in only 68 games, hitting seven home runs. Unfortunately, Easter—now 38—saw his career end with the exception of six games played early in the 1954 season. His legs gave out, his ankles were damaged in an auto accident, and he was sent to the minor leagues and retired shortly thereafter. Tragically, in 1979, 63-year old Luke Easter was murdered by two robbers as he exited a downtown bank in Cleveland where, as a union steward, he had cashed $40,000 worth of checks for his fellow workers. Over 4,000 fans passed by the casket of their hero.[42]

The 1953 season's highlight was Rosen's great performance. He made a valiant effort to capture the Triple Crown. The achievement of leading the league in batting average, home runs, and RBIs had occurred only twice since 1937, both times by Ted Williams of the Red Sox—in 1942 and 1947. Rosen edged out Philadelphia's Gus Zernial for the home run title, 43–42, and had no serious challenge to his league-leading 145 RBI. He also led the league in slugging percentage, .613, and runs scored, 115. The race for the batting title matched Rosen against former Indians teammate Mickey Vernon of the Senators. Vernon held off Rosen to win the crown, .337 to .336. Rosen's brilliant season earned him the American League's Most Valuable Player Award.[43]

However, Rosen reaped no financial benefit from this coveted award. Again, Greenberg showed his arrogance when he called Rosen into his office to discuss his 1954 contract. Rosen, after his successful season, expected a handsome raise. Instead, Greenberg opened a drawer of his desk and pulled out a green book with his own hitting statistics. "You just completed your fourth year," Hank said. "Let's see what I did in my fourth year."[44] Rosen had hit 43 home runs—a club record—three more than had Greenberg, and had one more hit—201–200. In every other category—batting average, runs scored, doubles, RBI—the former Tiger had edged out Rosen. Even though he had come so close to winning the Triple Crown, Rosen began to feel as if he had had a bad year. "He reduced me to ashes," he said. "It was absolutely devastating."[45] Instead of obtaining the $55,000 he had hoped for, Rosen signed for $37,000 plus a $5,000 bonus. As usual, the general manager had played hardball and won. As a player, Greenberg had always negotiated aggressively in his own interest. Now, he negotiated on the team's behalf at the player's expense, and Rosen resented the behavior of his former hero.

Rosen was not the only unhappy member of the Tribe family. Manager Lopez had tired of being a bridesmaid for three straight seasons and told Greenberg that perhaps it was time for a change. Cincinnati had contacted him about managing the Reds. However, the general manager would not hear of it. The Tribe had been winning 90 games a season under Lopez. El Señor was his man, and finally Lopez relented: "If you want me back, I'll be back."[46] Greenberg granted his manager a two-year contract.

Another unhappy member of the Tribe family who did not return was former Indians outfielder and long-time popular baseball announcer Jack Graney—the first former major leaguer to announce big league games starting with the Indians in 1932. Jimmy Dudley, Graney's cohort since 1948, became the Indians' bellwether broadcaster for the next 14 years.

Greenberg's recruiting strength in promoting and signing black players would be crucial for the 1954 season. Of the American League teams who reported for spring training, 18 black players were listed on the eight teams. When they began spring training at Hi Corbett

Field in Tucson, seven were with the Tribe. Neither Boston nor Detroit had yet signed a black player.

Greenberg made two important additions to the roster for the 1954 season. He acquired outfielder Dave Philley from the Athletics, and a few days later he signed Hal Newhouser, a former Detroit teammate. A two-time MVP, "Prince Hal" was one of baseball's best starting pitchers, winning 200 games during his 15 seasons with the Tigers. The 33-year-old started only one game for the Tribe in 1954 but provided valuable relief pitching throughout the season.

Now the Indians had considerable firepower, pitching capability, and a heavy hitting brigade to finally ambush the "Damn Yankees."[47] Manager Lopez called his pitching staff "the greatest ever assembled." The top twirlers were Early Wynn, Bob Lemon, and Mike Garcia, augmented by Bob Feller—the "Sunday pitcher," poised to go out in a blaze of glory. Additional weapons came in the form of Art Houtteman and three ace relievers, Hal Newhouser and two young, eager recruits, left-hander Don Mossi and fireballer Ray Narleski.

The hitting brigade was led by Larry Doby, Bobby Avila, and Al Rosen, who played most of the season with a broken finger and other assorted injuries. Timely hitting was provided by "Old Reliable" catcher Jim Hegan, Wally Westlake, Dave Philley, and Al Smith. Of course, no one underrated the Yankees. "Every spring," Lopez remembered, "writers ... asked if we were going to catch the Yankees this year. 'Yes, we will,' hoping that we could. The Yankees had great clubs, a tremendous organization. They used to get all the players they wanted from Kansas City, Washington—one year they came up with Johnny Mize and what players—Mantle, Berra. Reynolds, Raschi, Ford—they were great."[48]

In spite of these assets, both Lopez and Greenberg entered the 1954 season squarely on the spot, for the Indians looked like a team that could not win the games that counted. Gordon Cobbledick, predicting a sixth consecutive pennant for the Yankees, wrote, "The Indians will have to demonstrate they can win the 'big one.' They've been a long time earning a reputation as a team that looks like a champion until the chips are down." Harry Jones of the *Plain Dealer* provided an even harsher assessment: "You find little team spirit in the Indians. [They] are not a team at all, but a crowd of players, each striving for personal achievement."[49]

One newcomer to the team had an opportunity to taste the fruits of playing with a pennant-winning team, but the pleasures of night life left him on the outside looking in. In 1954, Rudy Regalado from San Diego called Greenberg to ask if he could stop in Tucson, where the Indians were training. He was on his way to the Tribe's minor league camp in Daytona Beach, Florida, and sought advice in helping hone his game. As fate would have it, when he arrived at Hi Corbett Field, the Indians needed a second baseman to play in an intrasquad game because Bobby Avila was late reporting to camp.

Regalado, a third baseman, played second base and hit the ball all over the park in several spring training games. For a whole month, he could do no wrong. "Rudy, the red-hot rapper" was batting .447 with 11 homeruns, and when the team went north, Regalado was given a major league contract. In order to insert Regalado's hot bat into the lineup, Lopez moved Rosen to first base.[50]

Unfortunately, Regalado turned out to be a mirage of the Arizona desert. Soon after

A drawing by Dick Dugan, sports illustrator for the Cleveland *Plain Dealer* in the 1950s and beyond, depicting one of the most distinguished pitching staffs in baseball history, with manager Al Lopez. This drawing was sold to raise funds for Mike "Bear" Garcia, who suffered from kidney failure and died in 1986 at 62. Garcia had a sterling pitching career, winning 142 and losing 96 with a 3.27 E.R.A. He was said to "walk like a bear and pitch like a lion" (author's collection).

the season started, it became obvious he lacked the talent. Greenberg learned via the grapevine that Regalado left his game in the Cleveland night clubs, dancing, drinking, and staying out late after curfew, and had come to the ballpark practically drunk from the lack of sleep. By midseason, he struggled with a .250 batting average and only two home runs in sixty-five games.

Greenberg called him into his office and told him that Cleveland was sending him to San Diego, an Indians' Triple-A affiliate. Greenberg advised the 24-year-old that he was abusing his body and being unfair to his teammates. Of course, Regalado resented these remarks.[51] He returned to Cleveland to play in the 1954 World Series, batting three times and garnering one hit. He played in 26 games in 1955 and 1956, and then drifted out of the majors. Several years later, Greenberg, no longer the general manager for the Tribe, was stunned by an apologetic letter from Regalado. Regalado said that Greenberg had been right in his decision to send him back to San Diego but that he was sorry he had made a fool of himself and had ruined his baseball career.[52] At the age of 84, Regalado still lives in San Diego.

Before Opening Day, while still in Tucson, Doby had decided to hold out, but once again, Greenberg callously reduced Doby's salary from $28,000 to $25,000. Doby had "slumped" from 32 to 29 home runs and from 104 to 102 RBI compared to the year before. (Such salary shenanigans would never succeed in present-day negotiations because of the players' unions and astute agents.) Doby threatened to go home to New Jersey, but shortly thereafter, Spud Goldstein, the Indians' all-purpose traveling secretary, conveyed an offer from Greenberg of $30,000 which Doby accepted, and in 1954 he proved to be well worth his salary.

Meanwhile, Harry Jones of the *Plain Dealer* intimated that Doby had rid himself of the chip that he had previously carried on his shoulder and now seemed less depressed when he had a hitless game. Jones added, "He is not the same Doby who would sulk and brood and sit alone and snap at people and give the impression the whole world was against him." Doby, in trying to recall his thoughts and feelings in the 1954 season, said, "I don't feel any different [this year]. As for Jones's comments, they don't make any sense to me."[53]

After a mediocre 13–16 spring training season, the Tribe limped out of the gate with a 3–6 record. But the pitching staff, deeper than ever before, began to right the ship. In late April and into May, the Indians beat up on second division teams and played .500 ball against pennant contenders, specifically the Yankees and Chicago White Sox. On June 1, Greenberg negotiated the last trade needed to put the team in the driver's seat. He acquired hard-hitting Vic Wertz from the Baltimore Orioles, now in their first year in the American League, in exchange for pitcher Bob Chakales, nicknamed "The Golden Greek." Wertz, formerly an outfielder, filled the hole at first base and proved to be a missing link. Al Rosen, with his broken right index finger, moved back to third base.

The first series with the Yankees took place in late June, with the Yankees four games behind the Tribe. The two teams had split eight games to date. The first two games left fans with the age-old feeling that "these are the same old Yankees." The Clevelanders were trounced, 11–0 and 11–9. Then the Tribe stemmed the slide, winning the third game of the series, 4–3, behind Hal Newhouser's strong relief pitching and home runs by Wally Westlake and Dave Philley.

The Yankees, however, were back in the race. A piece of doggerel warned, "No shaking that old Yankee hex, they'll soon be on the Redskins' neck." Yankees manager Casey Stengel added fuel to the fire; he regarded the Indians with derision and referred to Lopez's team as "those plumbers."

The Indians no longer drew gigantic crowds, so common during the Bill Veeck era. Gate receipts were down throughout the major leagues. Gallup's American Institute of Public

Opinion poll found in a coast-to-coast survey that more Americans than ever before followed major league baseball. One obvious reason for the declining attendance was that more fans were watching the game on television, hearing it on the radio, and reading about it in newspapers. Other factors were the effect of industrial layoffs and fan resentment of colored players in a game that had drawn a color line for nearly 60 years.

The Indians went into a funk during their visit to Chicago just before the All-Star Game. On a "lost weekend," the Tribe succumbed to the White Sox four straight games and lost their firm hold on first place, and with it the confidence that accompanies a comfortable lead. They now led the Yankees by only one-half game. The Clevelanders halted their pennant drive for the All-Star Game held in Cleveland's Municipal Stadium for the second time before 69,751 spectators.[54] Three Indians excelled in the 21st All-Star Game with the American League winning, 11–9. Al Rosen stroked two home runs and added five RBI, Larry Doby added a pinch-hit home run, and Avila's three hits and two RBI meant that the Tribesmen accounted for eight of the American League's 11 runs. Al Rosen earned the MVP Award.

A most unusual occurrence took place in Fenway Park in Boston on July 20 and 21. On the first night, the Indians and Red Sox staged a 16-inning marathon, deadlocked 5–5 after Bobby Avila tied the game with a two-run homer with two outs in the ninth inning. The thrilling battle was terminated at 12:58 a.m. due to a league curfew. The two teams tried again the following day, and in the ninth inning, with the score tied 7–7, the game was halted because of a downpour. The following afternoon, the Indians swept the Red Sox in a doubleheader before 17,000 fans—an attendance figure which is a far cry from present-day capacity crowds at nearly every game in Fenway Park.

Few teams can ride through a 154-game schedule without suffering injuries, and Cleveland was no exception. The most battered player was Al Rosen, who played the entire season, minus 17 games, with a broken finger, a bruised elbow, contusions to the chest, and bursitis of the left shoulder. This is the same stalwart who suffered through 13 broken noses—several from clubhouse fights—during his professional career.

On July 30, Larry Doby hit the newspaper headlines and television with a catch many claimed was the greatest they had ever seen. Cleveland was entertaining Washington, and the Indians were leading 5–3 in the third inning. Playing shallow against Tom Umphlett, Doby raced back into left-center field in pursuit of Umphlett's unexpected long drive. At the five-foot "Veeck" fence, Doby leaped high, placed his bare hand on the fence, pushed himself still higher, caught the ball, fell against the awning over the bullpen bench, and bounced back onto the field with the ball clutched in his glove. Leftfielder Al Smith snatched the ball from Doby, and as umpire John Flaherty threw his right hand up to signal an out, almost threw out base runner Jim Busby as he raced back to first base.

"That," Dizzy Dean declared to Hal Lebovitz, "was the greatest catch I ever saw as a player or a broadcaster. If I was the pitcher," Dean added, "I'd go up to Doby and say, 'Podner, here's half of my month's salary. You deserve it.'" In the dugout after the game, pitcher Art Houtteman cornered Doby and said, "I wanted to thank you for that catch. As long as I live, I'll never forget the greatness of that play."[55] After the catch, Doby received an ovation from the 17,500 fans every time he came to bat. He responded to the cheers in the fifth inning by slugging his 21st home run of the season.

On August 16, Cobbledick said in his column "Plain Dealing," that if there is a practicing psychologist in the house, he had a question:

> Which is a more frustrating experience—to play baseball ... at a .733 clip over a two-and-a-half-month period and gain only a half game on the team ahead of you?
> OR
> To play .730 ball in the same stretch and lose a half game to your relentless pursuers?[56]

On June 1, the Yankees were 3½ games behind the Indians. Thereafter, they traveled at a fantastic pace, winning 55 of 75 games through mid–August, and for their pains they remained three games out of first. The Yankees thought they were running on a treadmill. At the same time, the Indians won 54 of 74 games, which, if there had been any justice, normally would have left the runner-up team far back in the dust. Instead, Cleveland lost a half-game.

With just 12 games remaining, the Tribe was on the brink of clinching their third pennant. Despite the bitter second-place finishes of the three preceding seasons, northern Ohio anticipated a dramatic knockout against their vaunted rivals, the New York Yankees.

Possessing an astonishing 102–40 record on September 12, Cleveland hosted the Bronx Bombers for the 21st and 22nd times—that seems so much better than the ragged seven- or eight-game season series between the Indians and Yankees on present-day schedules. Cleveland, who had won nine of the first 20 games, held a 6½-game lead over New York, its largest lead of the season. Cleveland was in control of its destiny.

Bob Lemon and Early Wynn faced the Yankees' Whitey Ford and Tommy Byrne. Thousands of fans lined up at the ticket office that morning. The Cleveland Transit System organized a "Baseball Special," running trains between suburbs and downtown. Many fans came from outer burgs, arriving early in the afternoon, "giving the city the air of a midwest college town on a Saturday afternoon," the *Plain Dealer*'s Murray Seeger noted, "as they milled around the streets, restaurants and hotels waiting for game time."[57]

When the turnstile tally was completed, it stood at 86,563—including 10,000 fans behind the outfield fence—breaking baseball's attendance record set at the Stadium in the 1948 World Series. Fans were not disappointed. The Indians scored a run in the fifth inning of the first game; the Yankees retaliated with a run in the sixth inning. After Ford was lifted after six innings, the Tribe scored three runs off Allie Reynolds to secure a 4–1 victory. In the second game, after Yogi Berra stroked his 20th home run in the first inning, for two runs, Early Wynn caught fire, allowing only one more hit for the remainder of the game, and Cleveland scored three runs in the fifth inning off southpaw Byrne for a doubleheader victory.

The Cleveland players swarmed onto the field, drowned in a raucous ovation from their appreciative fans. With ten games to play, "They knew they had done it," Dan Cordtz wrote in the *Plain Dealer*, and in a fit of braggadocio, Murray Seegar added, "No gambler, actor, or politician ever had a funeral like the one that [the large throng] saw at the Stadium yesterday and never before have so many persons paid for the privilege of seeing a wake."[58]

On September 18, after the three straight second-place finishes, the Indians' hour was finally at hand. On a gloomy, rainy afternoon in the Motor City, they finally applied the coup de grâce to the tenacious New Yorkers. Ironically, three of the five remaining active members of the 1948 World Champion team were involved in this game. Pitcher Steve Gromek, who had spent 13 years in an Indians uniform, was pitching for the Tigers. Little-used veteran Dale Mitchell, another hero of the 1948 team, smashed his former teammate's pitch into the right field stands for his first home run of 1954—and the last of his career—to give the Tribe a 2–1 lead. Not to be outdone, catcher Jim Hegan, another stalwart of the 1948 team, followed with a home run to seal a pennant-clinching victory, 3–2.

Bobby Avila touched second base with extreme care for the final out, and team members poured out of the dugout for the traditional celebration. The rain-soaked team retreated to the clubhouse for a party, and a teammate wrote, "We're In" with lipstick atop first baseman Vic Wertz's bald scalp.

Yankees manager Casey Stengel sent a congratulatory telegram to Lopez, and the Yankees players wired one to their Cleveland counterparts. In the next few hours, dozens of Hollywood stars contacted comedian Bob Hope—a minority owner of the Indians—to hit him up for World Series tickets. "It's been a great season." Lopez reflected. "This is a great team. It's a greater team than anyone [knew]."[59]

Finishing with 111 victories and a .721 winning percentage, the Tribe had broken the American League record for victories in a season, one more than the Yankees' 110 wins in 1927. The five starting pitchers had accounted for 147 starts and 93 victories. Lemon and Wynn tied for the league lead in wins with 23 each; Garcia had 19 wins and led the American League with a 2.64 ERA. Feller, near the end of his career, finished with a laudable 13–3 record. Art Houtteman (15), Hal Newhouser (seven), Don Mossi (six), and Ray Narleski (three) accounted for 31 victories. These eight pitchers accounted for almost 95 percent of the total innings pitched. The key to the Tribe's success had been the ability to overwhelm the American League's lesser teams, racking up records of 18–4 against last-place Philadelphia and sixth-place Washington, 19–3 against seventh-place Baltimore, and an amazing 20–2 against fourth-place Boston.

On the offensive side, Cleveland led the American League in home runs for the fifth consecutive year, topped by Larry Doby's 32. He also led the league with 126 RBI. Bobby Avila won the batting title with a .341 average. Attendance increased a modest 266,296 for a total of 1,335,472 in 1954.

Having dethroned the Yankees at last, the Indians faced the Giants, a friendlier New York team. The Giants were a good team with adequate pitching which included 21-game winner Johnny Antonelli, Ruben Gomez, Sal "The Barber" Maglie, and two excellent relievers, Marv Grissom and Hoyt Wilhelm. The Giants' offense was led by Willie Mays, leading the National League in batting with a .345 average, a .667 slugging average, and 13 triples. In addition, the slugger stroked 41 round-trippers and 33 doubles. He was supported by outfielders Don Mueller with .342 batting average, 212 hits and 90 scored runs, Whitey Lockman, Hall of Famer Monte Irwin, Alvin Dark with 98 runs and the pesky spoiler Dusty Rhodes, though he only played 82 regular season games yet batted .341.

The Polo Grounds—where a polo match was never played—possessed many attributes and liabilities comparable to Cleveland's now deposed League Park. Ironically, both ball parks had been built in 1891. In the Polo Grounds, the distance was 279 feet to the left field bleachers and a mere 257 feet to right field; however, the distance was 483 feet to the center field bleachers and clubhouse. This venerable park was home to many historical moments provided by players and managers like Christy Mathewson, John McGraw, Miller Huggins, and Babe Ruth. The 1954 Series was the last one in the Polo Grounds.

The Tribe took the New York Central to Gotham, confident in the outcome. With Cleveland's outstanding pitching, Nevada odds-makers made them 9 to 5 favorites on the betting board. On Wednesday, September 29, a warm and sultry day, a crowd of 52,751 filled the stands. Popular crooner Perry Como led the crowd in singing the national anthem. The game was televised nationally, but most Americans followed the action by radio with Jimmy Dudley of Cleveland and Giants announcer Al Helfer describing play-by-play over the Mutual Broadcasting Network.

Opposed by right-hander Sal Maglie, Bob Lemon started for Cleveland. The Indians struck first in the initial inning when Vic Wertz tripled off the right field wall to score Bobby Avila and Al Smith. The New Yorkers retaliated with two runs in the third inning. Lemon settled down, and meanwhile, the Tribe threatened repeatedly to break open the game. In the eighth inning, Doby walked and Rosen singled. Giants relief pitcher Don Liddle came in to pitch to Wertz, who already had three hits. Next came the pivotal play of the four-game Series. Mark Winegardner, author of the novel *Crooked River Burning*, described what happened:

> Vic Wertz swings ... and connects: a smash, a screamer, a shot, a bomb, hissing and rising, to dead center.... As the ball rockets out of the infield, Doby and Rosen run. The ball is uncatchable. Willie Mays plays the shallowest, but also the best center field of his time, and he takes off running, running. His hat falls off. Back, back, back, back. A dead run.
>
> Forty feet from where the ball will eventually land, it passes a point that, in every other ballpark in the big leagues would have been over the outfield fence.[60]

Rosen recalled, "[The ball] went off Vic's bat like a cannon shot, I was on first base and I was off at the crack of the bat. I wanted to score." Rosen raced toward second, looked up, and lamented, "I had [this] sinking feeling. I could tell that if the ball stayed in the park, Willie would catch it." Feller added, "I felt the same way."[61] So did most of the guys in the dugout. The wind was blowing in, and that helped Mays. Everyone said it was the greatest catch ever, but Feller had seen Mays make better plays than that in spring training. Many other baseball aficionados agreed with Feller. Modern-day outfielders are making comparable outstanding plays on a regular basis.

According to Terry Pluto, Mays ran about 400 miles to track the ball down, which seems an exaggeration. Mark Winegardner is more realistic in his description:

> Mays is all elbows and knees and wind and grace, and with his back to the plate, *460 feet from home*, still on the pure dead run, he sticks up his glove and as the ball shoots over his left shoulder, he spears it—*spears it*—and in the same impossibly fluid motion, [nearly falling,] spins and fires the ball to the infield.[62]

Upon realizing Mays' play, Doby tagged up and made it to third, as Rosen—nearly thrown out—made it back to first base. Doby was one of the frustrating number of 37 Indians left on base during the Series. An objective evaluation of this figure is a major reason why Cleveland fell in the World Series.

"If" is a big word, but if this game had been played in Cleveland's Municipal Stadium, the score would have been 5–2 in favor of the Indians. Wertz should have been a hero with his fourth hit. Instead, after Mays' catch, Liddle was removed from the mound. Since Wertz was the only batter he faced, he smiled and said, "Well, I got my man."[63]

Two words Tribe fans will never forget from the 1954 World Series are Dusty Rhodes. According to Pluto, "[Fans] didn't say the name, they spat it. They cursed it. They dreaded the day they ever heard the name."[64] James Lamar Rhodes did not even start; he was supposed to be an outfielder, but he was not on speaking terms with his glove. Mostly, he could swing the bat.

In the bottom of the tenth inning, Lemon faced Rhodes, who had batted .341 in 82 games during the season. The Giants had two men on base as Rhodes stroked the first pitch into the short porch in right field. Avila drifted back from second base and thought he could catch the ball, but the same wind that had seemed to knock down Wertz's drive shifted, and Rhodes' fly ball sailed over the wall—260 feet—barely half as far as Wertz's drive. The winning run was scored by none other than Willie Mays. The final score was 5–2 for the Giants.

After the game, several politically incorrect reporters called Rhodes's hit a "Chinese homer."[65] Lopez called it a "wind-blown popup." In view of the final result of the Series, the Tribe may have been most accurate calling it "the crusher."

In Game Two, the Indians went ahead *early*, 1–0. "*Early*"—a good omen, with future Hall of Famer Early Wynn pitching. Wynn was in command until the fifth inning, when Giants manager Leo Durocher sent, of all people, Dusty Rhodes in to pinch-hit for Monte Irvin. Wynn decked him with the first pitch, then put the ball under his chin and again dropped his butt in the dirt. Rhodes did not say a word—he just dropped a Texas-Leaguer to center field, to score—you guessed it, Willie Mays. Rhodes stayed in the game, and in the seventh inning, as Winegardner described it, "stroked another cheap-ass homer" to right field.[66] The Giants won the second game, 3–1, and the Tribe was in deep trouble as they headed westward.

The Series went back to Cleveland without a day off. The dispirited Indians knew they had to awaken their silent bats. Reporters wanted to know the answer to this fallout. "We've been leaving too many men on the bases," said the besieged Señor. "Our hits have not been coming at the right time. We need more timely hitting and more speed."[67] With Cleveland leaving 13 men on base in each game, Lopez's critique of the club's troubles seemed right on the mark.

Although 71,555 fans turned out for Game Three, it was a smaller crowd than expected. To turn the tide, the Indians relied on Mike "Big Bear" Garcia. The momentum on the Giants' side was too much. After scoring a run in the first inning, Durocher, ridiculously, sent Rhodes in to pinch-hit for Irvin in the *third inning*. Keeping to form, he lashed a two-run single. By the end of the inning, the Giants had four runs, and they won the game, 6–2. The Indians were in a deep hole; no team had won the World Series after losing the first three games.

Rhodes's three pinch-hits are a World Series record, and the Alabaman retorted, "I ain't thinkin' about no record, all I care about is seein' us win."[68] It looked like the game-spoiler would get his wish. Wertz was batting .500 for the Series; but no other Tribesman besides Al Smith was hitting his weight.

On the eve of Game Four, Lopez felt the pressure increase. There was talk of starting Bob Feller and giving the 36-year-old a final chance to win a World Series game. Lopez decided to go with Lemon, commenting, "In a spot like this, you have to go with your best." The Señor also put injured Rosen back at third and Sam Dente at shortstop for more batting punch.

On a comfortably warm day on October 2, with not a cloud in sight, an enormous turnout of 78,102 loyal fans cheered as the beleaguered Indians took the field. But to no avail, even as Dusty Rhodes sat on the bench for this game. Durocher added insult to injury, starting Don Liddle, one of only two left-handers on his pitching roster. (Left-hander Johnny Antonelli finished the game, pitching 1.2 innings in relief of Liddle.) A few days before the World Series had begun, Lou Boudreau, in a charitable fashion, was quoted as saying, "the 29-year-old control artist could give the Indians trouble."[69]

The former Indians manager's observation rang true over the first four innings. Liddle held the Indians hitless except for Wertz's double. By then, the game was out of control and the underdog Giants won, 7–4, to deprive Cleveland of an opportunity for a third World Championship.

After the loss in the final game, the large crowd made this impression on Arthur Daley of the *New York Times*: "A breathless hush fell over this sprawling stadium. It was so quiet, you could almost hear a heart break. No one spoke a kind word about the deceased. The Indians died friendless and alone."[70]

The Tribe made no alibis. In spite of serious injuries to Doby, Rosen, and Wertz—the injury to Wertz's severely bruised index finger did not hinder him from registering a .500 batting average (8-for-16) in the Series—manager Lopez and Rosen analyzed the debacle: "If I could have changed anything about 1954, we'd have won a few less games. Going into the Series, maybe we were a little too confident. Everybody asks 'What happened?' It was simple. We went cold, the breaks went against us, and the Giants played good ball and beat us."[71]

Forty years later, Al Rosen reflected on the outcome. "I am still stunned by what happened." He praised Rhodes: "The guy caught lightning in a bottle and the 1954 World Series ... was Dusty Rhodes's time on earth." The star third baseman added what to fans was a truism: "It was a letdown, pure and simple," he said. "All year people kept waiting for us to fold and the Yankees to catch us. We were always the bridesmaids and we were sick of it. We had a chance to be one of the ten greatest teams of all time." Lopez added, "The only thing I can say, we had a slump at the absolute worst time."[72]

When the Tribe had clinched the pennant, more than 250,000 fans watched the players parade through the streets of Cleveland in convertibles. The 1954 Indians drove themselves to beat the Yankees, and when they did, it was like winning the World Series. Apparently, the Tribe had neglected to reset their goal for the ultimate conquest—the World Series Championship.

Epilogue

*"It breaks your heart. It is designed to break your heart. The game begins
in the spring, when everything else begins again, and it blossoms in the
summer, filling the afternoons and evening, and then as soon as the
chill rains come, it stops and leaves you to face the fall alone."*
—A. Bartlett Giamatti, from "The Green Fields of the Mind"

The Giants' four-game sweep of the Tribe in the 1954 World Series was an ominous sign for coming decades for the Cleveland franchise and the city of Cleveland, though for different reasons. Although the Tribe struggled valiantly to retain their winning ways, the Yankees would thwart their efforts, regaining their pennant-winning tradition in 1955. But there would be no World Championship for them either, as their cross-town rival Brooklyn Dodgers and Jackie Robinson would win the Series.

For the fourth time in the last five years, the Tribe had again finished second under the manager "Señor" Lopez. Now he planned to resign, citing stomach problems, and one may easily ascertain why. However, general manager Hank Greenberg talked Lopez into retaining his position for the 1956 season.

Bright times during the 1955 season included Bob Feller's 12th one-hitter, a record subsequently tied by Nolan Ryan. In the same doubleheader, Herb Score, a young left-handed "fireballer," struck out 16 Red Sox batters, en route to a league-leading 245 strikeouts and "Rookie of the Year" honors.

Lo and behold, the Indians finished in second place yet again in 1956, behind the New Yorkers, and Lopez, the most successful manager in Cleveland history with a winning percentage of .617 (570–354), resigned. Two positive highlights of this disappointing season were Score's 20 victories and the exploits of Rocky Colavito, who slugged 21 home runs. On a somber note, Bob Feller, the greatest pitcher in Cleveland history with 266 victories, a total restricted by four years of service in World War II, hung up his glove for the last time. He continues to hold a majority of Indians pitching records.

Attendance had dropped nearly in half since 1950 with only 865,000 filing through turnstiles in 1956. At the same time, ownership of the franchise changed hands again in February 1956, when Cleveland industrialist William R. Daley and partners purchased the franchise for $3,961,800, the highest price ever paid for a major league team. (The L.A. Dodgers were bought for $2 billion in 2012.) As manager, Greenberg hired Kerby Farrell, who led the Tribe's Triple-A farm team at Indianapolis to the American Association pennant and Junior World Series title in 1956.

The Tribe's impending demise was hastened by a critical loss of two players. On May 7, 1957, Herb Score was struck in the right eye by a scorching line drive off the bat of Yankees second baseman Gil McDougald. Eighteen thousand horrified spectators witnessed this devastating blow. Score did not pitch for the rest of the season, and never recovered enough to pitch effectively again. In 1964, he became a member of the Indians' broadcasting team on radio and TV, describing play-by-play action until 1998. He died on November 11, 2008, at 75.

At the end of the 1957 season, after Cleveland finished in sixth place and recorded a 12-year low in attendance (722,000), once again the managerial graveyard admitted a new member. Farrell was fired after only one season, and general manager Greenberg was fired as well, even though he was the second largest stockholder (19 percent) of the club. These management activities fed the rumor mill that the franchise might move, possibly to Minneapolis–St. Paul.

In 1958, "Trader" Lane or "Frantic" Lane, whose given name was Frank, replaced Greenberg as the Indians' new general manager. Lane became one of the most disliked general managers ever employed by the Cleveland franchise. He enjoyed a small respite in 1959 when the Indians delivered what would be their "last hurrah" for many years. The club finished in second place under the leadership of popular Joe Gordon, losing to the Chicago White Sox by three games. And the wonder of it all—the owner of the White Sox was Bill Veeck and the manager was Al Lopez.

However, next spring, Lane pulled the *coup de grâce* that would anger Indians fans for decades. He traded Rocky Colavito, then in the prime of his career and one of the most popular Cleveland players ever, for Harvey Kuenn of the Tigers. Like the fans, Colavito was crushed. He had led the American League in 1959 with 42 home runs and 111 RBI. As for Kuenn, he demonstrated little power even though he had led the American League in 1959 with a .353 batting average. During his one year with the Tribe (1960), he batted .308 in 126 games (Kuenn was injury-prone), and Cleveland fans never saw him again. Conversely, Colavito hit 370 home runs and drove in 1,159 runs in his 14-year career. Enough said!

During the next three decades, the Cleveland franchise descended into its Dark Ages. So, too, had the city of Cleveland fallen off the ladder at approximately the same time as the Tribe. For over 20 proud years, the slogans "The Best Location in the Nation" and "City of Champions" had defined the city. These accolades were replaced by slogans such as "the Mistake on the Lake," as the city lost its pride, particularly after the crooked Cuyahoga River caught fire.

Cleveland was plagued with two significant and negative qualities that made it different from cities of a similar size and background: political volatility and fragmentation. The emergence of large and politically powerful suburbs reflected the city's unsettled nature. Movement of industries and population to the suburbs served as a reminder of power, influence, and opportunity lost by the city's failure to incorporate these communities within the larger central city.

Two Clevelanders underscored the severity of their home city's dilemma. Hal Holbrook, "The Boy Who Became Mark Twain," recalled a visit to his lonely sister in the late

1950s. "[She] was off in a kind of a far country ... on the east side of Cleveland, the once proud city whose steel mills were closing down, leaving ... thousands of black migrants from the South stranded in decaying old houses and apartment buildings.... Down in the sooty darkness of [an] apartment courtyard, there was no clear and beautiful sky above ... just parked cars under blackened trees."

Mark Winegardner, noted author of *The Veracruz Blues* and *Crooked River Burning*, wrote that Cleveland in 1948 had been America's sixth largest city, but by 1968 it was 12th. For Easterners, Cleveland is where the Midwest begins; for Westerners, it is where the East begins. For Winegardner, nothing was ever the same after the Indians traded Rocky Colavito. Nothing was ever the same after Jim Brown, at the peak of his physical powers, retired from football. Nothing was ever the same after the Democratic machine failed to take into account the emerging political clout of the black population. Nothing was ever the same after Cleveland succumbed to an unfortunate tendency to look for one black person to speak for all black people. Nothing was the same when Euclid Beach Park closed forever. Nothing was the same after the Hough riots of 1967—just blocks west of old League Park. "Millionaire's Row" on Euclid Avenue was nearly gone. Nothing was the same after the Cuyahoga River caught on fire several times.

The dismal commentary of greater Cleveland's post–World War II economic, political and social decline is poignantly highlighted by Holbrook and Winegardner. The travails of the Cleveland Indians followed along the same path. The exploits of the Tribe during the first half of the twentieth century gave fans a wide swing between success and failure, individual accomplishments and fan interest in their teams. News about the Indians' fortunes was much more restrictive, however, conveyed primarily through local newspapers, radio, and *The Sporting News*.

Among baseball historians, sabermetrics[1] are often suspect. Yet an analysis of basic and traditional statistics suggests that the Indians, as charter members of the junior circuit, had been a strong force from 1901 through 1955. For example, Cleveland finished in the first division of the tight-knit American League in 38 of 55 seasons. The Tribe won their two World Championships in this time period. Both Series provided outstanding performances and heroes, including the 1948 appearance of Larry Doby, the first black player in the American League. Through 1959, the Tribe finished in second place 11 times, one more than the hated Yankees. The Tribe holds the record for the most threesomes to win 20 or more games in a season—1920, 1951, 1952, and 1956. Of a total of 16 owners, there had been only seven before 1957. However, 16 playing or bench managers had been hired in the first 55 years— 1901–1955. This turnover represented a 3.4-year average tenure for each manager. In the subsequent 59 years, 24 managers were employed with a 2.5-year average tenure.

The following names of this era flash across a fan's mind: Hall of Famers Nap Lajoie, Tris Speaker, Cy Young, Elmer Flick, Stanley Coveleski, Addie Joss, Joe Gordon, Joe Sewell, Satchel Paige, Early Wynn, Bill Veeck and Al Lopez. Six players are in Cleveland's Hall of Fame and have their uniform numbers retired: Bob Feller (#19), Earl Averill (#3), Lou Boudreau (#5), Larry Doby (#14), Bob Lemon (#21), and Mel Harder (#18), who spent all 20 years of his career with Cleveland, winning 223 games. And it would be proper to put Bill Veeck, everyone's Hall of Famer, in the Cleveland Hall of Fame.

Although it is interesting to analyze a team's statistics, there is more to consider for a fan who followed the Tribe during the early and mid–1900s. Following the Tribe meant forever looking for silver linings in storm clouds. Baseball has a certain air of timelessness cherished by fans to bring them back every spring. From the perspective of one's own life, particularly for this senior citizen, it is still easy to grasp how central baseball was to American life—emotionally dominant, unchallenged and saturating. Two major leagues were compact with all teams east of the Mississippi—St. Louis was just on the other side. Professional football and basketball were in their infancy. Collegiate football and basketball, now extremely popular, were growing adolescents. As the years went by, the play on the field, the sounds of the crowd, the cries of vendors and umpires would be reassuringly traditional in ways that other aspects of American society have failed to duplicate—two unfortunate examples are American jazz and the film industry.

During the 55-year period covered in this text, over 35,000,000 Tribe fans filed through the turnstiles. They experienced thrills and disappointments, through the exploits of Addie Joss and Nap Lajoie, the managership and play of Tris Speaker, the eventual World Championship of 1920 (one year before the New York Yankees' first title), the disappointing "Cry Baby" season of 1940, and the glory years of Bill Veeck and Al Lopez, during what many called the "Golden Age" of baseball. They represent a part of the glorious past in Cleveland Indians history.

For the decades from the 1960s into the mid–1990s, the Tribe and its fans suffered through the Dark Ages. A Renaissance occurred in the mid–1990s when the Tribe again became a formidable power under the leadership of the "H-Boys," general manager John Hart and manager Mike Hargrove.

The Alomar brothers, Omar Vizquel, Kenny Lofton, Manny Ramirez, Albert Belle, Jim Thome, and others provided another period of Tribal glory. Though the game is currently beset with serious problems such as parity between large market franchises and small market franchises, drug issues, the threat of changes in game management such as replays for the benefit of television, baseball will survive. True believers and real Indians fans hope that like the phoenix, Cleveland will rise again to compete with the best of the winning teams. "Wait 'Til Next Year!"

Chapter Notes

Chapter 1

1. Carol Miller and Robert Wheeler, *Cleveland: A Concise History* (Bloomington: Indiana University Press, 1990), 77.
2. William Ganson Rose, *Cleveland: The Making of a City* (Cleveland: World Publishing, 1950), 361.
3. Cleveland *Leader* in Miller and Wheeler, *Cleveland: A Concise History*, 76.
4. Forest City, Cleveland's longtime nickname, has murky origins. Credit for inspiring this name is generally given to William Case, Secretary of the Cleveland Horticultural Society in the 1840s, and mayor of Cleveland in 1850–1851. He encouraged the planting of fruit and shade trees in the city. In 1940, a count of 221,000 trees was recorded, in addition to 100,000 in parks. Forest City was the name of 35 large and small businesses in Greater Cleveland in 1895. (Excerpt from David D. Van Tassel and John J. Grabowski, *The Encyclopedia of Cleveland History*, 415.).
5. Philip W. Porter, *Cleveland: Confused City on a Seesaw* (Columbus: Ohio State University Press, 1976), 3.
6. Miller and Wheeler, *Cleveland: A Concise History*, 81.
7. George E. Condon, *Cleveland: The Best Kept Secret* (New York: Doubleday, 1967), 125, 142.
8. Rose, *Cleveland: The Making of a City*, 425.
9. Miller and Wheeler, *Cleveland: A Concise History*, 86.
10. Charles Alexander, *Our Game: An American Baseball History* (New York: Henry Holt, 1991), 349.
11. Johnathan Fraser Light, *The Cultural Encyclopedia of Baseball* (Jefferson, NC: McFarland, 1997), 68.
12. *Ibid.*
13. Charles Alexander. *Our Game,* 349.
14. Paul Dickson, *The Dickson Baseball Dictionary*, 3d edition (New York: W.W. Norton, 2009), 484. John Thorn, a preeminent baseball historian, presents in his book *Baseball in the Garden of Eden* the most objective and well-researched interpretation of the tangled history of baseball's beginnings in the United States, discarding many myths.
15. Rose, *Cleveland: The Making of a City*, 332.
16. Condon, *Cleveland: The Best Kept Secret*, 266.
17. Rose, *Cleveland: The Making of a City*, 356.
18. John Grabowski, *Sports in Cleveland: An Illustrated History* (Bloomington: Indiana University Press, 1992), 9.
19. *Ibid.*
20. *Ibid.*
21. Franklin Lewis, *The Cleveland Indians* (New York: G. P. Putnam's Sons, 1949), 17.
22. Harold Seymour, *Baseball: The Golden Age* (New York: Oxford University Press, 1971), 212–13.
23. *Ibid.*, 18–9.
24. Jonathan Fraser Light, *The Cultural Encyclopedia of Baseball*, 166.
25. Grabowski, *Sports in Cleveland, An Illustrated History*, 11–12.
26. Morris Eckhouse, *Legends of the Tribe: An Illustrated History of the Cleveland Indians* (Dallas: Taylor, 2000), 4.
27. Lewis, *The Cleveland Indians*, 25.
28. Lowell Reidenbaugh, *The Sporting News: Take Me Out to the Ballgame* (St. Louis: The Sporting News, 1983), 99.
29. *Ibid.*, 98.
30. Lewis, *The Cleveland Indians*, 26–27.
31. *1893 Spalding Baseball Guide* (St. Louis: The Sporting News, 1893).
32. Marshall D. Wright, *Nineteenth Century Baseball* (Jefferson, NC: McFarland, 1986), 261.
33. Lewis, *The Cleveland Indians*, 30.
34. Grabowski, *Sports in Cleveland, An Illustrated History*, 12.
35. Lewis, *The Cleveland Indians*, 30.
36. Condon, *Cleveland: The Best Kept Secret*, 267.
37. *Sporting Life*, March 1897. In 1896 and beyond, Gilbert Patten—alias Burt L. Standish—wrote pulp stories that introduced Frank Merriwell, star athlete and campus hero at Yale University. Later in the Frank Merriwell series, Patten introduced Joe Crowfoot, an intelligent, talented Indian who joined Merriwell at Yale. Possibly Patten created this character of Crowfoot in a thinly veiled homage to Sockalexis, a fellow Maine resident.
38. David L. Fleitz, *Louis Sockalexis* (Jefferson, NC: McFarland, 2002), 43.
39. *Ibid.*, 91.
40. Lewis, *The Cleveland Indians*, 31.

41. A detailed study of the 1899 Spiders is provided in J. Thomas Hetrick, *Misfits: The Cleveland Spiders in 1899* (Jefferson, NC: McFarland, 1991).

42. Brooklyn *Daily Eagle*, June 6, 1899.

43. Cleveland *Plain Dealer*, June 24, 1899.

44. Cleveland *Plain Dealer*, October 14, 1899.

45. *Ibid.*

46. *Ibid.*

Chapter 2

1. Leonard Koppett, *Koppett's Concise History of Major League Baseball* (Philadelphia: Temple University, 1998), 88–89.

2. Andrew Freedman, born in 1860, a life-long bachelor, made a fortune from real estate and transit contracts by "devious" means, "no longer traceable" and was connected to notorious Tammany Hall. (Dictionary of *American Biography*) After internal club disputes and a league power struggle, Freedman was forced to sell control of the New York Giants in 1903 to new ownership led by John T. Brush.

3. Russell Schneider, *The Cleveland Indians Encyclopedia* (Philadelphia: Temple University, 1996), 11.

4. Fred Lieb, "A.L. Fights for Major States," *Cleveland News*, July 3, 1946.

5. Lewis, *The Cleveland Indians*, 32.

6. Henry P. Edwards, "Saga of Cleveland Baseball," Cleveland *Plain Dealer*, December 24, 1943.

7. *Ibid.*, December 26, 1943.

8. Jonathan Knight, *Classic Tribe.* (Kent, OH: Kent State University Press, 2009), 151.

9. Henry P. Edwards, "Saga of Cleveland Baseball," Cleveland *Plain Dealer*, December 28, 1943.

10. Charles C. Alexander, *Spoke: A Biography of Tris Speaker* (Dallas: Southern Methodist University, 2007), 181–182.

11. Rich Blevins, *Addie Joss on Baseball.* Collected Newspaper Columns and World Series Reports, 1907–1909 (Jefferson, NC: McFarland), xviii.

12. *Ibid.*, xix.

13. Mark Stang, *Indians Illustrated* (Wilmington, OH: Orange Frazer Press, 2000), 11.

14. Henry P. Edwards, "Saga of Cleveland Baseball," Cleveland *Plain Dealer*, December 29, 1943.

15. Schneider, *The Cleveland Indians Encyclopedia*, 187.

16. David Fleitz, *Napoleon Lajoie: King of Ball Players* (Jefferson, NC: McFarland, 2013), 74.

17. Henry P. Edwards, "Saga of Cleveland Baseball," Cleveland *Plain Dealer*, December 29, 1943.

18. Fleitz, *Napoleon Lajoie: King of Ball Players*, 83.

19. *The Sporting News*, April 26, 1902.

20. Fleitz, *Napoleon Lajoie: King of Ball Players*, 83.

21. Henry P. Edwards, "Saga of Cleveland Baseball," Cleveland *Plain Dealer*, December 29, 1943.

22. Philadelphia *North American*, July 10, 1902.

23. Cleveland *Plain Dealer*, December 25, 1941, 36.

24. Schneider, *The Cleveland Indians Encyclopedia*, 13.

25. Eckhouse, *Legends of the Tribe*, 22–23.

26. Lewis, *The Cleveland Indians*, 44–45.

27. Schneider, *The Cleveland Indians Encyclopedia*, 13.

28. Lewis, *The Cleveland Indians*, 45.

29. Frank Gibbons, "Cleveland Muffs One, Refuses Trade for Ty Cobb," *Cleveland Press*, January 5, 1963.

30. Frank Gibbons, "Lajoie, Joss Arrive—a Dynasty Born," *Cleveland Press*, January 14, 1963.

31. Fleitz, *Napoleon Lajoie: King of Ball Players*, 130.

32. Emil H. Rothe, *Baseball's Most Historic Games* (Self-published, Society for American Baseball Research, Chicago Chapter, 1993), 54–55.

33. *Ibid.*, 64–65.

34. Henry P. Edwards, "Saga of Cleveland Baseball," Cleveland *Plain Dealer*, January 5, 1944.

35. Rick Wolff, Editorial Director, *The Macmillian Baseball Encyclopedia*. Eighth Edition (New York: Macmillan, 1990), 164.

36. Henry P. Edwards, "Saga of Cleveland Baseball," Cleveland *Plain Dealer*, January 5, 1944.

37. *Ibid.*

38. *Ibid.*

39. Cait Murphy, *Crazy '08* (New York: Harper-Collins, 2008), xiii–xiv.

40. Fleitz, *Napoleon Lajoie: King of Ball Players*, 117.

41. Henry P. Edwards, "Saga of Cleveland Baseball," Cleveland *Plain Dealer*, January 6, 1944.

42. Frank Gibbons, "Cleveland Muffs One, Refuses Trade for Ty Cobb," *Cleveland Press*, January 15, 1963.

43. Lewis, *The Cleveland Indians*, 52.

44. Cleveland *Plain Dealer*, September 13, 1908.

45. Cleveland *Plain Dealer*, September 22, 1908.

46. Cleveland *Plain Dealer*, September 27, 1908.

47. Scott Longert, *Addie Joss: King of the Pitchers* (Cleveland: Society for American Baseball Research, 1998), 18.

48. Jack DeVries, *Indians Baseball: 100 Years of Memories* (Cleveland: Cleveland Indians Baseball Company, 2002), 14–15.

49. *Ibid.*

50. Cleveland *Plain Dealer*, October 3, 1908.

51. Cy Young pitched the first perfect game in the modern era on May 5, 1904, for the Boston Red Sox, shutting out the Philadelphia Athletics, 3–0.

52. Scott Longert, *Addie Joss: King of the Pitchers*, 101.

53. Schneider, *The Cleveland Indians Encyclopedia*, 17.

54. Lewis, *The Cleveland Indians*, 63.

55. Schneider, *The Cleveland Indians Encyclopedia*, 17.

56. *Ibid.*

57. Fleitz, *Napoleon Lajoie: King of Ball*, 168–70.

58. *Ibid.*, 166; Lewis, *The Cleveland Indians*, 66.

59. *Cleveland Indians 2010 Information and Record Book*, 366.

60. Ken Krsolovic and Bryan Fritz, *League Park, 1891–1946* (Jefferson, NC: McFarland, 2013), 33–34.

61. Frank Gibbons, "18,832 Turn Out for Opener But Naps Find Poverty in New "Palace," *Cleveland Press*, January 17, 1953.

62. Cleveland *Plain Dealer*, April 21, 1910.

63. Jonathan Fraser Light, *The Cultural Encyclopedia of Baseball*, 438.

64. Frank Gibbons, "Shoeless Joe Joins Naps," *Cleveland Press*, January 19, 1963.

65. Steve P. Gietschier, "A Good Piece of Hitting: The 1910 American League Batting Race," The Ohio Historical Society: *Timeline* 27, October–December 2010, 35.

Chapter 3

1. Stanley Frank, "Bible of Baseball," *Saturday Evening Post* (June 20, 1942), 9; G. Edward White, *Creating the National Pastime: Baseball Transforms Itself, 1903–1953* (Princeton University Press, 1996), 190–191.

2. *Ibid.*, 191.

3. Stanley Frank, "Bible of Baseball," *Saturday Evening Post*, June 20, 1942, 9.

4. Jonathan Fraser Light, *The Cultural Encyclopedia of Baseball*, 429.

5. Taken from Ford Frick, *Games, Asterisks and People* (1973), in Jonathan Fraser Light, *The Cultural History of Baseball*, 72.

6. Peter Morris, *A Game of Inches* (Chicago: Ivan R. Dee, 2006), 309–312.

7. *Ibid.*

8. *Ibid.*

9. J. G. Taylor Spink, "It'll be an Odd Springtime for Henry," *The Sporting News*, January 29, 1942.

10. Cleveland *Plain Dealer*, January 25, 1948.

11. Henry P. Edwards, "Saga of Cleveland Baseball," Cleveland *Plain Dealer*, January 1, 1944.

12. Frank Gibbons, "Death Strikes Down Addie Joss," *Cleveland Press*, January 20, 1963.

13. *Ibid.*

14. Cait Murphy, *Crazy '08*, 292.

15. *Ibid.*

16. Scott Longert, *Addie Joss: King of the Pitchers* (Cleveland: Society for American Baseball Research, 1998), 121.

17. *Ibid.*

18. Frank Gibbons, "Chapman's Death Stunned Tribe," *Cleveland Press*, January 28, 1913.

19. Bob Feller and Nolan Ryan hold the record for most one-hitters with twelve, followed by Addie Joss and Walter Johnson with seven.

20. Scott Longert, *Addie Joss: King of the Pitchers*, 130.

21. *Ibid.*

22. Lewis, *The Cleveland Indians*, 69.

23. The *Plain Dealer* in Jack DeVries, *Indians Baseball: 100 Years of Memories*, 17.

24. Henry P. Edwards, "Those Were the Days," Cleveland *Plain Dealer*, January 4, 1948.

25. *Ibid.*

26. Frank Gibbons, "Naps Sputter with Davies as Pilot," *Cleveland Press*, January 22, 1963.

27. *Ibid.*

28. Norman L. Macht, *Connie Mack, and the Early Years of Baseball* (Lincoln: University of Nebraska Press, 2007), 547.

29. DeVries, *Indians Baseball: 100 Years of Memories*, 19.

30. *Ibid.*, 21.

31. *The Sporting News*, July 26, 1914.

32. Frank Gibbons, "Naps Era Ends as Lajoie Returns to A's, *Cleveland Press*, January 23, 1963.

33. Cleveland *Plain Dealer*, January 18, 1915.

34. David G. Fleitz, *Louis Sockalexis: The First Cleveland Indian* (Jefferson, NC: McFarland, 2002), 182.

35. Jeffrey Powers Beck, *The American Indian Integration of Baseball*. (Lincoln: University of Nebraska Press, 2004), 1; Louis A. Sockalexis Interview, June 19, 1897.

36. *Ibid.*, 175.

37. Frank Gibbons, "Naps Era Ends as Lajoie Returns to A's," *Cleveland Press*, January 23, 1963.

38. Lewis, *The Cleveland Indians*, 76.

39. Lest one shed tears for Charley Somers, the gray-haired, still-handsome coal baron recouped his fortune. He died at Put-in-Bay, Ohio, June 29, 1934, at the age of sixty-five, leaving behind approximately three million dollars and the New Orleans Pelicans minor league team, a notable comeback for a man who had been $1,750,000 in debt. Eckhouse, *An Illustrated History of the Cleveland Indians*, 23.

40. Lewis, *The Cleveland Indians*, 77.

41. *Ibid.*, 78.

42. Franklin Gibbons, "Somers Out, Dunn Buys Tribe," *Cleveland Press*, January 24, 1963.

43. *The Sporting News*, 1922.

44. Lewis, *The Cleveland Indians*, 78.

45. Henry P. Edwards, "Saga of Cleveland Baseball," Cleveland *Plain Dealer*. January 12, 1944.

46. *Ibid.*

47. Jonathan Fraser Light, *The Cultural Encyclopedia of Baseball*, 164.

48. Henry P. Edwards, "Saga of Cleveland Baseball," Cleveland *Plain Dealer*. January 12, 1944.

49. Lewis, *The Cleveland Indians*, 140.

50. Frank Gibbons, "Somers Out, Dunn Buys Tribe," *Cleveland Press*, January 24, 1963.

51. *Ibid.*

52. Lewis, *The Cleveland Indians*, 83–84.

53. Jack DeVries, *Indians Baseball: 100 Years of Memories*, 24.

54. *Ibid.*

55. *Ibid.*

56. Charles C. Alexander, *Spoke: A Biography of Tris Speaker* (Dallas: Southern Methodist University, 2007), 103–104.

57. Stang, *Indians Illustrated*, 40.

58. The story of Larry, the famous dog, is beautifully told in Barbara Gregorich's book entitled *Jack and Larry: Jack Graney and Larry, the Cleveland Baseball Dog*, self-published (Chicago, Illinois, 2012).

59. Ross Tenney, "Steve O'Neill Loses His Temper," *Cleveland Press*, April 28, 1917.

60. Lewis, *The Cleveland Indians*, 91–92.

61. *Ibid.*

62. Newton D. Baker spent most of his life in Cleveland, first as solicitor under Mayor Tom L. Johnson. Baker was elected mayor of Cleveland for two terms before joining President Wilson's cabinet as Secretary of War during World War I. In 1927, Baker became one of several wealthy members who purchased the Cleveland Indians.

63. Schneider, *The Cleveland Indians Encyclopedia*, 28.

64. Chuck Pezano, Paterson *Record*, NJ, August 3, 1968.

65. Cleveland *Plain Dealer*, May 9, 1919, 8.

66. Frank Gibbons, "Ruth's Homer Kayoed Fohl, Made Speaker Tribe Pilot," *Cleveland Press*, January 27, 1963.

67. *Ibid.*

68. *Ibid.*

69. *Ibid.*

70. Steve Steinberg, "Ray Caldwell" (Phoenix: Society for American Baseball Research: The Baseball Biography Project, 2002), 8.

71. *Ibid.*

72. *Ibid.*

73. Condon, *Cleveland: The Best Kept Secret*, 271.

74. Dallas *Morning News*, August 15, 1920.

75. Frank Gibbons, "Chapman's Death Stunned Tribe," *Cleveland Press*, January 28, 1963.

76. *2011 Cleveland Indians Information and Record Book, Media Guide*, 352.

77. *Cleveland Press*, August 17, 1920.

78. Cleveland *Plain Dealer*, August 22, 1920.

79. Schneider, *The Cleveland Indians Encyclopedia*, 27.

80. Frank Gibbons, "Ruth's Homer Kayoed Fohl, Made Speaker Tribe Pilot," *Cleveland Press*, January 29, 1963.

81. Frank Gibbons, "Rookies Sewell, Mails Spark '20 Drive," *Cleveland Press*, January 29, 1963.

82. *The Sporting News*, July 27, 1960.

83. *The Sporting News*, October 7, 1920.

84. *New York Times*, October 9, 1920.

85. *Ibid.*

86. Editor, *Reach Guide* in Lewis, *The Cleveland Indians*, 130–131.

87. DeVries, *Indians Baseball: 100 Years of Memories*, 42.

88. Cleveland *Plain Dealer*, October 12, 1920.

89. Lewis, *The Cleveland Indians*, 133.

Chapter 4

1. Lewis, *The Cleveland Indians*, 135.

2. Seymour, *Baseball: The Golden Age*, 212–213.

3. *Ibid.*

4. Charles Alexander, *Spoke: A Biography of Tris Speaker*, 184.

5. Frank Gibbons, "Uhle New Star of Tribe Staff," *Cleveland Press*, February 2, 1963.

6. Lewis, *The Cleveland Indians*, 136.

7. *Ibid.*

8. Alexander, *Spoke: A Biography of Tris Speaker*, 189.

9. Lewis, *The Cleveland Indians*, 142.

10. John Fraser Light, *The Cultural Encyclopedia of Baseball*, 233.

11. Gary Webster, *Tris Speaker and the Indians: Tragedy to Glory.* (Jefferson, NC: McFarland), 200.

12. George Burns's record-breaking doubles lasted only five years when Earl Webb of the Boston Red Sox stroked 67 doubles in 1931.

13. Alexander, *Spoke: A Biography of Tris Speaker*, 231.

14. *Ibid.*, 232.

15. Schneider, *The Cleveland Indians Encyclopedia*, 32.

16. Cleveland *Plain Dealer*, October 8, 1920.

17. Alexander, *Spoke: A Biography of Tris Speaker*, 238–39.

18. Timothy Gay, *Tris Speaker: The Rough and Tumble Life of a Baseball Legend* (Guilford, CT: Lyons Press, 2007), 244–45.

19. Gary Webster, *Tris Speaker and the Indians: Tragedy to Glory,* 207.

20. David D. Van Tassel and John J. Grabowski, *The Encyclopedia of Cleveland History*, 78–80.

21. Schneider, *The Cleveland Indians Encyclopedia*, 33.

22. Lewis, *The Cleveland Indians*, 156.

23. Fred Schuld, "Alva Bradley, Baseball's Last Purist," *Batting Four Thousand: Baseball in the Western Reserve* (Cleveland: Society for American Baseball Research, 2008), 46.

24. Gordon Cobbledick, "Evans Laid Foundation for Strong Teams," Cleveland *Plain Dealer*, January 25, 1956.

25. Henry Edwards, reference unlisted.

26. Jonathan Fraser Light, *The Cultural Encyclopedia of Baseball*, 235.

27. Fred Schuld, "Alva Bradley, Baseball's Last Purist," *Batting Four Thousand: Baseball in the Western Reserve*, 46.

28. Gordon Cobbledick, Cleveland *Plain Dealer*, January 24, 1928.

29. *Ibid.*, February 19, 1928.

30. *Ibid.*, January 25, 1956.

31. Fred Schuld, "Alva Bradley, Baseball's Last Purist," *Batting Four Thousand*, 46.

32. Lewis, *The Cleveland Indians*, 163.

33. DeVries, *Indians Baseball: 100 Years of Memories*, 54.

34. Lewis, *The Cleveland Indians*, 162.

35. Cleveland *Plain Dealer*, January 26, 1962.

36. *Ibid.*

37. Walter Langford, "Willis Hudlin," *Baseball Research Journal* 16 (Kansas City, MO, 1987), 81.

38. Cleveland *Plain Dealer*, January 26, 1962.

39. *Ibid.*, 11.

40. *Ibid.*, 14.

41. *Ibid.*, 19.

42. Hal Lebovitz, "How Could We Forget the 50th Anniversary?" Cleveland *Plain Dealer*, August 1, 1982.

43. *Ibid.*

44. Fred Schuld, "Alva Bradley, Baseball's Last Purist," 47.

45. Bill Livingston, "Tribe's Drafty Home Stores Memories Mostly Fading," Cleveland *Plain Dealer*, October 7, 1993.

46. Hal Lebovitz, "How Could We Forget the 50th Anniversary?" Cleveland *Plain Dealer*, August 1, 1982.

47. Bill Livingston, "Tribe's Drafty Home Stores Memories Mostly Fading," Cleveland *Plain Dealer*, October 7, 1993.

48. Jack DeVries, *1993 Indians Game Face Magazine*, 12.

49. Philip Lowry, *Green Cathedrals* (New York: Walker, 2006), 73–74.

50. Bill Livingston, "Tribe's Drafty Home Stores Memories Mostly Fading," Cleveland *Plain Dealer*, October 7, 1993.

51. Henry P. Edwards, "Saga of Cleveland Baseball," Cleveland *Plain Dealer*, January 19, 1994.

52. Lewis, *The Cleveland Indians*, 172.

53. Footnote Unavailable.

54. Dan Daniel, "Psychology Wins—The Cleveland Indians Move," *Baseball Magazine* 1 (December 1933), 308.

55. *Ibid.*

56. Bill Livingston, "Tribe's Drafty Home Stores Memories Mostly Fading," Cleveland *Plain Dealer*, October 7, 1993.

57. George E. Condon, in Miller and Wheeler, *Cleveland: A Concise History, 1796–1990*, 146.

58. Fred Schuld, "Alva Bradley, Baseball's Last Purist," *Batting Four Thousand: Baseball in the Western Reserve*, 47.

59. James DeVries, *1993 Indians Game Face Magazine*, 14.

60. James R. Toman and Gregory G. Deegan, *Cleveland Stadium: The Last Chapter*, 19.

61. Curt Smith, *Voice of the Game*. (South Bend, IN: Diamond Communication, 1987), 15.

62. David D. Van Tassel and Grabowski, *The Encyclopedia of Cleveland History*, 655.

63. *Ibid.*

64. Raymond P. Hart, "Jack Graney, Indians Voice for a Decade, Recalls Old Days," Cleveland *Plain Dealer*, June 11, 1973.

65. Russell Schneider, *Tribe Memories: The First Century*. (Hinchley, OH: Moonlight, 2000), 62.

66. *Ibid.*

67. Raymond P. Hart, "Jack Graney, Indians Voice for a Decade, Recalls Old Days," Cleveland *Plain Dealer*, June 11, 1973.

68. Jonathan Fraser Light, *The Cultural Encyclopedia of Baseball*, 117.

69. Jean Edward Smith, *FDR* (New York: Random House, 2007), 302.

70. Time Magnets from *Time Magazine*, 1936.

71. Porter, *Cleveland: Confused City on a Seesaw*, 53.

72. James DeVries, *1993 Indians Game Face Magazine*, 14.

73. Ed McAuley, "Tribe's First Stadium Test Cost $80,000," *Cleveland News*, February 1, 1951.

74. Ed McAuley, "Ferrell Takes His Last Cut as an Indian," *Cleveland News*, February 6, 1951.

75. Schneider, *Tribe Memories: The First Century*, 39.

Chapter 5

1. Letter from Maynard Brichford, Curator, University of Illinois Library, to author, May 15, 2003.

2. Cleveland *Plain Dealer*, October 6, 1969.

3. Lewis, *The Cleveland Indians*, 175.

4. Ed McAuley, "Johnson Fine Fellow, Not a Good Manager," *Cleveland News*, February 7, 1951.

5. Henry W. Thomas, *Walter Johnson: Baseball's Big Train* (Washington, DC: Farragut, 1995), 322.

6. Fred Lieb, "Cutting the Plate," Column located in Walter Johnson Scrapbook XXIX (1930–1946), Walter Johnson Archives, Washington, DC.

7. Washington *Star*, August 1935; Henry W. Thomas, *Walter Johnson*, 322–333.

8. Henry W, Thomas, *Walter Johnson*, 322.

9. *Ibid.*

10. Gordon Cobbledick, "Writers and Ball Players Were Close Friends in Era of Rail Travel," Cleveland *Plain Dealer*, September 3, 1963.

11. Lewis, *The Cleveland Indians*, 176.

12. *Ibid.*, 177.

13. Dick Thompson, *The Ferrell Brothers of Baseball* (Jefferson, NC: McFarland, 2005), 77.

14. *Ibid.*

15. Walter Langford, "A Conversation with Willis Hudlin," *Baseball Research Journal, 1998* (Cleveland: Society for American Baseball Research, 1987), 81.

16. Dick Thompson, *The Ferrell Brothers*, 114.

17. *Ibid.*

18. Lewis, *The Cleveland Indians*, 183–184.

19. *2011 Cleveland Indians Information and Record Book*, 352.

20. Jack Kavanagh, *Walter Johnson: A Life* (South Bend, IN: Diamond Communications, Inc., 1995), 260.

21. Ed Bang, "Between You and Me," *Cleveland News*, July 17, 1934.

22. Schneider, *The Cleveland Indians Encyclopedia*, 40.

23. *2011 Cleveland Indians Information and Record Book*, 366.

24. F. C. Lane, "The Storm Center of the Cleveland Club," *Baseball Magazine,* September, 1935.

25. Gordon Cobbledick, Letter to President Alva Bradley, Reprinted in James E. Odenkirk, *Plain Dealing, A Biography of Gordon Cobbledick*, 175–176.

26. Lane, "The Storm Center of the Cleveland Club."

27. *Ibid.*

28. Cleveland *Plain Dealer*, June 6, 1935.

29. Lewis, *The Cleveland Indians*, 181–182.

30. The Washington *Post*, July 22, 1935.

31. The *Baseball Magazine*, September 1934.

32. Cleveland *Plain Dealer*, July 4, 1946.

33. Herman Goldstein, *The Sporting News*, December 25, 1946.

34. Ed McAuley, "Johnson Fine Fellow, Not a Good Manager," *Cleveland News*, February 7, 1951.

35. *Ibid.*

36. Schneider, *The Cleveland Indians Encyclopedia*, 42.

37. Lewis, *The Cleveland Indians*, 184.

38. Unpublished papers by Gordon Cobbledick given to author by his son William in 1992.

39. *Ibid.*

40. Schneider, *The Cleveland Indians Encyclopedia*, 341.

41. Verona Gomez and Lawrence Goldstone, *Lefty, An American Odyssey* (New York: Ballantine, 2012), 79.

42. *Ibid.*

43. *Ibid.*

44. *The Sporting News*, March 25, 1937.
45. Brochure from the Norway (IA) Baseball Museum.
46. Bill Brancher, "Who May Be Who in 1935," *The Sporting News*, February 2, 1935.
47. Cleveland *Plain Dealer*, March 25, 1934.
48. Daniel M. Daniel, "Hal Trosky, Prize Rookie of the Year," *Baseball Magazine*, December 1934.
49. "Lou Gehrig's Leading Rivals," *Baseball Magazine*, March 1937, 443–444, 472.
50. Ira Berkow, *Hank Greenberg* (New York: Times Books, 1989), 58.
51. Lewis, *The Cleveland Indians*, 185.
52. Louis B. Seltzer, *The Years Were Good* (Cleveland: World Publishing, 1956), 304.
53. Idaho *Statesman*, November 7, 2010.
54. David D. Van Tassel and Grabowski, *The Encyclopedia of Cleveland History*, 468.
55. Gordon Cobbledick, Cleveland *Plain Dealer*, August 6, 1936.
56. Lewis, *The Cleveland Indians*, 194–195.
57. Schneider, *The Cleveland Indians Encyclopedia*. 218–219.
58. John Fleischman, "North Toward Home," *Ohio Magazine* (August 1991), 27.
59. Bud Collins, "Win or lose, It was an Indian Love Call," *The Boston Globe*, April 5, 1985.
60. Notes from Maynard Brichford, University Archivist, University of Illinois, Champaign, Illinois, 2003.
61. *Ibid.*
62. *Ibid.*
63. Correspondence with Robert Boynton, San Diego, California, 1993.
64. Jonathan Fraser Light, *The Cultural Encyclopedia of Baseball*, 363.
65. Lewis, *The Cleveland Indians*, 182–183.
66. Ed McAuley, "I Didn't Know Game, Men Around Me Did," *Cleveland News*, February 3, 1951.
67. Schneider, *The Cleveland Indians Encyclopedia*, 43.
68. *Ibid.*
69. Walter Langford, "A Conversation with Willis Hudlin," *Baseball Research Journal*, 1998, 82.
70. Unpublished notes from the files of Gordon Cobbledick, Cleveland.
71. John Sickels. *Bob Feller, Ace of the Greatest Generation* (Washington, DC: Brassey's, 2004). 49.
72. Lewis, *The Cleveland Indians*, 190.
73. Gordon Cobbledick, "Feller Skipped Minors Because O'Neill Visioned Bob's Rally-Stopping Strikeouts," Cleveland *Plain Dealer*, January 25, 1962.
74. *Ibid.*
75. Bob Feller with Bill Gilbert, *Now Pitching, Bob Feller*, 43.
76. Regis McAuley, "'Blankety-Blank Lie' Gave Feller to Tribe, Judge Says," *Cleveland News*, February 10, 1951.
77. David Pietrusza. *Judge and Jury: The Life and Times of Judge Kenesaw Mountain Landis* (South Bend, IN: Diamond Communications, 1998), 354.
78. Regis McAuley, "'Blankety-Blank Lie' Gave Feller to Tribe, Judge Says," *Cleveland News*, February 10, 1951.

79. *Ibid.*
80. John Sickels. *Bob Feller, Ace of the Greatest Generation*, 59; Bob Feller. *Bob Feller's Strikeout Story* (New York: Grosset and Dunlap, 1947), 58.
81. Brian McKenna, "Cy Slapnicka," from "Can He Play" in *Baseball Scouts and Their Profession*. (Phoenix: Society for American Baseball Research, 2011), 20.
82. Jonathan Fraser Light, *The Cultural Encyclopedia of Baseball*, 247.
83. Lewis, *The Cleveland Indians*, 197.
84. *Ibid.*
85. Billy Evans, "Hunting Baseball Ivory," *Saturday Evening Post*, April 27, 1935, 16, 17, 53, 55, 58.
86. Unpublished notes from the files of Gordon Cobbledick, Cleveland.
87. Tommy Henrich with Bill Gilbert. *Five O'clock Lightning, Ruth, Gehrig, Dimaggio, Mantle, and the Glory Years of the Yankees* (New York: Carol, 1992), 14; Unpublished notes from the files of Gordon Cobbledick, Cleveland.
88. Unpublished notes from the files of Gordon Cobbledick, Cleveland.
89. Lewis, *The Cleveland Indians*, 197.
90. *Ibid.*
91. Interview with Tommy Henrich by author in Prescott, Arizona, August 8, 1996.
92. Gordon Cobbledick in Cleveland *Plain Dealer*, May 8, 1936.
93. *Cleveland News*, July 4, 1940.
94. Schneider, *Tribe Memories: The First Century* (Hinckley, OH: Moonlight, 2000), 159.
95. "Lou Gehrig's Leading Rivals," *Baseball Magazine*, March 1936, 443–444, 472–473.
96. Franklin Gibbons, "Old League Park," *Cleveland Press*, February 10, 1953.
97. DeVries, *Indians Baseball: 100 Years of Memories*, 58.
98. Lewis, *The Cleveland Indians*, 198–199.
99. Frank Gibbons, "Old League Park: Vitt Takes Helm, Feller Strikes Out 18 for Record," *Cleveland Press*, February 10, 1953.
100. Gordon Cobbledick, "Plain Dealing: Death Erases Two Glamorous Names, O'Neill and Vosmik From the Sports Scene," Cleveland *Plain Dealer*, January 28, 1962.
101. Lewis, *The Cleveland Indians*, 200.

Chapter 6

1. The MacMillan *Baseball Encyclopedia*, Eighth Edition, 1558.
2. J. G. Taylor Spink, *The Sporting News*, May 26, 1938.
3. Frank Gibbons, "Old League Park: Vitt Takes Indians' Helm," The *Cleveland Press*, February 10, 1963.
4. DeVries, *Indians Baseball: 100 Years of Memories*, 59.
5. Lewis, *The Cleveland Indians*, 200.
6. *Ibid.*
7. *Ibid.*
8. J. G. Taylor Spink, *The Sporting News*, May 26, 1938.

9. Robert W. Feller, *Strikeout Story* (New York: A. S. Barnes, 1947), 121.

10. DeVries, *Indians Baseball: 100 Years of Memories*, 59.

11. Lewis, *The Cleveland Indians*, 188.

12. DeVries, *Indians Baseball: 100 Years of Memories*, 59.

13. John Stickels, *Bob Feller*, 81.

14. Robert W. Feller, *Strikeout Story*, 128.

15. John Stickels, *Bob Feller*, 81.

16. Talmadge Boston, *1939, Baseball's Tipping Point* (Albany, TX: Bright Sky Press, 2005), xiii.

17. *Ibid.*

18. *Ibid.*

19. *1998 National Baseball Hall of Fame and Museum Yearbook*, Cooperstown, NY, 18.

20. Burt Solomon, *The Baseball Time Line* (New York: Audio Books, 1995), 1018.

21. Talmadge Boston, *1939, Baseball's Tipping Point*, 249.

22. Jonathan Fraser Light, *The Cultural Encyclopedia of Baseball*, 512.

23. *Ibid.*

24. *Ibid.*, 509.

25. Ed McAuley, "Game More Commercial Than Sport," *Cleveland News*, January 31, 1951.

26. Daniel M. Daniel, "Mr. Bradley Gazes at the Stars," *Baseball Magazine*, February 1939, 391.

27. *Ibid.*

28. Talmadge Boston, *1939, Baseball's Tipping Point*, 143.

29. *2011 Cleveland Indians Information and Record Book*, 352.

30. Bud Collins, "Love for Indians Lasts a Lifetime," Cleveland *Plain Dealer*, August 19, 2001.

31. Peter Ledick, *League Park* (Cleveland: Society for American Baseball Research, 1990), 13.

32. Bill Lee, *The Baseball Necrology*, 156: Bob Dolgan, "Ex-Tribe Voice Graney, 91, Dies," Cleveland *Plain Dealer*, April 21, 1978.

33. *Ibid.*

34. Schneider, *Tribe Memories: The First Century*, 76.

35. *Ibid.*

36. "Tribute to Earl Averill," Cleveland *Plain Dealer*, August 17, 1983.

37. Ed Linn, *Rivalry: The Yankees and the Red Sox* (New York: Tickner and Fields, 1991), 129–30.

38. Larry R. Gerlach, *The Men in Blue* (Lincoln: University of Nebraska Press, 1994), 107.

39. Gordon Cobbledick, "Plain Dealing," Cleveland *Plain Dealer*, July 13, 1939.

40. *Ibid.*, August 3, 1939.

41. Schneider, *The Cleveland Indians Encyclopedia*, 47.

42. Clifford Bloodgood, "The Razzing of Big Hal," *The Sporting News*, July 1941, 354, 374.

43. Bob Dolgan, "A Hitter Retired by Pain," Cleveland *Plain Dealer*, September 24, 1996.

44. Schneider, "The Best Since Joe Jackson," *Tribe Memories: The First Century*, 158.

45. *Ibid.*

46. *Ibid.*

47. *Ibid.*

48. *Ibid.*

49. John Sickels, *Bob Feller: Ace of the Greatest Generation*, 88.

50. Rick Wolff, Editorial Director, *Macmillan Baseball Encyclopedia*, 8th Edition. (New York: Macmillan, 1993), 1820.

51. *Ibid.*

52. Gordon Cobbledick, "Plain Dealing" Cleveland *Plain Dealer*, July 23, 1939.

53. Fred Schuld, "Alva Bradley, Baseball's Last Purist," *Batting Four Thousand: Baseball in the Western Reserve*, 49.

54. Gordon Cobbledick, "Plain Dealing" Cleveland *Plain Dealer*, July 23, 1939.

55. Papers from the Gordon Cobbledick files (given to the author by Dorn, Cobbledick's son).

56. Lewis, *The Cleveland Indians*, 204–205.

57. *Ibid.*

58. *Ibid.*

59. Lou Boudreau with Russell Schneider, *Lou Boudreau: Covering All the Bases* (Champaign, IL: Sagamore, 1993), 15.

60. *Ibid.*, 10–11.

61. *Ibid.*, 12.

62. *Ibid.*, 11–12.

63. Lewis, *The Cleveland Indians*, 205.

64. James E. Odenkirk, unpublished satirical composition in verse (Chandler, AZ, 2012). Copyright Pending.

Chapter 7

1. John P. Rossi, *The National Game: Baseball and American Culture* (Chicago: Ivan R. Dee, 2001), 133.

2. Rick Wolff, Editorial Director, *The Macmillan Baseball Encyclopedia*, 8th Edition, 238–302.

3. Schneider, *The Cleveland Indians Encyclopedia*, 168.

4. Mel Antonen, "Rapid Robert, Still Hero at 88," *USA Today*, July 26, 2007.

5. Schneider, *Tribe Memories: The First Century*, 101.

6. Gordon Cobbledick, "I Just Pitched," in Jonathan Knight, *Classic Tribe*, 185.

7. Schneider, *The Cleveland Indians Encyclopedia*, 176.

8. Bob Feller with Bill Gilbert, *Bob Feller Now Pitching* (New York: Carol Publishing Group, 1990), 102.

9. Fred Schuld, "Alva Bradley Baseball's Last Purist," *Batting Four Thousand: Baseball in the Western Reserve*, 49.

10. Bob Feller, *Strikeout Story*, 180–181.

11. John Phillips, *The Crybaby Indians of 1940* (Cabin John, MD: Capital Publishing, 1990), 1.

12. John Sickels, *Bob Feller: Ace of the Greatest Generation*, 93.

13. Lewis, *The Cleveland Indians*, 210.

14. The Cleveland *Plain Dealer*, August 16, 1946.

15. Lou Boudreau with Russell Schneider, *Lou Boudreau: Covering All the Bases*, 29.

16. James E. Odenkirk, *Plain Dealing*, 31.

17. Lewis, *The Cleveland Indians*, 209.

18. *Ibid.*, 209–210.

19. DeVries, *1993 Indians Game Face Magazine*, 22.
20. Franklin Lewis, *The Cleveland Indians*, 210.
21. Cleveland *Plain Dealer*, August 16, 1964.
22. *Ibid.*
23. Author's interview with Lou Boudreau, Wrigley Field, Chicago, June 26, 1984.
24. James E. Odenkirk, *Plain Dealing* (Tempe, AZ: Spider Naps, 1990), 34.
25. *Ibid.*
26. Author's interview with Bob Feller, Hi Corbett Field, Tucson, AZ, March 30, 1985.
27. James E. Doyle, Cleveland *Plain Dealer*, October 4, 1969.
28. Hal Lebovitz, "Sport Scene," Mansfield (OH) *News-Journal*, May 25, 1987.
29. *Ibid.*
30. Hal Lebovitz, *The Best of Hal Lebovitz* (Cleveland: Gray and Company, 2004) 56.
31. Robert W. Creamer, *Baseball in 1941* (New York: Penguin, 1991), 161.
32. Terry Pluto, *Our Tribe: A Baseball Memoir* (New York: Simon & Schuster, 1999), 107.
33. *Ibid.*
34. Hal Lebovitz, *The Best of Hal Lebovitz*, 280.
35. Fred Schuld, "Alva Bradley Baseball's Last Purist," *Batting Four Thousand: Baseball in the Western Reserve*, 49.
36. Ed McAuley, *Cleveland News*, September 8, 1956.
37. Hal Lebovitz, *The Best of Lebovitz*, 284.
38. *Ibid.*, 283.
39. *Ibid.*
40. James E. Odenkirk, *Plain Dealing*, 35.
41. Bill McMahon, "The Cleveland Indians in 1940," *Baseball in Cleveland* (Cleveland: Jack Graney Chapter for Society for American Baseball Research, 1990), 3.
42. Robert W. Creamer, *Baseball in 1941,* 105.
43. Fred Schuld, "Alva Bradley, Baseball's Last Purist," *Batting Four Thousand: Baseball in the Western Reserve*, 50.
44. *Ibid.*, 49.
45. Ed McAuley, "Vitt Replaces O'Neill; Hold Your Hats!" *Cleveland News*, February 13, 1951.
46. *Ibid.*
47. DeVries, *Indians Baseball: 100 Years of Memories*, 68.
48. Ed McAuley, "Vitt Replaces O'Neill; Hold Your Hats!" *Cleveland News*, February 13, 1951.
49. *Ibid.*
50. James E. Doyle, "The Sports Trail," Cleveland *Plain Dealer*, June 26, 1940.
51. *1993 Indians Game Face Magazine*, 22.
52. Bob Dolgan, "Hitter Retired with Pain," Cleveland *Plain Dealer*, September 24, 1996.
53. *Ibid.*
54. John Sickels, *Bob Feller: Ace of the Greatest Generation*, 96.
55. Schneider, *Tribe Memories: The First Century*, 158.
56. *Ibid.*
57. Lewis, *The Cleveland Indians*, 211.
58. Bill Gilbert, *Now Pitching, Bob Feller*, 98.
59. Bob Dolgan, "This Day in Indians' History," The Cleveland *Plain Dealer*, September 20, 1995.

60. *1993 Indians Game Face Magazine*, 22–23.
61. Bill Gilbert, *Now Pitching, Bob Feller*, 101.
62. Frank Gibbons, "Indians Eliminated from Pennant Race, Admidst the Hail of Fruit and Eggs," Cleveland *Press*, September 28, 1940.
63. George Pipgras in Larry Gerlach's *Men in Blue*, 86–7.
64. Rick Wolff, Editorial Director, *The Macmillan Baseball Encyclopedia*, 8th Edition, 243–303.
65. *Cleveland Indians Media Guide*, 363.
66. Gordon Cobbledick, The Cleveland *Plain Dealer*, June 14, 1940.
67. Bill James, *The Bill James Guide to Baseball Managers, 1870–Present.* (Tappan, NJ: Scribner's, 1994), 106.
68. Bill McMahon, "The Cleveland Indians in 1940," *Baseball in Cleveland*, 4.
69. *Ibid.*
70. *Ibid.*
71. Lou Boudreau with Russell Schneider, *Lou Boudreau: Covering All the Bases*, 42.
72. Bud Collins, "Love for Indians Lasts a Lifetime," The Cleveland *Plain Dealer*, August 19, 2001.

Chapter 8

1. Miller and Wheeler, *Cleveland: A Concise History*, 146.
2. *Ibid.*, 147.
3. David D. Van Tassel and Grabowski, *The Encyclopedia of Cleveland History*, xlvii.
4. James E. Odenkirk, *Frank J. Lausche: Ohio's Great Political Maverick* (Wilmington, OH: Orange Frazer Press, 2003), 85.
5. Condon, *Cleveland: The Best Kept Secret*, 243.
6. *Ibid.*, 240–241.
7. Miller and Wheeler, *Cleveland: A Concise History*, 150.
8. *Ibid.*, 151–152.
9. Robert Creamer, *Baseball in '41*, 44.
10. *Ibid.*, 167.
11. Lewis, *The Cleveland Indians*, 215.
12. Alexander, *Our Game and American Baseball History*, 196.
13. *The 2010 Cleveland Indians Information and Record Book*, 408.
14. Lewis, *The Cleveland Indians*, 215.
15. Robert Creamer, *Baseball in '41*, 162.
16. Author's interview with Hal Trosky, Jr., Cedar Rapids, IA, October 5, 2000.
17. Bob Dolgan, "A Hitter Retired from Pain," Cleveland *Plain Dealer*, September 24, 1996.
18. *Ibid.*
19. *Ibid.*
20. Lou Boudreau with Russell Schneider, *Lou Boudreau: Covering All the Bases*, 45–46.
21. *Ibid.*
22. Mike Seidel, *Streak* (Lincoln: University of Nebraska Press, 2002), 68.
23. "Rusty Peters, Journey Ball Player," *Oldtyme Baseball News* 8, No. 2, 15.
24. Bob Feller with Bill Gilbert, *Now Pitching, Bob Feller*, 109.

25. Lewis, *The Cleveland Indians*, 216.
26. *Ibid.*
27. Bob Feller with Bill Gilbert, *Now Pitching, Bob Feller*, 109.
28. Robert Creamer, *Baseball in '41*, 238.
29. Bob Feller with Bill Gilbert, *Now Pitching, Bob Feller*, 113.
30. *Ibid.*
31. Terry Pluto, *Our Tribe*, 87.
32. *Ibid.*, 88.
33. Author's interview with Hal Trosky, Jr., Cedar Rapids, IA, October 5, 2000; DeVries, *Indians Baseball: 100 Years of Memories*, 73.
34. James E. Odenkirk, "Not Tolstoy, Trotsky, But Harold 'Hal' Trosky: The Rise and Fall of a Bona Fide Hall of Fame Candidate," Paper presented at NINE Conference, March 12, 2006, Tempe, AZ.
35. Richard Ruelas, "Riding the Tide of Immigration," Arizona *Republic*, January 5, 2001.
36. Clifford Bloodgood, "The Razzing of Big Hal," *Baseball Magazine*, July 1941, 354.
37. Steven A. Reiss, *Sport in Industrial America* (Wheeling, IL: Harlan Davidson, 1995), 102.
38. Bud Collins, "Love for Indians Lasts a Lifetime," Cleveland *Plain Dealer*, August 19, 2001.
39. Bob Feller with Bill Gilbert, *Bob Feller, Now Pitching*, 112.
40. Lewis, *The Cleveland Indians*, 217.
41. *Ibid.*, 219.
42. *Ibid.*
43. *Ibid.*
44. Lou Boudreau with Russ Schneider, *Lou Boudreau: Covering All the Bases*, 50.
45. Ed McAuley, "Biggest Word in Lou's Book Is 'Security,'" *Cleveland News*, February 17, 1951.
46. Lou Boudreau with Russ Schneider, *Lou Boudreau: Covering All the Bases*, 53.
47. *Ibid.*
48. *Ibid.*, 52.
49. Lewis, *The Cleveland Indians*, 219.
50. Lou Boudreau with Russ Schneider, *Lou Boudreau: Covering All the Bases*, 54.
51. Eugene Stack, a White Sox rookie, was the first player on a major league roster to enter the military for World War II. He enlisted in January 1941, and died on June 27, 1942. He did not play a game in the major leagues. Hugh Mulcahy, a pitcher for the Phillies, was the first major league player to be drafted on March 7, 1941. Hank Greenberg, with a high draft number, enlisted in early 1941. He was released from the service two days before Pearl Harbor. Greenberg reenlisted two days after Pearl Harbor and served for over two years in the China-Burma-India Theater.
52. Lou Boudreau with Russ Schneider, *Lou Boudreau: Covering All the Bases*, 54.
53. Talmadge Boston, *1939: Baseball's Tipping Point*, 148.
54. Lou Boudreau with Russ Schneider, *Lou Boudreau: Covering All the Bases*, 54–55.
55. Author's interview with Russ Schneider, Cleveland, Ohio, May 3, 1998; Lewis, *The Cleveland Indians*, 223.
56. David Pietrusza, *Judge and Jury: The Life and Times of Judge Kenesaw Mountain Landis* (South Bend, IN: Diamond Communications, 1998), 420–424.
57. Ed McAuley, "Tribe Chief Offers to Quit; Gets Spanked," *Cleveland News*, February 19, 1951.
58. *Cleveland Indians 2010 Information and Record Book*, 366.
59. Charles C. Alexander, *Our Game: An American Baseball History* (New York: Henry Holt, 1991), 196.
60. Jered Benjamin Kolbert, "Major League Baseball During World War II," *The National Pastime: A Review of Baseball History* (Cleveland: Society for American Baseball Research, 1994), 103.
61. Stephen R. Bullock, *Playing for the Nation* (Lincoln: University Nebraska Press, 2004), 30; Alexander, *Our Game: An American Baseball History*, 191–192.
62. Charles C. Alexander, *Our Game, An American Baseball History*, 192; Stephen R. Bullock, *Playing for Their Nation*, 30.
63. Jonathan Fraser Light, *The Cultural History of Baseball*, 472.
64. Benjamin G, Rader, *Baseball: A History of America's Game* (Urbana: University of Illinois Press, 1992), 150.
65. Ed McAuley, "Tribe Chief Offers to Quit; Gets Spanked," *Cleveland News*, February 19, 1951.
66. *Ibid.*
67. *Ibid.*
68. *Ibid.*
69. David Pietrusza, *Judge and Jury*, 418.
70. *Ibid.*, 419.
71. *The Sporting News*, August 6, 1942.
72. *Ibid.*
73. *Milwaukee Journal*, October 18, 1943.
74. Donn Rogosin, *Invisible Men: Life in Baseball's Negro League* (New York: Atheneum, 1985), 193.
75. Lee Lowenfish, *Branch Rickey, Baseball's Ferocious Gentleman* (Lincoln: University of Nebraska Press, 2007), 358.
76. *Ibid.*, 359.
77. Bill Veeck with Ed Linn, *Veeck—As in Wreck*, 171–172.
78. David Jordon, Larry Gerlach, and John Rossi, "The Truth About Bill Veeck and the '43 Phillies, *The National Pastime, a Review of Baseball History* (Cleveland: Society for American Baseball Research) 17, 1998, 3–13.
79. *Ibid.*
80. Jules Tygiel, "Revisiting Bill Veeck and the 1943 Phillies," *Baseball Research Journal*, 3 (Cleveland: Society for American Baseball Research, 2007), 114.
81. Chris Lamb, *Conspiracy of Silence: Sportswriters and the Long Campaign to Desegregate Baseball* (Lincoln, NE, 2011), 228–229; The controversy over whether Veeck's effort to purchase the Phillies in 1942 and field a team of players from the Negro Leagues is analyzed by Norman L. Macht and Robert D. Warrington, "The Veracity of Veeck," *The Baseball Research Journal*, published by Society for American Baseball Research, 42, #2, Fall 2013, 17–20. Another analysis of this controversy is found in Paul Dickson's excellent 2011 biography, *Bill Veeck, Baseball's Greatest Maverick*—see appendix, pages 357–66.
82. *Ibid.*

83. *Ibid.*

84. Lou Boudreau with Russell Schneider, *Lou Boudreau: Covering All the Bases*, 63.

85. *Ibid.*

86. *Ibid.*

87. Lou Boudreau with Russell Schneider, *Lou Boudreau: Covering All the Bases*, 68.

88. Steve Krah, "The Limestone League, Spring Training in Indiana in 1942," *Baseball Research Journal*, 1997, 119.

89. *Ibid.*, 120.

90. *Ibid.*

91. Fred Schuld, "Alva Bradley, "Baseball's Last Purist," *Batting Four Thousand: Baseball in the Western Reserve*, 50.

92. John Sickels, *Bob Feller*, 119.

93. *Ibid.*, 128.

94. Ed McAuley, "Cheery Word from Feller, Arm Is Okay," *Cleveland News*, February 21, 1951.

95. Mel Antonen, "Rapid Robert, Still Hero at 88," *USA Today*, July 26, 2006.

96. Bob Yonkers, "Only Six Members of 1941 Indians on Hand to Welcome Feller Back," Cleveland *Plain Dealer*, August 23, 1945.

97. Interview by author and John Sickels with Bob Feller, Cleveland, Ohio, October 2, 2002.

98. Ed McAuley, "It's the Same Feller, a Winner," *Cleveland News*, August 25, 1945.

Chapter 9

1. Frederick Turner, *When the Boys Came Back: Baseball and 1946* (New York: Henry Holt, 1996), 57.

2. John Rossi, *The National Game and American Culture*, 148.

3. *Cleveland News*, March 16, 1946.

4. John Sickles, *Bob Feller: Ace of the Great Generation*, 136.

5. Frederick Turner, *When the Boys Came Back: Baseball and 1946*, 56.

6. *Ibid.*, 54.

7. *Ibid.*

8. *Ibid.*

9. *Ibid.*, 38.

10. John L. Green, "A Review of 1946, When Johnny (Sain) and Hundreds More Come Marching Home Again," *The 27th Baseball Research Journal* (Cleveland: Society for American Baseball Research, 1997), 122.

11. Schneider, *The Cleveland Indians Encyclopedia*, 54–58.

12. Ed McAuley, "Tribe Chief Offers to Quit; Gets Spanked," *Cleveland News*, February 19, 1951.

13. Ed McAuley, "Club Not for Sale, but Veeck Drops By," *Cleveland News*, February 23, 1951.

14. *Ibid.*

15. *Ibid.*

16. Paul Dickson, *Bill Veeck: Baseball's Greatest Maverick* (New York: Walker, 2012), 8.

17. Gerald Eskenazi, *Bill Veeck: A Baseball Legend.* (New York: McGraw-Hill, 1988), 3.

18. Warren Brown, *The Chicago Cubs* (New York: G. P. Putnam's Sons, 1946), 80.

19. *Ibid.*, 30.

20. Chicago *American,* August 16, 1932.

21. Dickson, *Bill Veeck: Baseball's Greatest Maverick*, 20.

22. Bill Veeck with Ed Linn, *Veeck—As in Wreck.* (New York: G.P. Putnam's Sons, 1962), 35–6.

23. Dickson, *Bill Veeck: Baseball's Greatest Maverick*, 8–9.

24. Gerald Eskenazi, *Bill Veeck: A Baseball Legend*, 5.

25. Quote from an article Scott Jones wrote about his shared childhood with Veeck in the Hinsdale (IL) newspaper *The Doings* several days after Veeck's death, January 9, 1986, 102.

26. *Ibid.*

27. Chicago *Tribune*, December 6, 1935.

28. Bill Veeck with Ed Linn, *Veeck—As in Wreck,* 81.

29. *Ibid.*, 36.

30. *Ibid.*, 36–40.

31. Gerald Eskenazi, *Bill Veeck: A Baseball Legend*, 13.

32. Bill Veeck with Ed Linn, *Veeck—As in Wreck,* 81.

33. Gerald Eskenazi, *Bill Veeck: A Baseball Legend*, 15.

34. Bill Veeck with Ed Linn, *Veeck—As in Wreck*, 49.

35. Dickson, *Bill Veeck: Baseball's Greatest Maverick*, 67.

36. *Look*, September 7, 1943.

37. *Leatherneck*, April 1944, 49.

38. Milwaukee *Journal*, November 28, 1943.

39. Gerald Eskenazi, *Bill Veeck: A Baseball Legend*, 22; Bill Veeck with Ed Linn, *Veeck—As in Wreck*, 94.

40. *Ibid.*, 22; Dickson, *Bill Veeck: Baseball's Greatest Maverick*, 50.

41. Bill Veeck with Ed Linn, *Veeck—As in Wreck*, 94.

42. William Marshall, *Baseball's Pivotal Era, 1945–1951* (Lexington: University of Kentucky Press, 1999), 170–171.

43. Bill Veeck with Ed Linn, *Veeck—As in Wreck*, 94.

44. Mansfield (OH) *News Journal*, January 6, 1986. Veeck gave his recollection of the Lebovitz story: "While I was going into the second bank, Hal Lebovitz ... spotted me and tagged along.... He walked the rest of the way with me, along the wet sidewalk of a cool, clearing morning, wondering what in the world I was doing running in and out of banks."

45. Ed McAuley, "A Surprise for Bradley," The *Cleveland News*, July 3, 1946.

46. Ed Bang, "Bill Proves Ace David Harum," The *Cleveland News*, July 31, 1946.

47. Ed McAuley, "Veeck's Wampum in Indian Buy Nearer Million Than $1,750,000," The *Cleveland News*, July 31, 1946.

48. George Condon in Lewis, *The Cleveland Indians*, 237.

49. *Ibid.*

50. Bill Veeck with Ed Linn, *Veeck—As in Wreck*, 102.

51. Lou Boudreau with Russell Schneider, *Lou Boudreau: Covering All the Bases*, 80.

52. Ed McAuley, "Lou Remains as Tribe Pilot for Rest of '46," The *Cleveland News*, July 3, 1946.

53. *Ibid.*

54. Cleveland *Plain Dealer*, July 18, 1946.

55. Dickson, *Bill Veeck: Baseball's Greatest Maverick*, 115.

56. Lewis, *The Cleveland Indians*, 239.

57. Dickson, *Bill Veeck: Baseball's Greatest Maverick*, 112.

58. *Ibid.*

59. Bill Veeck with Ed Linn, *Bill Veeck—As in Wreck*, 105.

60. *New York Times*, March 14, 1971.

61. Ed McAuley, "Indians Stand on Head to Entertain the Fans," The *Cleveland News*, August 14, 1946.

62. Dickson, *Bill Veeck: Baseball's Greatest Maverick*, 113.

63. *Ibid.*, 113.

64. *Baseball Digest,* 1988.

65. *New York Times*, March 14, 1971.

66. Lou Boudreau with Russell Schneider, *Lou Boudreau: Covering All the Bases*, 82.

67. Jack Malany, "Lou Lines Up 'C' Formation," *Cleveland News*, July 24, 1946.

68. Lou Boudreau with Russell Schneider, *Lou Boudreau: Covering All the Bases*, 84.

69. Schneider, *Tribe Memories: The First Century*, 181.

70. Randy Merritt, "A Conversation with Bob Feller," *108, Celebrating Baseball*, Summer 2006, 1, no. 1, 102.

71. Frank Gibbons, "Veeck Ends Colorful League Park Era," *Cleveland Press*, February 13, 1953.

72. *2010 Cleveland Indians Media Guide*, 366.

73. Burton A. and Benita Boxerman, *Ebbets to Veeck to Busch: Eight Owners Who Saved Baseball* (Jefferson, NC: McFarland, 2003), 130.

74. *Ibid.*

75. Lou Boudreau with Russell Schneider, *Lou Boudreau: Covering All the Bases*, 86, 93.

76. *Ibid.*, 93.

77. Interview by author and son Tom with Bob Feller, Goodyear (AZ) Spring Training facility, March 26, 2008.

78. "Gordon, Overlooked Yankee, Gets His Due," *New York Times*, December 2008; Sol Gittleman, "One Trade, Three Teams, and a Reversal of Fortune," *The Baseball Research Journal*, 41, no. 1, Spring 2012, 86–89.

79. "Gordon, Overlooked Yankee, Gets His Due," *New York Times*, December 2008.

80. Gordon Cobbledick, "Plain Dealing," Cleveland *Plain Dealer*, October 12, 1946.

81. Lewis, *The Cleveland Indians*, 242.

82. Fred Schuld, "Alva Bradley, Baseball's Last Purist," *Batting Four Thousand: Baseball in the Western Reserve*, 51.

83. Alva Bradley interview with Howard Preston, *Cleveland News*, August 1, 1946.

84. Ed McAuley, *Cleveland News*, 1951.

85. Ed McAuley, "Thousands of Letters, but Only One to Mr. Veeck," *Cleveland News*, January 30, 1951.

86. *The Sporting News*, April 5, 1953.

Chapter 10

1. Grabowski, *Sports in Cleveland*, 83.

2. Miller and Wheeler, *Cleveland: A Concise History*, 157.

3. *Ibid.*, 147.

4. *Ibid.*, 155.

5. Miller and Wheeler, *Cleveland: A Concise History*, 155.

6. L. H. Robbins, *New York Times Magazine*, June 1946.

7. Porter, *Cleveland, Confused City on a Seesaw*, 3.

8. David D. Van Tassel and Grabowski, *The Encyclopedia of Cleveland History*, 206.

9. *Ibid.*

10. *Ibid.*

11. The fans' affair with the Cleveland Browns ended abruptly when owner Arthur Modell transferred the franchise to Baltimore prior to the 1996 NFL season.

12. Stephanie M. Liscio, *Integrating Cleveland Baseball Media Activism: The Integration of the Indians and the Demise of the Negro League Buckeyes* (Jefferson, NC: McFarland, 2010), 45–46.

13. *Ibid.*, 98.

14. *Ibid.*, 188.

15. *Ibid.*, 189.

16. The New England Watch and Ward Society, founded in the late 1800s in Boston, promoted the censorship of books and the performing arts and later condemned the spread of gambling.

17. George E. Condon, *Cleveland: The Best Kept Secret*, 279.

18. Mark Purdy, "Bill Veeck Deserves Special Corner in Baseball's Hall of Fame," Mansfield *News-Journal*, January 3, 1986.

19. Peter Axthelm, "The Outsider Who Was King," *Newsweek*, January 13, 1986.

20. Rick Ostrow, "Veeck's Passion for Baseball was Second to None," *USA Today*, January 3, 1986.

21. *Ibid.*

22. Hank Greenberg, "Unforgettable Bill Veeck," *Readers Digest,* July 1986, 67–72.

23. *Ibid.*

24. Gerald Eskenazi, *Bill Veeck: A Baseball Legend*, 60.

25. Tom Fitzgerald, "The Fan's Man," *New Times*, Phoenix, March 6–12, 2006.

26. *Ibid.*

27. Bill Veeck with Ed Linn, *Veeck—As in Wreck*, 128.

28. Hal Lebovitz, *The Best of Hal Lebovitz*, 78–79.

29. David D. Tassel and Grabowski, *The Encyclopedia of Cleveland History*, 98–99; Porter, *Cleveland, Confused City on a Seesaw*, 294.

30. Hal Lebovitz, "Recalling Early Days Writing About Indians in Tucson," Mansfield *News-Journal*, March 3, 1986.

31. Ed McAuley, "Notable Scribes, Fans Honor Prexy of Indians," *Cleveland News*, April 30, 1947.

32. Don Robertson, "A Sportswriter Is Saluted," May 22, 1968.

33. Gordon Cobbledick, "Plain Dealing," Cleveland *Plain Dealer*, August 6, 1946.

34. *Cleveland Press,* May 22, 1969.

35. Author's interview with announcer Jimmy Dudley, Tucson, Arizona, December 8, 1984.

36. Author's interview with Bill Veeck, Wrigley Field, Chicago, June 26, 1984.

37. Bill Veeck with Ed Linn, *Veeck—As in Wreck*, 201.

38. Edward Bellamy was an American author and socialist most famous for his Utopian novel, *Looking Backward*, a Rip Van Winkle–like tale set in the distant future of the year 2000. He had a vision of a harmonious future world.

39. Author's interview with Hal Lebovitz, Cleveland, Ohio, May 23, 1984.

40. *Ibid.*

41. James E. Odenkirk, *Plain Dealing*, 148.

42. Tad Dorgan was known for his cartoon panel "Indoor Sports" and many words and expressions he added to the language. He was linked with George Ade and Ring Lardner as a popularizer of "a new slang vernacular." He popularized such words and expressions as "dumbbell," "dumb Dora," "drugstore cowboy," and "cat's meow."

43. *Cleveland Press*, June 4, 1958.

44. Bill Dvorak, "Collector's Prize Lou's Cartoons," *Cleveland Press*, December 1, 1961.

45. Author's interview with Bob August, Wooster, Ohio, December 1, 2010.

46. Cleveland *Plain Dealer*, February 14, 1962.

47. Cleveland *Plain Dealer*, September 1974.

48. Robert Cole, "Baseball Cartoon Memories," *Baseball Research Journal*, 1983, 91.

49. James E. Odenkirk, *Plain Dealing*, 151.

50. The Terminal Tower and Union Terminal were Cleveland's most familiar landmarks. Located on Public Square, the Van Sweringen brothers planned and constructed this complex to counter difficulties with the lakefront railroad depot. Completed in 1927, the 708-foot Terminal Tower was until 1967 the tallest building in the world outside of New York City.

51. *Ibid.*

52. Robert Cole, "Baseball Cartoon Memories," *Baseball Research Journal*, 1983, 91.

53. Timothy D. Taylor, Mark Katz and Tony Grajeda, *Music, Sound and Technology in America: A Documentary History of Early Phonography, Cinema and Radio* (Durham, NC: Duke University Press, 2012), 3–4.

54. Adam Ulrey, "Jack Graney," in David Jones, ed. *Deadball Stars of the American League* (Washington, DC: Potomac Books, 2006).

55. Curt Smith, *Voices of the Game: The First Full-Scale Overview of Baseball Broadcasting, 1921 to the Present* (South Bend, IN: Diamond Communications, 1987), 168.

56. *Ibid.*

57. Author interview with Stephanie Liscio, Cleveland, August 5, 2013.

58. *2011 Cleveland Indians Information and Record Book*, 479.

59. Schneider, *The Cleveland Indians Encyclopedia*, 54–58.

60. *Ibid.*

61. Bill Veeck with Ed Linn, *Veeck—As in Wreck*, 159–160.

62. *Ibid.*

63. *Ibid.*

64. Frank Bowerman in John Sickels; *Bob Feller: Ace of the Greatest Generation*, 179.

65. *The Sporting News*, June 11, 1947.

66. John Sickels, *Bob Feller: Ace of the Greatest Generation*, 172; See Bill Gilbert, *Now Pitching, Bob Feller*, 136–144.

67. Schneider, *The Cleveland Indians Encyclopedia*, 59.

68. *Ibid.*

69. Dickson, *Bill Veeck: Baseball's Greatest Maverick*, 160–161.

70. Terry Pluto, *Our Tribe*, 132.

71. Miller and Wheeler, *Cleveland: A Concise History*, 157.

72. Terry Pluto, *Our Tribe*, 143.

73. *Ibid.*, 148.

74. *Ibid.*

75. Lou Boudreau with Russell Schneider, *Lou Boudreau: Covering All the Bases*, 95.

76. *Ibid.*

77. Ira Berkow, *New York Times*, February 23, 1997.

78. *Ibid.*

79. Terry Pluto, *Our Tribe*, 150.

80. Eddie Robinson with C. Paul Rogers III, *Lucky Me: My Sixty-Five Years in Baseball* (Dallas: Southern Methodist University Press, 2011), 49.

81. *Ibid.*

82. *Ibid.*

83. *Ibid.*

84. *Ibid.*

85. Lou Boudreau with Russell Schneider, *Lou Boudreau: Covering All the Bases*, 96.

86. Bill Veeck interview with William J. Marshall for the University of Kentucky Libraries, A.B. "Happy" Chandler oral history project, February 23, 1977, Tape 1, Side 2.

87. Terry Pluto, *Our Tribe*, 151.

88. Joseph Moore, *Pride and Prejudice: The Biography of Larry Doby*, 50.

89. Associated Press, *New York Times*, July 6, 1947.

90. Joseph Moore, *Pride and Prejudice: The Biography of Larry Doby*, 50–51.

91. Cleveland Jackson, Cleveland *Call and Post*, July 12, 1947.

92. Gordon Cobbledick, "Plain Dealing," Cleveland *Plain Dealer*, July 7, 1947.

93. J. G. Taylor Spink, "Once Again, the Negro Question," *The Sporting News*, July 16, 1947.

94. Gerald Eskenazi, *Bill Veeck: A Baseball Legend*, 41.

95. Cleveland *Plain Dealer*, August 5, 1947.

96. *Cleveland Indians 2011 Information and Record Book*, 352.

97. Schneider, *The Cleveland Indians Encyclopedia*, 59.

98. Lewis, *The Cleveland Indians*, 250.

99. Ed McAuley, *The Sporting News*, October 15, 1947, 11.

100. Lewis, *The Cleveland Indians*, 250.

101. Bob August, *Cleveland Press*, November 18, 1947.

102. Lou Boudreau with Russell Schneider, *Lou Boudreau: Covering All the Bases*, 102–3.

103. Cleveland *Plain Dealer*, November 25, 1947.

Chapter 11

1. William Marshall, *Baseball's Pivotal Era, 1945–1951* (Lexington: University of Kentucky Press, 1999), Preface.

2. J. Ronald Oakley, *Baseball's Last Golden Age, 1946–1960* (Jefferson, NC: McFarland, 1994), 81–82; G. Edward White, *Creating the National Pastime*, 316–330.

3. Ted Williams with John Underwood, *My Turn at Bat: The Story of My Life* (New York: Simon & Schuster, 1969), 166.

4. "In the News," *Cleveland News*, October 6, 1948.

5. Ed Bang, "Between You and Me," *Cleveland News*, October 12, 1948, 11.

6. Stephanie M. Liscio, *Integrating Cleveland Baseball: Media Activism, the Integration of the Indians and the Demise of the Negro League Buckeyes*, 144.

7. Author's interview with Bill Veeck, Wrigley Field, Chicago, June 24, 1984.

8. Bill Veeck with Ed Linn, *Bill Veeck—As in Wreck*, 147–148.

9. *Ibid.*

10. Joseph Thomas Moore *Pride Against Prejudice: The Biography of Larry Doby*, 69.

11. Jackie Robinson with Charles Dexter, *Baseball Has Done It* (Philadelphia: J. P. Lippencott, 1964).

12. *Ibid.*

13. Gordon Cobbledick, "Plain Dealing," Cleveland *Plain Dealer*, March 7, 1948.

14. Terry Pluto, *Our Tribe*, 153.

15. *Ibid.*, 155.

16. Ben Strauss, "Friendship Is Priceless as the National Pastime," *New York Times*, August 2, 2012.

17. Franklin Lewis, *Cleveland Press*, April 14, 1948.

18. Joseph Thomas Moore, *Pride Against Prejudice: The Biography of Larry Doby*, 73.

19. Ira Berkow, *New York Times*, August 22, 1997.

20. Gordon Cobbledick, "Plain Dealing," Cleveland *Plain Dealer*, April 8, 1960.

21. *Ibid.*

22. Franklin Lewis, "About Larry Doby, His Thoughts and His Problems," *Cleveland Press*, March 24, 1948.

23. *Ibid.*

24. Hank Greenberg with Ira Berkow, *Hank Greenberg: The Story of My Life* (Chicago: Triumph Books, 2001), 209.

25. *Ibid.*

26. *Ibid.*

27. Bill Plaschke, "Being Second Not Bad," Idaho *Statesman*, June 20, 2003.

28. Lou Boudreau with Russ Schneider, *Lou Boudreau: Covering All the Bases*, 109.

29. Bill Veeck with Ed Linn, *Veeck—As in Wreck*, 146.

30. David Kaiser, *Epic Season: The 1948 American League Pennant Race* (Amherst, MA: University of Massachusetts Press, 1998), 38.

31. Lou Boudreau with Russ Schneider, *Lou Boudreau: Covering All the Bases*, 109.

32. *New York Times*, October 3, 1948.

33. Pittsburgh *Courier*, May 15, 1948, 17.

34. Cleveland *Plain Dealer*, May 8, 1948.

35. *Ibid.*

36. Bill Veeck with Ed Linn, *Veeck—As in Wreck*, 150.

37. *The Sporting News*, March 3, 1948; May 5, 1948.

38. *Ibid.*

39. *The Sporting News*, June 30, 1948.

40. Ed McAuley, "Cautious Lou Admits This May Be the Year," *Cleveland News*, June 16, 1948.

41. Russell Schneider, *The Boys of '48* (Champaign, IL: Sports Publishing, 1998), 58.

42. Gordon Cobbledick, "Plain Dealing," Cleveland *Plain Dealer*, June 12, 1948; *Now Pitching, Bob Feller*, 153.

43. *Now Pitching, Bob Feller*, 153.

44. John Sickels, *Bob Feller: Ace of the Greatest Generation*, 194.

45. *The Sporting News*, July 21, 1948.

46. John Sickels, *Bob Feller: Ace of the Greatest Generation*, 194–195.

47. Lou Boudreau with Russ Schneider, *Lou Boudreau: Covering All the Bases*, 112.

48. Ben Strauss, "Friendship as Priceless as the National Pastime," *New York Times*, August 22, 2012.

49. Timothy M. Jay, *Satch, Dizzy & Rapid Robert* (New York: Simon & Schuster, 2010), 280.

50. Shirley Povich, *Washington Post*, July 15, 1948, 18.

51. *The Sporting News*, July 14, 1958.

52. *Ibid.*

53. *Ibid.*

54. Interview by author with Russ Schneider, Cleveland Ohio, July 2, 2002.

55. Terry Pluto, *Our Tribe*, 155.

56. Ed McAuley, The *Cleveland News*, August 9, 1948.

57. Doc Young, Cleveland *Call and Post*, August 9, 1948.

58. Lou Boudreau with Russ Schneider, *Lou Boudreau: Covering All the Bases*, 117.

59. *Ibid.*, 118.

60. *Ibid.*

61. The *Cleveland Press*, September 7, 1948.

62. Grabowski, *The Cleveland Indians*, 262.

63. *Ibid.*, 263.

64. Harry Jones, Cleveland *Plain Dealer*, September 14, 1948.

65. Gordon Cobbledick, "Plain Dealing," Cleveland *Plain Dealer*, September 15, 1948.

66. Dickson, *Bill Veeck: Baseball's Greatest Maverick*, 155.

67. Gordon Cobbledick, "Plain Dealing," Cleveland *Plain Dealer*, October 3, 1948.

68. *Ibid.*, 232.

69. *Ibid.*

70. Lou Boudreau with Russ Schneider, *Lou Boudreau: Covering All the Bases*, 120.

71. *Ibid.*, 121.

72. Lou Boudreau with Russ Schneider, *Lou Boudreau: Covering All the Bases*, 122.

73. David Kaiser, *Epic Season: The 1948 American League Pennant Race*, 238.

74. *Ibid.*, 242.

75. *Ibid.*, 243.

76. Hank Greenberg with Ira Berkow, *Hank Greenberg: The Story of My Life* (Chicago: Triumph Books, 2001), 193.

77. Lou Boudreau with Russ Schneider, *Lou Boudreau: Covering All the Bases*, 123.

78. Otherwise known as "The Wall," the Green Monster is synonymous with Fenway Park. The imposing 37-foot-high left field wall is 310 feet from home plate. The bane of pitchers, it has been blamed and credited for events ranging from turning line-driven home runs into sliding doubles, and converting high fly balls into home runs.

79. Lou Boudreau with Russ Schneider, *Lou Boudreau: Covering All the Bases*, 125.

80. DeVries, *Indians Baseball: 100 Years of Memories*, 98.

81. Lou Boudreau with Russ Schneider, *Lou Boudreau: Covering All the Bases*, 126.

82. *Ibid.*, 137.

83. Red Smith, New York *Herald Tribune*, October 5, 1948.

84. Lou Boudreau with Russ Schneider, *Lou Boudreau: Covering All the Bases*, 128.

85. David Anderson, *Pennant Races: Baseball at Its Best* (New York: Dell, 1994), 183.

86. *Ibid.*

Chapter 12

1. Jonathan Fraser Light, *The Cultural History of Baseball*, 105.

2. "Ask Hal Lebovitz," Cleveland *Plain Dealer*, January 20, 1958.

3. *Ibid.*

4. Lou Boudreau with Russell Schneider, *Lou Boudreau: Covering All the Bases*, 128.

5. Schneider, *The Boys of Summer of '48*, 28.

6. *Ibid.*

7. *Ibid.*

8. *Ibid.*

9. Grabowski, *The Cleveland Indians*, 270.

10. Lou Boudreau with Russell Schneider, *Lou Boudreau: Covering All the Bases,* 130.

11. *Ibid.*

12. *Ibid.*

13. Lou Boudreau with Ed Fitzgerald, *Player-Manager* (Boston: Little, Brown, 1952), 226.

14. Bob Feller with Bill Gilbert, *Now Pitching, Bob Feller*, 164.

15. *Ibid.*, 170.

16. Heath, previously a ten-year veteran with Cleveland, enjoyed a productive season with the Braves, hitting .319 with 76 RBIs. He suffered a broken ankle on September 29 at Ebbets Field.

17. David Kaiser, *Epic Season: The 1948 American League Pennant Race* Photo opposite page 186.

18. John Sickles, *Bob Feller: Ace of the Greatest Generation*, 170.

19. Lou Boudreau with Russell Schneider, *Lou Boudreau: Covering All the Bases*, 133.

20. Gordon Cobbledick, "Plain Dealing," Cleveland *Plain Dealer*, October 11, 1948.

21. Author interview with Lou Boudreau, Wrigley Field, Chicago, June 26, 1984.

22. Bob Yonkers, "Nobody Pitches Tuesday," Cleveland *Plain Dealer*, October 9, 1948.

23. Harry Jones, "Bearden's Series All the Way," Cleveland *Plain Dealer*, October 12, 1948.

24. Schneider, *The Boys of Summer of '48*, 126.

25. Frank Gibbons, *Cleveland Press*, October 12, 1948.

26. Oscar Fraley, *United Press*, October 12, 1948.

27. Grabowski, *The Cleveland Indians*, 274.

28. Author interview with Jimmy Dudley, Baseball Announcer, Tucson, AZ, December 8, 1984.

29. Jack Ledden, *The Sporting News*, October 13, 1948; Gerald Eskenazi, *Bill Veeck: A Baseball Legend*, 70.

30. Hal Lebovitz, *The Best of Hal Lebovitz* (Cleveland: Gray, 2004), 245–249.

31. Gerald Eskenazi, *Bill Veeck: A Baseball Legend*, 70; Bill Veeck with Ed Linn, *Veeck—As in Wreck*, 208.

32. George E. Condon, *Cleveland: The Best Kept Secret*, 282.

33. Dickson, *Bill Veeck: Baseball's Greatest Maverick*, 178.

34. Terry Pluto, *Our Tribe*, 141.

35. The six shortstops were Honus Wagner (.363), Arky Vaughan (.385), Luke Appling (.388), Cecil Travis (.359), Alex Rodriquez (.358), and Omar Garciapara (.372).

36. Gordon Cobbledick, "Plain Dealing," Cleveland *Plain Dealer*, October 26, 1948.

37. Associated *Press*, Miami *News*, February 12, 1949.

38. Dickson, *Bill Veeck: Baseball's Greatest Maverick*, 170.

39. St. Petersburg *Times*, February 12, 1949.

40. *New York Amsterdam News*, May 14, 1949; *The Sporting News*, April 13, 1949.

41. Schneider, *Cleveland Indians Encyclopedia*, 478.

42. Hank Greenberg with Ira Berkow, *Hank Greenberg: The Story of My Life*, 199.

43. Leo W. Banks, "An Oasis for Some Pioneers," *Sports Illustrated*, May 8, 1989, 116–117.

44. Dickson, *Bill Veeck: Baseball's Greatest Maverick*, 174.

45. Hank Greenberg with Ira Berkow, *Hank Greenberg: The Story of My Life*, 197.

46. *Cleveland Press*, September 5, 1949.

47. Lou Boudreau with Russell Schneider, *Lou Boudreau: Covering All the Bases*, 145.

48. Bosley Crowther, *New York Times*, September 5, 1949.

49. Milwaukee *Journal*, September 24, 1949.

50. Ed McAuley, *The Sporting News,* October 5, 1949.

51. Bruce Dudley, *Distant Drums, 1948 Cleveland Indians, Revisited* (Unpublished Monograph: Cleveland, 1989), 100.

52. Dickson, *Bill Veeck: Baseball's Greatest Maverick*, 177.

53. *Ibid.*, 178.

54. *Time*, December 5, 1949. Dickson, *Bill Veeck: Baseball's Greatest Maverick*, 179.

55. Gordon Cobbledick, "Plain Dealing," Cleveland *Plain Dealer*, November 17, 1949.

56. Dickson, *Bill Veeck: Baseball's Greatest Maverick*, 179.

57. Gordon Cobbledick, "Plain Dealing," Cleveland *Plain Dealer*, November 17, 1949.

58. Mike Veeck and Pete Williams, *Fun Is Good* (Emmaus, PA: Rodale, 2005), xxii.

59. Lou Boudreau with Russell Schneider, *Lou Boudreau: Covering All the Bases*, 146.

60. Larry Tye, *Satchel: The Life and Times of An American Legend* (New York: Random House, 2009), 219.

61. John E. Fuster, "Paige's Release May Give Minoso Better Chance," Cleveland *Call and Post*, February 19, 1950, 1B.

62. Hank Greenberg with Ira Berkow, *Hank Greenberg: The Story of My Life*, 210.

63. Schneider, *The Boys of Summer '48*, 131.

64. Lou Boudreau with Russell Schneider, *Lou Boudreau: Covering All the Bases*, 150.

65. Schneider, *The Cleveland Indians Encyclopedia*, 84.

66. Harry Jones, Cleveland *Plain Dealer*.

67. Gordon Cobbledick, "Plain Dealing," Cleveland *Plain Dealer*, November 7, 1950.

68. Lou Boudreau with Russell Schneider, *Lou Boudreau: Covering All the Bases*, 151.

69. Lou Boudreau with Ed Fitzgerald, *Player-Manager*, 249.

70. *Ibid.*

71. Schneider, *The Cleveland Indians Encyclopedia*, 125.

72. The five managers were: Connie Mack, 53 years, .486; Jimmy Dikes, 21 years, .477; Bucky Harris, 29 years, .473; Bill Rigney, 18 years, .484; and Gene Mauch, 26 years, .483.

73. Terry Pluto, *Our Tribe*, 105, 103.

Chapter 13

1. Jack Torry, *Endless Summers: The Fall and Rise of the Cleveland Indians* (South Bend, IN: Diamond Communications, 1992), 45.

2. Hank Greenberg with Ira Berkow, *Hank Greenberg: The Story of My Life*, 168–169.

3. *Ibid.*, 183.

4. John Rosengren, *Hank Greenberg: The Hero of Heroes.* (New York: New America's Library, 2013), 324.

5. Jack Torry, *Endless Summers: The Fall and Rise of the Cleveland Indians*, 5.

6. John Rosengren, *Hank Greenberg: The Hero of Heroes*, 321.

7. *Ibid.*

8. Jack Torry, *Endless Summers: The Fall and Rise of the Cleveland Indians*, 6.

9. *Ibid.*

10. Hank Greenberg with Ira Berkow, *Hank Greenberg: The Story of My Life*, 210.

11. Jack Torry, *Endless Summers: The Fall and Rise of the Cleveland Indians*, 8.

12. *Ibid.*

13. *Ibid.*, 9.

14. Ernest Havemann, "Low Pressure Lopez," *Sports Illustrated*, September 6, 1954.

15. *Ibid.*

16. *Ibid.*

17. *Ibid.*

18. Joseph Thomas Moore, *Pride Against Prejudice: The Biography of Larry Doby* (New York: Praeger, 1988), 95.

19. *New York Times*, May 1, 1951.

20. Author's on-the-scene observation of Reynolds' no-hitter, Municipal Stadium, July 12, 1951.

21. Franklin Lewis, *Cleveland Press*, October 12, 1957.

22. Gordon Cobbledick, "Is Larry Doby a Bust," *Sport*, February 1952.

23. *Ibid.*

24. Author's interview with Russell Schneider, Cleveland *Plain Dealer*, June 25, 2009.

25. Gordon Cobbledick, "Plain Dealing," The *Plain Dealer*, January 8, 1957.

26. Gordon Cobbledick, Cleveland *Plain Dealer*, December 12, 1951.

27. Jules Tygiel, *Baseball's Great Experiment* (London: Oxford University Press, 1983), 243.

28. Schneider, *The Cleveland Indians Encyclopedia*, 144.

29. *Pittsburgh Courier*, September 10, 1949.

30. Schneider, *The Cleveland Indians Encyclopedia*, 68.

31. Author Interview with Bob August, Wooster, Ohio, June 14, 1984.

32. John Rosengren, *Hank Greenberg: The Hero of Heroes*, 335–336.

33. Schneider, *The Cleveland Indians Encyclopedia*, 329.

34. *Ibid.*

35. John Rosengren, *Hank Greenberg: The Hero of Heroes*, 326.

36. *Ibid.*, 327. Five years after Jackie Robinson broke the color barrier, only five of 16 teams had added a negro player.

37. Stephen H. Norwood and Harold Brackman, "Going to Bat for Jackie Robinson, The Jewish Role in Breaking Baseball's Color Line," *Journal of Sport History* 26, no. 1, Spring 1999.

38. John Rosengren, *Hank Greenberg: The Hero of Heroes*, 327–328.

39. *Ibid.*, 328.

40. *Ibid.*

41. Schneider, *The Cleveland Indians Encyclopedia*, 66.

42. Schneider, *Tribe Memories: The First Century*, 51.

43. Schneider, *The Cleveland Indians Encyclopedia*, 67.

44. John Rosengren, *Hank Greenberg: The Hero of Heroes*, 326.

45. *Ibid.*

46. *Plain Dealer*, September 19, 1954.

47. For many years baseball fans called the New York team the "Damn Yankees" because of their pro-

pensity for winning. The name "Damn Yankees" did not become official until the 1955 Broadway musical of the same name. The musical was based on the novel, *The Year the Yankees Lost the Pennant* by Douglas Wallop.

48. DeVries, *Indians Baseball: 100 Years of Baseball*, 112.

49. Harry Jones, *The Plain Dealer*, April 11, 1954.

50. Bruce Dudley, *Bittersweet Season, Cleveland Indians Revisited* (Canton: Sliman's Printery, 1995), 17–18.

51. Hank Greenberg with Ira Berkow, *Hank Greenberg: The Story of My Life*, 202.

52. *Ibid.*

53. Harry Jones, "Explaining the Indians Success," *Cleveland Plain Dealer*, May 9, 1954.

54. Cleveland holds the record for the largest game attendance at any All-Star game, with 69,831 present in Municipal Stadium for the 1935 game.

55. Joseph Thomas Moore, *Pride Against Prejudice*, 103.

56. Gordon Cobbledick, "Plain Dealing," Cleveland *Plain Dealer*, August 16, 1954.

57. Murray Seegar, "Funeral for New Yorkers Brings Largest Turnout in Majors' History," The *Plain Dealer*, September 3, 1954.

58. *Ibid.*

59. Bill Chastain, "Cleveland's Dream Team," *Sports History*, November 1948, 23.

60. Mark Winegardner, *Crooked River Burning* (New York: Harcourt, 2001), 182. Researchers Bill Deane and Ron Seltzer claim to have proven conclusively that Wertz's shot traveled no more than 425–430 feet. Most journalist and eyewitness accounts suggest the drive went at least between 340–350 feet. Readers may take their pick. The drive was a long, long way.

61. Terry Pluto, *Our Tribe: A Baseball Memoir*, 169.

62. Mark Winegardner, *Crooked River Burning*, 184.

63. Terry Pluto, *Our Tribe: A Baseball Memoir*, 169.

64. *Ibid.*

65. The *Dickson Baseball Dictionary* defines a Chinese home run as a derogatory term for a home run over the portion of the outfield fence closest to home plate, often one that lands just inside (or hits) the foul pole in a park with small dimensions.

66. Mark Winegardner, *Crooked River Burning*, 185.

67. Bruce Dudley, *Bittersweet Season: Cleveland Indians Revisited*, 179.

68. Mark Winegardner, *Crooked River Burning*, 185.

69. Bruce Dudley, *Bittersweet Season: Cleveland Indians Revisited*, 183.

70. Arthur Daley, *New York Times*, October 13, 1954.

71. Terry Pluto, *Our Tribe: A Baseball Memoir*, 170.

72. *Ibid.*, 171, 167.

Epilogue

1. Sabermetrics is a popular subject for the Society for American Baseball Research, founded in 1971. Researchers use various forms of baseball statistics to ascertain objective performance of individual major league players and teams.

Bibliography

Books and Articles

Alexander, Charles C. *Our Game: An American Baseball History*. New York: Henry Holt, 1991.

_____. *Spoke: A Biography of Tris Speaker*. Dallas: Southern Methodist University Press, 2007.

Anderson, David. *Pennant Races: Baseball at Its Best*. New York: Bantam Doubleday Dell, 1994.

Barber, Red. *The Broadcasters*. New York: Dial Press, 1970

Beck, Jeffrey Powers. *The American Indian Integration of Baseball*. Lincoln: University of Nebraska Press, 2004.

Berkow, Ira. *Hank Greenberg*. New York: Times, 1989.

Blevins, Rich. *Addie Joss on Baseball: Collected Newspaper Columns and World Series Reports, 1907–1909*. Jefferson, NC: McFarland, 2012.

_____. *Ed McKean: Slugging Shortstop of the Cleveland Spiders*. Jefferson, NC: McFarland, 2015.

Borsvold, David. *Cleveland Indians: The Cleveland Press Years 1920–1982*. Charleston, SC: Arcadia, 2003.

Boston, Talmadge. *1939: Baseball's Tipping Point*. Albany, TX: Bright Sky Press, 2005.

Boudreau, Lou, with Ed Fitzgerald. *Player-Manager*. Boston: Little, Brown, 1949.

Boudreau, Lou, with Russell Schneider. *Lou Boudreau: Covering All the Bases*. Champaign, IL: Sagamore, 1993.

Brown, Warren. *The Chicago Cubs*. New York: G. P. Putnam's Sons, 1946.

Gordon Cobbledick, "Don Black's Greatest Victory," *American Weekly*, September 12, 1948.

Condon, George E. *Cleveland: The Best Kept Secret*. Garden City, NY: Doubleday, 1967.

Cormack, George, *Municipal Stadium: Memories on the Lakefront*, Vol. 1. Berea, OH: Instant Concepts, 1997.

Creamer, Robert W. *Baseball in 1941*. New York: Penguin, 1991.

_____. "Bill Veeck, 1914–86." *Sports Illustrated*, January 13, 1986.

Crepeau, Richard. *Baseball's Diamond Mind*. Lincoln, NE: Bison, 2000.

DeVries, Jack. *Indians Baseball: 100 Years of Memories*. Cleveland: Cleveland Indians Baseball, 2002.

Dickson, Paul. *Bill Veeck: Baseball's Greatest Maverick*. New York: Walker, 2012.

_____. *The Dickson Baseball Dictionary*, 3d ed. New York: W. W. Norton, 2009.

Dudley, Bruce. *Bittersweet Season: The 1954 Cleveland Indians Revisited*. Canton, OH: self-published, 1995.

_____. *Distant Drums: 1948 Cleveland Indians, Revisited*. Unpublished monograph. Cleveland: 1989.

Eckhouse, Morris, ed. *Baseball in Cleveland*. Cleveland: The Jack Graney Chapter of the Society for American Baseball Research, 1990.

_____ *Legends of the Tribe: An Illustrated History of the Cleveland Indians*. Dallas: Taylor, 2000.

Eskenazi, Gerald. *Bill Veeck: A Baseball Legend*. New York: McGraw-Hill, 1988.

Felber, Bill. *Under Pallor, Under Shadow: The 1920 American League Pennant Race That Rattled and Rebuilt Baseball*. Lincoln: University of Nebraska Press, 2011.

Feller, Bob. *Bob Feller's Strikeout Story*. New York: Grosset and Dunlap, 1947.

_____, with Bill Gilbert. *Now Pitching, Bob Feller*. New York: Carol Publishing Group, 1990.

Fleitz, David L. *Louis Sockalexis: The First Cleveland Indian*. Jefferson, NC: McFarland, 2002.

_____. *Napoleon Lajoie: King of Ball Players*. Jefferson, NC: McFarland, 2013.

Gay, Timothy M. *Tris Speaker: The Rough-and-Tumble Life of a Baseball Legend*. Lincoln: University of Nebraska Press, 2005.

Gerlach, Larry R. *The Men in Blue*. Lincoln: University of Nebraska Press, 1994.

Gietschier, Stephen P. "A Good Piece of Hitting: The 1910 Batting Race," *Timeline* 27, no. 4 (Oct./Dec. 2010): 20–33.

Gomez, Verona, and Lawrence Goldstone. *Lefty: An American Odyssey*. New York: Ballantine, 2012.

Grabowski, John J. *Sports in Cleveland: An Illustrated History*. Bloomington: Indiana University Press, 1992.

Greenberg, Hank, with Ira Berkow. *Hank Greenberg: The Story of My Life*. Chicago: Triumph, 2001.

Henrich, Tommy, with Bill Gilbert. *Five O'Clock Lightning: Ruth, Gehrig, DiMaggio, Mantle and the Glory Years of the Yankees*. New York: Birch Lane Press, 1992.

Hetrick, J. Thomas. *Misfits! The Cleveland Spiders in 1899*. Jefferson, NC: McFarland, 1991.

Holbrook, Hal. *Harold: The Boy Who Became Mark Twain*. New York: Farrar, Straus and Giroux, 2011.

Huhn, Rick. *The Chalmers Race: Ty Cobb, Napoleon Lajoie, and the Controversial 1910 Batting Title That Became a National Obsession*. Lincoln: University of Nebraska Press. 2014.

Jordan, David M., Larry Gerlach and John P. Rossi, "A Baseball Myth Exploded." *The National Pastime* 17 (1998): 3–13.

Kaiser, David. *Epic Season: The 1948 American League Pennant Race*. Amherst: University of Massachusetts Press, 1998.

Kavanagh, Jack. *Walter Johnson: A Life*. South Bend, IN: Diamond Communications, 1995.

Knight, Jonathan. *Classic Tribe: The 50 Greatest Games in Cleveland Indians History*. Kent, OH: Kent State University, 2009.

Kolbert, Jered Benjamin. "Major League Baseball During World War II." *The National Pastime* 14 (1994): 102–105.

Koppett, Leonard. *Koppett's Concise History of Major League Baseball*. Philadelphia: Temple University Press, 1998.

Krsolovic, Ken, and Bryan Fritz. *League Park, 1891–1946*. Jefferson, NC: McFarland, 2013.

Lamb, Chris. *Conspiracy of Silence: Sportswriters and the Long Campaign to Desegregate Baseball*. Lincoln: University of Nebraska Press, 2011.

Langford, Walter. "A Conversation with Willis Hudlin." *The Baseball Research Journal* 16 (1987): 80–82.

Lebovitz, Hal. *The Best of Hal Lebovitz*. Cleveland: Gray, 2004.

Ledick, Peter. *League Park*. Cleveland: Society for American Baseball Research, 1990.

Lee, Bill. *The Baseball Necrology*. Jefferson, NC: McFarland, 2003.

Lewis, Franklin. *The Cleveland Indians*. New York: G. P. Putnam's Sons, 1949.

Light, Jonathan Fraser. *The Cultural Encyclopedia of Baseball*. Jefferson, NC: McFarland, 1997.

Linn, Ed. *Rivalry: The Yankees and the Red Sox*. New York: Tickner and Fields, 1991.

Liscio, Stephanie M. *Integrating Cleveland Baseball: Media Activism, the Integration of the Indians and the Demise of the Negro League Buckeyes*. Jefferson, NC: McFarland, 2010.

Longert, Scott H. *Addie Joss: King of the Pitchers*. Cleveland: Society for American Baseball Research, 1998.

_____. *The Best They Could Be*. Dulles, VA: Potomac, 2013.

Lowenfish, Lee. *Branch Rickey: Baseball's Ferocious Gentleman*. Lincoln: University of Nebraska Press, 2007.

Lowry, Philip J. *Green Cathedrals*. New York: Walker, 2006.

McKenna, Brian. "Cy Slapnicka." In *"Can He Play?": Baseball Scouts and Their Profession*. Phoenix: Society for American Baseball Research, 2011.

McMahon, Bill. "The Cleveland Indians in 1940." In *Baseball in Cleveland*. Cleveland: Society for American Baseball Research, 1990.

Macht, Norman L. *Connie Mack and the Early Years Baseball*. Lincoln: University of Nebraska Press, 2007.

Marshall, William. *Baseball's Pivotal Era*. Lexington: University of Kentucky Press, 1999.

Miller, Carol Poh, and Robert Wheeler. *Cleveland: A Concise History*. Bloomington: Indiana University Press, 1990.

Moore, Joseph Thomas. *Pride Against Prejudice: The Biography of Larry Doby*. New York: Praeger, 1988.

Morris, Peter. *A Game of Inches*. Chicago: Ivan R. Dee, 2006.

Murphy, Cait. *Crazy '08*. New York: HarperCollins, 2008.

Odenkirk, James E. "The Cleveland Indians and the New York Yankees, 1947–1956." *The National Pastime* 28 (2008): 78–86.

_____. *Frank J. Lausche: Ohio's Great Political Maverick*. Wilmington, OH: Orange Frazer Press, 1993.

_____. *Plain Dealing: A Biography of Gordon Cobbledick*. Tempe, AZ: Spider Naps, 1990.

Phillips, John. *The Crybaby Indians of 1940*. Cabin John, MD: Capital Publishing, 1990.

Pietrusza, David. *Judge and Jury: The Life and Times of Judge Kenesaw Mountain Landis*. South Bend, IN: Diamond Communications, 1998.

Pluto, Terry. *The Curse of Rocky Colavito*. Cleveland: Gray, 1994.

_____. *Our Tribe: A Baseball Memoir*. New York: Simon & Schuster, 1999.

Porter, Philip W. *Cleveland, Confused City on a Seesaw*. Columbus: Ohio State University Press, 1976.

Rader, Benjamin G. *Baseball: A History of America's Game*. Urbana: University of Illinois Press, 1992.

Reidenbaugh, Lowell. *The Sporting News: Take Me Out to the Ballgame*. St. Louis: The Sporting News, 1983.

Reiss, Steven A. *Sport in Industrial America*. Wheeling, IL: Harlan Davidson, 1995.

Robinson, Eddie, with C. Paul Rogers III. *Lucky Me: My Sixty-Five Years in Baseball*. Dallas: Southern Methodist University Press, 2011.

Rogosin, Donn. *Invisible Men: Life in Baseball's Negro Leagues*. New York: Atheneum, 1985.

Rose, William Ganson. *Cleveland: The Making of a City*. Cleveland: World Publishing, 1950.

Rosengren, John. *Hank Greenberg: The Hero of Heroes*. New York: New American Library, 2013.

Rossi, John P. *The National Game: Baseball and American Culture*. Chicago: Ivan R. Dee, 2001.

Rothe, Emil H. *Baseball's Most Historic Games*. Chicago: self-published, 1993.

Schneider, Russell. *The Boys of Summer of '48*. Champaign, IL: Sports Publishing, 1998.

_____. *The Cleveland Indians Encyclopedia*. Philadelphia: Temple University Press, 1996.

_____. *Tales from the Tribe Dugout*. Champaign, IL: Sports Publishing, 2005.

_____. *Tribe Memories: The First Century*. Hinckley, OH: Moonlight Publishing, 2000.

Schuld, Fred. "Alva Bradley, Baseball's Last Purist." In *Batting Four Thousand: Baseball in the Western Reserve*, edited by Brad Sullivan. Cleveland: Society for American Baseball Research, 2008.

Seidel, Mike. *Streak*. Lincoln: University of Nebraska Press, 2002.

Seltzer, Louis B. *The Years Were Good*. Cleveland: World Publishing, 1956.

Seymour, Harold, and Dorothy Seymour Mills. *Base-

ball: The Golden Age. New York: Oxford University Press, 1971.

Sickels, John. *Bob Feller: Ace of the Greatest Generation*. Washington, DC: Brassey's, 2004.

Smith, Curt. *Voice of the Game*. South Bend, IN: Diamond Communication, 1987.

Smith, Jean Edward. *FDR*. New York: Random House, 2007.

Solomon, Burt. *The Baseball Time Line*. New York: Avon, 1997.

Stang, Mark. *Indians Illustrated: 100 Years of Cleveland Indians Photos*. Wilmington, OH: Orange Frazer Press, 2010.

Taylor, Timothy D., Mark Katz, and Grajeda Ajeda. *Music, Sound, and Technology in America: A Documentary History of Early Phonography, Cinema and Radio*. Durham, NC: Duke University Press, 2012.

Thomas, Henry W. *Walter Johnson: Baseball's Big Train*. Washington, DC: Farragut, 1995.

Thompson, Dick. *The Ferrell Brothers of Baseball*. Jefferson, NC: McFarland, 2005.

Torry, Jack. *Endless Summers: The Fall and Rise of the Cleveland Indians*. South Bend, IN: Diamond Communications, 1992.

Turner, Frederick. *When the Boys Come Home: Baseball and 1946*. New York: Henry Holt, 1996.

Tye, Larry. *Satchel: The Life and Times of an American Legend*. New York: Random House, 2009.

Tygiel, Jules. *Baseball's Great Experiment*. London: Oxford University Press, 1983.

Ulrey, Adam, "Jack Graney." In *Deadball Stars of the American League*, edited by David Jones. Dulles, VA: Potomac, 2006.

Veeck, Bill, with Ed Linn. *Veeck—as in Wreck*. New York: G. P. Putnam's Sons, 1962.

Veeck, Mike, and Pete Williams. *Fun Is Good*. Emmaus, PA: Rodale Publishers, 2005.

Wancho, Joseph, ed. *Pitching to the Pennant: The 1954 Cleveland Indians*. Lincoln: SABR and University of Nebraska Press, 2014.

Webster, Gary. *Tris Speaker and the 1920 Indians: Tragedy to Glory*. Jefferson, NC: McFarland, 2012.

Wertheim, Jon L. "The Amazing Race." *Sports Illustrated*. September 20, 1910, 76–86.

White, G. Edward. *Creating the National Pastime*. Princeton, NJ: Princeton University Press, 1996.

Wiley, George. *How to Win 111 Games: The Story of the 1954 Indians*. Cleveland: Society for American Baseball Research, 1990.

_____. *One Wall and 357 Doubles: The Story of the 1936 Cleveland Indians*. Cleveland: Society for American Research, 1990.

Winegardner, Mark. *Crooked River Burning*. New York: Harcourt, 2001.

Wolff, Rick, ed. *The Baseball Encyclopedia*, 8th Edition. New York: Macmillan, 1993.

Wright, Marshall D. *Nineteenth Century Baseball*. Jefferson, NC: McFarland, 1986.

Newspapers

Akron Beacon Journal
Arizona Republic
The Boston Globe
Brooklyn Daily Eagle
Chicago Tribune
Cincinnati Enquirer
Cleveland Call and Post
Cleveland News
Cleveland Press
Columbus Dispatch
Dallas Morning News
Detroit Free Press
Hinsdale, (IL) The Doings
Idaho Statesman
Mansfield News-Journal (Ohio)
Milwaukee Journal
New Times (Phoenix)
New York Times
Paterson (NJ) Record
Philadelphia Enquirer
Plain Dealer
The Sporting News
Toledo Blade
USA Today
Washington Post
Washington Star

Annuals and Media Guides

1998 National Baseball Hall of Fame and Museum Yearbook, Cooperstown, New York
2011 Cleveland Indians Information and Record Book
Indians Game Face Magazine, 1993

Interviews

August, Bob (sportswriter, *Cleveland Press*). Wooster, OH, June 14, 1984, and June 20, 2001.

Boone, Ray. Phoenix, AZ, March 12, 1993.

Boudreau, Lou. Phoenix, AZ, March 10, 1992.

Brichford, Maynard (archivist, University of Illinois). Champaign, IL, May 15, 2003.

Cobbledick, Dorn (son of sportswriter Gordon Cobbledick), Cleveland, OH, May 23, 1984.

Cobbledick, William (son of sportswriter Gordon Cobbledick). Tucson, AZ, October 22, 1982; May 7, 1984; December 8, 1984; and October 24, 1986.

DiBiasio, Robert (vice president of public relations, Cleveland Indians). Cleveland, OH, May 25, 1984.

Dudley, Jimmy (Cleveland Indians broadcaster). Tucson, AZ, December 8, 1984.

Feller, Bob. Tucson, AZ, March 30, 1985; Cleveland, OH, August 20, 1991; Winter Haven, FL, March 1994; and (with Tom Odenkirk), Goodyear, AZ, March 26, 2008.

Heaton, Charles (sportswriter, *Cleveland Plain Dealer*), Cleveland, May 23, 1984.

Hemond, Roland. Philadelphia, PA, July 30, 2013.

Henrich, Tommy. Prescott, AZ, August 8, 1996, and October 8, 2004.

Jones, Aldona (wife of Harry Jones, sportswriter and Cleveland Indians broadcaster). Sedona, AZ, January 2, 1986.

Killebrew, Harmon. Phoenix, AZ, February 20, 1996.
Lebovitz, Hal (sportswriter, *Cleveland Plain Dealer*). Cleveland, OH, May 22, 1984.
Paul, Gabe (president, Cleveland Indians). Cleveland, OH, May 27, 1984.
Russell, Schneider (sportswriter, *Cleveland Plain Dealer*). Cleveland, OH, May 3, 1998; July 10, 2003; and August 5, 2008.
Herb, Score. Chicago, IL, June 26, 1984.
Trosky, Hal, Jr. Cedar Rapids, IA, October 5, 2000.
Veeck, Bill. Chicago, IL, June 26, 1984.

Correspondence

Robert Boynton (baseball researcher), San Diego, CA, July 10, 1993.

Maynard Brichford (archivist, University of Illinois Library), Champaign, IL, May 15, 2003.
Rocky Colavito, December 4, 1989.

Special Collections and Archival Sources

Charles W. Mears and Eugene C. Murdock Collections, Cleveland Public Library
Fred Schuld Papers, Cleveland Baseball Heritage Museum
Gordon Cobbledick, unpublished papers, private collection of William Cobbledick
John Toland, correspondence with Cleveland Indians players, private collection of John Toland

Index